Sliding Mask

Exam Tips:

1. Read each question carefully before looking at the possible answers.

2. After formulating an answer, determine which of the choices most nearly corresponds with that answer. It should completely answer the question.

3. Answer each question according to the latest regulations and procedures. You will receive credit if the regulations or procedures have changed. Computerized exams may be updated as regulations and procedures change.

4. There is only one answer that is correct and complete. The other answers are either incomplete or are derived from popular misconceptions.

5. If you do not know the answer to a question, try not to spend too much time on it. Continue with those you can answer. Then, return to the unanswered or difficult questions.

6. Unanswered questions will be counted as incorrect.

7. On calculator problems, select the answer nearest your solution. If you have solved it correctly, your answer will be closer to the correct answer than the other choices.

Quizlet

FAA AIRMAN KNOWLEDGE
PRIVATE PILOT TEST GUIDE

ii

Jeppesen

Published in the United States of America
Jeppesen
55 Inverness Drive East, Englewood, CO 80112-5498
www.jeppesen.com

Cover Photo
Cirrus airplane in flight courtesy of Cirrus Aircraft

ISBN 978-0-88487-287-0

Jeppesen
55 Inverness Dr. East
Englewood, CO 80112-5498
Web Site: www.jeppesen.com
Email: Captain@jeppesen.com
Copyright © Jeppesen
All rights reserved. Published 1992-2009, 2014, 2015, 2018
Printed in the United States of America

10001387-023

PREFACE

Thank you for purchasing this Private Pilot FAA Airman Knowledge Test Guide. This test guide helps you understand the learning objectives for the test questions so that you can take the FAA knowledge test with confidence. The test guide contains sample FAA Private Pilot airplane test questions, with correct answers, explanations, and study references. Explanations of why the other choices are wrong are included where appropriate. Questions are organized by topic, with explanations located to the right side of each question. You can use the sliding mask to cover up the answers and test yourself. Full-color figures identical to the figures on the FAA test are included together in Appendix 1 and 2 in the back of the book. This test guide is intended to supplement your instructor-led flight and ground training—it is not a stand-alone learning tool.

THE JEPPESEN TRAINING PHILOSOPHY

Flight training is most effective when academic knowledge (ground training) is integrated with flight training in the aircraft. Jeppesen provides integrated preparation for the practical test, by coordinating academic content with flight training guidance. Some of the Jeppesen design features are:

- Objectives and completion standards included in every lesson.

- Teaching of complex skills using the **building block principle**.

- Incorporation of **meaningful repetition.** Each necessary concept or skill is presented several times throughout the instructional program.

You can find these features in Jeppesen syllabi, textbooks, online computer-assisted learning, exercises, exams, and in this test guide. Combine these elements with instructor-led class discussion and with the skills learned in the simulator and airplane, the result is an integrated training system with all materials coordinated.

People retain about 10 percent of what they read, 20 percent of what they hear, 30 percent of what they see, and 50 percent of what they hear and see together. These averages can be increased to as high as 90% by including active learning methods. Active learning includes exercises, stage exams, student/instructor discussions, computer-assisted learning, and practice in a simulator or airplane.

Levels of learning include rote, understanding, application, and correlation. One shortcoming of test preparation courses that concentrate only on passing the test is that they accomplish only rote learning, the lowest level of learning. The Jeppesen approach raises the standard by challenging students to learn at the application and correlation levels. Our materials are challenging and motivating, maximizing knowledge and skill retention. More than 3 million pilots have learned to fly using our materials, which include:

TEXTBOOKS — Jeppesen pilot and maintenance training textbooks and e-books contain the answers to many of the questions you might have as you begin your training program. They are based on the **study and review** concept of learning, which means detailed material is presented in an uncomplicated way, then important points are summarized using bold type and color. For best results, study the textbook as part of a coordinated package of materials. The textbook is the central component for academic study and is cross-referenced to the syllabus and to Jeppesen online computer-assisted training.

ONLINE COURSES — Available for private, instrument, and commercial students, these engaging courses teach the academic knowledge for your pilot certificate or rating in straightforward, no-nonsense lessons. Strategic use of animation helps you understand concepts beyond what you can learn by just reading about them. Built-in maneuvers lessons show an animated overview of each maneuver, plus pilot's-eye videos that put you in the cockpit with an instructor. This adds up to your best possible preparation before the actual flight lessons.

SUPPORT COMPONENTS — Supplementary items include training syllabi, booklets that contain stage and end-of-course exams, FAR/AIM manuals or e-books, these airman knowledge test guides, practical test study guides, the *Aviation Weather* textbook, the student record folder, mechanical flight computer, plotter, and logbook. The Jeppesen training products are the most comprehensive pilot training materials available. Together with your instructor, they help you prepare for the FAA exam and practical test. More importantly, they help you become a more proficient and safe pilot.

You can purchase our products and services through your Jeppesen dealer. For product, service, or sales information go to www.jeppdirect.com. If you have comments, questions, or need explanations about any component of our GFD Training System, contact us directly at: TrainingServices@Jeppesen.com, or go to www.jeppesen.com/testprep. You can also contact Jeppesen at the following addresses.

Jeppesen
55 Inverness Drive East
Englewood, CO 80112-5498
1-800-621-JEPP
303-799-9090

In Europe, Africa, or the Middle East, contact us at:

Jeppesen & Co., GmbH
Frankfurter Strasse 233
63263 Neu-Isenburg, Germany
Tel: 011-49-6102-5070
Fax: 011-49-6102-507-999

INTRODUCTION

The Private Pilot FAA Airman Knowledge Test Guide is designed to help you prepare for the Private Pilot Knowledge Test. It covers FAA exam material that applies to airplanes, including pertinent Federal Aviation Regulations (FARs). Questions about rotorcraft, gliders, balloons, powered-lift, and airships are not included.

We recommend that you use this test guide as part of the Guided Flight Discovery (GFD) Pilot Training System. The test guide is organized like the GFD Private Pilot Textbook, with 11 chapters and sections within each chapter. Questions are covered in the test guide in roughly the same sequence as the material in the textbook. References to applicable sections in the textbook are included along with the answers. An extra chapter in the test guide (Chapter 12) covers questions related to the regulations (14 CFR 1, 61, 91, and 49 CFR 830) that are not covered in other chapters.

Within the chapters, each section contains a brief introduction. FAA test questions appear in the left column and answers and explanations are in the right column. The following is an example of a typical reference for a question.

[1]	[2]	[3]	[4]	[5]	[6]	[7]
4-59	PLT025	PA.I.F.K6	4-59.	Answer C.	GFDPP 4B	AIM

(FAA Question)   *(Explanation of FAA Question)*

[1] Jeppesen designated test guide question number. The first number is the chapter where the question is located in the test guide, which usually corresponds to the chapter in the GFD textbook. The second number is the question number within the chapter. In this example, the question is the 59th question in chapter 4 of the test guide.

[2] The FAA learning statement code. You can find a list of learning statements with learning statement codes in Appendix 3. The FAA is phasing out these codes in favor of the new ACS codes.

[3] The new FAA airman certification standards (ACS) code is included on most questions. You can find these codes in the latest airman certification standards for the test you are preparing for. The FAA is still adjusting these codes between ACS releases. As a result, some codes in this Test Guide might not match the latest FAA content.

[4] The Jeppesen test guide number is repeated in the right-hand column above the explanation.

[5] The correct answer to the question, in this example, answer C is correct.

[6] The location where the question is covered in the GFD textbook. In this case, the question is covered in Chapter 4, Section B in the GFD Private Pilot textbook. In some cases, a page number might be included.

[7] Abbreviation for the FAA or other authoritative source document. In this example, the reference is the *Aeronautical Information Manual* (AIM). The following abbreviations can appear in Jeppesen test guides.

AC	—	Advisory Circular
A/FD	—	Airport/Facility Directory (section in Chart Supplement)
AFH	—	Airplane Flying Handbook, FAA-H-8083-3
AIM	—	Aeronautical Information Manual
ASI-SA##	—	Air Safety Institute (AOPA) Safety Advisor (by number ##)
AW	—	Aviation Weather, AC 00-6A
AWS	—	Aviation Weather Services, AC 00-45
FAR	—	Federal Aviation Regulation (14 CFR)
GFDIC	—	Guided Flight Discovery Instrument/Commercial Textbook
GFDPP	—	Guided Flight Discovery Private Pilot Textbook

IAP	—	Instrument Approach Procedure
IFH	—	Instrument Flying Handbook, FAA-H-8083-15
IPG	—	Instrument Procedures Guide (Jeppesen)
IPH	—	Instrument Procedures Handbook, FAA-H-8083-16
NAVWEPS	—	Aerodynamics for Naval Aviators
PHB	—	Pilot's Handbook of Aeronautical Knowledge, FAA-H-8083-25
RMH	—	Risk Management Handbook, FAA-H-8083-2
WBH	—	Aircraft Weight and Balance Handbook, FAA-H-8083-1
TERPS	—	U.S. Standard for Terminal Instrument Procedures

Below the reference line is the FAA question in the left column and the explanation in the right column. The explanation includes the correct answer followed by an explanation of why the answer is correct and if needed, why the other answers are wrong, unless the explanation of the correct answer makes it obvious. Wrong answers are not explained for calculated answers, unless a common error in the calculations leads to one of the wrong answers.

The answers in this test guide are based on official reference documents and, in our judgment, are the best choices of the available answers. Some questions that were valid when the FAA test was developed might no longer be appropriate due to ongoing changes in regulations or official operating procedures. The knowledge test that you take can be updated at any time. Therefore, when taking the FAA test, it is important to answer the questions according to the latest regulations or official operating procedures.

Three appendixes are included in the back of the test guide. Appendix 1 provides legends from the FAA airman knowledge testing supplement. The legends are an important resource for answering questions about charts and the *Chart Supplement*. If you do not know the answer to a chart-related question, look in the legends and remember that they are available during your test. Appendix 2 contains the figures from the airman knowledge testing supplement that are required to answer questions that refer to figures. A copy of this supplement is available during your test, Appendix 3 contains the FAA learning statement codes and learning statements. The FAA is replacing the learning statement codes with the new ACS codes, but during the transition, the legacy codes are useful for reference.

RECREATIONAL AND SPORT PILOT COVERAGE

The recreational pilot certificate limits a person to flying a basic, single-engine airplane with no more than 180 horsepower within 50 NM of their home airport. Mainly because of the 50 NM limitation, the recreational pilot certificate has not been practical. Because the number of applicants for recreational pilot certificates is negligible, we have removed all recreational pilot questions from this test guide. If you are interested in simplified training and do not need all the private pilot privileges, consider checking out the sport pilot requirements in FAR 61, Subpart J (FAR 61.301 - FAR 61.327). The sport pilot certificate allows you to fly certain light, two-place aircraft during daylight hours and does not have the 50 NM limitation. You can use this guide, together with the sport pilot regulations, to prepare for the Sport Pilot knowledge test for airplane.

HOW TO PREPARE FOR THE FAA TEST

To become a safe and competent pilot, you need more than just the academic knowledge required to pass a test. For a comprehensive ground training program, we recommend a structured ground school with a qualified flight or ground instructor. An organized course of instruction covers the content more quickly, and enables you to obtain answers to questions you think of as you learn the material. The additional instruction is beneficial in your flight training.

Whether or not you use a structured ground training program, this test guide is an excellent learning aid to help you prepare for the FAA airman knowledge test. The test guide contains sample airplane questions similar to questions in the FAA knowledge test. By reviewing the questions and studying the GFD Private Pilot textbook and other training materials, you can be well equipped to take the test.

You can benefit more from your study if you test yourself as using this test guide. Cover the answers in the right-hand column, read each question, and choose what you consider the best answer. A sliding mask is provided for this purpose. Move down the sliding mask and read the answer and explanation for that question. You might mark the questions you miss for further study and review before taking the knowledge test.

After you complete your study, schedule your knowledge test right away, while the information is fresh in your mind. This helps you have more confidence when you take the FAA test.

ESTABLISHING YOUR ELIGIBILITY TO TAKE THE TEST

When you show up for the FAA airman knowledge test, you must show that you have completed the appropriate ground instruction or home study course. You need a graduation certificate from a pilot training course, or a written statement or logbook entry by a certified ground or flight instructor. Although it is best to obtain ground training from a qualified instructor, you may also use a suitable home study course that generates a graduation certificate.

You also must provide evidence of a permanent mailing address, appropriate identification, and proof of your age. The identification must include a current photograph, your signature, and your residential address if different from your mailing address. You may use more than one form of identification—a driver's license, government identification card, passport, alien residency (green) card, or a military identification card.

FAA KNOWLEDGE TEST REGISTRATION

Schedule your knowledge test with a company that the FAA has authorized to give these tests. The FAA has designated an airman knowledge testing (AKT) organization designation authorization (ODA) holder, which sponsors hundreds of knowledge testing center locations. Contact information for the AKT ODA holder is included at the end of this introduction.

The first step in taking a knowledge test is registration. You may either call the central registration phone number for the AKT ODA holder, or walk in to a local testing center. Before you call or go online to register for your test, be prepared to select a test date, choose a testing center, and pay for the test. You may register for tests several weeks in advance, and you may cancel your appointment in accordance with the AKT ODA holder's cancellation policy. If you do not follow the cancellation policy, you might be charged for the canceled test.

DESCRIPTION OF THE TEST

The Private Pilot Airplane (PAR) test contains 60 multiple-choice questions, and you have 2 hours and 30 minutes to complete it. Each test question is independent of other questions—a correct response to one question does not depend on, or influence, the correct response to another. The minimum passing score is 70 percent.

TIPS FOR TAKING AN FAA KNOWLEDGE TEST

Before starting the actual test, the testing software gives you a few sample questions so that you can practice navigating through the test. The sample questions in your practice session have no relation to the content of the test. This "practice test" familiarizes you with the look and feel of the system screens, including how to select answers, mark questions for later review, view the time remaining in the test, and use other features of the testing software.

After you start the actual test, you answer the questions that appear on the screen. If you are prepared, you will likely have plenty of time to complete the test. After you begin the test, the screen will show you the time remaining for completion. When taking the test, keep the following points in mind:

1. Answer each question in accordance with the latest regulations and procedures. If a recent change invalidates a question, you receive credit if you answer it. However, the FAA normally deletes or updates these questions.

2. Read each question carefully before looking at the possible answers. Make sure you clearly understand the problem before attempting to solve it.

3. After formulating an answer, determine which of the alternatives most nearly corresponds with that answer. The answer chosen should completely resolve the problem.

4. A question might appear to have more than one possible answer; however, only one answer is correct and complete. The other answers are either incomplete or are derived from popular misconceptions.

5. Make sure that you select an answer for each question. Questions left unanswered are counted as incorrect.

6. If you find a certain question difficult, mark it for review and proceed to the next question. After you answer the less difficult questions, return to the questions you marked for review and answer them. The review marking procedure is explained before you start the test. Although the testing software alerts you to unanswered questions, make sure that every question has an answer recorded before submitting the test for grading.

7. After solving a calculation problem, select the answer nearest to your solution. The problem has been checked with various calculators. If you solve it correctly, your result will be closer to the correct answer than the other choices.

8. For graph type questions, you may request a printed copy of the graph on which you may draw and write to compute the answer. You must turn in all paper work when you complete the test.

TEST MATERIALS, REFERENCE MATERIALS, AND AIDS

You are allowed to use aids, reference materials, and test materials within specified guidelines, provided the actual test questions or answers are not revealed. You may use aviation-oriented computers, including hand-held computers designed expressly for aviation use, and also small electronic calculators that perform arithmetic functions. Simple programmable memories, which allow addition to, subtraction from, or retrieval of one number from the memory, are acceptable. Simple functions such as square root and percent keys are also acceptable. The following guidelines apply:

1. You may use any reference materials provided with the test. In addition, you may use scales, straightedges, protractors, plotters, navigation computers, log sheets, and electronic or mechanical calculators that are directly related to the test.

2. Manufacturer's permanently inscribed instructions on the front and back of such aids, such as formulas, conversions, regulations, signals, weather data, frequencies, and weight-and-balance formulas are permissible. However, you are not permitted to use any booklet or manual containing instructions on the use of test aids.

3. Testing centers may provide a calculator to you or deny use of your personal calculator based on the following limitations:

   • Before and after the test, while in the presence of the unit member (formerly a *proctor*), you must erase the device's memory. You may not use a device that has permanent memory, or when the unit member cannot determine the erasure capability.

   • If your calculator has a printer, you must surrender any hard copies at the completion of the test.

   • You may not use any device that can store pre-written programs or information related to the test.

4. Dictionaries are not allowed in the testing area.

5. The unit member makes the final determination of which test materials and personal possessions you may take into the testing area.

WHERE TO TAKE THE FAA TEST

To schedule your test, contact the following airman knowledge testing organization designation authorization holder. The designee has knowledge testing centers at various locations throughout the United States.

Computer Assisted Testing Service (CATS)
www.catstest.com/
Applicant inquiry and test registration: 1-800-947-4228
From outside the U.S. (650) 259-8550

YOUR TEST RESULTS

Upon completion of the knowledge test, you receive your airman knowledge test report with your score. The test report is stamped with the raised or embossed seal of the testing center. You present the airman knowledge test report to the examiner before taking your practical test. During the oral portion of the practical test, the examiner is required to evaluate the noted areas of deficiency. [Figure A]

U.S. DEPARTMENT OF TRANSPORTATION
Federal Aviation Administration
Airman Knowledge Test Report

NAME: Jeffrey Scott   APPLICANT ID: 123456789

EXAM: Private Pilot-Airplane   EXAM ID: 90121120070468013

EXAM DATE: 12/11/2007   EXAM SITE: ABS80102

SCORE: 75%   GRADE: PASS   TAKE: 1

Below are learning statement codes which represent learning statements for incorrectly answered questions. For code descriptions, refer to the Learning Statement Reference Guide for Airman Knowledge Testing on the Internet: **www.faa.gov/education_research/testing/airmen/media/LearningStatementReferenceGuide.pdf** .

A single code may represent more than one incorrect response.

PLT012 PLT023 PLT090 PLT091 PLT141 PLT161 PLT173 PLT263 PLT366 PLT369 PLT420 PLT446

PLT447 PLT514

DO NOT LOSE THIS REPORT   (emboss here)

(Place red stamp above here)

EXPIRATION DATE: 12/31/2009

- -

Authorized instructor's statement. (If applicable)

On_____(date) I gave the above named applicant _____ hours of additional instruction in each subject area shown to be deficient and consider the applicant competent to pass the test.

Last _____ Initial _____ Cert. No. _____ Type _____
(Print clearly)

Signature _____

FRAUDULENT ALTERATION OF THIS FORM BY ANY PERSON IS A BASIS FOR SUSPENSION OR REVOCATION OF ANY CERTIFICATES OR RATINGS HELD BY THAT PERSON.

ISSUED BY: Computer Assisted Testing Service, CATS (01/06)

FEDERAL AVIATION ADMINISTRATION

Figure A. This sample airman knowledge test report shows an applicant's test results. Take 1 indicates this is the first time the applicant has taken this test. Learning statement codes for incorrect answers are included in the report; your report might have the new ACS codes.

The airman knowledge test report includes learning statement codes (or ACS codes) for incorrect answers. To determine the knowledge areas in which question were missed, compare the codes on this report to the learning statement codes in Appendix 3 or to the ACS codes in the Private Pilot Airman Certification Standards.

Airman knowledge test reports are valid for 24 calendar months. **If the airman knowledge test report expires before you complete the practical test, you must retake the knowledge test.**

RETESTING AFTER FAILURE

An applicant may apply for retesting after an authorized instructor provides additional training and an endorsement that the applicant is competent to pass the test. Before retesting, the applicant must surrender the previous test report to the unit member, who will destroy that test report after administering the retest. The results from the latest test taken are the official score.

CHAPTER 1

DISCOVERING AVIATION

Each chapter and section in this *Private Pilot FAA Airmen Knowledge Test Guide* corresponds to the same chapter and section in *Private Pilot* Textbook, part of the Guided Flight Discovery pilot training system. The textbook, also available as an e-Book, explores in depth each topic presented in this guide. You are expected to demonstrate understanding of this content on your knowledge test and practical tests.

SECTION A — PILOT TRAINING

THE TRAINING PROCESS

- The Federal Aviation Administration (FAA) oversees all regulatory aspects of flight, including the process by which you obtain your private pilot certificate.

- Your training focuses on gaining the skills and knowledge that the FAA Private Pilot Airman Certification Standards (ACS) require for issuing a private pilot certificate.

- With respect to the certification of airmen, categories of aircraft are airplane, rotorcraft, powered lift, glider, lighter-than-air, weight-shift control, and powered parachute. This guide focuses on the knowledge requirements for the airplane category.

- For aircraft certification, category relates to the intended use of an aircraft and sets strict limits on its operation. Examples include transport, normal, utility, acrobatic, limited, restricted, and provisional.

- To be eligible for a student pilot certificate you must be at least 16 years of age and be able to read, speak, and understand the English language.

- In addition to the student pilot requirements, to be eligible for a private pilot certificate you must be at least 17 years of age, complete specific training and flight time requirements described in the FARs, pass a knowledge test, and successfully complete a practical test that consists of oral quizzing, performing pilot operations, and executing maneuvers in the airplane.

- To act as pilot in command of an aircraft carrying passengers, you must have performed at least three take-offs and landings in an aircraft of the same category and class within the preceding 90 days. If a type rating is required, the aircraft must be of the same type.

- To meet the recency of experience requirements to act as pilot in command carrying passengers at night, a pilot must have made at least three takeoffs and three landings to a full stop within the preceding 90 days in the same category and class of aircraft to be used. These takeoffs and landings must be done during the time period from one hour after sunset to one hour before sunrise.

- If recency of experience requirements for night flight are not met, the latest time passengers may be carried is one hour after official sunset.

- The takeoffs and landings required to meet the recency of flight experience requirements for carrying passengers in a tailwheel airplane must be in a tailwheel airplane and to a full stop.

- To continue acting as pilot in command of an aircraft, you must satisfactorily complete a flight review every 24 calendar months.

MEDICAL CERTIFICATES

- The three classes of medical certificates are: first-class, required for airline transport pilots; second-class, required for commercial pilot operations other than airline transport; and third-class for student and private pilots.

- A third-class medical certificate expires at the end of the 24th calendar month after the date of examination, if the pilot is age 40 or over at the time of the examination. It expires at the end of the 60th calendar month, if the pilot is under age 40.

- A second-class medical expires at the end of the 12th calendar month after the date of examination, for commercial pilot privileges. It expires at the end of the 24th calendar month for private pilot privileges, if age 40 or over, and at the end of the 60th month, if under age 40.

- A first-class medical certificate is valid to exercise the privileges of an ATP until the end of the sixth calendar month after the date of examination for pilots age 40 or over. At that point, the medical is valid for second-class privileges, such as those requiring a commercial certificate, until the end of the 12th calendar month. After that, the certificate is valid for third-class privileges, such as those requiring a private pilot certificate, until the end of the 24th calendar month after the month of the examination. If the pilot is under age 40, the first-class medical certificate is valid until the end of the 12th month for first and second class privileges, with third-class privileges available until the end of the 60th calendar month after the month of the examination.

- To continue acting as a pilot after your medical certificate expires, you must obtain a new exam from an aviation medical examiner or if you qualify, comply with the requirements of the BasicMed rule, which permits certain operations with a driver's license instead of a medical certificate.

- The FAA BasicMed rule allows pilots to operate small aircraft on certain personal flights using a driver's license instead of a medical certificate. To qualify, pilots must obtain a physical exam from a state-licensed physician every 48 months and have that physician complete an FAA-provided checklist, complete an approved online medical education course every 24 months, and consent to a National Driver Register check.

1-1   PLT371   PA.I.A.K1

With respect to the certification of airmen, which are categories of aircraft?

A – Gyroplane, helicopter, airship, free balloon

B – Airplane, rotorcraft, glider, lighter-than-air

C – Single-engine land and sea, multiengine land and sea

1-1. Answer B. GFDPPM 1A, FAR 1.1
Airmen are certificated according to five categories of aircraft: airplane, rotorcraft, glider, lighter-than-air, and a new category, powered lift. Gyroplane and helicopter are classes of aircraft within the rotorcraft category. Airship and balloon are classes of aircraft within the lighter-than-air category. Single-engine land and sea and multiengine land and sea are the four classes within the airplane category.

1-2   PLT371   PA.I.A.K1

With respect to the certification of airmen, which is a class of aircraft?

A – Airplane, rotorcraft, glider, lighter-than-air

B – Single-engine land and sea, multiengine land and sea

C – Lighter-than-air, airship, hot air balloon, gas balloon

1-2. Answer B. GFDPPM 1A, FAR 1.1
Each category of aircraft is broken down into classes. The airplane category is divided into single-engine land and sea, and multi-engine land and sea.

1-3   PLT371   PA.I.A.K1

With respect to the certification of aircraft, which is a category of aircraft?

A – Normal, utility, acrobatic

B – Airplane, rotorcraft, glider

C – Landplane, seaplane

1-3. Answer A. GFDPPM 1A, FAR 1.1

Normal, utility, and acrobatic are three of the categories under which aircraft are certified, based on their construction and use. Airplane, rotorcraft, and glider are categories of aircraft with respect to certification of AIRMEN. Landplane and seaplane are common, but incomplete, descriptions of CLASSES of airplanes based on airmen certification.

1-4   PLT371   PA.I.A.K1

With respect to the certification of aircraft, which is a class of aircraft?

A – Normal, utility, acrobatic, limited

B – Airplane, rotorcraft, glider, balloon

C – Transport, restricted, provisional

1-4. Answer B. GFDPPM 1A, FAR 1.1

FAR 1.1 defines "class" when used with respect to the certification of aircraft, as a broad grouping of aircraft having similar means of flight, propulsion or landing. These classes include: airplane, rotorcraft, glider, balloon, and powered-lift. In reality, however, class is not used as a designator in aircraft certification.

1-5   PLT427   PA.I.A.K3

A third-class medical certificate is issued to a 36-year-old pilot on August 10, this year. To exercise the privileges of a private pilot certificate, the medical certificate will be valid until midnight on

A – August 10, three years later

B – August 31, three years later

C – August 31, five years later

1-5. Answer C. FAR 61.23

For pilots who were under 40 years of age at the time of their medical exam, a third-class medical certificate expires at the end of the 60th month after the examination.

1-6   PLT427   PA.I.A.K3

A third-class medical certificate is issued to a 51-year-old pilot on May 3, this year. To exercise the privileges of a private pilot certificate, the medical certificate will be valid until midnight on

A – May 31, two years later

B – May 31, three years later

C – May 31, five years later

1-6. Answer A. FAR 61.23

For pilots who were 40 years of age or more at the time of their medical exam, a third-class medical certificate expires at the end of the 24th month after the examination.

1-7 PLT427 PA.I.A.K3

You were 40 years old when you obtained a second-class medical certificate on March 15, 2018. For exercising private pilot privileges, when does your medical certificate expire?

A – March 15, 2020

B – March 31, 2020

C – March 31, 2023

1-7. Answer B. FAR 61.23

For pilots who were 40 years of age or more at the time of their medical exam, second class privileges expire at the end of the 12th month after the month of the examination and third-class privileges expire at the end of the 24th month after the examination.

1-8 PLT427 PA.I.A.K3

For private pilot operations, a second-class medical certificate issued to a 42-year-old pilot on July 15, 2018, will expire at midnight on

A – July 31, 2019

B – July 15, 2020

C – July 31, 2020

1-8. Answer C. FAR 61.23

For a pilot age 40 or over to exercise the privileges of a commercial pilot, a second-class medical is valid until the end of the 12th calendar month after the date of examination. For private pilot operations, a second-class medical is valid until the end of the 24th calendar month after the date of examination.

1-9 PLT427 PA.I.A.K3

For private pilot operations, a first-class medical certificate issued to a 23-year-old pilot on October 21, this year, will expire at midnight on

A – October 31, next year.

B – October 21, two years later.

C – October 31, five years later.

1-9. Answer C. FAR 61.23

For pilots under 40 years of age, to exercise the privileges of an ATP, a first-class medical certificate is valid until the end of the 12th calendar month after the date of examination. From the beginning of the 13th month to the end of the 60th calendar month, a first-class medical is valid only for operations requiring a third-class medical certificate.

1-10 PLT427 PA.I.A.K9

A third-class medical certificate was issued to a 19-year-old pilot on August 10, this year. To exercise the privileges of a private pilot certificate, the medical certificate will expire at midnight on

A – August 10, two years later.

B – August 31, two years later.

C – August 31, five years later.

1-10. Answer C. FAR 61.23

A third-class medical, which is appropriate to exercise the privileges of a private pilot, expires at the end of the 60th calendar month after the date of examination, if under the age of 40 at the time of the examination.

1-11   PLT427   PA.I.A.K3

The FAA BasicMed rule allows pilots to operate small aircraft on certain personal flights

A – without a physical examination.

B – using a driver's license instead of a medical certificate.

C – after one-time completion of an approved online medical education course.

1-11. Answer B. FAR 61.23, 61.113

The FAA BasicMed rule allows pilots to operate small aircraft on certain personal flights using a driver's license instead of a medical certificate. To qualify, pilots must obtain a physical exam from a state-licensed physician every 48 months and have that physician complete an FAA-provided checklist; complete an approved BasicMed online medical education course every 24 months, and consent to a National Driver Register check.

1-12   PLT427   PA.I.A.K3

The BasicMed rule allows you to use a driver's license instead of an FAA medical certificate under what conditions?

A – You may operate below 18,000 feet MSL at a maximum airspeed of 250 knots.

B – You may operate outside the United States as long as the flight is not for compensation or hire.

C – You may carry up to 6 passengers in an aircraft with a maximum certificated takeoff weight of no more than 6,000 pounds.

1-12. Answer A. FAR 61.23, 61.113

Under the BasicMed rule, you may conduct flight operations:

- In an aircraft certificated to carry no more than 6 occupants, including the pilot, and with a maximum certificated takeoff weight of no more than 6,000 pounds.
- Below 18,000 feet MSL.
- At a maximum airspeed of 250 knots.
- That are entirely within the United States.
- That are not for compensation or hire.

Answer C is wrong because the aircraft may have a total of 6 occupants, not 6 passengers plus a pilot.

1-13   PLT427   PA.I.A.K3

What requirements must you meet to utilize the BasicMed rule?

A – You must have completed an approved BasicMed exam from an aviation medical examiner within the previous 48 months.

B – You must have completed an approved medical education course within the previous 24 calendar months and a comprehensive medical exam from a physician within the previous 48 months.

C – You must have completed an approved medical education course within the previous 48 months and a comprehensive medical exam from a physician within the previous 24 calendar months.

1-13. Answer B. FAR 61.23, 61.113

To qualify for the BasicMed rule, you must:

- Possess and carry a valid U.S. driver's license.
- Have completed an approved medical education course—available online from the Aircraft Owners and Pilots Association (AOPA)—within the previous 24 calendar months.
- Received a comprehensive medical exam from a state-licensed physician within the previous 48 months.
- Certify that you are under the care and treatment of a physician for any diagnosed medical condition that could impact your ability to fly and that you are medically fit to fly.
- Agree to a National Driver Register check.

Answer A is wrong because there is no such thing as an "approved BasicMed exam"; you obtain a normal physical exam from a state-licensed physician who does *not* have to be an aviation medical examiner.

1-14   PLT444   PA.I.A.K1

To act as pilot in command of an aircraft carrying passengers, a pilot must show by logbook endorsement the satisfactory completion of a flight review or completion of a pilot proficiency check within the preceding

A – 6 calendar months.

B – 12 calendar months.

C – 24 calendar months.

1-14. Answer C. FAR 61.56

To act as pilot in command of any aircraft, whether you are carrying passengers or not, you must have, within the preceding 24 calendar months, complied with the flight review requirements.

1-15   PLT444   PA.I.A.K1

If recency of experience requirements for night flight are not met and official sunset is 1830, the latest time passengers may be carried is

A – 1829.

B – 1859.

C – 1929.

1-15. Answer C. FAR 61.57

No person may act as pilot in command of an aircraft carrying passengers during the period beginning one hour after sunset and ending one hour before sunrise, unless that person meets night experience requirements.

1-16   PLT444   PA.I.A.K1

Your cousin wants you to take him flying. You must have made at least three takeoffs and three landings within the preceding

A – 90 days.

B – 12 calendar months.

C – 24 calendar months.

1-16. Answer A. FAR 61.57

To meet recent flight experience requirements for carrying passengers, you must have, within the preceding 90 days, made three takeoffs and landings in the same category and class of aircraft (to a full stop for night currency requirements).

1-17   PLT444   PA.I.A.K1

To act as pilot in command of an aircraft carrying passengers, a pilot must have made three takeoffs and three landings within the preceding 90 days in an aircraft of the same

A – make and model.

B – category and class, but not type.

C – category, class, and type, if a type rating is required.

1-17. Answer C. FAR 61.57

To meet the recency of experience requirements for carrying passengers, FAR 61.57(c) states that you must have made three takeoffs and landings within the preceding 90 days in an aircraft of the same category and class, and if a type rating is required, of the same type.

1-18 PLT451 PA.I.A.K1

The takeoffs and landings required to meet the recency of experience requirements for carrying passengers in a tailwheel airplane

A – may be touch and go or full stop.

B – must be touch and go.

C – must be to a full stop.

1-18. Answer C. FAR 61.57

On a tailwheel airplane, skillful handling is required to avoid ground looping the airplane, especially in adverse wind conditions. Touch-and-go landings, especially wheel landings, would be inadequate for obtaining this difficult practice. That is why the FAA requires full-stop landings for currency in a tail dragger.

1-19 PLT451 PA.I.A.K1

The three takeoffs and landings that are required to act as pilot in command at night must be done during the time period from

A – sunset to sunrise.

B – one hour after sunset to one hour before sunrise.

C – the end of evening civil twilight to the beginning of morning civil twilight.

1-19. Answer B. FAR 61.57

To act as pilot in command of an aircraft carrying passengers between one hour after sunset and one hour before sunrise, you must have, within the preceding 90 days, made three takeoffs and landings to a full stop.

1-20 PLT444 PA.I.A.K1

To meet the recency of experience requirements to act as pilot in command carrying passengers at night, a pilot must have made at least three takeoffs and three landings to a full stop within the preceding 90 days in

A – any aircraft.

B – the same type of aircraft to be used.

C – the same category and class of aircraft to be used.

1-20. Answer C. FAR 61.57

No person may act as pilot in command of an aircraft carrying passengers at night unless that person has made three takeoffs and three landings to a full stop within the preceding 90 days. The takeoffs and landings must be at night and in the same category and class of aircraft that is to be used for the carriage of passengers.

1-21 PLT407 PA.I.A.K1

If a private pilot had a flight review on August 8, this year, when is the next flight review required?

A – August 31, next year.

B – August 8, two years later.

C – August 31, two years later.

1-21. Answer C. FAR 61.56

To act as pilot in command of an aircraft, a private pilot must have, within the preceding 24 calendar months, complied with the flight review requirement. (Calendar month means the review is good until the end of the month in which it expires.)

1-22   PLT407   PA.I.A.K1

Each private pilot is required to have

A – an annual flight review.

B – a biennial flight review.

C – a semiannual flight review.

1-22. Answer B. FAR 61.56

For any pilot to act as pilot in command of an aircraft, that person must have, within the preceding 24 calendar months, complied with the flight review requirement. Because of the two-year interval, this flight review is sometimes called a biennial flight review.

1-23   PLT448   PA.I.A.K1

In regard to privileges and limitations, a private pilot may

A – not be paid in any manner for the operating expenses of a flight.

B – not pay less than the pro rata share of the operating expenses of a flight with passengers provided the expenses involve only fuel, oil, airport expenditures, or rental fees.

C – act as pilot in command of an aircraft carrying a passenger for compensation if the flight is in connection with a business or employment.

1-23. Answer B. FAR 61.113

A private pilot may not pay less than the pro rata share of the operating expenses of a flight with passengers, provided the expenses involve only fuel, oil, airport expenditures, or rental fees.

1-24   PLT448   PA.I.A.K1

According to regulations pertaining to privileges and limitations, a private pilot may

A – not pay less than the pro rata share of the operating expenses of a flight with passengers provided the expenses involve only fuel, oil, airport expenditures, or rental fees.

B – not be paid in any manner for the operating expenses of a flight.

C – be paid for the operating expenses of a flight if at least three takeoffs and three landings were made by the pilot within the preceding 90 days.

1-24. Answer A. FAR 61.113

A private pilot may not pay less than the pro rata share of the operating expenses of a flight with passengers, provided the expenses involve only fuel, oil, airport expenditures, or rental fees.

1-25   PLT448   PA.I.A.K1

What exception, if any, permits a private pilot to act as pilot in command of an aircraft carrying passengers who pay for the flight?

A – If the passengers pay all the operating expenses

B – If a donation is made to a charitable organization for the flight

C – There is no exception

1-25. Answer B. FAR 61.113

Paragraph 61.113 of the FARs indicates a private pilot may act as pilot in command of an aircraft used in a passenger-carrying airlift sponsored by a charitable organization, and for which the passengers make a donation to the organization.

SECTION B — AVIATION OPPORTUNITIES

ADDITIONAL TRAINING, FLIGHT EXPERIENCE AND RATINGS

- The pilot in command is required to hold a type rating for the operation of aircraft having a gross weight of more than 12,500 pounds.
- The definition of a high-performance airplane is an airplane that has an engine with more than 200 horsepower.
- Before a person holding a private pilot certificate may act as pilot in command of a high-performance airplane, that person must have received flight instruction from an authorized flight instructor, who then endorses that person's logbook. The instruction must be given in a high-performance airplane.
- The definition of a complex airplane is an airplane with retractable landing gear, flaps, and a controllable propeller or full authority digital engine control (FADEC).
- Before a person holding a private pilot certificate may act as pilot in command of a complex airplane, that person must have received flight instruction from an authorized flight instructor, who then endorses that person's logbook. The instruction must be given in a complex airplane.

1-26   PLT399   PA.I.A.K1

The pilot in command is required to hold a type rating in which aircraft?

A – Aircraft involved in ferry flights, training flights, or test flights

B – Aircraft having a gross weight of more than 12,500 pounds

C – Aircraft operated under an authorization issued by the Administrator

1-26. Answer B. FAR 1.1, FAR 61.5, FAR 61.31

FAR 61.31 indicates that a type rating is required for a large aircraft. FAR 1.1 defines large aircraft as having a gross weight greater than 12,500 pounds.

1-27   PLT399   PA.I.A.K8

What is the definition of a high-performance airplane?

A – An airplane with 180 horsepower, or retractable landing gear, flaps, and a fixed-pitch propeller

B – An airplane with a normal cruise speed of more than 200 knots

C – An airplane with an engine of more than 200 horsepower

1-27. Answer C. FAR 61.31

A high-performance airplane has an engine with more than 200 horsepower. A complex airplane has retractable landing gear, flaps, and a controllable propeller. Cruise speed is not used to determine whether an airplane is high performance.

1-28   PLT399   PA.I.A.K8

Before a person holding a private pilot certificate may act as pilot in command of a high-performance airplane, that person must have

A – passed a flight test in that airplane from an FAA inspector.

B – an endorsement in that person's logbook that he or she is competent to act as pilot in command.

C – received ground and flight instruction from an authorized flight instructor who then endorses that person's logbook.

1-28. Answer C. FAR 61.31

In order to act as pilot in command of a high-performance airplane, you must have received ground and flight instruction from an authorized flight instructor who then endorses that person's logbook. Answer B is partly correct, but is not the most complete answer.

1-29   PLT448   PA.I.A.K8

In order to act as pilot in command of a high-performance airplane, a pilot must have

A – received and logged ground and flight instruction in an airplane that has more than 200 horsepower.

B – made and logged three solo takeoffs and landings in a high-performance airplane.

C – passed a flight test in a high-performance airplane.

1-29. Answer A. FAR 61.31

No person may act as pilot in command of a high-performance airplane (an airplane with an engine of more than 200 horsepower) unless that person has received ground and flight instruction from an authorized flight instructor in a high-performance airplane and received a one-time endorsement in that person's logbook showing proficiency.

1-30   PLT399   PA.I.A.K8

What is the definition of a complex airplane?

A – An airplane with retractable landing gear, flaps, and a controllable-pitch propeller (or FADEC)

B – An airplane with a normal cruise speed of more than 200 knots

C – An airplane with an engine of more than 200 horsepower

1-30. Answer A. FAR 61.31

A complex airplane has retractable landing gear, flaps, and a controllable pitch propeller (or FADEC). A high-performance airplane has an engine with more than 200 horsepower. Cruise speed is not used to determine whether an airplane is high performance or complex.

1-31   PLT399   PA.I.A.K8

Before a person holding a private pilot certificate may act as pilot in command of a complex airplane, that person must have

A – passed a flight test in that airplane from an FAA inspector.

B – an endorsement in that person's logbook that he or she is competent to act as pilot in command.

C – received ground and flight instruction from an authorized flight instructor who then endorses that person's logbook.

1-31. Answer C. FAR 61.31

In order to act as pilot in command of a complex airplane (an airplane with retractable landing gear, flaps, and a controllable pitch propeller or full authority digital engine control (FADEC)), you must have received ground and flight instruction from an authorized flight instructor and received a one-time endorsement in your logbook showing proficiency.

1-32   PLT448   PA.I.A.K8

In order to act as pilot in command of a complex airplane, you must

A – receive and log ground and flight instruction in a complex airplane.

B – make and log three solo takeoffs and landings in a complex airplane.

C – pass a flight test in a complex airplane.

1-32. Answer A. FAR 61.31

To act as pilot in command of a complex airplane (an airplane with retractable landing gear, flaps, and a controllable pitch propeller or full authority digital engine control (FADEC)), you must receive ground and flight instruction from an authorized flight instructor with a one-time endorsement in your logbook showing proficiency.

SECTION C — INTRODUCTION TO HUMAN FACTORS

ELECTRONIC FLIGHT DISPLAY

- Pilots who are transitioning to an electronic flight display can experience information overload.
- A common error associated with using a moving map is overreliance on the moving map leading to complacency.
- Automation management typically applies to an airplane with an advanced avionics system that includes digital displays, GPS equipment, a moving map, and an integrated autopilot.
- To manage automation effectively, monitor the current mode, anticipate the next mode, and verify that mode changes occur as expected.
- To help manage automation and other avionics equipment, consider using one of three equipment operating levels during flight operations.

DRUGS AND ALCOHOL

- A person may not act as a crewmember of a civil aircraft if alcoholic beverages have been consumed within the preceding eight hours, or with 0.04 percent or more alcohol in the blood by weight.
- A pilot may not allow a person who is obviously under the influence of drugs to be carried aboard an aircraft except in an emergency, or if the person is a medical patient under proper care.
- A conviction for driving while intoxicated by alcohol or drugs shall be reported to the FAA Civil Aviation Security Division no later than 60 days after the motor vehicle action.

SINGLE-PILOT RESOURCE MANAGEMENT

- Single-pilot resource management (SRM) is the art and science of managing all available resources—both on board the airplane and from outside sources—prior and during flight to ensure the successful completion of a flight.

- Aeronautical decision making (ADM) is a systematic approach to the mental process used by aircraft pilots to consistently determine the best course of action in response to a given set of circumstances.

- Risk management involves making decisions about four fundamental risk elements: the pilot, the aircraft, the environment, and the type of operation. Sometimes these risk elements are classified using the 5Ps—pilot, passengers, plane, programming, plan.

1-33   PLT436   PA.I.H.K2

How soon after the conviction for driving while intoxicated by alcohol or drugs shall it be reported to the FAA, Civil Aviation Security Division?

A – No later than 60 days after the motor vehicle action

B – No later than 30 working days after the motor vehicle action

C – Required to be reported upon renewal of medical certificate

1-33. Answer A. FAR 91.15

Certificated pilots must provide a written report of each motor vehicle action to the FAA not later than 60 days after the action.

1-34   PA.I.A.R4

Pilots who are transitioning to an electronic flight display can experience information

A – inaccuracy.

B – overload.

C – deficiency.

1-34. Answer B. GFDPP 1C, PHB

A major benefit of an electronic flight display is the abundance of information the system provides. While this extra information can improve situational awareness, it can also overload a pilot, leading to distraction and loss of situational awareness. An important part of the training on these systems is focusing pilots on the information they need so that they can disregard extraneous data.

1-35   PA.I.A.R4

One hazard of flying an airplane with an autopilot and an electronic flight display is

A – lack of relevant flight information.

B – overreliance on hand-flying skills.

C – pilot complacency and loss of situational awareness.

1-35. Answer C. GFDPP 1C, PHB

Relying too heavily on automation can lead to complacency and a loss of situational awareness. If you become overly dependent on automation, equipment failure can have serious consequences. Maintain your flight skills and your ability to maneuver and navigate the airplane manually.

1-36 PLT463 PA.I.H.K2

A person may not act as a crewmember of a civil aircraft if alcoholic beverages have been consumed by that person within the preceding

A – 8 hours.

B – 12 hours.

C – 24 hours.

1-36. Answer A. FAR 91.17
A common saying used in aviation for this regulation is "eight hours from bottle to throttle." In other words, no person may act or attempt to act as a crewmember of a civil aircraft within eight hours after the consumption of any alcoholic beverage.

1-37 PLT463 PA.I.H.K2

Under what condition, if any, may a pilot allow a person who is obviously under the influence of drugs to be carried aboard an aircraft?

A – Under no condition.

B – In an emergency, or if the person is a medical patient under proper care.

C – Only if the person does not have access to the cockpit or pilot's compartment.

1-37. Answer B. FAR 91.17
Except in an emergency, no pilot of a civil aircraft may allow a person who appears to be intoxicated or who demonstrates by manner or physical indications that the individual is under the influence of drugs (except a patient under proper care) to be carried in that aircraft.

1-38 PLT463 PA.I.H.K2

No person may attempt to act as a crewmember of a civil aircraft with

A – 0.008 percent by weight or more alcohol in the blood.

B – 0.004 percent by weight or more alcohol in the blood.

C – 0.04 percent by weight or more alcohol in the blood.

1-38. Answer C. FAR 91.17
No person may act or attempt to act as a crewmember of a civil aircraft while having 0.04 percent by weight or more alcohol in the blood.

CHAPTER 2

AIRPLANE SYSTEMS

SECTION A — AIRPLANES

- The airframe on an airplane consists of the fuselage, wings, empennage, trim devices, and landing gear.
- The engine and propeller provide thrust.
- You can find the operating limitations for an aircraft in the current, FAA-approved flight manual, approved manual material, markings, and placards, or any combination of these items. On experimental and light-sport aircraft, these limitations are attached to the airworthiness certificate.
- The FAA-approved Airplane Flight Manual (AFM) is required to be carried in the airplane. On airplanes that are not required to have an AFM, such as airplanes certified before the AFM was a requirement, the limitations for the airplane must be available in approved manual material, markings, and placards, or a combination thereof.

MAINTENANCE

- Required inspections must be conducted by an appropriately certificated aviation maintenance technician (AMT) and documented in the maintenance records for the aircraft.
- You may not fly an aircraft unless it has received an annual inspection and an ELT inspection within the previous 12 calendar months.
- When the ELT has been in use for more than one cumulative hour, or if 50 percent of the useful life the batteries expires, the batteries must be replaced or recharged.
- Transponder inspections are required within the previous 24 calendar months. If the aircraft is flown under IFR, altimeter and static system inspections are also required within the previous 24 calendar months.
- 100-hour inspections are required on aircraft that are used for flight instruction for hire and provided by the flight instructor, or that carry any person, other than a crewmember, for hire. The aircraft may be flown up to 10 additional hours enroute to a place where service can be completed. However, the next 100-hour inspection must be completed within 100 hours of the original expiration time.
- To determine the expiration date of any inspection, refer to the aircraft maintenance records.
- When an unsafe condition might exist or develop in an aircraft or other aircraft of the same design, the FAA publishes an airworthiness directive (AD). ADs are legally enforceable rules and compliance is mandatory.
- FAR 91.205 requires specific equipment to be installed and operational for day and night VFR flight, which includes flight instruments, engine and system monitoring indicators, and safety equipment.
- If an airplane has inoperative equipment and does not have an MEL, you must determine whether the equipment affects flight safety and if it is required by the FARs.
- If inoperative equipment is not required, you may fly the airplane if the equipment is removed and the cockpit control placarded by an AMT or deactivated and placarded "inoperative" (by an AMT if deactivation involves maintenance).
- To fly an airplane that is not airworthy to a location where repairs can be made, you can apply to the nearest FAA flight standards district office (FSDO) for a special flight permit.

PREVENTIVE MAINTENANCE

After preventive maintenance is performed on an aircraft, the signature, certificate number, and kind of certificate held by the person approving the work must be entered in the aircraft maintenance records.

2-1   PLT373   PA.I.F.K1

Where can the operating limitations for an aircraft be found?

A – On the airworthiness certificate

B – In the aircraft airframe and engine logbooks

C – In the current, FAA-approved flight manual, approved manual material, markings, and placards, or any combination thereof

2-1. Answer C. GFDPP 2A (FAR 91.9)
You can find the operating limitations in the current, FAA-approved flight manual, approved manual material, markings, and placards, or any combination of these items. On experimental and light-sport aircraft, these limitations are attached to the airworthiness certificate.

2-2   PLT377   PA.I.F.K1

If an aircraft has an experimental or special light-sport airworthiness certificate, where can its operating limitations be found?

A – Attached to the airworthiness certificate

B – In the current, FAA-approved flight manual

C – In the aircraft airframe and engine logbooks

2-2. Answer A. GFDPP 2A, FAA Order 8130.2
Operating limitations for experimental aircraft are part of Form 8130-7, which is the special airworthiness certificate. As with all airworthiness certificates, this one must be carried in the aircraft, which ensures that the operating limitations of an experimental or light-sport aircraft are available to the pilot.

2-3   PA.I.B.K3

Which of the following are required to be carried in the aircraft during flight?

A – Pilot's information manual (PIM)

B – Pilot's operating handbook (POH)

C – FAA-approved Airplane Flight Manual (AFM)

2-3. Answer C. GFDPP 2A, FAR 91.9
The FAA-approved Airplane Flight Manual (AFM) must be carried in the aircraft. Although the PIM and the POH are derivatives of the AFM, they do not meet the legal requirement.

2-4   PA.I.B.K1b

An annual inspection was performed on an aircraft June 13, 2018. When is the next annual inspection due?

A – June 1, 2019

B – June 13, 2019

C – June 30, 2019

2-4. Answer C. GFDPP 2A, FAR 91.409
The annual inspection is due on the last day of the 12th month after the inspection.

2-5   PLT372   PA.I.B.K1b

An annual inspection was performed on an aircraft July 12, this year. The next annual inspection is due no later than

A – July 1, next year.

B – July 13, next year.

C – July 31, next year.

2-5. Answer C. GFDPP 2A, FAR 91.409

No person may operate an aircraft unless, within the preceding 12 calendar months, it has had an annual inspection. The term "calendar month" is defined as to the end of the month.

2-6   PLT372   PA.I.B.K1b

To determine the expiration date of the last annual aircraft inspection, a person should refer to the

A – airworthiness certificate.

B – registration certificate.

C – aircraft maintenance records.

2-6. Answer C. GFDPP 2A, FAR 91.417

The registered owner or operator shall keep records of the maintenance, preventive maintenance, alterations, records of the 100-hour, annual, progressive, and other required or approved inspections, as appropriate, for each aircraft. This information is found in the maintenance records for the aircraft.

2-7   PLT372   PA.I.B.K1b

What aircraft inspections are required for rental aircraft that are also used for flight instruction?

A – Annual and 100-hour inspections

B – Biannual and 100-hour inspections

C – Annual and 50-hour inspections

2-7. Answer A. GFDPP 2A, FAR 91.409

No person may operate an aircraft carrying any person (other than a crewmember) for hire, or give flight instruction for hire in an aircraft that person provides, unless within the preceding 100 hours of time in service, the aircraft has received an annual or 100-hour inspection.

2-8   PLT372   PA.I.B.K1b

An aircraft had a 100-hour inspection when the tachometer read 1259.6. When is the next 100-hour inspection due?

A – 1349.6 hours

B – 1359.6 hours

C – 1369.6 hours

2-8. Answer B. GFDPP 2A, FAR 91.409

No person may operate an aircraft carrying any person (other than a crewmember) for hire, or give flight instruction for hire in an aircraft, which that person provides, unless within the preceding 100-hours of time in service, the aircraft has received an annual or 100-hour inspection.

2-9   PLT372   PA.I.B.K1b

A 100-hour inspection was due at 2202.5 hours on the tachometer. The 100-hour inspection was performed at 2209.5 hours. When is the next 100-hour inspection due?

A – 2302.5 hours

B – 2309.5 hours

C – 2312.5 hours

2-9. Answer A. GFDPP 2A, FAR 91.409

The 100-hour limitation may be exceeded by not more than 10 hours while enroute to reach a place where the inspection can be done. However, the next inspection is still due 100 hours after the original inspection was due.

2-10   PLT372   PA.I.B.K1b

A 100-hour inspection was due at 3303 hours. The 100-hour inspection was actually done at 3300 hours. When is the next 100-hour inspection due?

A – 3400 hours

B – 3403 hours

C – 3413 hours

2-10. Answer A. GFDPP 2A, FAR 91.409

If the 100-hour inspection is delayed past the time it is due, the next inspection is due 100 hours after the *original* inspection was due. However, If the 100-hour inspection is done ahead of schedule, the next inspection is due 100 hours after the *actual* time of the inspection.

2-11   PLT374   PA.I.B.K1

The responsibility for ensuring that an aircraft is maintained in an airworthy condition is primarily that of the

A – pilot in command.

B – owner or operator.

C – mechanic who performs the work.

2-11. Answer B. FAR 91.403

The owner or operator of an aircraft is primarily responsible for maintaining that aircraft in an airworthy condition. The pilot in command is responsible for checking the condition of the aircraft before flying it. The mechanic is only responsible for the work performed.

2-12   PLT444

Who is responsible for determining if an aircraft is in condition for safe flight?

A – A certificated aircraft mechanic

B – The pilot in command

C – The owner or operator

2-12. Answer B. FAR 91.7

The pilot in command of a civil aircraft is responsible, and has final authority, for determining whether that aircraft is in condition for safe flight.

2-13   PLT372   PA.I.B.K1b

Maintenance records show the last transponder inspection was performed on September 1, 2017. The next inspection is due no later than

A – September 30, 2018.

B – September 1, 2019.

C – September 30, 2019.

2-13. Answer C. FAR 91.413
No person may use an ATC transponder unless, within the preceding 24 calendar months, that transponder has been tested and found to comply with the appropriate standards listed in Appendix F of 14 CFR Part 43. The term "calendar month" refers to the end of the month when an inspection is due.

2-14   PLT373   PA.I.B.K1

Unless otherwise specifically authorized, no person may operate an aircraft that has an experimental certificate

A – beneath the floor of Class B airspace.

B – over a densely populated area or in a congested airway.

C – from the primary airport within Class D airspace.

2-14. Answer B. FAR 91.319
Unless otherwise authorized by the Administrator in special operating limitations, no person may operate an aircraft that has an experimental certificate over a densely populated area or in a congested airway.

2-15   PLT426   PA.I.B.K1b

The responsibility for ensuring that maintenance personnel make the appropriate entries in the aircraft maintenance records indicating the aircraft has been approved for return to service lies with the

A – owner or operator.

B – pilot in command.

C – mechanic who performed the work.

2-15. Answer A. FAR 91.405
Each owner or operator of an aircraft shall ensure that maintenance personnel make appropriate entries in the aircraft maintenance record.

2-16   PLT374   PA.I.B.K1b

Who is responsible for ensuring appropriate entries are made in maintenance records indicating the aircraft has been approved for return to service?

A – Repair station

B – Certified mechanic

C – Owner or operator

2-16. Answer C. FAR 91.405
Each owner or operator of an aircraft shall ensure that maintenance personnel make appropriate entries in the aircraft maintenance records indicating the aircraft has been approved for return to service.

2-17   PLT402   PA.I.B.K3

When must batteries in an emergency locator transmitter (ELT) be replaced or recharged, if rechargeable?

A – After any inadvertent activation of the ELT

B – When the ELT has been in use for more than one cumulative hour

C – When the ELT can no longer be heard over the airplane's communication radio receiver

2-17. Answer B. FAR 91.207
Batteries used in the emergency locator transmitters must be replaced (or recharged, if the battery is rechargeable) when the transmitter has been in use for more than one cumulative hour.

2-18   PLT402   PA.I.B.K3

When are non-rechargeable batteries of an emergency locator transmitter (ELT) required to be replaced?

A – Every 24 months

B – When 50 percent of their useful life expires

C – At the time of each 100-hour or annual inspection

2-18. Answer B. FAR 91.207
Non-rechargeable batteries used in the ELT must be replaced when 50 percent of their useful life, as established by the manufacturer, has expired.

2-19   PA.I.B.K3a

You discover inoperative equipment on an airplane that you are planning to fly. Under what conditions can you complete the flight under VFR?

A – The equipment is not required by 14 CFR 91.205.

B – The pilot in command, who has at least a private pilot certificate, determines the airplane is in a safe condition for flight.

C – The equipment is not required by 14 CFR 91.205, an equipment list or KOEL, the VFR-day type certificate requirements, or an AD.

2-19. Answer C. GFDPP 2A, FAR 91. 213
You must determine that the inoperative equipment is not required by:

- The VFR-day type certificate requirements prescribed in the airworthiness certification regulations.
- FAR 91.205 for the specific kind of flight operation (e.g. day or night VFR) or by other flight rules for the specific kind of flight to be conducted.
- The equipment list or the kinds of operations equipment list (KOEL) for the aircraft.
- An airworthiness directive (AD).

The inoperative equipment must be deactivated and placarded as inoperative.

2-20   PLT374   PA.I.B.K1c

Which records or documents shall the owner or operator of an aircraft keep to show compliance with an applicable airworthiness directive?

A – Aircraft maintenance records

B – Airworthiness Certificate and Pilot's Operating Handbook

C – Airworthiness and Registration Certificates

2-20. Answer A. GFDPP 2A, FAR 91.417
The owner or operator of an aircraft shall keep a record of current status of applicable airworthiness directives (ADs) in the appropriate aircraft maintenance records.

2-21   PLT378   PA.I.B.K1c

What should an owner or operator know about Airworthiness Directives (ADs)?

A – They are for informational purposes only.

B – They are mandatory.

C – They are voluntary.

2-21. Answer B. GFDPP 2A, FAR 39
ADs are published as part of the FARs. You may not operate an aircraft to which an airworthiness directive applies, except in accordance with that airworthiness directive.

2-22   PLT377   PA.I.B.K1c

May a pilot operate an aircraft that is not in compliance with an Airworthiness Directive (AD)?

A – Yes, under VFR conditions only.

B – Yes, ADs are only voluntary.

C – Yes, if allowed by the AD.

2-22. Answer C. GFDPP 2A, FAR 39
ADs are published as part of the FARs. You may not operate an aircraft to which an airworthiness directive applies, except in accordance with that airworthiness directive. Some ADs ground an aircraft immediately, and others require actions to be taken on a future inspection.

2-23   PLT446   PA.I.B.K2

Which operation would be described as preventive maintenance?

A – Repair of landing gear brace struts

B – Replenishing hydraulic fluid

C – Repair of portions of skin sheets by making additional seams

2-23. Answer B. GFDPP 2A, FAR 1.1, FAR 43 App A
Replenishing hydraulic fluid is listed as preventive maintenance in FAR Part 43, Appendix A. Structural repairs, such as those to landing gear brace struts, or adding seams to skin, are *not* preventive maintenance and require an appropriate aircraft mechanic certificate.

2-24   PLT446   PA.I.B.K2

Preventive maintenance has been performed on an aircraft. What paperwork is required?

A – A full, detailed description of the work done must be entered in the airframe logbook.

B – The date the work was completed, and the name of the person who did the work must be entered in the airframe and engine logbook.

C – The signature, certificate number, and kind of certificate held by the person approving the work and a description of the work must be entered in the aircraft maintenance records.

2-24. Answer C. GFDPP 2A, FAR 43.9, FAR 91.417
FAR 91.417 states that records of preventive maintenance must include a description of the work performed, the date of completion, and the signature and certificate number of the person approving the aircraft for return to service. In addition, FAR 43.9 also indicates that the kind of certificate held by the person approving the work must be included in the record.

2-25   PLT446   PA.I.B.K2

What regulation allows a private pilot to perform preventive maintenance?

A – 14 CFR Part 43.7

B – 14 CFR Part 91.403

C – 14 CFR Part 61.113

2-25. Answer A. GFDPP 2A, FAR 43.7
14 CFR Part 43 covers preventive maintenance. If you hold at least a private pilot certificate, you may perform preventive maintenance such as replacing and servicing batteries, replacing spark plugs, servicing wheel bearings, etc.

2-26   PLT446   PA.I.B.K2

Who may perform preventive maintenance on an aircraft and approve it for return to service?

A – Student or Recreational pilot

B – Private or Commercial pilot

C – None of the above

2-26. Answer B. GFDPP 2A, FAR 43.7
14 CFR Part 43 covers preventive maintenance. If you hold at least a private pilot certificate, you may perform preventive maintenance such as replacing and servicing batteries, replacing spark plugs, servicing wheel bearings, etc.

2-27   PLT374   PA.I.B.K1c

Who is responsible for ensuring that airworthiness directives (ADs) are complied with?

A – Mechanic with inspection authorization (IA)

B – Owner or operator

C – Repair station

2-27. Answer B. GFDPP 2A, FAR 91.403
The owner or operator of an aircraft is primarily responsible for maintaining that aircraft in an airworthy condition, including compliance with 14 CFR Part 39 (ADs).

2-28   PLT375   PA.I.B.K1b

Completion of an annual inspection and the return of the aircraft to service should always be indicated by

A – the relicensing date on the Registration Certificate.

B – an appropriate notation in the aircraft maintenance records.

C – an inspection sticker placed on the instrument panel that lists the annual inspection completion date.

2-28. Answer B. GFDPP 2A, FAR 91.409
No person may operate an aircraft unless, within the preceding 12 calendar months it has had an annual inspection by a person authorized to do that type of inspection and is entered as an annual inspection in the required maintenance records.

2-29   PLT170   PA.IV.B.S9

To minimize the side loads placed on the landing gear during touchdown, the pilot should keep the

A – direction of motion of the aircraft parallel to the runway.

B – longitudinal axis of the aircraft parallel to the direction of its motion.

C – downwind wing lowered sufficiently to eliminate the tendency for the aircraft to drift.

2-29. Answer B. AFH

Having the direction of motion parallel to the runway will not reduce side loads; the aircraft has to point in the same direction as it is moving. When a crosswind exists, the upwind, not downwind, wing needs to be lowered to stop drift.

SECTION B — POWERPLANT AND RELATED SYSTEMS

The engine and propeller produce thrust, which is required for an airplane to fly. Related systems, such as the fuel system, are necessary for the powerplant to function.

ENGINES

You need to know how the combustion process works in a piston engine, how to avoid damaging the engine, and what you can do to maximize its efficiency.

FUEL, MIXTURE, AND INDUCTION SYSTEM

- On aircraft equipped with fuel pumps, the auxiliary electric pump is used if the engine-driven fuel pump fails.
- Float-type carburetors operate based on the difference in air pressure at the venturi throat and the air inlet. The decreased pressure caused by air flowing rapidly through the venturi tube draws fuel from the float chamber.
- Carburetors are more susceptible to icing than fuel-injected engines because the air cools as it expands leaving the carburetor venturi and fuel vaporization further reduces the temperature. Carburetor icing is most likely to occur when the outside air temperature is between 20° and 70°F with high humidity or visible moisture. Although uncommon, carburetor icing is possible at temperatures up to 100°F if the air is moist.
- On an airplane with a fixed-pitch propeller, the first indication of carburetor ice would most likely be a loss of RPM.
- Carbureted engines are equipped with carburetor heat to prevent ice from forming in the venturi. Turn on the heat when flying in conditions conducive to carburetor icing. This heats the air entering the engine, making it less dense, which enrichens the mixture and reduces engine performance and RPM.
- If carburetor ice is present, applying carburetor heat will cause a temporary decrease in RPM, followed by a gradual increase as the ice melts.
- The basic purpose of adjusting the fuel/air mixture at altitude is to decrease the fuel flow in order to compensate for decreased air density that occurs in warm temperatures and at higher altitudes.
- If you notice engine roughness during the runup at a high elevation airport, the mixture might be too rich. Try a leaner setting of the mixture.
- The fuel/air mixture must be enriched prior to descent. If you are at cruising with the mixture properly adjusted, and you descend to a lower altitude without readjusting it, the mixture could become excessively lean.
- Fuel injection, compared to a carburetor, offers lower fuel consumption, increased horsepower, lower operating temperatures, and longer engine life. The most significant safety advantage is the reduced risk of induction icing.
- On aircraft equipped with fuel pumps, running a fuel tank dry before switching tanks is not recommended because the engine-driven or electric boost fuel pump can draw air into the fuel system and cause vapor lock.

- Using fuel of a lower-than-specified grade can cause cylinder head and engine oil temperature gauges to exceed their normal operating ranges. Fuel of the next higher octane may be substituted if the recommended octane is not available.
- Filling the fuel tanks after the last flight of the day will prevent moisture condensation by eliminating air in the tanks.

IGNITION

- The main purpose of a dual-ignition system on an aircraft is to provide system redundancy.
- Another advantage of dual-ignition systems is improved engine performance.

ABNORMAL COMBUSTION

- Detonation occurs in a reciprocating aircraft engine when the unburned charge in the cylinders explodes instead of burning normally. It is most likely to occur at high power settings and when the engine is running hot.
- If you suspect that the engine is detonating during climb-out, richen the mixture and lower the nose slightly to increase airspeed. These actions can improve engine cooling whether or not you suspect detonation.
- Pre-ignition occurs when the fuel/air mixture ignites too soon, in advance of normal spark ignition. It can be caused by hot spots in the cylinder, or by using too low a grade of fuel.
- Using a grade of fuel that is lower than specified for the engine, can also cause detonation.

OIL SYSTEM

- For internal cooling, reciprocating aircraft engines rely on the circulation of lubricating oil.
- An abnormally high oil temperature indication can be caused by the oil level being too low.

COOLING SYSTEM

- Excessively high engine temperatures will cause loss of power, excessive oil consumption, and possible permanent internal engine damage.
- If the engine oil temperature and cylinder head temperature gauges exceed their normal operating range, you might be operating with too much power and the mixture set too lean.
- To aid engine cooling during climb, lower the nose, reduce the rate of climb and increase airspeed.
- One way to cool an engine that is overheating is to enrichen the fuel mixture.

PROPELLER

- Two basic types of propellers exist on single-engine airplanes—fixed-pitch and constant-speed.
- Fixed-pitch propellers are normally optimized either for climb or for cruise.
- A constant-speed propeller enables selecting an RPM that results in a blade pitch angle for most efficient performance.
- To operate the engine on an airplane with a constant-speed propeller use the throttle to control power output, as shown on the manifold pressure gauge, and the propeller control to regulate engine RPM.
- When operating an engine equipped with a constant-speed propeller, avoid a high manifold pressure setting with low RPM, as specified in your POH.
- Full authority digital engine control (FADEC) is a computer with associated systems that manage the engine and propeller of an aircraft, simplifying the engine controls to a single power lever. Because the engine will stop running if the FADEC engine control unit (ECU) fails, a back-up ECU is required.

2-30 PLT342 PA.I.G.K1c

Excessively high engine temperatures will

A – cause damage to heat-conducting hoses and warping of the cylinder cooling fins.

B – cause loss of power, excessive oil consumption, and possible permanent internal engine damage.

C – not appreciably affect an aircraft engine.

2-30. Answer B. GFDPP 2B, PHB

High temperature can cause detonation and a resulting loss of power, excessive oil consumption, and engine damage, including scoring of the cylinders and damage to pistons, rings, and valves.

2-31 PLT342 PA.I.G.K1c

If the engine oil temperature and cylinder head temperature gauges have exceeded their normal operating range, the pilot may have been operating with

A – the mixture set too rich.

B – higher-than-normal oil pressure.

C – too much power and with the mixture set too lean.

2-31. Answer C. GFDPP 2B, PHB

With high power settings and the mixture set too lean, overheating can result. This can be indicated by a high engine oil temperature and cylinder head temperature.

2-32 PLT478 PA.I.G.K1c

One purpose of the dual-ignition system on an aircraft engine is to provide for

A – improved engine performance.

B – uniform heat distribution.

C – balanced cylinder head pressure.

2-32. Answer A. GFDPP 2B, AFH

Dual-ignition systems fire two spark plugs on each cylinder. In addition to system redundancy, this improves combustion of the fuel/air mixture and results in slightly more power.

2-33 PLT253 PA.I.G.K1e

On aircraft equipped with fuel pumps, when is the auxiliary electric pump used?

A – In the event engine-driven fuel pump fails.

B – All the time to aid the engine-driven fuel pump.

C – Constantly except in starting the engine.

2-33. Answer A. GFDPP 2B, PHB

The auxiliary electric pump is a back-up for an engine-driven pump. Although labeling, procedures for use, and control switches differ between manufacturers, these auxiliary pumps can cause operational problems if used inappropriately. In some systems, continuous use of both the auxiliary pump and the engine-driven pump can cause an excessively rich mixture. Besides the back-up function, auxiliary pumps are commonly used to provide fuel under pressure for engine starting.

2-34   PLT191   PA.I.G.K1e

Float-type carburetors operate based on

A – automatic metering of air at the venturi as the aircraft gains altitude.

B – the difference in air pressure at the venturi throat and the air inlet.

C – increase in air velocity in the throat of a venturi causing an increase in air pressure.

2-34. Answer B. GFDPP 2B, PHB

The decreased pressure caused by air flowing rapidly through the venturi tube draws fuel from the float chamber.

2-35   PLT191   PA.I.G.K1e

The basic purpose of adjusting the fuel/air mixture at altitude is to

A – decrease the amount of fuel in the mixture in order to compensate for increased air density.

B – decrease the fuel flow in order to compensate for decreased air density.

C – increase the amount of fuel in the mixture to compensate for the decrease in pressure and density of the air.

2-35. Answer B. GFDPP 2B, AFH

If fuel flow is not decreased with altitude, the mixture becomes too rich with fuel. Therefore, the fuel mixture must be leaned to maintain the proper fuel/air ratio.

2-36   PLT249   PA.I.G.K1c

During the runup at a high elevation airport, you notice a slight engine roughness that is not affected by the magneto check but grows worse during the carburetor heat check. Under these circumstances, what would be the most logical initial action?

A – Check the results obtained with a leaner setting of the mixture.

B – Taxi back to the flight line for a maintenance check.

C – Reduce manifold pressure to control detonation.

2-36. Answer A. GFDPP 2B, AFH

In this case, engine roughness is probably caused by the mixture set too rich for the high altitude. When the carburetor heat is turned on, the warmer air entering the carburetor is less dense, and the mixture is further enriched. As a result, the engine roughness increases. The problem can usually be corrected by leaning the mixture.

2-37   PLT249   PA.I.G.K1c

While cruising at 9,500 feet MSL, the fuel/air mixture is properly adjusted. What will occur if a descent to 4,500 feet MSL is made without readjusting the mixture?

A – The fuel/air mixture can become excessively lean.

B – There can be more fuel in the cylinders than is needed for normal combustion, and the excess fuel will absorb heat and cool the engine.

C – The excessively rich mixture creates higher cylinder head temperatures and can cause detonation.

2-37. Answer A. GFDPP 2B, AFH
With a decrease in altitude, air density increases. This means you will have to enrich the mixture as you descend, otherwise the fuel/air mixture can become excessively lean.

2-38   PLT190   PA.IX.C.K1b

Which condition is most favorable to the development of carburetor icing?

A – Any temperature below freezing and a relative humidity of less than 50 percent

B – Temperature between 32 and 50°F and low humidity

C – Temperature between 20 and 70°F and high humidity

2-38. Answer C. GFDPP 2B, PHB
Carburetor icing is most likely between 20° and 70°F in high humidity conditions.

2-39   PLT190   PA.IX.C.K1b

The risk of carburetor ice is

A – high when the ambient temperature is between 20°F and 70°F and the relative humidity is high.

B – nonexistent at 95°F even when there is visible moisture.

C – high at 0°F when the relative humidity is high.

2-39. Answer A. GFDPP 2B, PHB
Carburetor icing is most probable between 20°F and 70°F with high humidity or visible moisture. It is a possibility even at 95°F because with a 70°F temperature drop in the venturi, the venturi temperature would be 25°F. Carburetor icing is not a high risk at low temperatures, at which the air cannot hold much moisture.

2-40   PLT190   PA.IX.C.K1b

If an aircraft is equipped with a fixed-pitch propeller and a float-type carburetor, the first indication of carburetor ice would most likely be

A – a drop in oil temperature and cylinder head temperature.

B – engine roughness.

C – loss of RPM.

2-40. Answer C. GFDPP 2B, PHB
The restricted airflow through the carburetor causes an enriched mixture and loss of RPM

2-41   PLT189   PA.IX.C.K1b

Applying carburetor heat will

A – result in more air going through the carburetor.

B – enrich the fuel/air mixture.

C – not affect the fuel/air mixture.

2-41. Answer B. GFDPP 2B, PHB
When the carburetor heat is turned on, the warmer air entering the carburetor is less dense, and the mixture is enriched.

2-42   PLT189   PA.IX.C.K1b

What change occurs in the fuel/air mixture when carburetor heat is applied?

A – A decrease in RPM results from the lean mixture.

B – The fuel/air mixture becomes richer.

C – The fuel/air mixture becomes leaner.

2-42. Answer B. GFDPP 2B, PHB
When the carburetor heat is turned on, the warmer air entering the carburetor is less dense, and with the same amount of fuel entering the carburetor, the mixture is enriched.

2-43   PLT189   PA.I.G.K1c

Generally speaking, the use of carburetor heat tends to

A – decrease engine performance.

B – increase engine performance.

C – have no effect on engine performance.

2-43. Answer A. GFDPP 2B, PHB
Because the warmer air entering the carburetor is less dense, the fuel/air mixture is enriched and power decreases.

2-44   PLT189   PA.IX.C.K1b

The presence of carburetor ice in an aircraft equipped with a fixed-pitch propeller can be verified by applying carburetor heat and noting

A – an increase in RPM and then a gradual decrease in RPM.

B – a decrease in RPM and then a constant RPM indication.

C – a decrease in RPM and then a gradual increase in RPM.

2-44. Answer C. GFDPP 2B, PHB
When carburetor heat is first applied, the mixture is enriched, and RPM decreases. Then, as the ice melts, airflow into the carburetor increases, leaning the mixture, and RPM increases.

2-45   PLT191   PA.IX.C.K1b

With regard to carburetor ice, float-type carburetor systems in comparison to fuel injection systems are generally considered to be

A – more susceptible to icing.

B – equally susceptible to icing.

C – susceptible to icing only when visible moisture is present.

2-45. Answer A. GFDPP 2B, PHB

Because the fuel is introduced directly into the hot cylinders instead of vaporizing in a cold venturi throat, fuel injection systems are not as susceptible to icing as float-type carburetors.

2-46   PLT250   PA.I.G.K1e

If the grade of fuel used in an aircraft engine is lower than specified for the engine, it will most likely cause

A – detonation.

B – a mixture of fuel and air that is not uniform in all cylinders.

C – lower cylinder head temperatures.

2-46. Answer A. GFDPP 2B, PHB

The higher the grade of fuel, the more pressure it can withstand without detonating. Conversely, lower fuel grades are more prone to detonation with accompanying higher engine temperatures.

2-47   PLT115   PA.I.G.K1c

Detonation occurs in a reciprocating aircraft engine when

A – the spark plugs are fouled or shorted out or the wiring is defective.

B – hot spots in the combustion chamber ignite the fuel/air mixture in advance of normal ignition.

C – the unburned charge in the cylinders explodes instead of burning normally.

2-47. Answer C. GFDPP 2B, PHB

Detonation occurs when the fuel/air mixture suddenly explodes in the cylinders instead of burning smoothly. Hot spots in the combustion chamber are normally responsible for preignition, not detonation.

2-48   PLT115   PA.I.G.K1c

Detonation may occur at high-power settings as

A – the fuel mixture ignites instantaneously instead of burning progressively and evenly.

B – an excessively rich fuel mixture causes an explosive gain in power.

C – the fuel mixture is ignited too early by hot carbon deposits in the cylinder.

2-48. Answer A. GFDPP 2B, PHB

Detonation occurs when the fuel/air mixture suddenly explodes in the cylinders instead of burning smoothly. Detonation is caused by excessively lean mixtures while hot spots in the cylinder cause preignition.

2-49   PLT115   PA.I.G.K1c

You suspect that your engine (with a fixed-pitch propeller) is detonating during climb-out after takeoff. Your initial corrective action would be to

A – lean the mixture.

B – lower the nose slightly to increase airspeed.

C – apply carburetor heat.

2-49. Answer B. GFDPP 2B, PHB

Detonation can occur when the engine overheats. One action to help cool the engine is to increase airspeed, which increases the cooling airflow around the engine.

2-50   PLT249   PA.I.G.K1c

The uncontrolled firing of the fuel/air charge in advance of normal spark ignition is known as

A – combustion.

B – preignition.

C – detonation.

2-50. Answer B. GFDPP 2B, PHB

Preignition occurs when the fuel/air mixture ignites too soon.

2-51   PLT250   PA.I.G.K1c

Which would most likely cause the cylinder head temperature and engine oil temperature gauges to exceed their normal operating ranges?

A – Using fuel that has a lower-than-specified fuel rating

B – Using fuel that has a higher-than-specified fuel rating

C – Operating with higher-than-normal oil pressure

2-51. Answer A. GFDPP 2B, PHB

Lower grade fuels detonate under less pressure. Using a lower fuel rating than specified can cause detonation, which in turn leads to excessive engine temperatures.

2-52   PLT250   PA.I.G.K1e

What type fuel can be substituted for an aircraft if the recommended octane is not available?

A – The next higher octane aviation gas

B – The next lower octane aviation gas

C – Unleaded automotive gas of the same octane rating

2-52. Answer A. GFDPP 2B, PHB

If the manufacturer's recommendations are followed, the next higher grade of fuel may normally be used. Autogas is not permitted unless the aircraft has a supplemental type certificate (STC) permitting its use.

2-53   PLT250   PA.I.G.K1e

Filling the fuel tanks after the last flight of the day is considered a good operating procedure because this will

A – force any existing water to the top of the tank away from the fuel lines to the engine.

B – prevent expansion of the fuel by eliminating airspace in the tanks.

C – prevent moisture condensation by eliminating airspace in the tanks.

2-53. Answer C. GFDPP 2B, PHB)

As the airplane cools overnight, water condenses in the tanks from vapor in the air and enters the fuel. Filling the tanks eliminates the air space and prevents this condensation.

2-54   PLT324   PA.I.G.K1c

For internal cooling, reciprocating aircraft engines are especially dependent on

A – a properly functioning thermostat.

B – air flowing over the exhaust manifold.

C – the circulation of lubricating oil.

2-54. Answer C. GFDPP 2B, PHB

Engine oil lubricates moving parts, reduces friction, and carries heat from interior portions of the engine to the oil cooler.

2-55   PLT324   PA.I.G.K1c

An abnormally high engine oil temperature indication may be caused by

A – the oil level being too low.

B – operating with a too high viscosity oil.

C – operating with an excessively rich mixture.

2-55. Answer A. GFDPP 2B, PHB

Engine oil lubricates moving parts, reduces friction, and carries heat from interior portions of the engine to the oil cooler. If the oil level is too low, it reduces its effectiveness cooling the engine.

2-56   PLT342   PA.I.G.K1c

What action can a pilot take to aid in cooling an engine that is overheating during a climb?

A – Reduce rate of climb and increase airspeed.

B – Reduce climb speed and increase RPM.

C – Increase climb speed and increase RPM.

2-56. Answer A. GFDPP 2B, PHB

Reducing the rate of climb and increasing airspeed increases the cooling airflow around the engine.

2-57   PLT342   PA.I.G.K1c

What is one procedure to aid in cooling an engine that is overheating?

A – Enrichen the fuel mixture.

B – Increase the RPM.

C – Reduce the airspeed.

2-57. Answer A. GFDPP 2B, PHB

A richer fuel mixture burns at a lower temperature and reduces heat in the engine. Increasing the RPM in and of itself does not significantly affect the airflow through the engine and on a fixed-pitch propeller, it means increasing power, which would worsen the overheating problem. Reducing airspeed would also worsen the problem because it would result in reduced airflow through the engine.

2-58   PLT342   PA.I.G.K1c

How is engine operation controlled on an engine equipped with a constant-speed propeller?

A – The throttle controls power output as registered on the manifold pressure gauge and the propeller control regulates engine RPM

B – The throttle controls power output as registered on the manifold pressure gauge and the propeller control regulates a constant blade angle

C – The throttle controls engine RPM as registered on the tachometer and the mixture control regulates the power output

2-58. Answer A. GFDPP 2B, PHB

The throttle controls the power output of the engine, which is indicated on the manifold pressure gauge. The propeller control changes engine RPM, which is indicated on the tachometer, by adjusting the pitch of the propeller.

2-59   PLT350   PA.I.G.K1c

What is an advantage of a constant-speed propeller?

A – Permits the pilot to select and maintain a desired cruising speed.

B – Permits the pilot to select the blade angle for the most efficient performance.

C – Provides a smoother operation with stable RPM and eliminates vibrations.

2-59. Answer B. GFDPP 2B, PHB

By setting propeller RPM, the pilot indirectly sets blade angle. Selecting the optimal blade angle enables a high percentage of engine power to be converted into thrust over a wide range of RPM and airspeed combinations. This enables the best performance to be gained from the engine.

2-60   PLT351   PA.I.G.K1c

A precaution for the operation of an engine equipped with a constant-speed propeller is to

A – avoid high RPM settings with high manifold pressure.

B – avoid high manifold pressure settings with low RPM.

C – always use a rich mixture with high RPM settings.

2-60. Answer B. GFDPP 2B, PHB

For a given RPM setting, there is a maximum allowable manifold pressure. Generally, high manifold pressures with low RPM should be avoided to prevent internal stress within the engine.

2-61 PA.I.G.K1c

Which preflight checks should be made on an airplane with full-authority digital engine control (FADEC)?

A – Verify proper operation of both ECUs as well as their back-up power sources.

B – Ensure that engine RPM drops sufficiently when the propeller control is pulled back.

C – Ensure that the mixture control is adjusted for highest RPM with smooth engine operation.

2-61. Answer A. GFDPP 2B, PHB
On an airplane equipped with FADEC, the engine control units (ECUs) completely manage the engine and propeller operation, eliminating the need for a propeller or mixture control. Because the engine stops running if an ECU fails, redundant systems are required with back-up power. These systems should be checked for proper operation before flight.

2-62 PLT479 PA.I.G.K1c

What should be the first action after starting an aircraft engine?

A – Adjust for proper RPM and check for desired indications on the engine gauges.

B – Place the magneto or ignition switch momentarily in the OFF position to check for proper grounding.

C – Test each brake and the parking brake.

2-62. Answer A. GFDPP 2B, PHB
Immediately after starting an engine, set the proper RPM and check engine gauges for proper indications. Turning the magnetos off could cause a backfire and testing the brakes occurs after the airplane starts moving.

2-63 PLT479 PA.II.C.K2

If it become necessary to hand-prop an airplane engine, it is extremely important that a competent pilot

A – call "contact" before touching the propeller.

B – be at the controls in the cockpit.

C – be in the cockpit and call out all commands.

2-63. Answer B. GFDPP 2B, PHB
When hand-propping an airplane, a qualified pilot must be at the controls to prevent the airplane from moving and to set the engine controls properly. The person who is turning the propeller calls out the commands.

2-64 PLT342 PA.I.G.K1c

Excessively high engine temperatures, either in the air or on the ground, will

A – increase fuel consumption and may increase power due to the increased heat.

B – result in damage to heat-conducting hoses and warping of cylinder cooling fans.

C – cause loss of power, excessive oil consumption, and possible permanent internal engine damage.

2-64. Answer C. GFDPP 2-34
High temperatures can cause detonation and a resulting loss of power, excessive oil consumption, and engine damage, including scoring of the cylinders and damage to piston, rings, and valves.

2-65   PLT254   PA.I.G.K1e

To properly purge water from the fuel system of an aircraft equipped with fuel tank sumps and a fuel strainer quick drain, it is necessary to drain fuel from the

A – fuel strainer drain.

B – lowest point in the fuel system.

C – fuel strainer drain and the fuel tank sumps.

2-65. Answer C. GFDPP 2-29, PHB
Fuel needs to be drained from both the fuel tank sumps and the fuel strainer drain. The fuel strainer drain might be the lowest point in the fuel system, but draining it without draining the fuel tank sumps is insufficient.

SECTION C — FLIGHT INSTRUMENTS

The instruments in the airplane cockpit that indicate the airplane's attitude, direction, altitude, and speed are collectively referred to as the flight instruments. The flight instruments are classified according to their method of operation.

PITOT-STATIC INSTRUMENTS

Pilot-static instruments measure air pressure, and are also affected by temperature.
- The standard temperature and pressure at sea level are 59°F (15°C) and 29.92 inches Hg (1013.2 hPa).
- The pitot-static system supplies ambient air pressure to operate the altimeter and vertical speed indicator (VSI), and both ambient and ram air to the airspeed indicator.
- The pitot system provides impact pressure for the airspeed indicator.
- The static system is connected to all three instruments—the altimeter, vertical speed indicator (VSI), and airspeed indicator.

V-SPEEDS

- The red line on an airspeed indicator represents never-exceed speed—the maximum speed at which the airplane may be operated under any conditions.
- The yellow arc is the caution range—operating at these speeds is permissible only in smooth air.
- The green arc is the normal operating range, with the bottom of the arc representing the power-off stalling speed in a specified configuration, and the upper limit representing the maximum structural cruising speed.
- The white arc identifies the normal flap operating range. The bottom of the white arc is the power-off stall speed in the landing configuration.
- V_A is defined as maneuvering speed. It is an important airspeed limitation that is not marked on the airspeed indicator. Avoid abrupt control movements above this speed, and also limit your airplane to this speed to protect the airframe during significant turbulence.
- The indicated airspeed at which a given airplane stalls in a particular configuration is not affected by altitude.
- V_{FE} represents the maximum flap operating speed.
- V_{LE} represents the maximum landing gear extended speed.
- V_{NO} is defined as the maximum structural cruising speed.
- V_{SO} is defined as the stalling speed or minimum steady flight speed in the landing configuration.

TYPES OF ALTITUDE

- Altimeter setting is the value to which the barometric pressure scale of the altimeter is set so that the altimeter indicates true altitude at field elevation.
- True altitude is the vertical distance of the aircraft above sea level.
- Absolute altitude is the vertical distance of the aircraft above the surface.
- Pressure altitude is the altitude indicated when the barometric pressure scale is set to 29.92.
- Density altitude is the pressure altitude corrected for nonstandard temperature.
- Indicated altitude is the same as true altitude when at sea level under standard conditions.
- Pressure altitude equals true altitude under standard conditions.
- One inch of change of Hg in the altimeter causes 1,000 feet of altitude change in the same direction.
- Variations in temperature affect the altimeter, because pressure levels are raised on warm days and the indicated altitude is lower than the true altitude.
- The true altitude of an aircraft is lower than the indicated altitude when it is flown into an area of colder-than-standard air temperature, or an area of lower pressure.
- An increase in ambient temperature increases the density altitude at a given airport.
- If the pitot tube becomes clogged, only the airspeed indicator is affected; if the static vents are clogged, the altimeter, airspeed indicator, and vertical speed indicator are all affected.

GYROSCOPIC INSTRUMENTS

Gyroscopic instruments include the turn coordinator, attitude indicator and heading indicator. They operate off of a gyro's tendency to remain rigid in space.

- A turn coordinator provides an indication of the rate of movement of an aircraft about the yaw and roll axes.
- To properly adjust the attitude indicator during level flight, align the miniature airplane to the horizon bar.
- A pilot determines the direction of bank from the attitude indicator by the relationship of the miniature airplane to the deflected horizon bar.
- A nonslaved heading indicator must be periodically realigned with the magnetic compass as the gyro precesses.

MAGNETIC COMPASS

- The magnetic compass contains a bar magnet, which swings freely to align with the Earth's magnetic field.
- Deviation in a magnetic compass is caused by the magnetic fields in the aircraft distorting the lines of magnetic force.
- In the Northern Hemisphere, a magnetic compass shows a turn toward the west if rolling into a right turn from a north heading, and a turn toward the east if rolling into a left turn.
- While on an east or west heading, the compass indicates a turn toward the north if accelerating the aircraft, and a turn toward the south if decelerating the aircraft. It indicates correctly if accelerating or decelerating the aircraft on a north or south heading. Generally, in-flight indications of a magnetic compass are correct only when the aircraft is in straight-and-level, unaccelerated flight.

DIGITAL FLIGHT DISPLAYS

- The digital flight instrument systems used in light general aviation airplanes typically have two screens: a primary flight display (PFD) and a multifunction display (MFD).
- The PFD contains digital versions of traditional flight instruments, including the attitude indicator, airspeed indicator, altimeter, vertical speed indicator, and HSI.
- The attitude and heading reference system (AHRS) uses inertial sensors such as electronic gyroscopes, accelerometers, and a magnetometer to determine the attitude of an aircraft relative to the horizon and heading.
- A magnetometer senses the earth's magnetic field to function as a magnetic compass, but without some of the errors associated with a conventional compass.
- The AHRS instruments are the attitude indicator, HSI and turn indicator.

- A slip/skid indicator below the roll pointer of the attitude indicator helps you maintain coordinated flight.
- In addition to a compass card, the digital HSI displays the current airplane heading in a window, a course indicator arrow and CDI, and a rate-of-turn indicator.
- When the AHRS system detects a problem, it places a red X over the display of the affected instruments to alert you that the indications are unreliable.
- The pitot tube, static source, and outside air temperature probe provide information to the air data computer (ADC), which drives the airspeed indicator, altimeter, and VSI.
- On the digital airspeed indicator, a window and a pointer on the airspeed tape show the indicated airspeed.
- A trend vector on the digital airspeed indicator shows the future airspeed (typically six seconds) if the acceleration or deceleration continues at the same rate.
- The trend vector on the digital altimeter shows the future altitude (typically six seconds) if it continues to climb or descend at the same rate.
- The trend vector on the heading indicator (HSI) shows the future heading (typically six seconds) if the aircraft continues turning at the same rate. This trend vector acts as a rate-of-turn indicator with calibration marks for a standard-rate turn.
- On the digital VSI, you read vertical speed in feet per minute in a window that also serves as a pointer.
- If one or more sensors stops providing input, or if the ADC determines that its own internal operations are not correct, it places a red X over the display of the affected instrument.
- On an integrated flight display, if the PFD fails, you can typically display PFD instruments on the MFD screen.
- If you lose all electric power to a digital flight display, you must use your back-up instruments. The back-up attitude indicator is vacuum- or electrically-powered. If it is electrically powered, that instrument must have a separate power source that is isolated from the main electrical system.

2-66   PLT506   PA.I.G.K1h

Which V-speed represents maneuvering speed?

A – V_A

B – V_{LO}

C – V_{NE}

2-66. Answer A. GFDPP 2C, FAR 1.2

V_A is defined as the design maneuvering speed. V_{LO} is maximum gear operating speed and V_{NE} is never-exceed speed.

2-67   PLT506   PA.I.G.K1h

Which V-speed represents maximum flap extended speed?

A – $V_{FE.}$

B – $V_{LOF.}$

C – $V_{FC.}$

2-67. Answer A. FAR 1.2

V_{FE} is defined as maximum flap extended speed.

2-68   PLT506   PA.I.G.K1h

Which V-speed represents maximum landing gear extended speed?

A – V_{LE}.

B – V_{LO}.

C – V_{FE}.

2-68. Answer A. FAR 1.2

V_{LE} is defined as maximum landing gear extended speed.

2-69   PLT506   PA.I.G.K1h

V_{NO} is defined as the

A – normal operating range.

B – never-exceed speed.

C – maximum structural cruising speed.

2-69. Answer C. FAR 1.2

V_{NO} is defined as maximum structural cruising speed. It is at the upper end of the green arc, the normal operating range.

2-70   PLT506   PA.I.G.K1h

V_{S0} is defined as the

A – stalling speed or minimum steady flight speed in the landing configuration.

B – stalling speed or minimum steady flight speed in a specified configuration.

C – stalling speed or minimum takeoff safety speed.

2-70. Answer A. FAR 1.2

V_{S0} is stalling speed or minimum steady flight speed in a landing configuration. V_{S1} is the stall speed in a specified configuration. Takeoff safety speed (V_1) normally does not apply to light general aviation airplanes.

2-71   PLT166   PA.I.G.K1h

If an altimeter setting is not available before flight, to which altitude should the pilot adjust the altimeter?

A – The elevation of the nearest airport corrected to mean sea level

B – The elevation of the departure area

C – Pressure altitude corrected for nonstandard temperature

2-71. Answer B. GFDPP 2C, FAR 91.121

If unable to obtain a local altimeter setting, you should set the altimeter to the field elevation prior to departure. If an airport chart or airport signs show the elevation of the departure area, then use that elevation. Field elevation is already referenced to mean sea level and does not need to be corrected, plus you should use the elevation of your airport, not a nearby airport. Pressure altitude corrected for nonstandard temperature is density altitude and that is not an altitude that can or should be displayed on an altimeter—you need *true altitude*.

2-72   PLT166   PA.I.G.K1h

Prior to takeoff, the altimeter should be set to

A – the current local altimeter setting, if available, or the departure airport elevation.

B – the corrected density altitude of the departure airport.

C – the corrected pressure altitude for the departure airport.

2-72. Answer A. GFDPP 2C, FAR 91.121

If unable to obtain a local altimeter setting, you should set the altimeter to the field elevation prior to departure. Corrected density altitude and corrected pressure altitudes are not valid terms.

2-73   PLT337   PA.I.G.K1h

If the pitot tube and outside static vents become clogged, which instruments would be affected?

A – The altimeter, airspeed indicator, and turn-and-slip indicator

B – The altimeter, airspeed indicator, and vertical speed indicator

C – The altimeter, attitude indicator, and turn-and-slip indicator

2-73. Answer B. GFDPP 2C, PHB

The altimeter, the airspeed indicator, and the vertical speed indicator all use static air and would therefore be affected. The turn-and-slip indicator and attitude indicator are gyroscopic instruments and are not affected by any clogs in the pitot-static system.

2-74   PLT337   PA.I.G.K1h

Which instrument becomes inoperative if the pitot tube becomes clogged?

A – Altimeter

B – Vertical speed

C – Airspeed

2-74. Answer C. GFDPP 2C, PHB

The airspeed indicator is the only pitot-static instrument that is connected to the pitot tube. It operates by sensing impact pressure (ram air) in the pitot tube and comparing it to static pressure.

2-75   PLT337   PA.I.G.K1h

Which instrument(s) become inoperative if the static vents become clogged?

A – Airspeed only

B – Altimeter only

C – Airspeed, altimeter, and vertical speed

2-75. Answer C. GFDPP 2C, PHB

The altimeter, the airspeed indicator, and the vertical speed indicator all use static air and would therefore be affected.

2-76   PLT041   PA.I.G.K1h

(Refer to Figure 3.) Altimeter 1 indicates

A – 500 feet.

B – 1,500 feet.

C – 10,500 feet.

2-76. Answer C. GFDPP 2C, PHB
The small 10,000 ft pointer is just above the 1, indicating that the altitude is above 10,000 feet. The wide 1,000 ft pointer is between 0 and 1, which indicates less than 1,000 feet. Finally, the 100 ft pointer is on 5. The altimeter reading is 10,500 feet.

2-77   PLT041   PA.I.G.K1h

(Refer to Figure 3.) Altimeter 2 indicates

A – 1,500 feet.

B – 4,500 feet.

C – 14,500 feet.

2-77. Answer C. GFDPP 2C, PHB
The 10,000 ft pointer is above 1, the 1,000 ft pointer is above 4, and the 100 ft pointer is on 5. This indicates an altitude of 14,500 feet.

2-78   PLT041   PA.I.G.K1h

(Refer to Figure 3.) Altimeter 3 indicates

A – 9,500 feet.

B – 10,950 feet.

C – 15,940 feet.

2-78. Answer A. GFDPP 2C, PHB
The 10,000 ft pointer is near 1, the 1,000 ft pointer is above 9, and the 100 ft pointer is on 5. This indicates the altitude is 9,500 feet.

2-79   PLT041   PA.I.G.K1h

(Refer to Figure 3.) Which altimeter(s) indicate(s) more than 10,000 feet?

A – 1, 2, and 3

B – 1 and 2 only

C – 1 only

2-79. Answer B. GFDPP 2C, PHB
On Altimeter 1, the small 10,000 ft pointer is just beyond the 1, indicating that the altitude is above 10,000 feet. The wide 1,000' pointer is between 0 and 1, which indicates less than 1,000 feet. Finally, the 100' pointer is on 5. The altimeter reading is 10,500 feet. On Altimeter 2, the 10,000 ft pointer is above 1, the 1,000' pointer is above 4, and the 100' pointer is on 5. This indicates an altitude of 14,500 feet. On Altimeter 3, the 10,000 ft pointer is near 1, the 1,000' pointer is above 9, and the 100 ft pointer is on 5. This indicates the altitude is 9,500 feet.

2-80   PLT166   PA.I.G.K1h

Altimeter setting is the value to which the barometric pressure scale of the altimeter is set so the altimeter indicates

A – calibrated altitude at field elevation.

B – absolute altitude at field elevation.

C – true altitude at field elevation.

2-80. Answer C. GFDPP 2C, AW

When the current altimeter setting is set on the ground, the altimeter reads true altitude of the field, which is the actual height above mean sea level. Calibrated altitude is not a valid term and absolute altitude at field elevation doesn't make sense, because absolute altitude is height above ground level (AGL). If the airplane is sitting on the ground at the field, the absolute altitude would be zero.

2-81   PLT165   PA.I.G.K1h

How do variations in temperature affect the altimeter?

A – Pressure levels are raised on warm days and the indicated altitude is lower than true altitude.

B – Higher temperatures expand the pressure levels and the indicated altitude is higher than true altitude.

C – Lower temperatures lower the pressure levels and the indicated altitude is lower than true altitude.

2-81. Answer A. GFDPP 2C, PHB

Because atmospheric pressure levels are raised on warm days, the aircraft is at a higher altitude than indicated. In other words, the indicated altitude is lower than true altitude. When lower temperatures lower the pressure levels, the indicated altitude is higher, not lower, than true altitude.

2-82   PLT023   PA.I.G.K1h

What is true altitude?

A – The vertical distance of the aircraft above sea level

B – The vertical distance of the aircraft above the surface

C – The height above the standard datum plane

2-82. Answer A. GFDPP 2C, PHB

True altitude is the actual height (vertical distance) above mean sea level. The vertical distance above the surface is *absolute altitude* and the height above the standard datum plane is *pressure altitude.*

2-83   PLT023   PA.I.G.K1h

What is absolute altitude?

A – The altitude read directly from the altimeter

B – The vertical distance of the aircraft above the surface

C – The height above the standard datum plane

2-83. Answer B. GFDPP 2C, PHB

Absolute altitude, often referred to as altitude above ground level (AGL), is the height (vertical distance) above the surface. The altitude read directly from the altimeter is *indicated altitude*, and the height above the standard datum plane is *pressure altitude.*

2-84   PLT023   PA.I.G.K1h

What is density altitude?

A – The height above the standard datum plane

B – The pressure altitude corrected for nonstandard temperature

C – The altitude read directly from the altimeter

2-85   PLT023   PA.I.G.K1h

What is pressure altitude?

A – The indicated altitude corrected for position and installation error

B – The altitude indicated when the barometric pressure scale is set to 29.92

C – The indicated altitude corrected for nonstandard temperature and pressure

2-86   PLT023   PA.I.G.K1h

Under what condition is indicated altitude the same as true altitude?

A – If the altimeter has no mechanical error.

B – When at sea level under standard conditions.

C – When at 18,000 feet MSL with the altimeter set at 29.92.

2-87   PLT167   PA.I.G.K1h

If it is necessary to set the altimeter from 29.15 to 29.85, what change occurs?

A – 70-foot decrease in indicated altitude

B – 700-foot decrease in indicated altitude

C – 700-foot increase in indicated altitude

2-84. Answer B. GFDPP 2C, PHB
You can find *density altitude* by applying a correction for nonstandard temperature to the pressure altitude. *Pressure altitude* is the height above the standard datum plane, which is indicated when 29.92 is set in the scale. *Indicated altitude* is the altitude read directly from the altimeter.

2-85. Answer B. GFDPP 2C, PHB
Pressure altitude is the height above the standard datum plane, which is indicated when 29.92 is set in the scale.

2-86. Answer B. GFDPP 2C, AW
The goal of the altimeter is to indicate true altitude as closely as possible. However, some amount of error always occurs, except when at sea level under standard conditions.

2-87. Answer C. GFDPP 2C, PHB
A one inch of mercury (1 inch Hg) change in the Kollsman window setting on the altimeter equals 1,000 feet of altitude change in the same direction. In this case, you increase the setting on the altimeter by 0.700 inches (29.850 – 29.150 = 0.700), therefore, the indicated altitude increases by 700 feet.

2-88   PLT337   PA.I.G.K1h

The pitot system provides impact pressure for which instrument?

A – Altimeter

B – Vertical-speed indicator

C – Airspeed indicator

2-88. Answer C. GFDPP 2C, PHB
The airspeed indicator senses impact pressure to provide an airspeed reading.

2-89   PLT123   PA.I.G.K1h

As altitude increases, the indicated airspeed at which a given airplane stalls in a particular configuration will

A – decrease as the true airspeed decreases.

B – decrease as the true airspeed increases.

C – remain the same regardless of altitude.

2-89. Answer C. GFDPP 2C, PHB
Because airspeed indicators are calibrated to read true airspeed only under standard sea level conditions, the indicated airspeed does not reflect lower air density at higher altitudes. As a result, the indicated airspeed of a stall remains the same.

2-90   PLT088   PA.I.B.S5

What does the red line on an airspeed indicator represent?

A – Maneuvering speed

B – Turbulence or rough-air speed

C – Never-exceed speed

2-90. Answer C. GFDPP 2C, PHB
The red line is the never-exceed speed.

2-91   PLT088   PA.I.B.S5

(Refer to Figure 4.) What is the full flap operating range for the airplane?

A – 55 to 100 knots

B – 55 to 208 knots

C – 55 to 165 knots

2-91. Answer A. GFDPP 2C, PHB
The white arc indicates the flap operating range. On this instrument, it is 55 to 100 knots.

2-92   PLT088   PA.I.G.K1h

(Refer to Figure 4.) What is the caution range of the airplane?

A – 0 to 55 knots

B – 100 to 165 knots

C – 165 to 208 knots

2-92. Answer C. GFDPP 2C, PHB
The yellow arc indicates the caution range. On this instrument, it is 165 to 208 knots.

2-93   PLT088   PA.I.G.K1h

(Refer to Figure 4.) The maximum speed at which the airplane can be operated in smooth air is

A – 100 knots

B – 165 knots

C – 208 knots

2-93. Answer C. GFDPP 2C, PHB
In smooth air, an airplane can be operated in the yellow arc up to the red line, in this case, 208 knots.

2-94   PLT088   PA.I.G.K1h

(Refer to Figure 4.) Which marking identifies the never-exceed speed?

A – Upper limit of the green arc

B – Upper limit of the white arc

C – The red radial line

2-94. Answer C. GFDPP 2C, PHB
The red line is the never-exceed speed, the yellow arc is the caution range, the green arc is the normal operating range, and the white arc is the flap operating range.

2-95   PLT088   PA.I.G.K1h

(Refer to Figure 4.) Which color identifies the power-off stalling speed in a specified configuration?

A – Upper limit of the green arc

B – Upper limit of the white arc

C – Lower limit of the green arc

2-95. Answer C. GFDPP 2C, PHB
The lower limit of the green arc represents the power-off stall speed in a specified configuration (usually flaps up, gear retracted).

2-96   PLT088   PA.I.G.K1h

(Refer to Figure 4.) What is the maximum flaps-extended speed?

A – 58 knots

B – 100 knots

C – 165 knots

2-96. Answer B. GFDPP 2C, PHB
This is represented by the upper limit of the white arc, which in this case is 100 knots.

2-97   PLT088   PA.I.G.K1h

(Refer to Figure 4.) Which color identifies the normal flap operating range?

A – The lower limit of the white arc to the upper limit of the green arc

B – The green arc

C – The white arc

2-97. Answer C. GFDPP 2C, PHB
The white arc indicates the normal flap operating range.

2-98   PLT088   PA.I.G.K1h
(Refer to Figure 4.) Which color identifies the power-off stalling speed with wing flaps and landing gear in the landing configuration?

A – Upper limit of the green arc

B – Upper limit of the white arc

C – Lower limit of the white arc

2-98. Answer C. GFDPP 2C, PHB
Stall speed with flaps and gear down is represented by the lower limit of the white arc.

2-99   PLT088   PA.I.G.K1h
(Refer to Figure 4.) What is the maximum structural cruising speed?

A – 100 knots

B – 165 knots

C – 208 knots

2-99. Answer B. GFDPP 2C, PHB
This speed is indicated by the upper limit of the green arc, which in this case is 165 knots

2-100   PLT088   PA.I.G.K1h
What is an important airspeed limitation that is not color coded on airspeed indicators?

A – Never-exceed speed

B – Maneuvering speed

C – Maximum structural cruising speed

2-100. Answer B. GFDPP 2C, PHB
The maneuvering speed of an airplane is not shown on the airspeed indicator. It can be found in the airplane manual or on placards.

2-101   PLT086   PA.I.G.K1h
(Refer to Figure 5.) A turn coordinator provides an indication of the

A – angle of bank up to but not exceeding 30°.

B – movement of the aircraft about the yaw and roll axes.

C – attitude of the aircraft with reference to the longitudinal axis.

2-101. Answer B. GFDPP 2C, PHB
The turn coordinator senses movement about both the vertical axis (yaw) and the longitudinal axis (roll).

2-102   PLT278   PA.I.G.K1h

(Refer to Figure 7.) The proper adjustment to make on the attitude indicator during level flight is to align the

A – horizon bar to the level-flight indication.

B – horizon bar to the miniature airplane.

C – miniature airplane to the horizon bar.

2-102. Answer C. GFDPP 2C, PHB
The miniature airplane is adjustable and should be set to match the level flight indication of the horizon bar.

2-103   PLT278   PA.I.G.K1h

(Refer to Figure 7.) How should a pilot determine the direction of bank from an attitude indicator such as the one illustrated?

A – By the direction of deflection of the banking scale (A)

B – By the direction of deflection of the horizon bar (B)

C – By the relationship of the miniature airplane (C) to the deflected horizon bar (B)

2-103. Answer C. GFDPP 2C, PHB
As the airplane banks, the relationship between the miniature airplane and the horizon bar depict the direction of turn.

2-104   PLT215   PA.VI.A.K2

Deviation in a magnetic compass is caused by the

A – presence of flaws in the permanent magnets of the compass.

B – difference in the location between true north and magnetic north.

C – magnetic fields within the aircraft distorting the lines of magnetic force.

2-104. Answer C. GFDPP 2C, PHB
Metal and electronic components in the aircraft create magnetic fields which distort the lines of magnetic force. This causes deviation errors in the compass readings.

2-105   PLT215   PA.VI.A.K2

In the Northern Hemisphere, a magnetic compass will normally indicate initially a turn toward the west if

A – a left turn is entered from a north heading.

B – a right turn is entered from a north heading.

C – an aircraft is accelerated while on a north heading.

2-105. Answer B. GFDPP 2C, PHB
When turning from a northerly heading, the compass initially indicates a turn in the opposite direction. When starting a right turn, toward the east, the compass begins to show a turn to the west.

2-106   PLT215   PA.VI.A.K2

In the Northern Hemisphere, a magnetic compass will normally indicate initially a turn toward the east if

A – an aircraft is decelerated while on a south heading.

B – an aircraft is accelerated while on a north heading.

C – a left turn is entered from a north heading.

2-106. Answer C. GFDPP 2C, PHB

When turning from a northerly heading, the compass initially indicates a turn in the opposite direction. When starting a right turn, toward the east, the compass begins to show a turn to the west.

In this question, during a left turn toward the west, the magnetic compass would initially indicate a turn to the east.

2-107   PLT215   PA.VI.A.K2

In the Northern Hemisphere, a magnetic compass will normally indicate a turn toward the north if

A – a right turn is entered from an east heading.

B – an aircraft is decelerated while on an east or west heading.

C – an aircraft is accelerated while on an east or west heading.

2-107. Answer C. GFDPP 2C, PHB

Acceleration error is most pronounced on east/west headings. Using the acronym ANDS (Accelerate — North, Decelerate — South), acceleration will show a turn to the north, and deceleration will show a turn to the south.

2-108   PLT215   PA.VI.A.K2

In the Northern Hemisphere, the magnetic compass will normally indicate a turn toward the south when

A – a left turn is entered from an east heading.

B – a right turn is entered from a west heading.

C – the aircraft is decelerated while on a west heading.

2-108. Answer C. GFDPP 2C, PHB

Acceleration error is most pronounced on east/west headings. Using the acronym ANDS (Accelerate — North, Decelerate — South), acceleration will show a turn to the north, and deceleration will show a turn to the south.

2-109   PLT215   PA.VI.A.K2

In the Northern Hemisphere, if an aircraft is accelerated or decelerated, the magnetic compass will normally indicate

A – a turn momentarily.

B – correctly when on a north or south heading.

C – a turn toward the south.

2-109. Answer B. GFDPP 2C, PHB

Because acceleration and deceleration errors are most pronounced on east/west headings, accelerating or decelerating on a north or south heading will not show much of an error on the magnetic compass.

2-110   PLT215   PA.VI.A.K2

During flight, when are the indications of a magnetic compass accurate?

A – Only in straight-and-level unaccelerated flight.

B – As long as the airspeed is constant.

C – During turns if the bank does not exceed 18°.

2-110. Answer A. GFDPP 2C, PHB
Magnetic dip causes turning and acceleration/deceleration errors. For this reason, magnetic compass indications are accurate only in straight-and-level unaccelerated flight.

2-111   PLT206   PA.I.F.K1

If the outside air temperature (OAT) at a given altitude is warmer than standard, the density altitude is

A – equal to pressure altitude.

B – lower than pressure altitude.

C – higher than pressure altitude.

2-111. Answer C. GFDPP 2C, PHB
When the OAT is warmer than standard, the density altitude (DA) is higher than pressure altitude.

2-112   PLT173   PA.I.G.K1h

What are the standard temperature and pressure values for sea level?

A – 15°C and 29.92 inches Hg

B – 59°C and 1013.2 millibars

C – 59°F and 29.92 millibars

2-112. Answer A. GFDPP 2C, PHB
The standard atmosphere is a temperature of 15°C (59°F) and 29.92" Hg (1013.2 millibars).

2-113   PLT173   PA.I.G.K1h

If a pilot changes the altimeter setting from 30.11 to 29.96, what is the approximate change in indication?

A – Altimeter will indicate .15 inches Hg higher.

B – Altimeter will indicate 150 feet higher.

C – Altimeter will indicate 150 feet lower.

2-113. Answer C. GFDPP 2C, PHB
The indicated altitude changes by about 1,000 feet for each one-inch change in the altimeter's setting and in the same direction. Increasing the setting in the altimeter setting window by 0.100 inch increases the indicated altitude by about 100 feet. In this case, the setting is decreased 0.150 inch, so the indicated altitude is 150 feet lower.

2-114   PLT023   PA.I.G.K1h

Under which condition will pressure altitude be equal to true altitude?

A – When the atmospheric pressure is 29.92 inches Hg.

B – When standard atmospheric conditions exist.

C – When indicated altitude is equal to the pressure altitude.

2-114. Answer B. GFDPP 2C, AW
Pressure altitude equals true altitude when standard atmospheric conditions exist. When nonstandard conditions exist, true altitude will not equal pressure altitude.

2-115   PLT023   PA.I.G.K1h

Under what condition is pressure altitude and density altitude the same value?

A – At sea level, when the temperature is 0°F.

B – When the altimeter has no installation error.

C – At standard temperature.

2-115. Answer C. GFDPP 2C, PHB
Because density altitude is pressure altitude corrected for nonstandard temperature, DA and PA are equal only at standard temperature.

2-116   PLT041   PA.I.G.K1h

If a flight is made from an area of low pressure into an area of high pressure without the altimeter setting being adjusted, the altimeter will indicate

A – the actual altitude above sea level.

B – higher than the actual altitude above sea level.

C – lower than the actual altitude above sea level.

2-116. Answer C. GFDPP 2C, AW
The aircraft is at a higher true (actual) altitude above sea level than is indicated. In other words, the altimeter indicates lower than the actual altitude.

2-117   PLT041   PA.I.G.K1h

If a flight is made from an area of high pressure into an area of low pressure without the altimeter setting being adjusted, the altimeter will indicate

A – lower than the actual altitude above sea level.

B – higher than the actual altitude above sea level.

C – the actual altitude above sea level.

2-117. Answer B. GFDPP 2C, AW
Remember, "from high to low, look out below." In other words, the aircraft is at a lower true (actual) altitude than indicated, because the altimeter indicates higher than actual altitude.

2-118 PLT165   PA.I.G.K1h

Under what condition will true altitude be lower than indicated altitude?

A – In colder than standard air temperature.

B – In warmer than standard air temperature.

C – When density altitude is higher than indicated altitude.

2-118. Answer A. GFDPP 2C, AW
When the air is colder than standard, the actual (true) altitude of an aircraft is lower than indicated.

2-119 PLT165   PA.I.G.K1h

Which condition would cause the altimeter to indicate a lower altitude than true altitude?

A – Air temperature lower than standard

B – Atmospheric pressure lower than standard

C – Air temperature warmer than standard

2-119. Answer C. GFDPP 2C, AW
When the air is colder than standard, the actual (true) altitude of an aircraft is lower than indicated. Conversely, when the air temperature is warmer than standard, indicated altitude is lower than actual (true) altitude.

2-120 PLT023   PA.I.G.K1h

Which factor would tend to increase the density altitude at a given airport?

A – An increase in barometric pressure

B – An increase in ambient temperature

C – A decrease in relative humidity

2-120. Answer B. GFDPP 2C, AW
The factors that decrease air density, increasing density altitude, are increased ambient temperature, decreased barometric pressure, and increased relative humidity.

2-121 PLT215   PA.VI.A.K2

The angular difference between true north and magnetic north is

A – magnetic deviation.

B – magnetic variation.

C – compass acceleration error.

2-121. Answer B. GFDPP 2C, 9A, PHB
Magnetic variation occurs because the earth's magnetic poles do not coincide with its geographic poles, and a magnetic compass aligns with the magnetic poles. You can determine local magnetic variation by referencing the isogonic lines on aeronautical charts, which are represented by dashed magenta lines.

2-122 PLT215   PA.VI.A.K2

In the Northern Hemisphere, a magnetic compass will normally indicate a turn toward the north if

A – a left turn is entered from a west heading.

B – an aircraft is decelerated while on an east or west heading.

C – an aircraft is accelerated while on an east or west heading.

2-123 PLT215   PA.VI.A.K2

What should be the indication on the magnetic compass as you roll into a standard rate turn to the right from a south heading in the Northern Hemisphere?

A – The compass will initially indicate a turn to the left.

B – The compass will indicate a turn to the right, but at a faster rate than is actually occurring.

C – The compass will remain on south for a short time, then gradually catch up to the magnetic heading of the airplane.

2-124 PLT215   PA.VI.A.K5a

When converting from true course to magnetic heading, a pilot should

A – subtract easterly variation and right wind correction angle.

B – add westerly variation and subtract left wind correction angle.

C – subtract westerly variation and add right wind correction angle.

2-122. Answer C. GFDPP 2C, PHB
An acronym to easily remember acceleration errors is ANDS (Accelerate North Decelerate South). Acceleration errors occur primarily due the weights added to offset magnetic dip.

2-123. Answer B. GFDPP 2C, PHB
When turning from a southerly heading, the compass moves the correct direction, faster than the actual change in heading. Various compass errors arise due to magnetic dip and from the compass weights that are added to offset magnetic dip.

2-124. Answer B. GFDPP 2C, PHB
Remember, "east is least, west is best" to recall that easterly variation is subtracted and westerly variation is added. This calculation is often performed in conjunction with wind correction calculations using the formula:

TC ± WCA = TH ± VAR = MH ± DEV = CH

When using the wind side of a flight computer, add wind correction if your wind dot is to the right of the centerline, and subtract if it's to the left. You can easily visualize this by remembering that compass headings decrease as you turn left, so a correction to the left requires that you subtract the correction angle.

2-125   PLT215   PA.VI.A.K2

Deviation error of the magnetic compass is caused by

A – northerly turning error.

B – certain metals and electrical systems within the aircraft.

C – the difference in location of true north and magnetic north.

2-125. Answer B. GFDPP 2C, PHB
Metal and electronic components in the aircraft create magnetic fields that cause deviation errors in the compass readings. The difference between true north and magnetic north is *variation*, not deviation.

2-126   PA.IX.C.K2d

If the AHRS detects a problem with the integrity of the sensor information for a digital flight display, what occurs?

A – The system reverts to reversionary mode and PFD information is displayed on the MFD.

B – A red X is placed over the display of the affected instrument (attitude indicator or HSI).

C – After an alert message appears, you must determine the affected instrument by comparing the indications of all instruments.

2-126. Answer B. GFDPP 2C PHB
If either the AHRS or the ADC fails its integrity checks, the associated instruments become unreliable and the system normally marks out the affected instruments with red Xs. When this happens, use the back-up instruments.

2-127   PA.IX.C.K2d

You are flying an airplane with an integrated digital flight display and the PFD screen fails. What are typical back-up options for these instruments?

A – Switch the display of these instruments to the MFD.

B – Monitor traditional back-up instruments that are powered from the main electrical bus.

C – Reset the AHRS and the ADC and observe whether the PFD turns back on.

2-127. Answer A. GFDPP 2C PHB
Airplanes with integrated digital displays normally have a means of switching the essential instruments on the primary flight display (PFD) to the multifunction display (MFD), or they do it automatically. In addition, the magnetic compass and other normally "traditional" instruments are available as a back-up. The back-up airspeed indicator and altimeter are pitot-static instruments that don't require power. The back-up attitude indicator can be vacuum powered or electrically powered, but must have a power source that is isolated from the electrical system of the aircraft.

2-128   **PA.I.G.K1h**

How do you conduct a standard-rate turn on an airplane with a digital flight display.

A – Monitor the digital turn coordinator and adjust the angle of bank as needed.

B – Monitor the trend vector on the HSI and adjust the angle of bank as needed.

C – Monitor the trend indicator on the digital attitude indicator and adjust the bank as needed.

2-128. Answer A. GFDPP 2C PHB

An integrated digital flight instrument display normally does not have a turn coordinator. Instead, a trend indicator shows the future heading above the heading indicator (HSI). Calibration marks show a standard-rate turn.

2-129   **PA.IX.C.K2d**

Which electronic flight instruments are related to the air data computer (ADC)?

A – Attitude indicator, heading indicator, and turn indicator

B – Compass, magnetometer, and ground track indicator

C – Airspeed tape, altitude tape, and VSI

2-129. Answer C. GFDPP 2C PHB

The air data computer (ADC) is connected to the pitot-static system and works with the same instruments as a pitot-static system would.

CHAPTER 3

AERODYNAMIC PRINCIPLES

SECTION A — FOUR FORCES OF FLIGHT

- The four forces that act on an airplane in flight are lift, weight, thrust, and drag.
- The forces are in equilibrium when the airplane is in unaccelerated flight.
- During straight-and-level flight, lift equals weight, and thrust equals drag. This is also true during climbs and descents and any time the airplane is not accelerating.
- Bernoulli's principle states that as the velocity of a fluid (including air) increases, its pressure decreases. It provides an explanation of lift produced by an airfoil that is curved more on the top than on the bottom. Air travels faster over the curved upper surface, causing lower pressure on the top surface.
- Another explanation for lift is provided by Newton's Third Law—For every action, there is an equal and opposite reaction. Newton's law explains why upward force is generated as the lower surface of the wing deflects air downward.
- The angle of attack is the angle between the wing chord line and the relative wind.
- The angle of attack affects lift by changing the amount of air that is deflected downward.
- The angle of attack at which an airplane wing stalls is the same regardless of weight or load factor.

FLAPS

- Flaps enable steeper approaches to a landing without increasing airspeed.

GROUND EFFECT

- Ground effect is the result of the interference of the surface of the Earth with the airflow patterns about an airplane.
- Ground effect reduces induced drag on the airplane, increasing performance.
- An adverse consequence of ground effect is that an airplane can become airborne before reaching the recommended takeoff speed, but then be unable to climb out of ground effect.
- Another undesirable consequence of ground effect is that any excess speed at the point of flare can cause considerable floating.

3-1   PLT247

The four forces acting on an airplane in flight are

A – lift, weight, thrust, and drag.

B – lift, weight, gravity, and thrust.

C – lift, gravity, power, and friction.

3-1. Answer A. GFDPP 3A, AFH

Lift is the upward force created by airflow over and under the wings. Weight, caused by the downward pull of gravity, opposes lift. Thrust is the forward force that propels the airplane forward, and drag is the retarding force that opposes thrust.

3-2   PLT247
When are the four forces that act on an airplane in equilibrium?

A – During unaccelerated flight

B – When the aircraft is accelerating

C – When the aircraft is at rest on the ground

3-2. Answer A. GFDPP 3A, AFH
In straight-and-level, unaccelerated flight, the four forces are in equilibrium. Lift equals weight, and thrust equals drag.

3-3   PLT168   PA.I.F.K3
(Refer to Figure 1.) The acute angle A is the angle of

A – incidence.

B – attack.

C – dihedral.

3-3. Answer B. GFDPP 3A, PHB
The angle between the chord line and the relative wind is the angle of attack.

3-4   PLT168   PA.I.F.K3
The term "angle of attack" is defined as the angle between the

A – airplane's center line and the relative wind.

B – chord line of the wing and the relative wind

C – airplane's longitudinal axis and that of the air striking the airfoil.

3-4. Answer B. GFDPP 3A, PHB
The angle of attack is the angle between the chord line of the wing and the relative wind. The other answers are wrong because the angle of attack is *not* measured from parts of the airplane other than the wing.

3-5   PLT168   PA.I.F.K6
The angle between the chord line of an airfoil and the relative wind is known as the angle of

A – lift.

B – attack.

C – incidence.

3-5. Answer B. GFDPP 3A, PHB
The angle of attack is the angle between the wing chord line and the relative wind. The angle of incidence is the angle between the chord line and the longitudinal access of the airplane, which normally provides some small angle of attack while the airplane is in level flight.

3-6   PLT247   PA.I.F.K3
What is the relationship of lift, drag, thrust, and weight when the airplane is in straight-and-level flight?

A – Lift, drag, and weight equal thrust.

B – Lift and weight equal thrust and drag.

C – Lift equals weight and thrust equals drag.

3-6. Answer C. GFDPP 3A, AFH
Assuming the airplane is not accelerating, thrust equals drag, and lift equals weight.

3-7   PLT473   PA.I.G.K1b
One of the main functions of flaps during approach and landing is to

A – decrease the angle of descent without increasing the airspeed.

B – enable a touchdown at a higher indicated airspeed.

C – increase the angle of descent without increasing the airspeed.

3-7. Answer C. GFDPP 3A, AFH
Flaps increase both lift and drag, enabling a steeper angle of descent without increasing airspeed. The increased lift also enables touchdown at a lower indicated airspeed.

3-8   PLT473   PA.I.G.K1b
What is one purpose of wing flaps?

A – To decrease wing area to vary the lift.

B – To relieve the pilot of maintaining continuous pressure on the controls.

C – To enable the pilot to make steeper approaches to a landing without increasing the airspeed.

3-8. Answer C. GFDPP 3A, AFH
Flaps increase both lift and drag, enabling a steeper approach without increasing airspeed. Trim controls, not flaps, relieve the pilot of maintaining continuous pressure on the controls. Some types of flaps increase wing area when deployed to increase lift.

3-9   PLT168   PA.I.F.K3
The angle of attack at which an airplane wing stalls

A – increases if the CG is moved forward.

B – changes with an increase in gross weight.

C – remains the same regardless of gross weight.

3-9. Answer C. GFDPP 3A, PHB
The critical angle of attack (angle of attack at which an airplane wing stalls) is determined by the lift coefficient of a particular wing configuration. An airplane stalls when the critical angle of attack is exceeded, regardless of weight or airspeed.

3-10   PLT131   PA.I.F.K3
What is ground effect?

A – The result of the interference of the surface of the Earth with the airflow patterns about an airplane

B – The result of an alteration in airflow patterns increasing induced drag about the wings of an airplane

C – The result of the disruption of the airflow patterns about the wings of an airplane to the point where the wings can no longer support the airplane in flight

3-10. Answer A. GFDPP 3A, AFH
When flying close to the ground, the airflow around an airplane is altered by interference with the surface of the earth. The resulting ground effect reduces the induced drag on the airplane.

3-11   PLT131   PA.I.F.K3
Floating caused by the phenomenon of ground effect is most realized during an approach to land when at

A – a higher-than-normal angle of attack.

B – less than the length of the wingspan above the surface.

C – twice the length of the wingspan above the surface.

3-11. Answer B. GFDPP 3A, AFH
Ground effect becomes noticeable when the height of the airplane above the ground is less than the length of the wingspan.

3-12   PLT131   PA.I.F.K3
What must a pilot be aware of as a result of ground effect?

A – Wingtip vortices increase, creating wake turbulence problems for arriving and departing aircraft.

B – Induced drag decreases; therefore, any excess speed at the point of flare may cause considerable floating.

C – A full stall landing requires less up elevator deflection than a full stall that is done free of ground effect.

3-12. Answer B. GFDPP 3A, AFH
Because ground effect decreases induced drag, the airplane tends to float during the flare. This especially affects low-wing airplanes.

3-13   PLT131   PA.I.F.K3
Ground effect is most likely to result in which problem?

A – Setting to the surface abruptly during landing

B – Becoming airborne before reaching recommended takeoff speed

C – Inability to get airborne even though airspeed is sufficient for normal takeoff needs

3-13. Answer B. GFDPP 3A, AFH
The decreased induced drag while in ground effect enables the airplane to become airborne at a lower airspeed than the recommended takeoff speed, but the airplane might not be able to climb out of ground effect. On landing, ground effect can lead to floating, especially on low-wing airplanes.

3-14   PLT025   PA.I.F.K6
Which statement relates to Bernoulli's principle?

A – For every action, there is an equal and opposite reaction.

B – An additional upward force is generated as the lower surface of the wing deflects air downward.

C – Air traveling faster over the curved upper surface of an airfoil causes lower pressure on the top surface.

3-14. Answer C. GFDPP 3A, PHB
Bernoulli's principle states that as the velocity of a fluid (including air), increases, its pressure decreases. The explanations of lift that relate to Bernoulli focus on the higher velocity of air over the upper surface of an airfoil. The other two answers are also valid explanations for lift, but are related to Newton's Third Law rather than Bernoulli's principle.

3-15   PLT236   PA.I.F.K3

Changes in the center of pressure of a wing affect the aircraft's

A – lift/drag ratio.

B – lifting capacity.

C – aerodynamic balance and controllability.

3-15. Answer C. GFDPP 3A, PHB

A wing's center of pressure moves forward and back with changing angles of attack (forward for high angles and back for lower). This movement changes the position of the airloads on the wing, which results in changes to an airplane's aerodynamic balance and controllability.

SECTION B — STABILITY

- An airplane cannot be completely stable, or it would not be possible to maneuver it. However, some stability is needed for desirable handling characteristics.
- An aircraft that is inherently stable requires less effort to control.
- Longitudinal stability involves the pitching motion or tendency of the airplane to move about its lateral axis.

LOCATION OF THE CENTER OF GRAVITY (CG)

- The location of the CG, with respect to the center of lift (CL), determines the longitudinal stability of the airplane. The airplane is more stable when the CG is forward of the CL.
- Loading an aircraft to the most aft CG causes the airplane to be less stable at all speeds.
- An airplane loaded with the CG aft of the approved CG range is difficult to recover from a stalled condition.

STALLS

- The inherent stability of an airplane is important because it relates to the aircraft's ability to avoid stalls and spins. Familiarization with the causes and effects of stalls is especially important during flight at slow airspeeds, such as during takeoff and landing, where the margin above the stall speed is small.
- When you reduce power without adjusting the controls, an airplane pitches nose down because the downwash on the elevator from the propeller slipstream is reduced, which reduces elevator effectiveness. This behavior discourages stalls.

SPINS

- You must stall an airplane before it can spin.
- During a spin, both wings are stalled, but one wing is more stalled than the other.

3-16   PLT213   PA.I.F.K3

An airplane said to be inherently stable

A – will not spin.

B – is difficult to stall.

C – requires less effort to control.

3-16. Answer C. GFDPP 3B, PHB

An airplane that is inherently stable tends to return to its original attitude after it has been displaced, which makes it easier to control.

3-17   PLT213   PA.I.F.K3

What determines the longitudinal stability of an airplane?

A – The location of the CG with respect to the center of lift

B – The effectiveness of the horizontal stabilizer, rudder, and rudder trim tab

C – The relationship of thrust and lift to weight and drag

3-17. Answer A. GFDPP 3B, PHB

The longitudinal stability of an airplane is determined primarily by the location of the center of gravity (CG) in relation to the center of lift (CL). The airplane is more stable when the CG is forward of the CL.

3-18   PLT351   PA.I.F.K3

What causes an airplane (except a T-tail) to pitch nose down when power is reduced and controls are not adjusted?

A – The CG shifts forward when thrust and drag are reduced.

B – The downwash on the elevators from the propeller slipstream is reduced and elevator effectiveness is reduced.

C – When thrust is reduced to less than weight, lift is also reduced and the wings can no longer support the weight.

3-18. Answer B. GFDPP 3B, PHB

At higher power settings, in airplanes other than T-tail designs, the propeller slipstream causes a greater downward force on the horizontal stabilizer. When power is reduced, this downward force on the tail is also reduced, and the nose pitches down.

3-19   PLT240   PA.I.F.K2e

An airplane has been loaded in such a manner that the CG is located aft of the aft CG limit. One undesirable flight characteristic a pilot might experience with this airplane would be

A – a longer takeoff run.

B – difficulty in recovering from a stalled condition.

C – stalling at higher-than-normal airspeed.

3-19. Answer B. GFDPP 3B, AFH

With a CG aft of the rear CG limit, the airplane becomes tail heavy and unstable in pitch because the horizontal stabilizer is less effective. This condition makes it difficult, if not impossible, to recover from a stall or spin. The other two answers are wrong because an aft CG, although dangerous, results in reduced drag, which could result in a shorter takeoff run and stalling at a lower-than normal airspeed.

3-20   PLT240   PA.I.F.K2e

Loading an airplane to the most aft CG causes the airplane to be

A – less stable at all speeds.

B – less stable at slow speeds, but more stable at high speeds.

C – less stable at high speeds, but more stable at low speeds.

3-20. Answer A. GFDPP 3B, AFH

In an airplane loaded to the aft CG limit, the horizontal stabilizer is less effective, causing the airplane to be less stable at all speeds.

3-21   PLT245   PA.I.F.K3

In what flight condition must an aircraft be placed in order to spin?

A – Partially stalled with one wing low

B – In a steep diving spiral

C – Stalled

3-21. Answer C. GFDPP 3B, AFH

An airplane must be stalled before it can spin. The spin progresses when one wing becomes more stalled than the other, which leads to rotation. A steep diving spiral is different than a spin because the airplane is not stalled, even though it is descending and turning.

3-22   PLT245   PA.I.F.K3

During a spin to the left, which wings are stalled?

A – Both wings are stalled.

B – Neither wing is stalled.

C – Only the left wing is stalled.

3-22. Answer A. GFDPP 3B, AFH

In any spin, both wings are stalled but in a spin to the left, the left wing is more stalled.

SECTION C — AERODYNAMICS OF MANEUVERING FLIGHT

The four flight fundamentals involved in maneuvering an aircraft are straight-and-level flight, turns, climbs, and descents.

LEFT-TURNING TENDENCY

Left-turning tendency, sometimes referred to as "torque," is made up of four elements that produce a twisting or rotating motion around at least one of the airplane's three axes. These elements are:
* Torque reaction from engine and propeller.
* Corkscrewing effect of the slipstream.
* Gyroscopic action of the propeller.
* Asymmetric loading of the propeller, or P-factor, which is the result of the propeller blade descending on the right producing more thrust than the ascending blade on the left.
* P-factor is the most prominent of the left-turning tendencies.
* P-factor is most pronounced at low airspeeds, high power settings, and high angles of attack.

TURNS AND LOAD FACTOR

* The horizontal component of lift is what makes an airplane turn.
* Load factor is the ratio of the load supported by the airplane's wings to the actual weight of the aircraft and its contents.
* Turns increase the load factor on an airplane, as compared to straight-and-level flight.
* The amount of excess load that can be imposed on an airplane depends on its speed.
* At 60 degrees of bank, 2 Gs are required to maintain level flight. To determine how much weight the airplane's wing structure must support, multiply the airplane's weight by the number of Gs.
* An increased load factor, whether it is experienced in a turn, or by a pull-up out of a descent, causes an airplane to stall at a higher airspeed.
* V_A is defined as maneuvering speed.

3-23   PLT243   PA.IV.C.K2

In what flight condition is torque effect the greatest in a single-engine airplane?

A – Low airspeed, high power, high angle of attack

B – Low airspeed, low power, low angle of attack

C – High airspeed, high power, high angle of attack

3-23. Answer A. GFDPP 3C, PHB

Torque effect is greatest at low airspeeds, high power settings, and high angles of attack.

3-24   PLT243   PA.IV.C.K2

The left-turning tendency of an airplane caused by P-factor is the result of the

A – clockwise rotation of the engine and the propeller turning the airplane counter-clockwise.

B – propeller blade descending on the right, producing more thrust than the ascending blade on the left.

C – gyroscopic forces applied to the rotating propeller blades acting 90° in advance of the point the force was applied.

3-24. Answer B. GFDPP 3C, PHB

P-factor, or asymmetric propeller loading, normally occurs at a high angle of attack. The descending propeller blade on the right side takes a larger "bite" of the air, and produces more thrust than the ascending blade on the left. The result is a left-turning tendency of the airplane.

3-25   PLT243   PA.IV.C.K2

When does P-factor cause the airplane to yaw to the left?

A – When at low angles of attack

B – When at high angles of attack

C – When at high airspeeds

3-25. Answer B. GFDPP 3C, PHB

P-factor is most pronounced at high angles of attack, which cause the descending propeller blade to produce more thrust.

3-26   PLT309   PA.VII.A.K2

(Refer to Figure 2.) If an airplane weighs 2,300 pounds, what approximate weight would the airplane structure be required to support during a 60° banked turn while maintaining altitude?

A – 2,300 pounds

B – 3,400 pounds

C – 4,600 pounds

3-26. Answer C. GFDPP 3C, PHB

At 60 degrees of bank, 2 Gs are required to maintain level flight, which means that the wing structure must support twice the airplane's weight— 2,300 lb × 2 = 4,600 lb.

3-27 PLT309 PA.VII.A.K2

(Refer to Figure 2.) If an airplane weighs 3,300 pounds, what approximate weight would the airplane structure be required to support during a 30° banked turn while maintaining altitude?

A – 1,200 pounds

B – 3,100 pounds

C – 3,800 pounds

3-27. Answer C. GFDPP 3C, PHB
The load factor for 30 degrees of bank is 1.154 [(1 ÷ Cos (30°)]. The airplane weight (3,300 lb) multiplied by the load factor (1.154) is 3,810 lb, which the wing structure must support.

3-28 PLT309 PA.VII.A.K2

(Refer to Figure 2.) If an airplane weighs 4,500 pounds, what approximate weight would the airplane structure be required to support during a 45° banked turn while maintaining altitude?

A – 4,500 pounds

B – 6,400 pounds

C – 7,200 pounds

3-28. Answer B. GFDPP 3C, PHB
At 45 degrees of bank, the load factor is 1.414. The wing loading would be 4,500 lb × 1.414, or 6,365 lb.

3-29 PLT311 PA.VII.A.K2

The amount of excess load that can be imposed on the wing of an airplane depends upon the

A – position of the CG.

B – speed of the airplane.

C – abruptness at which the load is applied.

3-29. Answer B. GFDPP 3C, PHB
The amount of excess load that can be imposed on an airplane depends on its speed. If abrupt control movements or strong gusts are applied at low airspeeds, the airplane stalls before the load becomes excessive. At higher airspeeds, the increased airflow causes a greater lifting capacity. A sudden control input or gust at a high airspeed may result in an excessive load factor beyond safe limits.

3-30 PLT310 PA.VII.A.K2

Which basic flight maneuver increases the load factor on an airplane as compared to straight-and-level flight?

A – Climbs

B – Turns

C – Stalls

3-30. Answer B. GFDPP 3C, PHB
In a level turn, lift must be increased to compensate for the loss of vertical lift and overcome centrifugal force. Because the wings must support not only the airplane's weight, but also the load imposed by centrifugal force, the load factor is greater than one G.

3-31   PLT242

What force makes an airplane turn?

A – The horizontal component of lift

B – The vertical component of lift

C – Centrifugal force

3-31. Answer A. GFDPP 3C, PHB

In a turn, lift has both a vertical and a horizontal component. The horizontal component of lift, which is also referred to as centripetal force, opposes centrifugal force and causes the airplane to turn. The vertical component of lift opposes gravity and enables the airplane to maintain altitude.

3-32   PLT018

During an approach to a stall, an increased load factor causes the airplane to

A – stall at a higher airspeed.

B – have a tendency to spin.

C – be more difficult to control.

3-32. Answer A. GFDPP 3C, PHB

Stall speed increases in proportion to the square root of the load factor. Added G-forces cause an airplane to stall at an airspeed higher than the normal 1 G airspeed.

3-33   PLT219

What are the four flight fundamentals that are involved in maneuvering an aircraft?

A – Aircraft power, pitch, bank, and trim

B – Starting, taxiing, takeoff, and landing

C – Straight-and-level flight, turns, climbs, and descents

3-33. Answer C. GFDPP 3C, AFH

All controlled flight consists of one of the four fundamental maneuvers or some combination of them.

THE FLIGHT ENVIRONMENT

SECTION A — SAFETY OF FLIGHT

COLLISION AVOIDANCE

- Most midair collisions occur during daylight hours, in VFR conditions, and within 5 miles of an airport.

- You might not notice objects in your peripheral vision without some relative motion. However, an aircraft on a collision course with your aircraft shows little relative movement but gradually increases in size.

- The most effective method of scanning for other aircraft for collision avoidance during daylight hours is to use a series of short, regularly spaced eye movements to search each 10-degree sector of the sky.

- The FAA's voluntary pilot safety program, *operation lights on*, encourages pilots to turn on their landing lights when operating below 10,000 feet, day or night, especially within 10 miles of any airport. *Lights on* also applies in conditions of reduced visibility and in areas where flocks of birds can be expected, such as coastal areas, lake areas, and around trash dumps.

- A cockpit display of traffic information is a dedicated screen, multi-function display, or GPS moving map that depicts traffic threats, so that you can concentrate your scan near the threat and avoid a collision.

- Haze reduces visibility, and makes objects appear to be farther away than they really are.

- When climbing or descending VFR along an airway, execute gentle banks left and right to enable continuous scanning of the area in front of the airplane.

- Before beginning a maneuver, make clearing turns to scan the entire area for other traffic.

RIGHT-OF-WAY RULES

- An aircraft in distress has right-of-way over all other aircraft.

- When two aircraft of the same category are converging, the aircraft on the right has right-of-way. When an aircraft and a watercraft are on crossing courses, the aircraft or vessel to the right has the right-of-way.

- When aircraft of different categories are converging: a glider has right-of-way over an airship, powered parachute, weight-shift-control aircraft, airplane, or rotorcraft; and an airship has the right-of-way over a powered parachute, weight-shift-control aircraft, airplane, or rotorcraft.

- An aircraft that is towing or refueling another has the right-of-way over other engine-driven aircraft.

- When aircraft are approaching head-on, each shall give way to the right.

- When two or more aircraft are approaching the airport with the intention of landing, the one at the lower altitude has the right-of-way.

MINIMUM SAFE ALTITUDES

- Except during takeoff or landing, you must maintain enough altitude to allow for an emergency landing in the event of an engine failure, without creating an undue hazard to people or property on the surface.

- Over a congested area, such as a city, you must maintain an altitude of 1,000 feet above the highest obstacle within a horizontal distance of 2,000 feet.

- Over other-than congested areas, you must maintain an altitude of at least 500 feet above the surface, except over sparsely populated areas or open water, where you must stay at least 500 feet away from any person, vessel, vehicle, or structure.
- If you are unable to obtain a local altimeter setting before departing, set the altimeter to the local field elevation.

TAXIING IN WIND

- When taxiing with a quartering headwind, hold the aileron up on the side from which the wind is blowing.
- A quartering tailwind is the most critical wind condition to a tricycle-gear, high-wing airplane.
- When taxiing with a quartering tailwind, hold the aileron down on the side from which the wind is blowing.

POSITIVE EXCHANGE OF FLIGHT CONTROLS

To avoid any misunderstanding as to who is operating the flight controls of an aircraft, the FAA recommends the use of a three-step process when exchanging the flight controls with your instructor or any other pilot.

1. The pilot passing control says: "You have the flight controls."
2. The pilot taking control says: "I have the flight controls."
3. The pilot passing control says: "You have the flight controls."

4-1   PLT414   PA.III.B.K4

Which aircraft has the right-of-way over all other air traffic?

A – A balloon

B – An aircraft in distress

C – An aircraft on final approach to land

4-1. Answer B. GFDPP 4A FAR 91.113C
An aircraft in distress has the right-of-way over all other aircraft.

4-2   PLT414   PA.III.B.K4

What action is required when two aircraft of the same category converge, but not head-on?

A – The faster aircraft shall give way.

B – The aircraft on the left shall give way.

C – Each aircraft shall give way to the right.

4-2. Answer B. GFDPP 4A, FAR 91.113
The aircraft on the right has the right-of-way and the aircraft on the left shall give way.

4-3   PLT414   PA.III.B.K4

Which aircraft has the right-of-way over the other aircraft listed?

A – Glider

B – Airship

C – Aircraft refueling other aircraft

4-3. Answer A. GFDPP 4A, FAR 91.113
In general, the least maneuverable or nonpowered aircraft have the right-of-way. A glider has the right-of-way over an airship, airplane, or rotorcraft. An aircraft that is towing or refueling another aircraft has the right-of-way over all other engine-driven aircraft (but not a glider).

4-4   PLT414   PA.III.B.K4

An airplane and an airship are converging. If the airship is left of the airplane's position, which aircraft has the right-of-way?

A – The airship.

B – The airplane.

C – Each pilot should alter course to the right.

4-4. Answer A. GFDPP 4A, FAR 91.113

In general, the least maneuverable aircraft normally has the right-of-way. A glider has the right-of-way over an airship, airplane, or rotorcraft. An aircraft that is towing or refueling another aircraft has the right-of-way over all other engine-driven aircraft (but not a glider).

Because an airship is less maneuverable than an airplane, the airship has the right-of-way.

4-5   PLT414   PA.III.B.K3

A seaplane and a motorboat are on crossing courses. If the motorboat is to the left of the seaplane, which has the right-of-way?

A – The motorboat.

B – The seaplane.

C – Both should alter course to the right.

4-5. Answer B. FAR 91.115

When an aircraft, or an aircraft and a vessel, are on crossing courses, the aircraft, or vessel, to the right has the right-of-way.

4-6   PLT414   PA.III.B.K4

Which aircraft has the right-of-way over the other aircraft listed?

A – Airship

B – Aircraft towing other aircraft

C – Gyroplane

4-6. Answer B. GFDPP 4A, FAR 91.113

An aircraft towing or refueling another aircraft has the right-of-way over all other engine-driven aircraft.

4-7   PLT414   PA.III.B.K4

What action should the pilots of a glider and an airplane take if on a head-on collision course?

A – The airplane pilot should give way to the left.

B – The glider pilot should give way to the right.

C – Both pilots should give way to the right.

4-7. Answer C. GFDPP 4A, FAR 91.113

When any aircraft are approaching each other head-on, both pilots should alter their course to the right. For aircraft approaching head-on, the FARs do not differentiate between aircraft categories.

4-8   PLT414   PA.III.B.K4

When two or more aircraft are approaching an airport for landing, the right-of-way belongs to the aircraft

A – that has the other to its right.

B – that is the least maneuverable.

C – at the lower altitude, but it shall not take advantage of this rule to cut in front of or to overtake another.

4-8. Answer C. GFDPP 4A, FAR 91.113

When two or more aircraft are approaching an airport for landing, the one at the lower altitude has the right-of-way, but do not use this rule to cut in front of another aircraft.

4-9   PLT430   PA.IV.E.K7

Except when necessary for takeoff or landing, what is the minimum safe altitude for a pilot to operate an aircraft anywhere?

A – An altitude allowing, if a power unit fails, an emergency landing without undue hazard to persons or property on the surface

B – An altitude of 500 feet above the surface and no closer than 500 feet to any person, vessel, vehicle, or structure

C – An altitude of 500 feet above the highest obstacle within a horizontal radius of 1,000 feet

4-9. Answer A. GFDPP 4A, FAR 91.119
Maintain enough altitude to allow an emergency landing in the event of an engine failure without undue hazard to people or property on the surface.

4-10   PLT430   PA.IV.E.K7

Except when necessary for takeoff or landing, what is the minimum safe altitude required for a pilot to operate an aircraft over congested areas?

A – An altitude of 1,000 feet above any person, vessel, vehicle, or structure

B – An altitude of 500 feet above the highest obstacle within a horizontal radius of 1,000 feet

C – An altitude of 1,000 feet above the highest obstacle within a horizontal radius of 2,000 feet

4-10. Answer C. GFDPP 4A, FAR 91.119
The minimum safe altitude required over a congested area is 1,000 feet above any obstacle within a horizontal radius of 2,000 feet of the aircraft.

4-11   PLT430   PA.IV.E.K7

Except when necessary for takeoff or landing, what is the minimum safe altitude for a pilot to operate an aircraft over other than a congested area?

A – An altitude of 1,000 feet above the highest obstacle within a horizontal radius of 2,000 feet

B – An altitude of 500 feet AGL, except over open water or a sparsely populated area, which requires 500 feet from any person, vessel, vehicle, or structure

C – An altitude of 500 feet above the highest obstacle within a horizontal radius of 1,000 feet

4-11. Answer B. GFDPP 4A, FAR 91.119
The minimum safe altitude over a noncongested area is 500 feet AGL, except over open water or a sparsely populated area, which requires 500 feet (horizontally or vertically) from any person, vessel, vehicle, or structure.

4-12   PLT430   PA.IV.E.K7

Except when necessary for takeoff or landing, an aircraft may not be operated closer than what distance from any person, vessel, vehicle, or structure?

A – 500 feet

B – 700 feet

C – 1,000 feet

4-12. Answer A. GFDPP 4A, FAR 91.119

Over a sparsely populated or open water area, you must remain at least 500 feet (horizontally or vertically) from any person, vessel, vehicle, or structure.

4-13   PLT485   PA.II.D.K1

When taxiing with strong quartering tailwinds, which aileron positions should be used?

A – Aileron down on the downwind side

B – Ailerons neutral

C – Aileron down on the side from which the wind is blowing

4-13. Answer C. GFDPP 4A, AFH

With a quartering tailwind, the aileron should be down on the side from which the wind is blowing to prevent the wind from flowing under the wing and lifting it.

4-14   PLT485   PA.II.D.K1

Which aileron positions should a pilot generally use when taxiing in strong quartering headwinds?

A – Aileron up on the side from which the wind is blowing

B – Aileron down on the side from which the wind is blowing

C – Ailerons neutral

4-14. Answer A. GFDPP 4A, AFH

To counteract the lifting tendency of a quartering headwind, the aileron should be up on the side from which the wind is blowing.

4-15   PLT485   PA.II.D.K1

Which wind condition would be most critical when taxiing a nosewheel equipped high-wing airplane?

A – Quartering tailwind

B – Direct crosswind

C – Quartering headwind

4-15. Answer A. GFDPP 4A, AFH

A tricycle-gear, high-wing airplane is most susceptible to a quartering tailwind because a strong airflow beneath the wing and horizontal stabilizer can lift the airplane and tip or nose it over.

4-16   PLT485   PA.II.D.K1

(Refer to Figure 9, area A.) How should the flight controls be held while taxiing a tricycle-gear equipped airplane into a left quartering headwind?

A – Left aileron up, elevator neutral

B – Left aileron down, elevator neutral

C – Left aileron up, elevator down

4-16. Answer A. GFDPP 4A, AFH

While taxiing a tricycle-gear airplane in a quartering headwind, the aileron should be up on the side from which the wind is blowing, and the elevator neutral to prevent any lifting force on the tail. In this case, the wind is from the left, so the left aileron should be up.

4-17   PLT485   PA.II.D.K1

(Refer to Figure 9, area B.)
How should the flight controls be held while taxiing a tailwheel airplane into a right quartering headwind?

A – Right aileron up, elevator up

B – Right aileron down, elevator neutral

C – Right aileron up, elevator down

4-17. Answer A. GFDPP 4A, AFH

In a tailwheel airplane, hold the aileron up on the upwind side, that is move the control stick into the wind. Hold the elevator up (pull back on the stick) to prevent the tail from lifting. Because the tail of most tailwheel airplanes is lower than the nose while taxiing, a strong headwind with a neutral or down elevator could lift the tail.

4-18   PLT485   PA.II.D.K1

(Refer to Figure 9, area C.)
How should the flight controls be held while taxiing a tailwheel airplane with a left quartering tailwind?

A – Left aileron up, elevator neutral

B – Left aileron down, elevator neutral

C – Left aileron down, elevator down

4-18. Answer C. GFDPP 4A, AFH

For a quartering tailwind, the controls are held the same for both tailwheel and tricycle-gear airplanes. Ailerons are down on the side from which the wind is blowing. The elevator is down to prevent the wind from lifting the tail.

4-19   PLT194   PA.V.A.R7

Before starting each maneuver, pilots should

A – check altitude, airspeed, and heading indications.

B – visually scan the entire area for collision avoidance.

C – announce their intentions on the nearest CTAF.

4-19. Answer B. GFDPP 4A, AIM

To ensure you can see other aircraft that might be blocked by blind spots, make clearing turns and scan the area.

4-20   PA.V.A.R4

Your instructor has demonstrated a maneuver and wants you to try it. What steps should you complete to assume control of the airplane?

A – Tell the instructor that you are ready to try the maneuver and start performing the maneuver when the airplane is stabilized.

B – Start performing the maneuver after your instructor says, "you have the flight controls," and let the instructor monitor your performance.

C – After your instructor says, "you have the flight controls", say "I have the flight controls", and watch for your instructor to confirm again, "you have the flight controls."

4-20. Answer C. GFDPP 4A, PHB
To ensure that it is clear who has control of the airplane, the FAA recommends the use of a three-step process when exchanging the flight controls.

4-21   PLT125   PA.III.B.R1

What collision avoidance procedure is recommended when climbing or descending VFR on an airway?

A – Execute gentle banks, left and right for continuous visual scanning of the airspace.

B – Advise the nearest FSS of the altitude changes.

C – Fly away from the centerline of the airway before changing altitude.

4-21. Answer A. GFDPP 4A, AIM
Because of potential traffic on airways, it is important to scan. Making shallow turns enables you to compensate for blind spots.

4-22   PLT194   PA.I.H.K1j

What effect does haze have on your ability to see traffic or terrain features during flight?

A – Haze causes the eyes to focus at infinity.

B – The eyes tend to overwork in haze and do not detect relative movement easily.

C – All traffic or terrain features appear to be farther away than their actual distance.

4-22. Answer C. GFDPP 4A, AIM
Haze reduces the clarity with which you see objects, which is similar to the way you see them when they are farther away. Because of this effect, haze creates the illusion that objects are farther away than their actual distance.

4-23   PLT194   PA.III.B.R1

The most effective method of scanning for other aircraft for collision avoidance during daylight hours is to use

A – regularly spaced concentration on the 3-, 9-, and 12-o'clock positions.

B – a series of short, regularly spaced eye movements to search each 10-degree sector.

C – peripheral vision by scanning small sectors and utilizing off-center viewing.

4-23. Answer B. GFDPP 4A, AIM
The eyes are able to focus clearly only on a small area, approximately 10°, so a series of short eye movements is most effective.

4-24   PLT194   PA.III.B.R1

Which technique should you use to scan for traffic to the right and left during straight-and-level flight?

A – Systematically focus on different segments of the sky for short intervals.

B – Concentrate on relative movement detected in the peripheral vision area.

C – Continuous sweeping of the windshield from right to left.

4-24. Answer A. GFDPP 4A, AIM
The eyes are able to focus clearly only on a small area, approximately 10°, so a series of short eye movements is most effective.

4-25   PLT194   PA.III.B.R1

How can you determine if another aircraft is on a collision course with your aircraft?

A – The other aircraft always appears to get larger and closer at a rapid rate.

B – The nose of each aircraft is pointed at the same point in space.

C – No relative motion is apparent between your aircraft and the other aircraft.

4-25. Answer C. GFDPP 4A, AIM
A lack of relative movement can indicate that the two aircraft are moving toward one another on a collision course.

4-26   PLT194   PA.III.B.R1

Most midair collision accidents occur during

A – foggy days.

B – clear days.

C – cloudy nights.

4-26. Answer B. GFDPP 4A, AFH
Most midair collisions occur near airports, in daytime VFR weather conditions.

4-27 PLT119 PA.III.B.R1

The FAA specifically encourages pilots to turn on their landing lights when operating below 10,000 feet, day or night, and especially when operating

A – in Class B airspace.

B – in conditions of reduced visibility.

C – within 15 miles of a towered airport.

4-27. Answer B. AIM

The FAA's voluntary pilot safety program, *Operation Lights On*, encourages pilots to turn on their landing lights when operating below 10,000 feet, day or night, especially within 10 miles of any airport; also in conditions of reduced visibility and in areas where flocks of birds can be expected, such as coastal areas, lake areas, and around trash dumps.

4-28 PLT119 PA.VI.A.R1

What is the appropriate way to use a cockpit display of traffic information (CDTI) to avoid a collision?

A – Monitor the CDTI and if you receive a traffic alert, turn away from target shown on the display.

B – Continuously scan for traffic by looking outside and cross check the CDTI to learn what areas need increased attention.

C – To avoid complacency, use the CDTI only after you are instrument rated and flying IFR.

4-28. Answer B. GFDPP 4A, AIM

General aviation traffic systems are advisory only, to help you locate traffic. You may not fly any avoidance maneuvers without first seeing the traffic out the window.

4-29 PLT208 PA.IX.B.K3

When executing an emergency approach to land in a single-engine airplane, it is important to maintain a constant glide speed because variations in glide speed

A – increase the chances of shock cooling the engine.

B – assure the proper descent angle is maintained until entering the flare.

C – nullify all attempts at accuracy in judgment of gliding distance and landing spot.

4-29. Answer C. GFDPP 4A, AFH

Maintain a constant gliding speed because variations of gliding speed nullify all attempts at accuracy in judgment of gliding distance and the landing spot. Factors such as altitude, obstructions, wind direction, landing direction, landing surface and gradient, and landing distance of the airplane determines the pattern and approach procedures to use.

SECTION B — AIRPORTS

RUNWAY LAYOUT AND MARKINGS

- Runway numbers correspond to the magnetic direction of the runway and are rounded to the nearest 10 degrees, with the last zero dropped. For example, a runway that is oriented to 357 degrees is numbered 36.
- Traffic pattern indicators on the segmented circle show the final and base legs to various runways on the airport. The wind cone or sock in the center gives current wind direction.
- The area before a displaced threshold may be used for taxi and takeoff.
- Landings should be made after the displaced threshold.
- A closed runway is marked with Xs painted on its surface at each end.

AIRPORT LIGHTING

- When a beacon at an airport is on during the day, it usually means that the weather is below basic VFR minimums (ceiling less than 1,000 feet or visibility less than 3 miles).
- A military airport beacon alternates two quick flashes of white with one green flash.
- Taxiway edge lights are blue, and runway edge lights are white, except that on instrument runways, yellow replaces white on the last 2,000 feet or half the runway length, whichever is less.
- At airports with a three-step pilot-controlled lighting system, seven clicks of the microphone sets the lights to high intensity, five clicks turns them to medium, and three clicks turns the lights to low.

VISUAL GLIDEPATH INDICATORS

- Pilots should fly on or above the glide path when approaching an airport with a visual approach slope indicator (VASI) to ensure safe obstruction clearance in the approach area.
- On a two-bar VASI, red over white indicates that you are on the glide path. White over white is above the glide path, and red over red is below the glide path.
- A precision approach path indicator (PAPI) has lights installed in a single row instead of far and near bars. On a four-light PAPI, an on-glide-path indication is two white lights and two red lights. Above the glide path, you see more white lights and below the glide path you see more red lights.
- A pulsating approach slope indicator provides a pulsating red light when below the glide path. Pulsating white is above glide path, and steady white is on the glide path.

AIRPORT OPERATIONS

- The correct traffic pattern procedure to use at a noncontrolled airport is to comply with any FAA traffic pattern established for the airport.
- Pilots should state their position on the airport when calling the tower for takeoff, particularly when at a runway intersection.
- At controlled airports, air traffic control can clear a pilot to land and hold short. Pilots may accept a land and hold short (LAHSO) clearance if they can determine that the aircraft can safely land and stop within the available landing distance (ALD).
- Student pilots or pilots who are not familiar with LAHSO should not accept a land and hold short clearance.
- The pilot-in-command has the final authority to accept or decline any land and hold short clearance. Pilots should decline a LAHSO clearance if they do not believe the operation can be done safely.
- Pilots should report any suspicious activity at their airport to the Transportation Security Administration by calling 1-866-GA-SECURE (1-866-427-3287), and also notify airport management. In addition, if witnessing criminal activity, pilots should call 911 and talk to local law enforcement followed by calling 1-866-GA-SECURE.

4-30   PLT435

Which is the correct traffic pattern departure procedure to use at a noncontrolled airport?

A – Depart in any direction consistent with safety, after crossing the airport boundary.

B – Make all turns to the left.

C – Comply with any FAA traffic pattern established for the airport.

4-30. Answer C. GFDPP 4B, FAR 91.127
Each person operating an aircraft to or from an airport without an operating control tower shall, in the case of an aircraft departing the airport, comply with any traffic patterns established for that airport in Part 93.

4-31   PLT147   PA.III.B.K2

While operating in class D airspace, each pilot of an aircraft approaching to land on a runway served by a visual approach slope indicator (VASI) shall

A – maintain a 3° glide until approximately 1/2 mile to the runway before going below the VASI.

B – maintain an altitude at or above the glide slope until a lower altitude is necessary for a safe landing.

C – stay high until the runway can be reached in a power-off landing.

4-31. Answer B. GFDPP 4B, AR 91.129
The VASI glide path provides safe obstruction clearance to the runway. Therefore, the pilot should fly at or above the glide path.

4-32   PLT147   PA.III.B.K2

When approaching to land on a runway served by a visual approach slope indicator (VASI), the pilot shall

A – maintain an altitude that captures the glide slope at least 2 miles downwind from the runway threshold.

B – maintain an altitude at or above the glide slope.

C – remain on the glide slope and land between the two-light bar.

4-32. Answer B. GFDPP 4B, FAR 91.129
The VASI glide path provides safe obstruction clearance to the runway. Therefore, the pilot should fly at or above the glide path.

4-33   PLT147   PA.III.B.K2

Which approach and landing objective is assured when the pilot remains on the proper glidepath of the VASI?

A – Runway identification and course guidance

B – Safe obstruction clearance in the approach area

C – Lateral course guidance to the runway

4-33. Answer B. GFDPP 4B, AIM
Remaining on the proper glidepath ensures obstruction clearance in the approach area.

4-34   PLT141   PA.II.D.K3
Airport taxiway edge lights are identified at night by

A – white directional lights.

B – blue omnidirectional lights.

C – alternate red and green lights.

4-34. Answer B. GFDPP 4B, AIM
Taxiway edge lights are blue.

4-35   PLT147   PA.III.B.K2
A slightly high glide slope indication from a precision approach path indicator is

A – four white lights.

B – three white lights and one red light.

C – two white lights and two red lights.

4-35. Answer B. GFDPP 4B, AIM
A slightly high indication on a precision approach path indicator is three white lights and one red light.

4-36   PLT147   PA.III.B.K2
A below glide slope indication from a pulsating approach slope indicator is a

A – pulsating white light.

B – steady white light.

C – pulsating red light.

4-36. Answer C. GFDPP 4B, AIM
A pulsating approach slope indicator provides a pulsating red light when below glide slope.

4-37   PLT147   PA.III.B.K2
(Refer to Figure 47.)
Illustration A indicates that the aircraft is

A – above the glide slope.

B – on the glide slope.

C – below the glide slope.

4-37. Answer B. GFDPP 4B, AIM
A red over white indication is on glide slope.

4-38   PLT147   PA.III.B.K2
(Refer to Figure 47.) VASI lights as shown by illustration C indicate that the airplane is

A – above the glide slope.

B – on the glide slope.

C – below the glide slope.

4-38. Answer A. GFDPP 4B, AIM
A white over white indication is above glide slope.

4-39   PLT147   PA.III.B.K2
(Refer to Figure 47.)
While on final approach to a runway equipped with a standard two-bar VASI, the lights appear as shown by illustration D. This means that the aircraft is

A – above the glide slope.

B – on the glide slope.

C – below the glide slope.

4-39. Answer C. GFDPP 4B, AIM
A red over red indication is below the glide slope.

4-40   PLT145   PA.III.B.K2
To set the high intensity runway lights on medium intensity, the pilot should click the microphone seven times, then click it

A – one time within four seconds.

B – three times within three seconds.

C – five times within five seconds.

4-40. Answer C. GFDPP 4B, AIM
At airports with three-step pilot-controlled runway lighting system, seven clicks turns all the lights on to the maximum intensity. Five clicks turns the lights to medium.

4-41   PLT141   PA.III.B.K2
An airport's rotating beacon operated during daylight hours indicates

A – there are obstructions on the airport.

B – that weather at the airport located in Class D airspace is below basic VFR weather minimums.

C – the air traffic control tower is not in operation.

4-41. Answer B. GFDPP 4B, AIM
When the airport beacon is on during the daytime, it means that the ceiling is less than 1,000 feet or the visibility is less than 3 miles—below basic VFR minimums.

4-42   PLT141   PA.III.B.K2
You can identify a military air station by a rotating beacon that emits

A – white and green alternating flashes.

B – two quick white flashes between each green flash.

C – green, yellow, and white flashes.

4-42. Answer B. GFDPP 4B, AIM
A military airport beacon has two quick flashes of white light between each green flash.

4-43　PLT141　　PA.III.B.K2
How can a military airport be identified at night?

A – Alternate white and green light flashes

B – Dual peaked (two quick) white flashes between each green flash

C – White flashing lights with steady green at the same location

4-43. Answer B. GFDPP 4B, AIM
A military airport beacon has two quick flashes of white light between each green flash.

4-44　PLT141　　PA.II.D.K3
(Refer to Figure 48.) The portion of the runway identified by the letter A may be used for

A – landing.

B – taxiing and takeoff.

C – taxiing and landing.

4-44. Answer B. GFDPP 4B, AIM
The area before a displaced threshold may be used for taxi and takeoff, and roll-out after landing in the opposite direction, but not for landing.

4-45　PLT141　　PA.II.D.K3
The "yellow demarcation bar" marking indicates

A – runway with a displaced threshold from a blast pad, stopway, or taxiway that precedes the runway.

B – a hold line from a taxiway to a runway.

C – the beginning of available runway for landing on the approach side.

4-45. Answer A. GFDPP 4B, AIM
This double bar delineates a runway with a displaced threshold from a blast pad, stopway, or taxiway that precedes the runway.

4-46　PLT141　　PA.II.D.K3
(Refer to Figure 65, item E.)
This sign is a visual clue that

A – confirms the aircraft's location to be on taxiway "B."

B – warns the pilot of approaching taxiway "B."

C – indicates "B" holding area is ahead.

4-46. Answer A. GFDPP 4B, AIM
A location sign has a black background with a yellow border and yellow numbers or letters inscribed in the center. A yellow letter designates a taxiway on which the aircraft is located.

4-47　PLT141　　PA.II.D.K3
(Refer to Figure 65, item F.)
This sign confirms your position on

A – runway 22.

B – routing to runway 22.

C – taxiway 22.

4-47. Answer A. AIM
A location sign has a black background with a yellow border and yellow numbers or letters inscribed in the center. The yellow number designates a runway on which the aircraft is located.

4-48   PLT141   PA.II.D.K3

(Refer to Figure 65, item G.) From the cockpit, this sign confirms the aircraft to be

A – on a taxiway, about to enter runway zone.

B – on a runway, about to clear.

C – near an instrument approach clearance zone.

4-48. Answer B. AIM

This sign is a runway boundary sign, which faces the runway and is visible to the pilot exiting the runway. It is located adjacent to the holding position marking on the pavement. The sign is intended to provide pilots with a visual cue they can use as a guide in deciding when they are "clear of the runway."

4-49   PLT077   PA.II.D.K6

(Refer to Figure 48.) According to the airport diagram, which statement is true?

A – Takeoffs may be started at position D on Runway 30, but the landing portion of this runway begins at position E.

B – Takeoffs may be started at position A on Runway 12, and the landing portion of this runway begins at position B.

C – The takeoff and landing portion of Runway 12 begins at position B.

4-49. Answer B. GFDPP 4B, AIM

At many airports, the area before a displaced threshold may be used for taxi and takeoff (and roll-out after landing in the opposite direction). Landings may be made after the displaced threshold at position "B" on Runway 12.

4-50   PLT077   PA.II.D.K6

(Refer to Figure 48.) What is the difference between area A and area E on the airport depicted?

A – "A" may be used for taxi and takeoff; "E" may be used only as an overrun.

B – "A" may be used for all operations except heavy aircraft landings; "E" may be used only as an overrun.

C – "A" may be used only for taxiing; "E" may be used for all operations except landings.

4-50. Answer A. GFDPP 4B, AIM

At many airports, the area before a displaced threshold may be used for taxi and takeoff (and roll-out after landing). Area "E" is a blastpad/stopway, and is not designed with the pavement strength to support continuous operations, but it may be used as an overrun.

4-51   PLT077   PA.II.D.K6

(Refer to Figure 48.)
Area C on the airport depicted is a

A – stabilized area.

B – multiple heliport.

C – closed runway.

4-51. Answer C. GFDPP 4B, AIM

A closed runway is depicted by Xs.

4-52   PLT141   PA.II.D.K3
(Refer to Figure 64.)
Which marking indicates a vehicle lane?

A – A

B – C

C – E

4-52. Answer B. GFDPP 4B AIM
Lanes for ground vehicles look something like a road painted on the airport surface.

4-53   PLT141   PA.II.D.K3
(Refer to Figure 49.)
The arrows that appear on the ends of the north/south runway indicate that these areas

A – may be used only for taxiing.

B – is usable for taxiing, takeoff, and landing.

C – cannot be used for landing, but may be used for taxiing and takeoff.

4-53. Answer C. GFDPP 4B, AIM
At many airports, the area before a displaced threshold may be used for taxi and takeoff, and for roll-out after landing in the opposite direction.

4-54   PLT141   PA.II.D.K3
The numbers 9 and 27 on a runway indicate that the runway is oriented approximately

A – 009° and 027° true.

B – 090° and 270° true.

C – 090° and 270° magnetic.

4-54. Answer C. GFDPP 4B, AIM
Runway numbers correspond to the magnetic, not true, direction, and are rounded to the nearest 10°, with the last zero omitted.

4-55   PLT077   PA.III.B.K2
(Refer to Figure 49.) Select the proper traffic pattern and runway for landing.

A – Left-hand traffic and Runway 18.

B – Right-hand traffic and Runway 18.

C – Left-hand traffic and Runway 22.

4-55. Answer B. GFDPP 4B, AIM
The wind tetrahedron indicates that landing should be to the southwest, but Runway 22 is closed. Runway 18 is the next best choice, and the "L" mark at that end of the circle shows right-hand traffic for Runway 18.

4-56   PLT077   PA.III.B.K1
(Refer to Figure 49.) If the wind is as shown by the landing-direction indicator, the pilot should land on

A – Runway 18 and expect a crosswind from the right.

B – Runway 22 directly into the wind.

C – Runway 36 and expect a crosswind from the right.

4-56. Answer A. GFDPP 4B, AIM
The wind tetrahedron indicates that landing should be to the southwest, but Runway 22 is closed. Runway 18 is the next best choice, with a crosswind from the right.

4-57   PLT039
(Refer to Figure 50.) The segmented circle indicates that the airport traffic is

A – left hand for Runway 18 and right hand for Runway 36.

B – right hand for Runway 9 and left hand for Runway 27.

C – left hand for Runway 36 and right hand for Runway 18.

4-57. Answer C. GFDPP 4B, AIM
The segmented circle indicates left-hand traffic for Runways 9 and 36, and right-hand traffic for Runways 18 and 27.

4-58   PLT039   PA.III.B.K2
(Refer to Figure 50.)
The traffic patterns indicated in the segmented circle have been arranged to avoid flights over an area to the

A – south of the airport.

B – north of the airport.

C – southeast of the airport.

4-58. Answer C. GFDPP 4B, AIM
Because the traffic pattern for the north-south runway is west of the field, and the pattern for the east-west runway is north of the field, no traffic patterns for landing should be flown southeast of the airport.

4-59   PLT039   PA.XII.A.K5
(Refer to Figure 50.) The segmented circle indicates that a landing on Runway 26 is with a

A – right-quartering headwind.

B – left-quartering headwind.

C – right-quartering tailwind.

4-59. Answer A. GFDPP 4B, AIM
Because the wind cone shows wind from the northwest, a landing to the west experiences a right-quartering headwind.

4-60   PLT039   PA.XII.A.K5
(Refer to Figure 50.)
Which runway and traffic pattern should be used as indicated by the wind cone in the segmented circle?

A – Right-hand traffic on Runway 18

B – Left-hand traffic on Runway 36

C – Right-hand traffic on Runway 9

4-60. Answer B. GFDPP 4B, AIM
With wind exactly from the northwest, you might choose either Runway 27 or 36, depending on runway length and other factors. Runway 27 is not an available answer choice, leaving Runway 36. A landing on Runway 36 would require a left-hand traffic pattern and would encounter a left-quartering headwind.

4-61   PLT140   PA.IV.B.R3b

How can you determine whether your destination airport uses land and hold short operations (LAHSO)?

A – The notation "L" preceding the runway length on a VFR chart

B – LAHSO information published in the Airport/ Facility Directory listing in the Chart Supplement

C – NOTAMs from Flight Service during your preflight weather briefing

4-61. Answer B. GFDPP 4B, AIM

LAHSO information is published in the Airport/ Facility Directory listing for that airport in the Chart Supplement. The ATIS announces whether LAHSO is in use at the time you are preparing to land. An "L" preceding the runway length on a VFR chart indicates that runway lighting is available at that airport.

4-62   PLT140   PA.IV.B.R3b

Who has final authority to accept or decline any land and hold short (LAHSO) clearance?

A – Pilot-in-command

B – Owner or operator

C – Second-in-command

4-62. Answer A. GFDPP 4B, AIM

The pilot in command (PIC) has the final authority to accept or decline any LAHSO clearances. The PIC should decline a LAHSO clearance if determining that it compromises safety.

4-63   PLT140   PA.IV.B.R13

When should pilots decline a land and hold short (LAHSO) clearance?

A – When it compromises safety.

B – Only when the tower operator concurs.

C – Pilots may not decline a LAHSO clearance.

4-63. Answer A. GFDPP 4B, AIM

The pilot in command (PIC) has the final authority over the flight, and should decline a LAHSO clearance if determining that it compromises safety.

4-64   PLT078   PA.IV.B.K1

Where is the "Available Landing Distance" (ALD) data published for an airport that utilizes Land and Hold Short Operations (LAHSO) published?

A – Airport/Facility Directory (A/FD) listings in the Chart Supplement

B – 14 CFR Part 91, General Operating and Flight Rules

C – Aeronautical Information Manual (AIM)

4-64. Answer A. GFDPP 4B, AIM

ALD data is published in the listing for an airport that has LAHSO. Airport listings are in the Airport/Facility Directory (A/FD) section of the Chart Supplement.

4-65   PLT140   PA.IV.B.R3b

What is the minimum visibility for a pilot to receive a land and hold short (LAHSO) clearance?

A – 3 nautical miles

B – 3 statute miles

C – 1 statute mile

4-65. Answer B. AIM
Pilots should only receive a LAHSO clearance when there is a minimum ceiling of 1,000 feet and 3 statute miles visibility.

4-66   PLT141   PA.II.D.K3

At a towered airport, when approaching taxiway holding lines from the side with the continuous lines, you

A – may continue taxiing.

B – should not cross the lines without an ATC clearance.

C – should continue taxiing until all parts of the aircraft have crossed the lines.

4-66. Answer B. GFDPP 4B, AIM
When approaching a taxiway hold line from the side with the continuous (solid) line at a towered airport, pilots should not cross the hold line without ATC clearance. At a non-towered airport, stop and check for traffic before crossing any hold line.

4-67   PLT141   PA.II.D.K3

The numbers 8 and 26 on the approach ends of a runway indicate that the runway is orientated approximately

A – 008° and 026° true.

B – 080° and 260° true.

C – 080° and 260° magnetic.

4-67. Answer C. GFDPP 4B, PHB
Runway numbers indicate the MAGNETIC direction of a runway to the nearest 10 degrees. Runway 8 would have a magnetic direction of approximately 080°, and 26 would be approximately 260° magnetic.

4-68   PLT150   PA.III.B.K2

The recommended entry position to an airport traffic pattern is

A – 45° to the base leg just below traffic pattern altitude.

B – 45° at the midpoint of the downwind leg at traffic pattern altitude.

C – to cross directly over the airport at traffic pattern altitude, and then join the downwind leg.

4-68. Answer B. GFDPP 4B, PHB
Always descend to traffic pattern altitude and level off before entering the traffic pattern. The recommended traffic pattern entry is 45 degrees at the midpoint of the runway on the downwind leg. If it is necessary to cross over the airport to join a downwind leg on the opposite side, you should cross at 500 feet above the traffic pattern altitude.

4-69   PLT141   PA.II.D.K3

What is the purpose of the runway/runway hold position sign?

A – Denotes entrance to runway from a taxiway.

B – Denotes area protected for an aircraft approaching or departing a runway.

C – Denotes intersecting runways.

4-69. Answer C. GFDPP Chap 4B, AIM
These signs are installed together with pavement markings only on runways that are used for land and hold short operations (LAHSO) or taxiing operations. Like other holding position signs, they consist of white runway numbers on a red background.

4-70   PLT141   PA.II.D.K3

What does the outbound destination sign identify?

A – Identifies entrance to the runway from a taxiway.

B – Identifies direction to takeoff runways.

C – Identifies runway on which an aircraft is located.

4-70. Answer B. PHB, AIM
An outbound destination sign displays black text on a yellow background, and a vertical black arrow. These signs always have an arrow showing the direction of the taxing route to that destination.

4-71   PLT222   PA.IV.A.S2

Pilots state their position on the airport when calling the tower for takeoff, especially when

A – visibility is less than 1 mile.

B – parallel runways are in use.

C – departing from a runway intersection.

4-71. Answer C. AIM
It is always good practice to state your position, but the AIM specifically requests pilots to do so when calling from a runway intersection. For example: "Centennial Tower, Cessna 5238-Kilo, at Alpha 3."

4-72   PA.II.A.R5

You observe someone breaking into an airplane. What should you do?

A – Call 1-866-GA SECURE and then call 911.

B – Call 911 and then call 1-866-GA SECURE.

C – Call 1-866-GA SECURE and then try to detain the suspected criminal.

4-72. Answer B. GFDPP 4B, TSA
Be able to recognize suspicious activity and know how to alert authorities. For criminal activity, such as someone breaking into an aircraft, call 911—do not confront the person—and then call 1-866-GA-Secure (1-866-427-3287), and your airport, FBO, or flight school manager. Call 1-866-GA-Secure, but not 911, if you observe suspicious, but not criminal, activity.

SECTION C — AERONAUTICAL CHARTS

- In the northern hemisphere, latitude increases as you travel north.
- In the western hemisphere, longitude increases as you travel west.
- Each tick mark on the sectional chart represents one minute of latitude or longitude.
- One minute of latitude is one nautical mile; one minute of longitude is approximately one nautical mile but varies with latitude, decreasing farther the equator.
- A blue segmented circle on a sectional chart depicts Class D airspace. A blue airport symbol depicts a tower-controlled airport.
- A common traffic advisory frequency (CTAF) is shown in the airport information followed by the circled letter "C."
- You can answer many of the questions on the FAA knowledge test by referring to the figures and legends that are available during the test. Also refer to these resources during flight if you are unsure of the meaning of a symbol on the chart.

4-73   PLT064   PA.I.E.K2
(Refer to Figure 20, area 3.)
Determine the approximate latitude and longitude of Currituck County Airport.

A – 36°24'N - 76°01'W

B – 36°48'N - 76°01'W

C – 47°24'N - 75°58'W

4-73. Answer A. GFDPP 4B, PHB
This airport is located northeast of the number "3." Starting near the top of the chart excerpt, near number "1" find the labels for the 37° latitude line and the 76° longitude line. That means the latitude line through the middle of the picture is 36°30'N. Count down the tick marks—one minute per tick mark—until abeam Currituck County Airport at 36°24'N. At one tick mark west of the 76° longitude line, the longitude of the airport is 76°01'W.

4-74   PLT064   PA.I.E.K2
(Refer to Figure 21, area 3.)
Which airport is located at approximately 47°21'30"N latitude and 101°01'30"W longitude?

A – Poleschook

B – Washburn

C – Johnson

4-74. Answer B. GFDPP 4B, PHB
The 48° latitude line crosses the top third of the chart. The latitude line along the bottom third is 30' less, or 47°30'N. Count down 9-1/2 tick marks (minutes) for 47°21'30"N. Because the longitude of the airport is more than 101°W, move to the left of the 101° line 1-1/2 tick marks to arrive at 101°01'30"W. This intersection is at Washburn Airport (5C8).

4-75   PLT064   PA.I.E.K2
(Refer to Figure 59, area 3.)
Which airport is located at approximately 41°02'00"N latitude and 83°59'00"W longitude?

A – Ruhes

B – Putnam

C – Bluffton

4-75. Answer B. GFDPP 4B, PHB
The 41° latitude line and the 84° longitude line are labeled near area 3. The airport is two tick marks above the 41° latitude line, which might be difficult to see, so count down from the 5-minute tick mark. At 83°59'00"W longitude, the airport is one tick mark east of the 84° longitude line.

4-76   PLT064   PA.I.E.K2
(Refer to Figure 21, area 2.) The CTAF/MULTICOM frequency for Garrison Airport is

A – 123.0 MHz.

B – 122.8 MHz

C – 122.9 MHz.

4-76. Answer C. GFDPP 4B, AIM
The frequency next to the CTAF symbol (the letter "C" in a dark circle) is the multicom frequency of 122.9 MHz.

4-77   PLT064   PA.I.E.K2
(Refer to Figure 59, area 3.) The CTAF/MULTICOM frequency for Wyandot County Airport (56D) is

A – 123.0 MHz.

B – 122.8 MHz

C – 122.9 MHz.

4-77. Answer C. GFDPP 4B, AIM
The frequency next to the CTAF symbol (the letter "C" in a dark circle) is the multicom frequency of 122.9 MHz.

4-78   PLT064   PA.I.E.K2
(Refer to Figure 22, area 2 and Figure 31.)
At Coeur D'Alene, which frequency should be used as a Common Traffic Advisory Frequency (CTAF) to self-announce position and intentions?

A – 122.05 MHz.

B – 108.8 MHz.

C – 122.8 MHz.

4-78. Answer C. GFDPP 4B, AIM
In this example, the airport data block located near Coeur D'Alene airport lists 122.8 as the CTAF frequency that should be used to self-announce your position and your intentions. The Chart Supplement excerpt also shows 122.8 as the CTAF/UNICOM frequency. 122.05 is the Flight Service frequency (Boise Radio) and 135.075 is the AWOS frequency, also available at telephone number (208) 772-8215.

4-79   PLT064   PA.I.E.K2
(Refer to Figure 22, area 2 and Figure 31.)
At Coeur D'Alene, which frequency should be used as a Common Traffic Advisory Frequency (CTAF) to monitor airport traffic?

A – 122.05 MHz.

B – 122.8 MHz.

C – 135.075 MHz

4-79. Answer B. GFDPP 4B, AIM
At non-towered airports, the CTAF frequency is used to self-announce position or intentions. The Chart Supplement lists the CTAF/Unicom Frequency as 122.8 MHz. The CTAF symbol on the sectional chart is beside the frequency of 122.8 MHz.

4-80   PLT064   PA.III.A.K2

(Refer to Figure 22, area 2 and Figure 31.)
What is the correct UNICOM frequency to be used at
Coeur D'Alene to request fuel?

A – 108.8 MHz.

B – 122.8 MHz.

C – 135.075 MHz.

4-80. Answer B. GFDPP 4B AIM

Use the Unicom/CTAF frequency of 122.8 to request
fuel, transportation, or other airport information.

4-81   PLT064   PA.III.A.K2

(Refer to Figure 59, area 1 and Figure 63.)
What is the correct frequency to be used to contact
Toledo Approach if approaching the Toledo Express
Class C airspace from the east?

A – 123.975 MHz.

B – 126.1 MHz.

C – 134.35 MHz.

4-81. Answer B. GFDPP 4B, AIM

You can find the frequency in both the Airport/Facility
Directory (A/FD) entry in the Chart Supplement
and on the sectional chart. On the chart, a box
east of the Class C airspace says to contact Toledo
Approach within 20 NM on 126.1... In the A/FD, under
Communications, The Approach/Departure control
frequency is 121.1 on radials 360°-179°, the east side
of the airport. The frequency is 134.35 on the west
side (radials 180°-359°). A third frequency, 123.975
is also available, but not associated with any specific
direction from the airport.

4-82   PLT064   PA.III.A.K2

(Refer to Figure 25, area 3.) If Dallas Executive
Tower is not in operation, which frequency should
be used as a Common Traffic Advisory Frequency
(CTAF) to monitor airport traffic?

A – 122.95 MHz.

B – 126.35 MHz.

C – 127.25 MHz.

4-82. Answer C. GFDPP 4-47, AIM

The star next to the tower frequency, "CT 127.25"
indicates that the tower operates part-time. You can
find the hours of operation in the Chart Supplement.
The circled "C" indicates that 127.25 is the CTAF
frequency when the tower is not operating.

4-83   PLT064   PA.III.A.K2

(Refer to Figure 26, area 4.) The CTAF/UNICOM
frequency at Jamestown Airport is

A – 118.425 MHz.

B – 122.2 MHz.

C – 123.0 MHz.

4-83. Answer C. GFDPP 4-47, AIM

The CTAF symbol, the circled C, is next to the
frequency 123.0. The frequency 118.425 for ASOS
weather broadcasts and the frequency 122.2 is for
Flight Service.

4-84   PLT064   PA.III.A.K2
(Refer to Figure 26, area 5.) What is the CTAF/ UNICOM frequency at Barnes County Airport?

A – 118.725 MHz.

B – 122.8 MHz.

C – 1402 kHz.

4-84. Answer B. GFDPP 4-47, AIM
The CTAF symbol, the circled C, is next to the frequency 122.8. The frequency 118.725 for ASOS weather broadcasts and 1402 is the field elevation.

4-85   PLT376   PA.I.D.K2
Refer to Figure 26, area 3.)
When flying over Arrowwood National Wildlife Refuge, a pilot should fly no lower than

A – 2,000 feet AGL.

B – 2,500 feet AGL.

C – 3,000 feet AGL.

4-85. Answer A. GFDPP 4-44, AIM
Pilots are requested to maintain a minimum of 2,000 feet above National Wildlife Refuges.

4-86   PLT064   PA.III.A.K2
(Refer to Figure 21.) On what frequency can a pilot receive hazardous in-flight weather advisory service (HIWAS) near area 1?

A – 122.0 MHz.

B – 118.725 MHz.

C – The Minot VOR frequency.

4-86. Answer C. GFDPP 4-48, Chart Legend
The circled "H" in the corner of the Minot VORTAC indicates that weather information (HIWAS) is available over the VOR frequency.

4-87   PLT064   PA.I.E.K2
(Refer to Figure 20, area 5.)
The CAUTION box denotes what hazard to aircraft?

A – Unmarked balloon on cable to 3,008 feet MSL.

B – Unmarked balloon on cable to 3,008 feet AGL.

C – Unmarked blimp hangers at 308 feet MSL.

4-87. Answer A. GFDPP 4-51, Chart Legend
The CAUTION box indicates an unmarked balloon on a cable to 3,008 feet MSL.

4-88 PLT064 PA.I.E.K2
(Refer to Figure 20, area 2.)
The flag symbol at Lake Drummond represents a

A – compulsory reporting point for the Norfolk Class C Airspace.

B – compulsory reporting point for Hampton Roads Airport.

C – visual checkpoint used to identify position for initial callup to Norfolk Approach Control.

4-88. Answer C. GFDPP 4-51, Chart Legend
The flag represents a visual checkpoint used to identify your position for approach control. Because the flag is 22 nautical miles southwest of Norfolk International Airport, it can be assumed that the checkpoint is used when contacting Norfolk Approach.

4-89 PLT064 PA.I.E.K2
(Refer to Figure 20, area 2.)
The elevation of the Chesapeake Regional Airport is

A – 19 feet.

B – 23 feet.

C – 55 feet.

4-89. Answer A. GFDPP 4-47, Chart Legend
The elevation is the first number listed before the runway information. In this case, it is 19 feet.

4-90 PLT064 PA.I.E.K2
(Refer to Figure 20, area 1.) The NALF Fentress (NFE) Airport is in what type of airspace?

A – Class C.

B – Class D.

C – Class E.

4-90. Answer C. GFDPP 4C, Chart Legend
NFE is outside the solid magenta lines delineating the Norfolk Class C airspace, but inside a dashed magenta circle indicating Class C airspace at the surface.

4-91 PLT012 PA.I.E.K2
(Refer to Figure 21.) The terrain elevation of the light tan area between Minot (area 1) and Audubon Lake (area 2) varies from

A – sea level to 2,000 feet MSL.

B – 2,000 feet to 2,500 feet MSL.

C – 2,000 feet to 2,700 feet MSL.

4-91. Answer B. GFDPP 4-43, Chart Legend
The colored scale shows that the tan area represents terrain above 2,000 feet MSL. In addition, the legend states that the contour interval is 500 feet. Between Minot and Audubon Lake, there are no contour lines in the tan area, which indicates that no terrain exists above 2,500 feet. Checking the airports in this area reveals that their elevations are all less than 2,500 feet. In addition, tower and windmill heights in MSL minus their AGL heights all yield base elevations less than 2,500 feet.

4-92   PLT064   PA.I.E.K2
(Refer to Figure 21.) Which public use airports depicted are indicated as having fuel?

A – Minot Intl. (area 1).

B – Minot Intl. (area 1) and Mercer County Regional Airport (area 3).

C – Mercer County Regional Airport (area 3) and Garrison (area 2).

4-92. Answer A. GFDPP 4-46, Chart Legend
Tick marks around an airport symbol indicate that fuel is available.

4-93   PLT064   PA.I.E.K2
(Refer to Figure 23, areas 2 and 3.) The flag symbols at Statesboro Bullock County Airport, Claxton-Evans County Airport, and Ridgeland Airport are

A – airports with special traffic patterns.

B – outer boundaries of Savannah Class C airspace.

C – visual checkpoints to identify position for initial callup before to entering Savannah Class C airspace.

4-93. Answer C. GFDPP 4-47, Chart Legend
The flag symbols represent checkpoints used to identify the aircraft position for Approach Control. In this case, they are visual checkpoints used when contacting Savannah Approach Control.

4-94   PLT064   PA.I.E.K2
(Refer to Figure 23, area 3.) What is the elevation of the obstacle with strobe lights that is approximately 6 nautical miles southwest of Savannah International?

A – 1,531 feet MSL

B – 1,534 feet AGL

C – 1,548 feet MSL

4-94. Answer C. GFDPP 4-51, Chart Legend
About 6 nautical miles southwest of the center of Savannah International airport is an obstacle with a strobe light symbol—its elevation marked as 1,548 (1,534). The first number is the elevation in MSL, and the number in parentheses is height AGL. Other nearby numbers mark a group of obstacles about 10 miles away that do not have strobe lights.

4-95   PLT064   PA.I.E.K2
(Refer to Figure 23, area 3.) The top of the group obstruction approximately 11 nautical miles from the Savannah VORTAC on the 010° radial is

A – 454 feet AGL

B – 454 feet MSL

C – 559 feet MSL

4-95. Answer B. GFDPP 4-51, Chart Legend
At 11 NM, this obstruction is just outside the VOR compass rose. It is labeled "stacks" and has the number 454 next to it. When only one number is printed, not in parentheses, it is the MSL altitude. The nearby 559 (505) foot group is inside the edge of the Savannah Class C airspace—noticeably closer to the VOR than 11 NM. The Class C airspace does not line up with the Savannah VORTAC because the VORTAC is north of the center of Savannah/Hilton Head International Airport, as shown by the dot on the airport symbol.

4-96   PLT064   PA.I.E.K2
(Refer to Figure 24, area 1.)
What minimum altitude is required to vertically clear the obstacle in the uncongested area on the northeast side of Airpark East Airport?

A – 1,010 feet MSL.

B – 1,273 feet MSL.

C – 1,283 feet MSL.

4-96. Answer B. GFDPP 4-51, Chart Legend
Start by correctly identifying Airpark East. Its symbol is below, not above the label, and has an obstacle immediately northeast of it. In other-than-congested areas, the FARs require 500 feet of obstacle clearance. Add 500 feet to the obstacle elevation of 773 feet MSL.

4-97   PLT064   PA.I.E.K2
(Refer to Figure 24, area 2.)
What minimum altitude is necessary to vertically clear the obstacle in the uncongested area on the southeast side of Winnsboro Airport by 500 feet?

A – 823 feet MSL.

B – 1,013 feet MSL.

C – 1,403 feet MSL.

4-97. Answer C. GFDPP 4-51, Chart Legend
In other than congested areas, the FARs require 500 feet of obstacle clearance. Add 500 feet to the obstacle elevation of 903 feet MSL.

4-98   PLT101   PA.I.E.K2
(Refer to Figure 25, area 2.)
The control tower frequency for Addison Airport is

A – 122.95 MHz.

B – 126.0 MHz.

C – 133.4 MHz

4-98. Answer B. GFDPP 4-47, Chart Legend
The tower frequency at Addison Airport is 126.0 as indicated by the letters "CT."

4-99   PLT101   PA.I.E.K2
(Refer to Figure 25, area 8.) What minimum altitude is required to fly over the Cedar Hill TV towers in the congested area east of Joe Pool Lake?

A – 2,731 feet MSL.

B – 3,049 feet MSL.

C – 3,549 feet MSL.

4-99. Answer C. GFDPP 4-51, FAR 91.119
Because this area is a congested area, add 1,000 feet to the elevation of the highest obstacle. The highest elevation (height) of these towers is 2,549 feet MSL (1,731 feet AGL), so the minimum altitude would be 3,549 feet MSL. You would need an ATC clearance to fly at this altitude because the floor of Class B airspace here is 3,000 feet MSL.

4-100   PLT064   PA.I.E.K2

(Refer to Figure 25, area 5.) The navigation facility at Dallas-Ft. Worth International (DFW) is a

A – VOR.

B – VORTAC.

C – VOR/DME.

4-100. Answer C. GFDPP 4-48, Chart Legend

This symbol appears immediately south of the runways at DFW. According to Legend 1, a hexagon surrounded by a square is a VOR/DME symbol.

4-101   PLT064   PA.I.E.K1

Pilots flying over a national wildlife refuge are requested to fly no lower than

A – 1,000 feet AGL.

B – 2,000 feet AGL.

C – 3,000 feet AGL.

4-101. Answer B. GFDPP 4-44, AIM

Pilots should fly no lower than 2,000 feet AGL over a national wildlife area.

4-102   PLT064   PA.I.E.K2

Which is true concerning the blue and magenta colors used to depict airports on sectional aeronautical charts?

A – Airports with control towers underlying Class A, B, and C airspace are shown in blue, Class D and E airspace are magenta.

B – Airports with control towers underlying Class C, D, and E airspace are shown in magenta

C – Airports with control towers underlying Class B, C, D, and E airspace are shown in blue.

4-102. Answer C. GFDPP 4-46

Airports with control towers are depicted in blue on sectional charts.

4-103   PLT064   PA.I.E.K2

Which statement about longitude and latitude is true?

A – Lines of longitude are parallel to the Equator.

B – Lines of longitude cross the Equator at right angles.

C – The 0° line of latitude passes through Greenwich, England.

4-103. Answer B. GFDPP 4-40

Lines of longitude connect the poles, and therefore, are perpendicular to the equator.

SECTION D — AIRSPACE

To efficiently manage the large amount of air traffic that traverses the sky each day, the airspace above the United States is divided into several classes. In each airspace class, specific rules apply, such as varying VFR weather minimums. In some areas, you must communicate with ATC and comply with pilot certification and aircraft equipment requirements. In addition, special use airspace areas can restrict flight for safety and national security reasons.

CLASS G AIRSPACE

- VFR flight in Class G (uncontrolled) airspace requires one statute mile of visibility and clear of clouds.
- Night VFR in Class G airspace requires 3 statute miles visibility, 500 feet below, 1,000 feet above, and 2,000 feet horizontal distance from clouds.

CONTROLLED AIRSPACE

- Below 10,000 feet MSL in Class C, D and E airspace, the cloud clearances are 500 feet below, 1,000 feet above and 2,000 feet horizontal. Flight visibility is 3 statute miles. Above 10,000 feet MSL in Class C, D and E airspace, the cloud clearances are 1 mile horizontal and 1,000 feet above and below. Flight visibility is 5 statute miles.
- An operable 4096-code or Mode S transponder with an encoding altimeter is required in Class A, Class C and within 30 NM of a primary Class B airport. As of the year 2020, ADS-B Out is also required in this airspace.
- Federal Airways are Class E airspace, and Class E airspace minimums apply. The airspace extends four nautical miles on each side of the airway centerline. Altitudes normally include 1,200 feet AGL up to 17,999 feet MSL.

CLASS D AIRSPACE

- VFR flight minimums in Class D airspace are 3 statute miles visibility and a 1,000-foot ceiling. Airspace becomes Class D only when a control tower is operating.
- Two-way radio communications are required for taking off and landing at an airport with an operating control tower.
- When approaching Class D airspace, you must contact the control tower of the primary airport.
- When departing a non-towered satellite airport, you must contact the control tower of the primary airport as soon as practicable after takeoff.
- Class D airspace is normally a circle with a 4 nautical mile radios, but these areas can be different shapes based on the instrument procedures for which the controlled airspace is established.

CLASS C AIRSPACE

- Two-way radio communications must be established with approach control before entering Class C airspace.
- Two-way radio communications and an operable 4096-code transponder with an encoding altimeter are required for operating in Class C airspace.
- Class C airspace usually consists of a 5 NM radius core surface area that extends from the surface up to 4,000 feet above the primary airport elevation, and a 10 NM radius shelf area that extends from 1,200 feet up to 4,000 feet above the airport elevation. An "outer area" extends to 20 NM from the airport, where radar service is available, but contact with ATC is not required.

CLASS B AIRSPACE

- A pilot must have either a private pilot certificate, or a student pilot certificate with a logbook endorsement from an appropriately rated instructor.
- You must establish two-way radio communication and obtain an ATC clearance before entering Class B airspace.
- Class B day VFR minimums are 3-miles visibility and clear of clouds.

CLASS A AIRSPACE

- The altimeter must be set to 29.92 at and above 18,000 feet MSL.
- VFR flight is prohibited in Class A airspace.

SPECIAL VFR

- A special VFR clearance allows the pilot to operate VFR within Class D airspace when the visibility is at least 1 mile and the aircraft can remain clear of clouds.
- To operate under special VFR at night you must have a current instrument rating, and the airplane must be equipped for instrument flight.
- Special VFR for fixed-wing aircraft is not authorized at airports with "No Special VFR" written over the airport identification name.

AIRSPEED

- Unless otherwise authorized, the maximum indicated airspeed at which a person may operate an aircraft below 10,000 feet MSL is 250 knots. This is also the maximum indicated airspeed within Class B airspace.
- Under Class B airspace, or in a VFR corridor through a Class B area, no person shall operate at an indicated airspeed of more than 200 knots.

SPECIAL USE AIRSPACE

- Special use airspace serves to confine certain flight activities and to place limitations on aircraft operations which are not part of these activities.
- All pilots flying within an alert area are equally responsible for collision avoidance.
- Warning areas often contain hazards such as aerial gunnery and guided missiles.
- Pilots may not fly through a restricted area unless authorized to do so by the controlling agency.
- Temporary flight restrictions are imposed by the FAA to protect persons or property on the surface or in the air from a specific hazard or situation.
- Emergency air traffic rules are established by the FAA immediately after determining that, without such action, the air traffic control system could not operate at the required level of safety and efficiency.
- Air defense identification zones (ADIZs) are established to facilitate identification of aircraft in the vicinity of U.S. international airspace boundaries.
- Security-related restricted airspace is created in sensitive areas to protect persons or objects on the ground from general aviation aircraft. It is normally published as a temporary flight restriction (TFR).
- Presidential TFRs prohibit all flight training activity within 30 miles of the president and create 10-mile radius no-fly zones that ban almost all general aviation activity.
- You are responsible for knowing about and avoiding TFR airspace. It is important to obtain a preflight weather briefing before every flight and to ask for TFRs if the briefer does not offer them.
- The Washington DC Special Flight Rules Area requires pilots to be in contact with ATC and squawking a discrete transponder code within 30 NM of DCA VOR up to 18,000 feet MSL; in the flight restricted zone, 13-15 miles from the DCA VOR, general aviation flight is prohibited.
- Aircraft that are within security-related restricted airspace without authorization may be intercepted by law enforcement or military aircraft. Pilots must comply with visual instructions from that aircraft while attempting contact on 121.5 MHz.

MOAS AND MILITARY TRAINING ROUTES

- A military operations area (MOA) is a block of airspace in which military training and other military maneuvers are conducted.
- When operating VFR in an MOA, pilots should exercise extreme caution when military training is being conducted.
- IR designates an IFR military training route, where aircraft may fly at speeds of more than 250 knots.
- When the route is a three-digit number, the route contains one or more segments above 1,500 feet AGL.

4-104 PLT040   PA.I.E.S1

(Refer to Figure 26, area 2.)
The day VFR visibility and cloud clearance requirements to operate over the town of Cooperstown, after departing and climbing out of the Cooperstown Airport at and above 700 feet AGL are

A – 1 mile and clear of clouds.

B – 3 miles and 500 feet below, 1,000 feet above, and 2,000 feet horizontally from clouds.

C – 3 miles and clear of clouds.

4-104. Answer B. GFDPP 4D, FAR 91.155
This area is inside a magenta shaded ring, meaning that Class E airspace begins at 700 feet AGL.

4-105 PLT161   PA.I.E.K1

Unless otherwise specified, Federal Airways include that Class E airspace extending upward from

A – 700 feet above the surface up to and including 17,999 feet MSL.

B – 1,200 feet above the surface up to and including 17,999 feet MSL.

C – the surface up to and including 18,000 feet MSL.

4-105. Answer B. GFDPP 4D, AIM
Federal Airways normally begin at 1,200 feet AGL and extend up to, but not including, 18,000 feet MSL.

4-106 PLT162   PA.I.E.K1

The width of a federal airway from either side of the centerline is

A – 4 nautical miles.

B – 6 nautical miles.

C – 8 nautical miles.

4-106. Answer A. GFDPP 4D, AIM
A Federal airway is normally 8 NM wide (4 NM each side of the centerline).

4-107   PLT163   PA.I.E.S1

Normal VFR operations in Class D airspace with an operating control tower require the ceiling and visibility to be at least

A – 1,000 feet and 1 mile

B – 1,000 feet and 3 miles

C – 2,500 feet and 3 miles

4-107. Answer B. GFDPP 4D, FAR 91.155

To operate in Class D airspace, the VFR visibility minimum is three statute miles. In addition, the ceiling must be at least 1,000 feet.

4-108   PLT163   PA.I.E.S2

At what altitude shall the altimeter be set to 29.92, when climbing to cruising flight level?

A – 14,500 feet MSL.

B – 18,000 feet MSL.

C – 24,000 feet MSL.

4-108. Answer B. GFDPP 4D, FAR 91.121

To standardize altimeter settings in Class A airspace, all pilots are required to set their altimeters to 29.92 at and above 18,000 feet MSL.

4-109   PLT040   PA.I.E.K2

A blue segmented circle on a sectional chart depicts which class airspace?

A – Class B

B – Class C

C – Class D

4-109. Answer C. GFDPP 4D, Chart Legend

Class D airspace is designated on sectional charts by a blue segmented circle. Class B airspace is indicated by a solid blue line. Class C airspace is designated by a solid magenta line.

4-110   PLT163   PA.I.E.K1

Airspace at an airport with a part-time control tower is classified as Class D airspace only

A – when the weather minimums are below basic VFR.

B – when the associated control tower is in operation.

C – when the associated Flight Service Station is in operation.

4-110. Answer B. GFDPP 4D, AIM

In order for airspace to be classified as Class D, a control tower must be operating.

4-111   PLT434   PA.III.A.K2

Unless otherwise authorized, two-way radio communications with air traffic control are required for landings or takeoffs at all towered airports

A – regardless of weather conditions.

B – only when weather conditions are less than VFR.

C – within Class D airspace only when weather conditions are less than VFR.

4-111. Answer A. GFDPP 4D, FAR 91.129

When operating at an airport where a control tower is in operation, you must be in radio contact with ATC whether or not VFR conditions exist.

4-112   PLT434   PA.III.A.K2

Two-way radio communication must be established with the air traffic control facility having jurisdiction over the area before entering which class airspace?

A – Class C

B – Class E

C – Class G

4-112. Answer A. GFDPP 4D, FAR 91-130

You must establish two-way radio communications before entering a Class C airspace area, and maintain it while operating within the Class C airspace.

4-113   PLT434   PA.I.E.K1

What minimum radio equipment is required for operation within Class C airspace?

A – Two-way radio communications equipment and a 4096-code transponder.

B – Two-way radio communications equipment, a 4096-code transponder, and DME.

C – Two-way radio communications equipment, a 4096-code transponder, and an encoding altimeter.

4-113. Answer C. GFDPP 4D, FAR 91.130, 91.215

To operate in a Class C airspace area, you are required to have both a two-way radio and a 4096-code transponder with encoding altimeter.

4-114   PLT161   PA.I.E.K1

What minimum pilot certification is required for operation within Class B airspace?

A – Sport pilot certificate

B – Private pilot certificate or student pilot certificate with appropriate logbook endorsements

C – Private Pilot Certificate with an instrument rating.

4-114. Answer B. GFDPP 4D, FAR 91.131

To operate in a Class B airspace area, a pilot must hold a private pilot certificate. However, within certain Class B airspace areas, student pilot operations may be conducted after receiving specific training and a logbook endorsement from an authorized flight instructor.

4-115 PLT161   PA.I.E.K1

What minimum pilot certification is required for operation within Class B airspace?

A – Private Pilot Certificate or Student Pilot Certificate with appropriate logbook endorsements.

B – Commercial Pilot Certificate.

C – Private Pilot Certificate with an instrument rating.

4-115. Answer A. GFDPP 4D, FAR 91.131
To operate in a Class B airspace area, a pilot must hold a private pilot certificate. However, within certain Class B airspace areas, student pilot operations may be conducted after receiving specific training and a logbook endorsement from an authorized flight instructor.

4-116 PLT161   PA.I.E.K1

What minimum radio equipment is required for VFR operation within Class B airspace?

A – Two-way radio communications equipment and a 4096-code or Mode S transponder.

B – Two-way radio communications equipment, a 4096-code or Mode S transponder, and an encoding altimeter.

C – Two-way radio communications equipment, a 4096-code or Mode S transponder, an encoding altimeter, and a VOR or TACAN receiver.

4-116. Answer B. GFDPP 4D, FAR 91.131
VFR operations within Class B airspace areas require a two-way radio and a 4096-code or Mode S transponder with an encoding altimeter. As of 2020, ADS-B Out is also required.

4-117 PLT161   PA.I.E.K1

An operable 4096-code or Mode S transponder and Mode C encoding altimeter are required in

A – Class B airspace and within 30 miles of the Class B primary airport.

B – Class D airspace.

C – Class E airspace below 10,000 feet MSL.

4-117. Answer A. GFDPP 4D, FAR 91.131
A 4096-code or Mode S transponder with an encoding altimeter is required for operations within a Class B airspace area. It is not required in Class D airspace or Class E airspace below 10,000 feet MSL.

4-118 PLT161   PA.I.B.K3

All operations within Class C airspace must be in

A – accordance with instrument flight rules.

B – compliance with ATC clearances and instructions.

C – an aircraft equipped with a Mode A or Mode S transponder with Mode C altitude encoding capability.

4-118. Answer C. GFDPP 4D, FAR 91.215, 91.130
All aircraft must have an altitude encoding transponder to operate within or above Class C airspace. A clearance is *not* required to operate in Class C airspace, only two-way radio communications with ATC.

4-119 PLT161   PA.I.E.K1

Unless otherwise authorized, the maximum indicated airspeed at which aircraft may be flown when at or below 2,500 feet AGL and within 4 nautical miles of the primary airport of Class C airspace is

A – 200 knots.

B – 230 knots.

C – 250 knots.

4-119. Answer A. GFDPP 4D, FAR 91.117

The maximum indicated airspeed inside or within 4 NM of the primary airport in Class C airspace is 200 knots.

4-120 PLT383   PA.I.E.K1

Unless otherwise authorized, what is the maximum indicated airspeed at which a person may operate an aircraft below 10,000 feet MSL?

A – 200 knots.

B – 250 knots.

C – 288 knots.

4-120. Answer B. GFDPP 4D, FAR 91.117

Unless otherwise authorized by the Administrator, no person may operate an aircraft below 10,000 feet MSL at an indicated airspeed of more than 250 knots.

4-121 PLT161   PA.I.E.K1

When flying in the airspace underlying Class B airspace, the maximum speed authorized is

A – 200 knots.

B – 230 knots.

C – 250 knots.

4-121. Answer A. GFDPP 4D, FAR 91.117

No person may operate an aircraft in the airspace underlying a Class B airspace area, or in a VFR corridor designated through a Class B airspace area, at an indicated airspeed of more than 200 knots.

4-122 PLT161   PA.I.E.K1

When flying in a VFR corridor designated through Class B airspace, the maximum speed authorized is

180 knots.

200 knots.

250 knots.

4-122. Answer B. FAR 91.117

No person may operate an aircraft in a VFR corridor designated through a Class B airspace area, or in the airspace underlying a Class B airspace area, at an indicated airspeed of more than 200 knots.

4-123   PLT101   PA.I.E.K2

(Refer to Figure 69, area 4.) You are in the uncongested area about 7 NM SW of Corpus Christi International Airport, and unable to reach Corpus Christi Approach because of radio congestion. What altitude or course should you use to avoid the tall TV towers in this area?

A – Maintain at least 1,604 feet MSL; it is not necessary to contact ATC for obstacle clearance.

B – Fly over the TV towers at 1,499 feet MSL to remain under the floor of the Class C airspace.

C – Remain under the floor of Class C airspace and maintain a safe lateral distance from all the TV towers.

4-123. Answer C. GFDPP 4B, FAR 91.119

Because this is an uncongested area, you should be 500 feet above the elevation of the highest obstacle, which is 1,104 feet MSL. However, the minimum safe altitude of 1,604 feet MSL is above the floor of the Class C airspace, and two-way radio communications with ATC is required. If you cannot climb to the minimum safe altitude, you must maintain a safe *horizontal* clearance from these towers, but notice there are several sets of nearby towers that are almost as tall. If you are unable to reach ATC and climb into Class C airspace, deviating to the south and remaining below 1,200 feet MSL could be the best course action, particularly in lower visibility, or if you are unfamiliar with the TV towers in the area.

4-124   PLT161   PA.I.E.K1

In which type of airspace are VFR flights prohibited?

A – Class A

B – Class B

C – Class C

4-124. Answer A. GFDPP 4D, FAR 91.135

Only IFR operations are allowed in Class A airspace. VFR flights are allowed in Class B and C airspace if authorized by ATC.

4-125   PLT434   PA.I.E.S1

During operations within controlled airspace at altitudes of less than 1,200 feet AGL, the minimum horizontal distance from clouds requirement for VFR flight is

A – 1,000 feet.

B – 1,500 feet.

C – 2,000 feet.

4-125. Answer C. GFDPP 4D, FAR 91.155

In controlled airspace, other than Class B, below 10,000 feet, it does not matter whether you are above or below 1,200 feet AGL. The VFR cloud clearance is 2,000 feet horizontal.

4-126   PLT016   PA.I.E.S1

What minimum visibility and clearance from clouds are required for VFR operations in Class G airspace at 700 feet AGL or below during daylight hours?

A – 1-mile visibility and clear of clouds.

B – 1-mile visibility, 500 feet below, 1,000 feet above, and 2,000 feet horizontal clearance from clouds.

C – 3-miles visibility and clear of clouds.

4-126. Answer A. GFDPP 4D, FAR 91.155

For VFR flight in uncontrolled or class G airspace below 1,200 feet during daytime, you are only required to have 1-mile visibility and remain clear of clouds.

4-127   PLT064   PA.I.E.S1

(Refer to Figure 78, coordinates 42°00'N - 96°06'W.) What basic VFR weather minima are required to take off from the Onawa, IA (K36) airport during the day?

A – 3 statute miles visibility, 500 feet below the clouds, 1,000 feet above the clouds, and 2,000 feet horizontally from the clouds

B – 1 statute mile visibility, 500 feet below the clouds, 1,000 feet above the clouds, and 2,000 feet horizontally from the clouds

C – 1 statute mile visibility, clear of clouds

4-127. Answer C. GFDPP 4D, FAR 91.155

This airport is in Class G airspace (uncontrolled) from the surface up to 1,200 feet AGL. For VFR flight in uncontrolled airspace below 1,200 feet AGL during daytime, you are required to have 1-mile visibility and remain clear of clouds.

4-128   PA.I.E.K3

What are the restrictions to general aviation flight in the vicinity of the president?

A – All flight training activity is prohibited within 30 NM and nearly all general aviation flight is prohibited within 10 NM.

B – You must squawk an assigned transponder code within 30 NM and obtain an ATC clearance to operate within 10 NM.

C – Nearly all general aviation flight is prohibited within 30 NM, and all flight activity, except for Secret Service activity supporting the president, is prohibited within 10 NM.

4-128. Answer A. GFDPP 4D, FAR 91.141

You may not operate an aircraft over or near any area to be visited or traveled by the president, the vice president, or other public figures contrary to the restrictions established by the administrator and published in a notice to airmen (NOTAM). Restrictions for the president typically ban all flight training activity within 30 NM and all general aviation flight within 10 NM.

4-129   PA.I.E.K3

What is the approved method of learning the time and location of temporary flight restrictions (TFRs)?

A – Obtain a weather briefing from Flight Service and ask for TFRs.

B – Obtain a weather briefing from AviationWeather. gov and select TFRs.

C – Check TFRs and their effective times at faa.gov or in your flight planning application.

4-129. Answer A. GFDPP 4D, AIM

Although the graphical TFR listings at faa.gov and in flight planning programs and applications provide excellent situational awareness of TFRs, official dissemination is through Flight Service by telephone at 1-800-wx-brief or at website 1800wxbrief.com.

4-130   PA.I.E.K3

You are flying VFR and not talking to ATC and observe a military jet fighter off your left wingtip rocking its wings and then making a slow left turn away from you. What action should you take?

A – Land at the nearest airport and wait for authorities to meet you.

B – Follow the aircraft, squawk 7700, and contact them on 121.5 MHz.

C – Proceed on course, you are free to go because the intercepting aircraft has turned away from you.

4-130. Answer B. GFDPP 4D, AIM

When the intercepting aircraft rocks its wings and makes a *slow* turn away from you, it means that you are intercepted and must follow it. An *abrupt* breakaway turn that does not cross your flight path means that you are free to proceed on course.

4-131   PA.I.E.K3

What must you do before flying anywhere within 60 miles of the Washington (DCA) VOR?

A – Take special awareness training from the FAA and have a certificate of completion in your possession.

B – Take an orientation flight with an authorized flight instructor, obtain a logbook endorsement, and carry your logbook.

C – Obtain ground instruction from an authorized ground or flight instructor, obtain a logbook endorsement, and carry your logbook.

4-131. Answer A. GFDPP 4D, FAR 91.161

You may not act as a pilot of an aircraft while flying within a 60-nautical mile radius of the DCA VOR under VFR unless you have completed Special Awareness Training and hold a certificate of training completion.

This training is available at the FAAsafety.gov website. Upon completion of the training, print a copy of the completion certificate and be able to present it to an authorized representative of the FAA, NTSB, TSA, or to a law enforcement officer.

4-132   PLT163   PA.I.E.S1

What minimum visibility and clearance from clouds are required for VFR operations on an airway below 10,000 feet MSL is

A – 1-mile visibility and clear of clouds.

B – 3-miles visibility, 500 feet below, 1,000 feet above, and 2,000 feet horizontally from clouds.

C – 3-miles visibility, 500 feet above, 1,000 feet below, and 2,000 feet horizontally from clouds.

4-132. Answer B. GFDPP 4D, FAR 91.155

The VFR cloud clearances for Class E airspace apply. Below 10,000 feet MSL, you must maintain 3-miles visibility and 500 feet below, 1,000 feet above, and 2,000 feet horizontally from clouds.

4-133 PLT163 PA.I.E.S1

During operations within controlled airspace at altitudes of more than 1,200 feet AGL, but less than 10,000 feet MSL, the minimum distance above clouds requirement for VFR flight is

A – 500 feet.

B – 1,000 feet.

C – 1,500 feet.

4-133. Answer B. GFDPP 4D, FAR 91.155
Below 10,000 feet MSL in Class C and D airspace, the cloud clearances are 500 feet below, 1,000 feet above, and 2,000 feet horizontal. In Class B airspace, however, the cloud clearance is just "clear of clouds."

4-134 PLT163 PA.I.E.S1

VFR flight in controlled airspace above 1,200 feet AGL and below 10,000 feet MSL requires a minimum visibility and vertical cloud clearance of

A – 3 miles, and 500 feet below or 1,000 feet above the clouds in controlled airspace.

B – 5 miles, and 1,000 feet below or 1,000 feet above the clouds at all altitudes.

C – 5 miles, and 1,000 feet below or 1,000 feet above the clouds only in Class A airspace.

4-134. Answer A. GFDPP 4D, FAR 91.155
Below 10,000 feet MSL in Class C and D Airspace, the cloud clearances are 500 feet below, 1,000 feet above, and 2,000 feet horizontal. In Class B airspace, however, the cloud clearance is just "clear of clouds."

4-135 PLT163 PA.I.E.S1

During operations outside controlled airspace at altitudes of more than 1,200 feet AGL, but less than 10,000 feet MSL, the minimum flight visibility for VFR flight at night is

A – 1 mile.

B – 3 miles.

C – 5 miles.

4-135. Answer B. GFDPP 4D, FAR 91.155
In Class G airspace at these altitudes, night VFR operations require 3-miles visibility.

4-136 PLT163 PA.I.E.S1

During operations outside controlled airspace at altitudes of more than 1,200 feet AGL, but less than 10,000 feet MSL, the minimum flight visibility for day VFR is

A – 1 mile.

B – 3 miles.

C – 5 miles.

4-136. Answer A. GFDPP 4D, FAR 91.155
In uncontrolled airspace below 10,000 feet MSL and above 1,200 feet AGL, required daytime visibility is 1 mile.

4-137   PLT163   PA.I.E.S1

During operations outside controlled airspace at altitudes of more than 1,200 feet AGL, but less than 10,000 feet MSL, the minimum distance below clouds requirement for VFR flight at night is

A – 500 feet.

B – 1,000 feet.

C – 1,500 feet.

4-137. Answer A. GFDPP 4-82, FAR 91.155

At night, in uncontrolled airspace below 10,000 feet MSL (both above and below 1,200 feet AGL), the VFR cloud clearance is 500 feet below.

4-138   PLT163   PA.I.E.S1

The minimum flight visibility required for VFR flights above 10,000 feet MSL and more than 1,200 feet AGL in controlled airspace is

A – 1 mile.

B – 3 miles.

C – 5 miles.

4-138. Answer C. GFDPP 4-82, FAR 91.155

At or above 10,000 feet MSL and above 1,200 feet AGL, the required visibility is 5 statute miles, whether in controlled or uncontrolled airspace.

4-139   PLT163   PA.I.E.S1

For VFR flight operations above 10,000 feet MSL and more than 1,200 feet AGL, the minimum horizontal distance from clouds required is

A – 1,000 feet.

B – 2,000 feet.

C – 1 mile.

4-139. Answer C. GFDPP 4-82, FAR 91.155

Whether in controlled or uncontrolled airspace at these altitudes, the minimum VFR horizontal distance from clouds is 1 statute mile.

4-140   PLT163   PA.I.E.S1

During operations at altitudes of more than 1,200 feet AGL and at or above 10,000 feet MSL, the minimum distance above clouds requirement for VFR flight is

A – 500 feet.

B – 1,000 feet.

C – 1,500 feet.

4-140. Answer B. GFDPP 4-82, FAR 91.155

For VFR flights at these altitudes, whether in controlled airspace or not, you are required to remain 1,000 feet above clouds. The only exception is for daytime operations below 1,200 feet AGL in uncontrolled airspace. In this case, it is clear of clouds.

4-141   PLT163   PA.I.E.S1

No person may take off or land an aircraft under basic VFR at an airport that lies within Class D airspace unless the

A – flight visibility at that airport is at least 1 mile.

B – ground visibility at that airport is at least 1 mile.

C – ground visibility at that airport is at least 3 miles.

4-141. Answer C. GFDPP 4-63, FAR 91.155

To take off or land under VFR in a Class D airspace area, the ceiling must be at least 1,000 feet and the ground visibility must be at least 3 statute miles. Flight visibility may be used if ground visibility is not available.

4-142   PLT163   PA.I.E.S1

The basic VFR weather minimums for operating an aircraft within Class D airspace are

A – 500-foot ceiling and 1-mile visibility.

B – 1,000-foot ceiling and 3-miles visibility.

C – clear of clouds and 2-miles visibility.

4-142. Answer B. GFDPP 4-82, FAR 91.155

To take off or land under VFR in a Class D airspace area, the ceiling must be at least 1,000 feet and the ground visibility must be at least 3 statute miles. Flight visibility may be used if ground visibility is not available.

4-143   PLT163   PA.I.E.S1

A special VFR clearance authorizes the pilot of an aircraft to operate VFR while within Class D airspace when the visibility is

A – less than 1 mile and the ceiling is less than 1,000 feet.

B – at least 1 mile and the aircraft can remain clear of clouds.

C – at least 3 miles and the aircraft can remain clear of clouds.

4-143. Answer B. GFDPP 4-71, FAR 91.157

When authorized by ATC, special VFR allows you to operate with one statute mile visibility as long as you can remain clear of clouds.

4-144   PLT163   PA.I.E.S1

What is the minimum weather condition required for airplanes operating under special VFR in Class D airspace?

A – 1-mile flight visibility.

B – 1-mile flight visibility and 1,000-foot ceiling.

C – 3-miles flight visibility and 1,000-foot ceiling.

4-144. Answer A. GFDPP 4-71, FAR 91.157

When authorized by ATC, special VFR allows you to operate with one statute mile visibility as long as you can remain clear of clouds.

4-145   PLT161   PA.I.E.S2

What are the minimum requirements for airplane operations under special VFR in Class D airspace at night?

A – The airplane must be under radar surveillance at all times while in Class D airspace.

B – The airplane must be equipped for IFR and with an altitude reporting transponder.

C – The pilot must be instrument rated, and the airplane must be IFR equipped.

4-145. Answer C. GFDPP 4-72, FAR 91.157

For special VFR at night, you must have a current instrument rating, and the airplane must be equipped for IFR operations.

4-146   PLT161   PA.I.E.S1

No person may operate an airplane within Class D airspace at night under special VFR unless the

A – flight can be conducted 500 feet below the clouds.

B – airplane is equipped for instrument flight.

C – flight visibility is at least 3 miles.

4-146. Answer B. GFDPP 4-72, FAR 91.157

For special VFR at night, you must have a current instrument rating, and the airplane must be equipped for IFR operations.

4-147   PLT161   PA.I.E.S2

An operable 4096-code or Mode S transponder with an encoding altimeter is required in which airspace?

A – Class A, Class B (and within 30 miles of the Class B primary airport), and Class C.

B – Class D and Class E (below 10,000 feet MSL).

C – Class D and Class G (below 10,000 feet MSL).

4-147. Answer A. GFDPP 4-59, FAR 91.215

A transponder with an encoding transponder is required in Class A, Class B, and Class C airspace.

4-148   PLT161   PA.I.E.S2

With certain exceptions, all aircraft within 30 miles of a Class B primary airport from the surface upward to 10,000 feet MSL must be equipped with

A – an operable VOR or TACAN receiver and an ADF receiver.

B – instruments and equipment required for IFR operations.

C – an operable transponder having either Mode S or 4096-code capability with Mode C automatic altitude reporting capability.

4-148. Answer C. GFDPP 4-59, FAR 91.215

An appropriate transponder capable of providing altitude encoding is required to be in use when within 30 miles of a Class B primary airport.

4-149   PLT040   PA.I.E.K1

(Refer to Figure 25, area 4) The floor of Class B airspace overlying Hicks Airport (T67) north-northwest of Fort Worth Meacham Field is

A – at the surface

B – 3,200 feet MSL

C – 4,000 feet MSL

4-149. Answer C. GFDPP 4-67, Chart Legend

The altitudes of this sector of the Class B airspace are indicated by "110" over "40." This means the Class B airspace extends from a floor of 4,000 feet MSL up to 11,000 feet MSL.

4-150   PLT040   PA.I.E.K2

(Refer to Figure 25, area 2.) The floor of Class B airspace at Addison Airport is

A – at the surface

B – 3,000 feet MSL

C – 3,100 feet MSL

4-150. Answer B. GFDPP 4-67, Chart Legend

The altitudes of this portion of the Class B airspace are indicated by "110" over "30." This means the Class B airspace extends from a floor of 3,000 feet MSL up to 11,000 feet MSL. In addition, the [–30] indicates that the Class D airspace at Addison extends up to, but does not include 3,000 feet, which is the floor of the overlying Class B airspace.

4-151   PLT064   PA.I.E.K3

(Refer to Figure 20, area 4.) What hazards to aircraft may exist in restricted areas such as R-5302B?

A – Military training activities that require acrobatic or abrupt flight maneuvers.

B – Unusual, often invisible, hazards such as aerial gunnery or guided missiles.

C – High volume of pilot training or an unusual type of aerial activity.

4-151. Answer B. GFDPP 4-75, AIM

Restricted areas can have invisible hazards to aircraft, such as artillery firing, aerial gunnery, or guided missiles.

4-152   PLT393   PA.I.E.K3

(Refer to Figure 21, area 2.) What hazards to aircraft may exist in areas such as Devils Lake West MOA?

A – Military training activities that require acrobatic or abrupt flight maneuvers.

B – High volume of pilot training or an unusual type of aerial activity.

C – Unusual, often invisible, hazards to aircraft such as artillery firing, aerial gunnery, or guided missiles.

4-152. Answer A. GFDPP 4-74, AIM

Most training activities in a military operations area (MOA) involve acrobatic or abrupt flight maneuvers.

4-153   PLT064   PA.I.D.K1
(Refer to Figure 21, area 3.) What type military flight operations should a pilot expect along IR 644?

A – VFR training flights above 1,500 feet AGL at speeds less than 250 knots.

B – IFR training flights above 1,500 feet AGL at speeds more than 250 knots.

C – Instrument training flights below 1,500 feet AGL at speeds more than 150 knots.

4-153. Answer B. GFDPP 4-77, AIM
IR routes are designed to be flown by military aircraft at speeds often more than 250 knots. An IR Route with three letters in the designator (IR 644) indicates one or more segments are above 1,500 feet AGL.

4-154   PLT163   PA.I.E.S1
(Refer to Figure 22, area 1.)
The visibility and cloud clearance requirements to operate VFR during daylight hours over Sandpoint Airport at 1,200 feet AGL are

A – 1 mile and 1,000 feet above, 500 feet below, and 2,000 feet horizontally from each cloud.

B – 1 mile and clear of clouds.

C – 3 miles and 1,000 feet above, 500 feet below, and 2,000 feet horizontally from each cloud.

4-154. Answer C. GFDPP 4D, FAR 91.155
The airspace is Class E above 700 feet AGL. The day VFR minimums are 3 miles and 1,000 feet above, 500 feet below, and 2,000 feet horizontally from all clouds.

4-155   PLT163   PA.I.E.S1
(Refer to Figure 27, area 2.) The visibility and cloud clearance requirements to operate VFR during daylight hours over the town of Cooperstown between 1,200 feet AGL and 10,000 feet MSL are

A – 3 miles and 1,000 feet above, 500 feet below, and 2,000 feet horizontally from clouds

B – 1 mile and clear of clouds.

C – 1 mile and 1,000 feet above, 500 feet below, and 2,000 feet horizontally from clouds.

4-155. Answer A. GFDPP 4D, FAR 91.155
Cooperstown is within the Class E airspace of the Cooperstown Airport. The floor of this airspace is 700 feet AGL. Visibility of 3 miles and 1,000 feet above, 500 feet below, and 2,000 feet horizontally from clouds is required to operate VFR in controlled airspace below 10,000 feet MSL.

4-156   PLT161   PA.I.E.S2
(Refer to Figure 27, area 1.)
Identify the airspace over the town of McHenry.

A – Class G airspace — surface up to but not
including 700 feet MSL, Class E airspace — 700
feet to 14,500 feet MSL.

B – Class G airspace — surface up to but not
including 1,200 feet AGL, Class E airspace —
1,200 feet AGL up to but not including 18,000
feet MSL.

C – Class G airspace — surface up to but not
including 18,000 feet MSL.

4-156. Answer B. GFDPP 4D, Chart Legend
The lower left corner of the sectional chart excerpt
shows a blue shaded area indicating that in the area
covered by this chart, Class E airspace extends from
1,200 ft AGL to 18,000 MSL unless otherwise marked.

4-157   PLT040   PA.I.E.K2
(Refer to Figure 26, area 5.) The airspace overlying
and within 5 miles of Barnes County Airport is

A – Class D airspace from the surface to the floor of
the overlying Class E airspace.

B – Class E airspace from the surface to 1,200 feet
MSL.

C – Class G airspace from the surface to 700 feet
AGL.

4-157. Answer C. GFDPP 4D, Chart Legend
The magenta shading around the airport indicates
that Class E airspace begins at 700 feet AGL.
Below 700 feet the airspace is uncontrolled (Class
G) airspace. Class D airspace, marked with a
blue dashed line around the airport, is not shown
anywhere on this chart.

4-158   PLT101   PA.I.E.K2
(Refer to Figure 25, area 7.)
The airspace overlying Collin County Mc Kinney
Airport (TKI) is controlled from the surface to

A – 2,900 feet MSL.

B – 2,500 feet MSL.

C – 700 feet AGL.

4-158. Answer A. GFDPP 4D, Chart Legend
The controlled airspace this question is referring to is
Class D airspace. The top of Class D airspace (MSL)
is shown within the square dashed box.

4-159   PLT101   PA.I.E.K2
(Refer to Figure 25, area 4.) The airspace directly
overlying Fort Worth Meacham is

A – Class B airspace to 10,000 feet MSL.

B – Class C airspace to 5,000 feet MSL.

C – Class D airspace to 3,200 feet MSL.

4-159. Answer C. GFDPP 4D, Chart Legend
The blue segmented circle indicates that Fort Worth
Meacham is located in Class D airspace. The [32]
indicates that the ceiling of the Class D airspace is
3,200 feet MSL.

4-160 PLT161   PA.I.E.K2
(Refer to Figure 23, area 3.)
What is the floor of the Savannah Class C airspace at the shelf area (outer circle)?

A – 1,300 feet AGL

B – 1,300 feet MSL

C – 1,700 feet MSL

4-160. Answer B. GFDPP 4D, AIM
The floor of the shelf area of most Class C airspace is around 1,200 feet AGL, rounded to an exact MSL altitude. At Savannah, it is 1,300 feet MSL, about 1,250 feet above the airport elevation. The exact upper and lower limits in MSL are depicted on the chart (41/13).

4-161 PLT064   PA.I.E.K1
(Refer to Figure 20, area 1.)
What minimum radio equipment is required to land and take off at Norfolk International?

A – Mode C transponder and VOR

B – Mode C transponder and two-way radio

C – Mode C transponder, VOR, and DME.

4-161. Answer B. GFDPP 4D, FAR 91.130
The area depicted is Class C airspace. Aircraft operating in Class C airspace must be equipped with a Mode C transponder and pilots are required to maintain two-way radio communications. A VOR is not required to operate in Class C airspace.

4-162 PLT064   PA.I.E.K1
(Refer to Figure 25.) At which airports is fixed-wing Special VFR not authorized?

A – Fort Worth Meacham and Fort Worth Spinks

B – Dallas-Fort Worth International and Dallas Love Field

C – Addison and Dallas Executive

4-162. Answer B. GFDPP 4D, Chart Legend
The "NO SVFR" above the airport name indicates that fixed-wing special VFR is not authorized.

4-163 PLT064   PA.I.E.K1
(Refer to Figure 22, area 3.) The vertical limits of that portion of Class E airspace designated as a Federal Airway over Magee Airport are

A – 1,200 feet AGL to 17,999 feet MSL.

B – 7,500 feet MSL to 17,999 feet MSL.

C – 700 feet MSL to 12,500 feet MSL.

4-163. Answer A. GFDPP 4D, Chart Legend
Class E airspace includes Federal, or Victor, airways that usually extend to 4 nautical miles on each side of the airway centerline and, unless otherwise indicated, extends from 1,200 feet AGL up to, but not including, 18,000 feet MSL.

4-164   PLT161   PA.I.E.K1

The vertical limit of Class C airspace above the primary airport is normally

A – 1,200 feet AGL.

B – 3,000 feet AGL.

C – 4,000 feet AGL.

4-164. Answer C. GFDPP 4D, AIM

The vertical limit of Class C airspace is approximately 4,000 feet above the primary airport in both the inner and outer circles. This altitude is rounded to an even 100-foot MSL altitude and shown as an MSL altitude on charts.

4-165   PLT161   PA.I.E.K1

The radius of the procedural outer area of Class C airspace is normally

A – 10 NM.

B – 20 NM.

C – 30 NM.

4-165. Answer B. GFDPP 4D, AIM

Class C airspace areas have a procedural outer area not shown on charts. Normally this area extends 20 NM from the primary Class C airspace airport. You may obtain radar services in this area, but are not required to contact ATC to operate here.

4-166   PLT161   PA.I.E.K1

Under what condition may an aircraft operate from a satellite airport within Class C airspace?

A – The pilot must file a flight plan before departure.

B – The pilot must monitor ATC until clear of the Class C airspace.

C – The pilot must contact ATC as soon as practicable after takeoff.

4-166. Answer C. GFDPP 4D, FAR 91.130

A pilot must establish two-way communications with ATC as soon as practical after takeoff.

4-167   PLT064   PA.I.E.K3

Under what condition, if any, may pilots fly through a restricted area?

A – When flying on airways with an ATC clearance.

B – With authorization from the controlling agency.

C – Regulations do not allow this.

4-167. Answer B. GFDPP 4D, FAR 91.133

The controlling agency may grant permission to fly through a restricted area.

4-168   PLT064   PA.I.E.K3

What action should a pilot take when operating under VFR in a military operations area (MOA)?

A – Obtain a clearance from the controlling agency before entering the MOA.

B – Operate only on the airways that transverse the MOA.

C – Exercise extreme caution when military activity is being conducted.

4-168. Answer C. GFDPP 4D, AIM

Due to the possibility of military training activities, pilots operating in a MOA should use extra caution and be vigilant for military traffic.

4-169   PLT444   PA.I.E.K3

Responsibility for collision avoidance in an alert area rests with

A – the controlling agency.

B – all pilots.

C – Air Traffic Control.

4-169. Answer B. GFDPP 4D, AIM

All pilots flying in an alert area, whether participating in activities or transitioning the area, are equally responsible for collision avoidance.

4-170   PLT161   PA.I.E.K1

The lateral dimensions of Class D airspace are based on

A – the number of airports that lie within the Class D airspace.

B – 5 statute miles from the geographical center of the primary airport.

C – the instrument procedures for which the controlled airspace is established.

4-170. Answer C. GFDPP 4D, AIM

The actual lateral dimensions of Class D airspace varies with each location, but, in general, Class D airspace is based on the instrument procedures for the airports in that area.

4-171   PLT435   PA.I.E.K1

A non-towered satellite airport, within the same Class D airspace as that designated for the primary airport, requires two-way radio communications be established and maintained with the

A – satellite airport's UNICOM.

B – associated Flight Service facility.

C – primary airport's control tower.

4-171. Answer C. GFDPP 4D, FAR 91.129

When approaching Class D airspace, you must contact the control tower of the primary airport before entering the airspace. When departing a nontowered satellite airport, contact the controlling tower as soon as practical after takeoff.

4-172   PLT161   PA.I.E.K1

Which initial action should a pilot take before entering Class C airspace?

A – Contact approach control on the appropriate frequency.

B – Contact the tower and request permission to enter.

C – Contact the FSS for traffic advisories.

4-172. Answer A. GFDPP 4D, AIM
Before entering Class C airspace, you must establish contact with approach control.

4-173   PLT161   PA.I.E.K1

What ATC facility should the pilot contact to receive a special VFR departure clearance in Class D airspace?

A – Flight Service

B – Air traffic control tower

C – Air route traffic control center

4-173. Answer B. GFDPP 4D, FAR 91.157
The control tower is the ATC facility that issues a special VFR clearance.

4-174   PLT040   PA.I.E.K3

You should not fly through a restricted area unless you have

A – filed an IFR flight plan.

B – received prior authorization from the controlling agency.

C – received prior permission from the commanding officer of the nearest military base.

4-174. Answer B. GFDPP 4D, FAR 91.133, AIM
You must receive prior authorization from the controlling agency before operating in a restricted area. If you are operating on an IFR flight plan and ATC clears you through that airspace, then they are acting as the controlling agency and providing you the needed authorization. The FAA is not the controlling agency when the restricted area is "hot" and may not clear you through the airspace at those times.

4-175   PLT162   PA.I.E.K1

When a control tower on an airport within Class D airspace ceases operation for the day, what happens to the airspace designation?

A – The airspace designation normally does not change.

B – The airspace remains Class D airspace as long as a weather observer or automated weather system is available.

C – The airspace reverts to Class E or a combination of Class E and G airspace during the hours the tower is not in operation.

4-175. Answer C. GFDPP 4D, AIM
Class D Airspace exists only when the control tower is operating. When the tower shuts down, the airspace becomes Class E or sometimes Class G and you normally continue to use the tower frequency as a common traffic advisory frequency (CTAF).

4-176 PLT161   PA.I.E.K1

With certain exceptions, Class E airspace extends upward from either 700 feet or 1,200 feet AGL to, but does not include,

A – 10,000 feet MSL.

B – 14,500 feet MSL.

C – 18,000 feet MSL.

4-176. Answer C. GFDPP 4D, AIM

Unless otherwise indicated, E airspace begins at 700 feet or 1,200 feet AGL and continues up to, but not including 18,000 MSL. Notice that the upper limit is defined by MSL, while the lower limit is typically defined by AGL.

4-177 PLT281   PA.I.E.K3

Information concerning regularly used parachute jumping sites may be found in the

A – NOTAMs publications.

B – Aeronautical Information Manual.

C – Associated Data section of the Chart Supplement.

4-177. Answer C. GFDPP 4D, PHB

Established parachute sites are listed in the Airport/Facility Directory listings of the Chart Supplement, and in the Associated Data section. Frequently used sites are also depicted on aeronautical charts and single events or infrequently used sites are listed in NOTAMS.

COMMUNICATION AND FLIGHT INFORMATION

SECTION A — ATC SERVICES

AUTOMATIC DEPENDENT SURVEILLANCE-BROADCAST (ADS-B)

- In addition to aircraft Mode S transponders, the automatic dependent surveillance-broadcast (ADS-B) system consists of ADS-B ground stations; and in each aircraft a GPS receiver, ADS-B Out transmitter, and ADS-B In receiver.
- The ADS-B system relies on the GPS in each aircraft for position information. This system is intended as a more accurate replacement for the ATC radar system.
- ADS-B Out transmits line-of-sight signals from the aircraft to ATC ground receivers and to receivers in other aircraft.
- ADS-B In receives the lateral position, altitude, and velocity of transmitting aircraft and presents this data on a cockpit display of traffic information (CDTI) or integrated into your MFD moving map.
- ADS-B provides precise real-time data to controllers that immediately indicates when an aircraft deviates from its assigned flight path.
- ADS-B offers an effective range of 100 nautical miles, providing ATC a large area in which to implement traffic conflict detection and resolution.
- In addition to traffic information, ADS-B can provide the flight information service broadcast (FIS-B) to suitably equipped aircraft. FIS-B delivers textual and graphical weather products, as well as TFR locations and special use airspace status.

TRANSPONDER OPERATIONS

- Your ATC transponder must have been tested and inspected within the preceding 24 calendar months, or its use is not permitted.
- Unless otherwise required, set the transponder to squawk 1200 when operating under VFR.
- When leaving Class B, C or D airspace and being advised that radar service is terminated, squawk 1200.
- Avoid inadvertently selecting the transponder codes 7500, the code for hijacking; 7600, the code for communication failure; or 7700, the code for emergency.

VFR RADAR SERVICES

- ATC tells you the position of other traffic using the face of a clock as a reference, with your aircraft at the center. An aircraft at the 12 o'clock position is straight ahead, 6 o'clock is directly behind, 3 o'clock is 90 degrees to the right, and 9 o'clock 90 is degrees to the left. This position is based on your ground track and not your heading.
- Basic radar service for VFR aircraft provides traffic advisories and limited vectoring on a workload permitting basis.
- To request VFR radar service and a transponder code, contact ground control or clearance delivery, and request the appropriate radar service.
- A small number of terminal radar service areas (TRSAs) exist that provide sequencing and separation for participating VFR aircraft. Class B and C areas also provide these services, but "participation" is mandatory.

AUTOMATIC TERMINAL INFORMATION SERVICE (ATIS)

- Automatic terminal information service (ATIS) is the continuous broadcast of recorded information concerning noncontrol data in selected high-activity terminal areas.
- Absence of the sky condition and visibility on an ATIS broadcast indicates that the ceiling is at least 5,000 feet and visibility is 5 miles or more.

FLIGHT SERVICE (FSS)

- Flight Service, also called a flight service station (FSS), provides weather briefings, NOTAMs, and flight plan filing at 1-800-WX-BRIEF (1-800-992-7433) or 1800wxbrief.com.
- Flight Service can provide updated weather information and take your pilot reports during flight. The call sign for a flight service station is its name, followed by the word "radio." On initial call-up, provide the full call sign of your aircraft, using the phonetic alphabet.

5-1   PLT426   PA.I.B.K1b

An ATC transponder was tested and inspected on March 15, 2018. The next test is due on

A – September 30, 2018.

B – March 31, 2019.

C – March 31, 2020

5-1. Answer C. GFDPP 5A, FAR 91.413

An ATC transponder must have been tested and inspected within at least the preceding 24 calendar months, or its use is not permitted.

5-2   PLT196   PA.I.C.R2b

Automatic terminal information service (ATIS) is the continuous broadcast of recorded information concerning

A – pilots of radar-identified aircraft whose aircraft is in dangerous proximity to terrain or to an obstruction.

B – nonessential information to reduce frequency congestion.

C – noncontrol information in selected high-activity terminal areas.

5-2. Answer C. GFDPP 5A

ATIS is broadcast at certain busy airports, and provides noncontrol weather and runway information.

5-3   PLT370   PA.VI.C.K2

When an ATC clearance has been obtained, no pilot in command may deviate from that clearance, unless that pilot obtains an amended clearance. The one exception to this regulation is

A – an emergency.

B – when the clearance states "at pilot's discretion."

C – if the clearance contains a restriction.

5-3. Answer A. GFDPP 5A, FAR 91.123

When an ATC clearance has been obtained, a pilot in command may not deviate from that clearance, except in an emergency, unless an amended clearance is obtained. A "pilot's discretion" clearance still must be followed, even though the pilot has more latitude in complying with that clearance.

5-4   PLT194   PA.VI.B.K3

An ATC radar facility issues the following advisory to a pilot flying on a heading of 090°: "TRAFFIC 3 O'CLOCK, 2 MILES, WESTBOUND..." Where should the pilot look for this traffic?

A – East

B – South

C – West

5-4. Answer B. GFDPP 5A, AIM

Because the pilot is heading east, the 3 o'clock position is to the right, which is south.

5-5   PLT194   PA.VI.B.K3

An ATC radar facility issues the following advisory to a pilot flying on a heading of 360°: "TRAFFIC 10 O'CLOCK, 2 MILES, SOUTHBOUND..." Where should the pilot look for this traffic?

A – Northwest

B – Northeast

C – Southwest

5-5. Answer A. GFDPP 5A, AIM

Because the pilot's 12 o'clock position is north, the 10 o'clock position is northwest.

5-6   PLT194   PA.VI.B.K3

An ATC radar facility issues the following advisory to a pilot during a local flight: "TRAFFIC 2 O'CLOCK, 5 MILES, NORTHBOUND..." Where should the pilot look for this traffic?

A – Between directly ahead and 90° to the left

B – Between directly behind and 90° to the right

C – Between directly ahead and 90° to the right

5-6. Answer C. GFDPP 5A, AIM

The pilot's 12 o'clock position is directly ahead, and the 3 o'clock position is 90° to the right. The 2 o'clock position is approximately 60° right.

5-7   PLT194   PA.VI.B.K3

An ATC radar facility issues the following advisory to a pilot flying north in a calm wind: "TRAFFIC 9 O'CLOCK, 2 MILES, SOUTHBOUND..." Where should the pilot look for this traffic?

A – South

B – North

C – West

5-7. Answer C. GFDPP 5A AIM

The pilot's 12 o'clock position is north, so the 9 o'clock position is west.

5-8   PLT172   PA.VI.B.K3

What basic terminal radar services does ATC provide to VFR aircraft?

A – Traffic advisories, safety alerts, limited vectoring, and, in Class B airspace, separation between all aircraft

B – Sequencing and separation between all aircraft operating in Class B and C airspace

C – Wind shear warning at participating airports

5-8. Answer A. GFDPP 5A, AIM

Basic radar service for VFR aircraft provides safety alerts, traffic advisories, and limited vectoring on a workload-permitting basis. In Class B airspace, ATC provides sequencing and separation for all aircraft. In Class C airspace, ATC provides sequencing for all aircraft and separation of VFR aircraft only from IFR aircraft; not other VFR aircraft.

5-9   PLT172   PA.VI.B.K3

During ground operations, from whom should a departing VFR aircraft request radar traffic information?

A – Flight Service

B – Ground control, on initial contact

C – Tower, just before takeoff

5-9. Answer B. GFDPP 5A, AIM

Request radar traffic information by notifying ground control on initial contact with your request and proposed direction of flight. At airports in Class B or C airspace, you might make this request from clearance delivery. Flight Service does not provide radar services and requesting radar service from the tower just before takeoff, could delay your departure or availability of the service.

5-10   PLT172   PA.VI.B.K3

TRSA Service in the terminal radar program provides

A – sequencing and separation for all VFR aircraft.

B – IFR separation (1,000 feet vertical and 3 miles lateral) between all aircraft.

C – warning to pilots when their aircraft are in unsafe proximity to terrain, obstructions, or other aircraft.

5-10. Answer C. GFDPP 5A, AIM

Terminal radar service areas (TRSAs) are airspace areas surrounding about 30 U.S. airports that offer radar services, but where contact with ATC is not mandatory outside of the Class D airspace that exists normally within 4 NM of the primary airport.

TRSA provides basic radar service, which provides safety alerts—warnings to pilots when their aircraft are in unsafe proximity to terrain, obstructions, or other aircraft. In addition, TRSA service provides sequencing and separation of all IFR and *participating* VFR aircraft to the primary airport. IFR separation is provided between *IFR* aircraft, not all aircraft.

5-11   PLT497   PA.VI.B.K4

When making routine transponder code changes, pilots should avoid inadvertent selection of which code?

A – 7200

B – 7000

C – 7500

5-11. Answer C. GFDPP 5A AIM

Avoid inadvertent selection of transponder codes that set off alarms at ATC facilities. These codes are: 7500 for hijacking, 7600 for two-way radio communications failure, and 7700 for other emergencies.

5-12   PLT497   PA.III.A.K4

When operating under VFR below 18,000 feet MSL, unless otherwise authorized, what transponder code should be selected?

A – 1200

B – 7600

C – 7700

5-12. Answer A. GFDPP 5A, AIM

The transponder code for standard VFR is 1200. Aircraft operating above 18,000 feet MSL are in Class A airspace and must have an IFR clearance. Code 7700 is to communicate an emergency and 7600 is for two-way radio communications failure.

5-13   PLT497   PA.III.A.K4

Unless otherwise authorized, if flying a transponder-equipped aircraft, a pilot should squawk which VFR code?

A – 1200

B – 7600

C – 7700

5-13. Answer A. GFDPP 5A, AIM

The transponder code for VFR aircraft is 1200. Code 7700 is to communicate an emergency and 7600 is for two-way radio communications failure.

5-14   PLT497   PA.VI.B.K3

What happens when you activate the IDENT function on your transponder?

A – A data block appears on the ATC display that contains your aircraft call sign and type.

B – The transponder return from your aircraft momentarily blossoms on the ATC display to enable easy identification.

C – The ATC display momentarily zooms in on the transponder return from your aircraft to enable easy identification.

5-14. Answer B. GFDPP 5A, AIM

Pressing the IDENT button or softkey on your transponder system causes the transponder return to blossom on the ATC display and enables easy identification of your aircraft. It does not cause any change to the data block or zoom level on the ATC display.

5-15   PLT497   PA.III.A.K4

When should you activate the IDENT function on your transponder?

A – On initial callup

B – On ATC request

C – When setting or changing a transponder code

5-15. Answer B. GFDPP 5A, AIM

Press the IDENT button or softkey on your transponder system only when ATC asks you to "Ident."

5-16   PLT497   PA.VI.B.K4

If air traffic control advises that radar service is terminated when the pilot is departing Class C airspace, the transponder should be set to code

A – 0000.

B – 1200.

C – 4096.

5-16. Answer B. GFDPP 5A, AIM

When radar service is terminated, you no longer squawk a discrete code, but the standard VFR code of 1200. Never use code 0000.

5-17   PLT497   PA.VI.B.K3

ATC issues a safety alert to aircraft under their control

A – that are at an altitude believed to place the aircraft in unsafe proximity to terrain or obstructions.

B – when another aircraft under their control is at an altitude that places the aircraft in unsafe proximity to each other.

C – if radar shows that the aircraft is headed into level 5 or 6 convective activity.

5-17. Answer A. GFDPP 5A, AIM

The types of safety alerts are:

Terrain or Obstruction Alert. Immediately issued to an aircraft under ATC control if ATC is aware that the aircraft is at an altitude believed to place the aircraft in unsafe proximity to terrain or obstructions.

Aircraft Conflict Alert. Immediately issued to an aircraft under ATC control if ATC is aware of an aircraft *not under their control* at an altitude believed to place the aircraft in unsafe proximity to each other.

ATC *does not* provide convective thunderstorm avoidance assistance unless a pilot requests it and ATC agrees to provide the service based on workload.

5-18   PLT497   PA.VI.B.K3

In addition to aircraft Mode S transponders, the automatic dependent surveillance-broadcast (ADS-B) system includes what primary components?

A – ADS-B radar transmitter; aircraft radar receiver, ADS-B Out transmitter, and ADS-B In receiver

B – ADS-B ground station; aircraft GPS receiver, ADS-B Out transmitter, and ADS-B In receiver

C – ADS-B ground station; aircraft VOR/DME or GPS receiver, and ADS-B In receiver

5-18. Answer B. GFDPP 5A, AIM

The ADS-B system depends on accurate GPS positions transmitted from each aircraft—GPS is a core component. The ADS-B Out transmitter in your aircraft sends your GPS position to ATC through the ADS-B ground station, which transmits information back to aircraft through the ADS-B In receiver.

5-19   PLT497   PA.VI.B.K3

Automatic dependent surveillance-broadcast (ADS-B) provides what services?

A – Weather products on FIS-B through your ADS-B Out transceiver.

B – Traffic alert and collision avoidance system (TCAS) with conflict resolution through your ADS-B In receiver.

C – Traffic information service-broadcast (TIS-B) through your ADS-B Out transmitter and ADS-B In receiver.

5-19. Answer C. GFDPP 5A, AIM

The ADS-B ground station receives the position that each aircraft transmits through ADS-B out, integrates it with non-ADS-B radar targets, and transmits the complete traffic picture back to aircraft. Properly equipped aircraft receive the traffic information broadcast through their ADS-B In receivers. Aircraft equipped with ADS-B In and Out can also receive traffic information directly from other aircraft, but this capability is not the same as the TCAS system that is required on airliners.

5-20   PLT078   PA.III.A.K5

(Refer to Figure 52.)
Which type radar service is provided to VFR aircraft at Lincoln Municipal?

A – Sequencing to the primary Class C airport and standard separation

B – Sequencing to the primary Class C airport and conflict resolution so that radar targets do not touch, or 1,000 feet vertical separation

C – Sequencing to the primary Class C airport, traffic advisories, conflict resolution, and safety alerts

5-20. Answer C. GFDPP 5A, AIM

The VFR services provided within a Class C airspace area include: sequencing all arriving aircraft to the primary Class C airport; providing traffic advisories and conflict resolutions between IFR and VFR aircraft so that radar targets do not touch, or 500 feet vertical separation, and between VFR aircraft, traffic advisories, and safety alerts.

5-21   PLT044   PA.VI.B.K3

When an air traffic controller issues radar traffic information in relation to the 12-hour clock, the reference the controller uses is the aircraft's

A – true course.

B – ground track.

C – magnetic heading.

5-21. Answer B. GFDPP 5A, PHB

Controllers can see the ground track of an aircraft on radar, but cannot factor in any crab angle applied for wind correction. Pilots should consider this when interpreting ATC traffic advisories.

5-22   PLT044   PA.I.C.K2

You can obtain pilot reports and updated weather information during flight by contacting

A – HIWAS

B – Flight Watch

C – Flight Service

5-22. Answer C. GFDPP 5A, AIM

Flight service stations (FSS) provide all non-ATC services to pilots before and during flight. Hazardous in-flight weather advisory service (HIWAS) provides automated inflight weather advisories over selected VORs, but that service is limited to specific weather products and does not replace preflight or inflight weather briefings from FSS.

5-23   PLT196   PA.III.A.K7
Absence of the sky condition and visibility on an
ATIS broadcast indicates that

A – weather conditions are at or above VFR
minimums.

B – the sky condition is clear and visibility is
unrestricted.

C – the ceiling is at least 5,000 feet and visibility is 5
miles or more.

5-23. Answer C. GFDPP 5A, AIM
If the ceiling is at least 5,000 feet and visibility is 5
miles or more, reporting of the ceiling/sky condition,
visibility, and obstructions to vision is optional.

SECTION B — RADIO PROCEDURES

Pilots use standard terminology to ensure that communication between aircraft and ground facilities is smooth and
concise. This section covers VHF radio characteristics, common terms, and proper phraseology. Coordinated universal time (UTC), radio procedures, and ground radio facilities are also included.

ATC CLEARANCES

An air traffic control clearance is an authorization by ATC for you to proceed under specified traffic conditions within
controlled airspace. Its purpose is to prevent collisions between known aircraft.
- When an ATC clearance has been obtained, no pilot may deviate from that clearance, unless that pilot obtains
an amended clearance. The exception to this regulation is in an emergency.
- A pilot who deviates from a clearance, and is given priority by ATC because of that emergency, shall submit a
detailed report of that emergency within 48 hours to the manager of that facility, if requested by ATC.

USING NUMBERS ON THE RADIO

State altitudes as individual numbers, with the word "thousand" included as appropriate. At altitudes of 10,000 feet and
above, each digit of the thousands is pronounced, for example "one zero thousand."

COORDINATED UNIVERSAL TIME (UTC)

To convert the local departure or arrival time to UTC, add the hours of difference from the number on the time conversion table. For example, to convert MST to UTC, add seven hours to MST.

ATC LIGHT SIGNALS

If you experience two-way communications failure, and need to land at a tower-controlled airport, determine the direction and flow of the traffic, join the pattern, and look for the following light signals from the tower.

COLOR AND TYPE OF SIGNAL	MEANING	
	On the Ground	**In Flight**
Steady Green	Cleared for takeoff	Cleared to land
Flashing Green	Cleared to taxi	Return for landing (to be followed by steady green at proper time)
Steady Red	Stop	Give way to other aircraft and continue circling
Flashing Red	Taxi clear of landing area (runway) in use	Airport unsafe — do not land
Flashing White	Return to starting point on airport	(No assigned meaning)
Alternating Red and Green	Exercise extreme caution	Exercise extreme caution

OTHER PROCEDURES

- After landing at a tower-controlled airport, contact ground control when advised by the tower to do so.
- The call sign for a flight service station is its name, followed by the word "radio." Give your full call sign of your aircraft, using the phonetic alphabet.
- If instructed by ground control to taxi to a runway, you should read back the assigned route and proceed to the next intersecting runway where further clearance is required to continue.
- If you are not already in contact with ATC, the frequency you use in an emergency is 121.5 MHz.
- An emergency locator transmitter (ELT) may be tested during the first 5 minutes after the hour.

5-24   PLT044   PA.I.A.K2

As pilot in command of an aircraft, under which situation may you deviate from an ATC clearance?

A – In an emergency

B – When operating in Class A airspace at night

C – If an ATC clearance is not understood and in VFR conditions

5-24. Answer A. GFDPP 5B, AIM

A pilot is expected to do what is necessary in an emergency. For example, in rare instances you might have to deviate from an ATC clearance to avoid a collision with terrain or with another aircraft. Any pilot deviating from an ATC clearance must report the deviation to ATC as soon as possible and obtain a new clearance. Airline pilots are required to comply with a resolution advisory from a TCAS II system, even if it conflicts with an ATC clearance.

5-25   PLT502   PA.III.A.K3

A steady green light signal directed from the control tower to an aircraft in flight is a signal that the pilot

A – is cleared to land.

B – should give way to other aircraft and continue circling.

C – should return for landing.

5-25. Answer A. GFDPP 5B, FAR 91.125

A steady green light while in flight means that you are cleared to land.

5-26   PLT502   PA.III.A.K3

Which light signal from the control tower clears a pilot to taxi?

A – Flashing green

B – Steady green

C – Flashing white

5-27   PLT502   PA.III.A.K3

If the control tower uses a light signal to direct a pilot to give way to other aircraft and continue circling, the light is

A – flashing red.

B – steady red.

C – alternating red and green.

5-28   PLT502   PA.III.A.K3

A flashing white light signal from the control tower to a taxiing aircraft is an indication to

A – taxi at a faster speed.

B – taxi only on taxiways and not cross runways.

C – return to the starting point on the airport.

5-29   PLT502   PA.III.A.K3

An alternating red and green light signal directed from the control tower to an aircraft in flight is a signal to

A – hold position.

B – exercise extreme caution.

C – not land; the airport is unsafe.

5-26. Answer A. GFDPP 5B, FAR 91.125
While on the ground, a flashing green light means cleared to taxi.

5-27. Answer B. GFDPP 5B, FAR 91.125
While in flight, a steady red light means give way and continue circling.

5-28. Answer C. GFDPP 5B, FAR 91.125
A flashing white light while operating on the ground means return to the starting point on the airport.

5-29. Answer B. GFDPP 5B, FAR 91.125
An alternating red and green signal means the same whether you are in flight or on the ground — exercise extreme caution.

5-30   PLT502   PA.III.A.K3

While on final approach for landing, an alternating green and red light followed by a flashing red light is received from the control tower. Under these circumstances, the pilot should

A – discontinue the approach, fly the same traffic pattern and approach again, and land.

B – exercise extreme caution and abandon the approach, realizing the airport is unsafe for landing.

C – abandon the approach, circle the airport to the right, and expect a flashing white light when the airport is safe for landing.

5-30. Answer B. GFDPP 5B, FAR 91.125
An alternating red and green signal means exercise extreme caution. The flashing red signal that follows means that the airport is unsafe.

5-31   PLT012   PA.I.D.K3

(Refer to Figure 27.) An aircraft departs an airport in the eastern daylight time zone at 0945 EDT for a 2-hour flight to an airport located in the central daylight time zone. The landing should be at what coordinated universal time?

A – 1345Z

B – 1445Z

C – 1545Z

5-31. Answer C. GFDPP 5B, AIM
To convert the local departure time to UTC, add four hours (0945 + 4:00 = 1345). Two hours later is 1545Z.

5-32   PLT012   PA.I.D.K3

(Refer to Figure 27.) An aircraft departs an airport in the central standard time zone at 0930 CST for a two-hour flight to an airport located in the mountain standard time zone. The landing should be at what time?

A – 0930 MST

B – 1030 MST

C – 1130 MST

5-32. Answer B. GFDPP 5B, AIM
To find the arrival time, add two hours to the 0930 departure time to get 1130 CST. Because mountain time is one hour earlier than central time, subtract one hour, for a landing time of 1030 MST.

5-33   PLT012   PA.I.D.K3
(Refer to Figure 27.) An aircraft departs an airport in the central standard time zone at 0845 CST for a 2-hour flight to an airport located in the mountain standard time zone. The landing should be at what coordinated universal time?

A – 1345Z

B – 1445Z

C – 1645Z

5-33. Answer C. GFDPP 5B, AIM
Departure time (0845) plus two hours is 1045 CST. Convert CST to UTC by adding six hours, for a landing time of 1645Z.

5-34   PLT012   PA.I.D.K3
(Refer to Figure 27.) An aircraft departs an airport in the mountain standard time zone at 1615 MST for a 2-hour 15-minute flight to an airport located in the Pacific standard time zone. The estimated time of arrival at the destination airport should be

A – 1630 PST.

B – 1730 PST.

C – 1830 PST.

5-34. Answer B. GFDPP 5B, AIM
Add 2:15 to 1615 MST to find the arrival time of 1830 MST. Because pacific time is one hour earlier than MST, the arrival time is 1730 PST.

5-35   PLT012   PA.I.D.K3
(Refer to Figure 27.) An aircraft departs an airport in the Pacific standard time zone at 1030 PST for a 4-hour flight to an airport located in the central standard time zone. The landing should be at what coordinated universal time?

A – 2030Z

B – 2130Z

C – 2230Z

5-35. Answer C. GFDPP 5B, AIM
Add four hours to 1030 PST to find the arrival time of 1430 PST. To convert PST to UTC, add eight hours. The landing time is 2230Z.

5-36   PLT012   PA.I.D.K3
(Refer to Figure 27.) An aircraft departs an airport in the mountain standard time zone at 1515 MST for a 2-hour 30-minute flight to an airport located in the Pacific standard time zone. What is the estimated time of arrival at the destination airport?

A – 1645 PST

B – 1745 PST

C – 1845 PST

5-36. Answer A. GFDPP 5B, AIM
Add 2:30 to 1515 MST to find the arrival time of 1745 MST. Convert MST to PST by subtracting one hour. The answer is 1645 PST.

5-37 PLT064 PA.III.A.K2

(Refer to Figure 20, area 3.)
What is the recommended communication procedure for a landing at Currituck County Airport?

A – Transmit intentions on 122.9 MHz when 10 miles out and give position reports in the traffic pattern.

B – Contact Elizabeth City Tower on 120.5 MHz for airport and traffic advisories.

C – Contact FSS for area traffic information.

5-37. Answer A. GFDPP 5B, AIM
The CTAF symbol is next to the frequency of 122.9. The normal procedure is to transmit intentions when 10 miles out and give position reports in the pattern.

5-38 PLT064 PA.III.A.K2

(Refer to Figure 27, area 2.)
What is the recommended communication procedure when inbound to land at Cooperstown Airport?

A – Broadcast intentions when 10 miles out on the CTAF/MULTICOM frequency, 122.9 MHz.

B – Contact UNICOM when 10 miles out on 122.8 MHz.

C – Circle the airport in a left turn before entering traffic.

5-38. Answer A. GFDPP 5B, AIM
The CTAF/MULTICOM frequency, 122.9, is depicted next to the CTAF symbol. Pilots should broadcast intentions on this frequency when 10 miles from the field.

5-39 PLT204 PA.III.A.K2

When flying HAWK N666CB, the proper phraseology for initial contact with McAlester FSS is

A – "MCALESTER RADIO, HAWK SIX SIX SIX CHARLIE BRAVO, RECEIVING ARDMORE VORTAC, OVER."

B – "MCALESTER STATION, HAWK SIX SIX SIX CEE BEE, RECEIVING ARDMORE VORTAC, OVER."

C – "MCALESTER FLIGHT SERVICE STATION, HAWK NOVEMBER SIX CHARLIE BRAVO, RECEIVING ARDMORE VORTAC, OVER."

5-39. Answer A. GFDPP 5B, AIM
The call sign for a flight service station is its name, followed by the word "radio." Give the full call sign of your aircraft, using the phonetic alphabet.

5-40 PLT204 PA.III.A.K2

The correct method of stating 4,500 feet MSL to ATC is

A – "FOUR THOUSAND FIVE HUNDRED."

B – "FOUR POINT FIVE."

C – "FORTY-FIVE HUNDRED FEET MSL."

5-40. Answer A. GFDPP 5B, AIM
Altitudes should be stated as individual numbers with the word hundreds or thousands added as appropriate. In this case, 4,500 feet should be read as "FOUR THOUSAND FIVE HUNDRED."

5-41   PLT204   PA.III.A.K2
The correct method of stating 10,500 feet MSL to ATC is

A – "TEN THOUSAND, FIVE HUNDRED FEET."

B – "TEN POINT FIVE."

C – "ONE ZERO THOUSAND, FIVE HUNDRED."

5-41. Answer C. GFDPP 5B, AIM
For altitudes at 10,000 feet MSL and above, pronounce each digit of the thousands, so that 10,500 becomes "ONE ZERO THOUSAND FIVE HUNDRED."

5-42   PLT391   PA.III.A.K1
While on a VFR cross-country flight and not in contact with ATC, what frequency would you use in the event of an emergency?

A – 121.5 MHz

B – 122.5 MHz

C – 128.725 MHz

5-42. Answer A. GFDPP 5B, AIM
If you are not already talking to ATC on another frequency, squawk 7700 and use the emergency frequency, 121.5, to obtain assistance.

5-43   PLT150   PA.III.A.K5
If the radio fails in an aircraft, what is the recommended procedure when landing at a controlled airport?

A – Observe the traffic flow, enter the pattern, and look for a light signal from the tower.

B – Enter a crosswind leg and rock the wings.

C – Flash the landing lights and cycle the landing gear while circling the airport.

5-43. Answer A. GFDPP 5B, AIM
To avoid conflicts and cause the least disruption in the traffic flow, determine the landing direction, and enter the pattern. Watch the tower for a light signal and acknowledge by rocking the wings. At night, acknowledge by flashing the landing or navigation lights.

5-44   PLT044   PA.III.A.K2
After landing at a tower-controlled airport, when should the pilot contact ground control?

A – When advised by the tower to do so

B – Before turning off the runway

C – After reaching a taxiway that leads directly to the parking area

5-44. Answer A. GFDPP 5B, AIM
The tower normally instructs you to exit the runway and contact ground control.

5-45   PLT502

If instructed by ground control to taxi to Runway 9, the pilot may proceed

A – via taxiways and across runways to, but not onto, Runway 9.

B – to the next intersecting runway where further clearance is required.

C – via taxiways and across runways to Runway 9, where an immediate takeoff may be made.

5-45. Answer B. GFDPP 5B, AIM

You must have an explicit clearance to cross any runway enroute to your departure runway, and you must have a clearance to taxi onto the departure runway.

5-46   PLT402   PA.IX.A.K9

When activated, an emergency locator transmitter (ELT) transmits on

A – 118.0 MHz and 118.8 MHz.

B – 121.5 MHz and 243.0 MHz.

C – 123.0 MHz and 119.0 MHz.

5-46. Answer B. GFDPP 5B, AIM

The frequencies used for ELTs are the emergency frequencies of 121.5 MHz (VHF) and 243.0 MHz (UHF).

5-47   PLT402

When must the battery in an emergency locator transmitter (ELT) be replaced (or recharged if the battery is rechargeable)?

A – After one-half of the battery's useful life

B – During each annual and 100-hour inspection

C – Every 24 calendar months

5-47. Answer A. GFDPP 5B, FAR 91.207

The ELT battery must be replaced or recharged after one-half of the useful life of the battery has passed.

5-48   PLT402   PA.II.F.K5

When may an emergency locator transmitter (ELT) be tested?

A – Any time

B – At 15 and 45 minutes past the hour

C – During the first 5 minutes after the hour

5-48. Answer C. GFDPP 5B, AIM

To prevent false alerts, ELT testing should be conducted only during the first 5 minutes after any hour.

5-49   PLT402   PA.II.F.K5

Which procedure is recommended to ensure that the emergency locator transmitter (ELT) has not been activated?

A – Turn off the aircraft ELT after landing.

B – Ask the airport tower if they are receiving an ELT signal.

C – Monitor 121.5 before engine shutdown.

5-49. Answer C. GFDPP 5B, AIM
By monitoring 121.5, you can hear the ELT signal if it is activated.

5-50   PLT370   PA.III.A.K2

An ATC clearance provides

A – priority over all other traffic.

B – adequate separation from all traffic.

C – authorization to proceed under specified traffic conditions in controlled airspace.

5-50. Answer C. GFDPP 5B, AIM
A clearance is authorization from ATC to operate under specific conditions in controlled airspace.

5-51   PLT078   PA.I.D.S2

(Refer to Figure 52.) When approaching Lincoln Municipal from the west at noon for landing, initial communication should be with

A – Lincoln Approach Control on 124.0 MHz.

B – Minneapolis Center on 128.75 MHz.

C – Lincoln Tower on 118.5 MHz.

5-51. Answer A. GFDPP 5B, Chart Supplement
The Communications section of the Chart Supplement Airport/Facility Directory entry indicates that the airport is in Class C airspace, and that you should contact approach control. When west of the airport (180°-359°), the frequency to use is 124.0. The Lincoln Approach Control hours of operation are 1130-0600Z (5:30 a.m. - midnight local time).

5-52   PLT078   PA.III.A.K2

(Refer to Figure 52.)
What is the recommended communication procedure for landing at Lincoln Municipal during the hours when the tower is not in operation?

A – Monitor airport traffic and announce your position and intentions on 118.5 MHz.

B – Contact UNICOM on 122.95 MHz for traffic advisories.

C – Monitor ATIS for airport conditions, then announce your position on 122.95 MHz.

5-52. Answer A. GFDPP 5B, Chart Supplement
The CTAF frequency is listed as 118.5, and is used when the tower is not in operation. Standard procedures are to monitor airport traffic and announce your position on CTAF.

5-53   PLT435   PA.III.A.K2

As standard operating practice, all inbound traffic to an airport without a control tower should continuously monitor the appropriate facility from a distance of

A – 25 miles.

B – 20 miles.

C – 10 miles.

5-53. Answer C. GFDPP 5-25, AIM

In addition to monitoring a CTAF within 10 miles when inbound or outbound from a non-towered airport, pilots should also make an initial call to announce their intention if they plan to land at the airport. They should then report on each leg of the pattern.

SECTION C — SOURCES OF FLIGHT INFORMATION

Aviation publications exist to aid you in planning a flight. These resources, many of which are available online, include the Aeronautical Information Manual (AIM), the Chart Supplement (including the Airport/Facility Directory), Federal Aviation Regulations, advisory circulars, Jeppesen pilot resources, and notices to airmen.

CHART SUPPLEMENT

- A Chart Supplement publication includes an Airport/Facility Directory section, plus sections providing other information for the region covered in that volume.
- The Chart Supplement includes information about parachute jumping areas both in individual airport listings in the Airport/Facility Directory section and in the Associated Data section.
- Nonstandard traffic patterns are included in the remarks following the runway data for each runway.
- Information regarding parachute jumping is also listed in the Chart Supplement.

ADVISORY CIRCULARS

- You can obtain FAA advisory circulars from the FAA website (**FAA.gov**).
- FAA advisory circulars (ACs) that relate to certain subject matters are identified by numeric codes. ACs pertaining to airmen are issued under subject number 60 (example AC 60-22). Airspace ACs are issued under subject number 70. ATC and General Operations ACs are issued under subject number 90.

5-54   PLT435   PA.I.D.S2

(Refer to Figure 22, area 2.)
For information about the parachute jumping and glider operations at Silverwood Airport, refer to

A – notes on the border of the chart.

B – the Silverwood Airport entry in the A/FD section of the Chart Supplement.

C – the Notices to Airmen (NOTAM) publication.

5-54. Answer B. GFDPP 5-39, Chart Legend

The Chart Supplement includes information about parachute jumping areas both in individual airport listings in the Airport/Facility Directory section and in the Associated Data section.

5-55   PLT116   PA.I.D.S2*
You can obtain FAA advisory circulars by

A – distribution from the nearest FAA district office.

B – searching for them at FAA.gov.

C – subscribing to the Federal Register.

5-55. Answer B. GFDPP 5C, PHB
Although you might be able to buy some advisory circulars in paper form, the FAA website is by far the most efficient way to obtain the most current version of most ACs. Search for the AC by name or number at FAA.gov. The Federal Register includes changes to regulations, but not the content of ACs.

5-56   PLT078   PA.I.D.S2
(Refer to Figure 52.) Where is Loup City Municipal located with relation to the city?

A – Northeast approximately 3 miles

B – Northwest approximately 1 mile

C – East approximately 10 miles

5-56. Answer B. GFDPP 5-38, A/FD
The first line of the A/FD includes the distance and direction from the associated city. The entry 1 NW indicates that the airport is 1 mile northwest of the city.

5-57   PLT078   PA.I.D.S2
(Refer to Figure 52.) The landing distance available on Rwy 17 at Lincoln Airport is

A – 5,400 feet.

B – 5,800 feet.

C – 8,286 feet.

5-57. Answer A. A/FD Legend.
The landing distance available (LDA) appears under Runway Declared Distance Information. For Rwy 17, it is 5,400 feet.

5-58   PLT078   PA.I.D.S2
(Refer to Figure 52.) The landing distance available on Rwy 32 at Lincoln Airport is

A – 7,816 feet.

B – 8,286 feet.

C – 8,649 feet.

5-58. Answer A. A/FD Legend.
The landing distance available (LDA) appears under Runway Declared Distance Information. For Rwy 32, it is 7,816 feet.

5-59   PLT078   PA.I.D.S2
(Refer to Figure 52.)
Traffic patterns in effect at Lincoln Municipal are

A – to the right on Runway 17L and Runway 35L; to the left on Runway 17R and Runway 35R.

B – to the left on Runway 17L and Runway 35L; to the right on Runway 17R and Runway 35R.

C – to the right on Runways 14-32.

5-59. Answer B. GFDPP 5-38, A/FD
Remarks following the runway data for each runway include nonstandard traffic patterns. If not otherwise stated, left-hand patterns are used. Right-hand traffic is noted for Runway 17R and Runway 35R. Left traffic is used for Runways 17L, 35L, 14, and 32.

5-60   PLT116   PA.I.D.S2
FAA advisory circulars containing subject matter related to Airmen are issued under which subject number?

A – 60

B – 70

C – 90

5-60. Answer A. GFDPP 5-45, AC 00-2
Advisory circulars relating to Airmen are issued under subject number 60.

5-61   PLT116   PA.I.D.S2*
FAA advisory circulars containing subject matter related to Air Traffic Control and General Operations are issued under which subject number?

A – 60

B – 70

C – 90

5-61. Answer C. GFDPP 5-45, AC 00-2
Advisory circulars relating to Air Traffic Control and General Operations are issued under subject number 90.

5-62   PLT323   PA.I.D.S2
What information is contained in the Notices to Airmen Publication (NTAP)?

A – Current NOTAM (D) and FDC NOTAMs

B – All current NOTAMs

C – Current Chart Supplement information and FDC NOTAMs

5-62. Answer A. GFDPP 5-47, AIM
The Notices to Airmen Publication (NTAP) contains all current NOTAM (D)s and FDC NOTAMs (except FDC NOTAMs for temporary flight restrictions) available for publication.

METEOROLOGY FOR PILOTS

SECTION A — BASIC WEATHER THEORY

- Atmospheric circulation refers to the movement of air relative to the surface of the earth.
- Every physical process of weather is accompanied by, or is the result of, a heat exchange.
- Unequal heating of the surface of the earth leads to variations in pressure, which is why altimeter settings differ between weather reporting points.
- Coriolis force deflects winds to the right in the northern hemisphere as they flow from high-pressure to low-pressure areas. However, below 2,000 feet AGL, friction with the surface of the earth reduces the effect of Coriolis force, so winds at the surface generally are different in direction from the winds aloft.
- Convective circulation patterns associated with sea breezes are caused by cool, dense air moving inland from over the water.

6-1   PLT512   PA.I.C.K3c

What causes variations in altimeter settings between weather reporting points?

A – Unequal heating of the earth's surface

B – Variation of terrain elevation

C – Coriolis force

6-1. Answer A. GFDPP 6-7, AW

Temperature changes cause variations in air pressure and density. Because the surface of the earth is heated unevenly, altimeter settings are different between weather stations.

6-2   PLT516   PA.I.C.K3b

The wind at 5,000 feet AGL is southwesterly while the surface wind is southerly This difference in direction is primarily due to

A – stronger pressure gradient at higher altitudes.

B – friction between the wind and the surface.

C – stronger Coriolis force at the surface.

6-2. Answer B. GFDPP 6-9, AW

Above 2,000 feet AGL, wind flows along isobars because of Coriolis force. Below that altitude, friction with the surface of the earth weakens Coriolis force and allows the wind to flow more directly toward the low pressure area. In the northern hemisphere, this action results in a counterclockwise shift in wind direction closer to the surface.

6-3   PLT494   PA.I.C.K3b

Convective circulation patterns associated with sea breezes are caused by

A – warm, dense air moving inland from over the water.

B – water absorbing and radiating heat faster than the land.

C – cool, dense air moving inland from over the water.

6-3. Answer C. GFDPP 6-11, AW

During the day, land surfaces become warmer than the adjacent water surfaces—warming the air above the land and causing it to rise. The rising air is replaced by the inland flow of cooler, denser air located over the water. The warm air then flows out over the water where it cools and descends. This action starts the cycle all over again. During the night, the process is reversed as the land cools off faster than the water.

6-4   PLT512   PA.I.C.K3c

Every physical process of weather is accompanied by, or is the result of, a

A – movement of air.

B – pressure differential.

C – heat exchange.

6-4. Answer C. GFDPP 6-19, AW

Every physical process of weather such as heating, cooling, evaporation, and condensation, is caused by, or is the result of, a heat exchange.

SECTION B — WEATHER PATTERNS

ATMOSPHERIC STABILITY

- Stability of air can be determined by its actual lapse rate.
- A characteristic of stable air is the presence of stratiform clouds.
- When moist, stable air flows upslope, you can expect the formation of stratus type clouds.
- Characteristics of unstable air include turbulence and good surface visibility.

TEMPERATURE INVERSIONS

- A temperature inversion means that temperature increases as altitude increases. An inversion is associated with a stable layer of air.
- The most frequent type of ground or surface-based temperature inversion is produced by terrestrial radiation on clear and relatively still nights.
- The weather conditions that can be expected beneath a low-level temperature inversion layer when the relative humidity is high are smooth air, poor visibility, fog, haze, or low clouds.

MOISTURE

- The processes by which moisture is added to unsaturated air are evaporation and sublimation.
- The dewpoint is the temperature to which the air must be cooled to become saturated.
- The amount of water vapor which air can hold depends on the air temperature.

- If the temperature of the collecting surface is at or below the dewpoint of the adjacent air, and the dewpoint is below freezing, frost forms.
- Frost on the wings affects takeoff performance by disrupting the smooth flow of air over the airfoil, adversely affecting its lifting capacity. Frost may prevent the airplane from becoming airborne at normal takeoff speed. Frost is considered a hazard to flight for this reason.

CLOUDS AND FOG

- Clouds are divided into four families according to their height range—low clouds, middle clouds, high clouds, and clouds with vertical development.
- Clouds, fog, or dew always form when water vapor condenses. Air cools when lifted and moisture condenses out of the air as the relative humidity reaches 100 percent.
- You can estimate the bases of cumulus clouds using the convergence rate of temperature and dewpoint of lifted air—4.4°F per 1,000 feet. Divide the temperature/dewpoint spread at the surface by 4.4 to find the height of the cloudbase above the surface, in thousands of feet.
- The suffix "nimbus," used in naming clouds, means a rain cloud.
- Stratus clouds form when moist, stable air is lifted.
- If the temperature/dewpoint spread is small and decreasing, and the temperature is above freezing, fog or low clouds are likely to develop.
- Radiation fog forms as warm, moist air lies over flatland areas on clear, calm nights.
- Advection fog forms when a warm air mass moves inland from the coast in winter.
- Advection fog and upslope fog depend upon wind to exist.
- Low-level turbulence can occur, and icing can become hazardous in steam fog.
- Clouds with extensive vertical development and associated turbulence can be expected when an unstable air mass is forced upward.
- Precipitation can range from light rain that is easy to fly through, to freezing rain that poses a serious hazard to all aircraft, even aircraft with deice and anti-ice equipment.
- The presence of ice pellets at the surface is evidence that a temperature inversion exists with freezing rain at a higher altitude.

AIR MASSES AND FRONTS

- Air masses are large-scale parcels of air that have a set of characteristics (i.e. moist, unstable) that distinguishes them from one another.
- Characteristics of a moist, unstable air mass are cumuliform clouds and showery precipitation.
- A stable air mass generally contains smooth air.
- The boundary between two different air masses is referred to as a front.
- One of the most easily recognizable discontinuities across a front is a change in temperature.
- One weather phenomenon that always occurs when flying across a front is a change in the wind direction.
- Steady precipitation preceding a front is an indication of stratiform clouds with little or no turbulence.

6-5   PLT301   PA.I.C.K3c

When a temperature inversion exists, you would expect to experience

A – clouds with extensive vertical development above an inversion aloft.

B – good visibility in the lower levels of the atmosphere and poor visibility above an inversion aloft.

C – an increase in temperature as altitude is increased.

6-5. Answer C. GFDPP 6-17, AW

Normally, temperature decreases with altitude. During an inversion, cooler air is trapped beneath a warmer layer of air. Therefore, temperature increases with altitude.

6-6   PLT512   PA.I.C.K3c

The most frequent type of ground or surface-based temperature inversion is that which is produced by

A – terrestrial radiation on a clear, relatively still night.

B – warm air being lifted rapidly aloft in the vicinity of mountainous terrain.

C – the movement of colder air under warm air, or the movement of warm air over cold air.

6-6. Answer A. GFDPP 6-18, AW

An inversion commonly forms on clear, cool nights when the ground radiates heat and cools faster than the overlying air.

6-7   PLT512   PA.I.C.K3c

Which weather conditions should be expected beneath a low-level temperature inversion layer when the relative humidity is high?

A – Smooth air, poor visibility, fog, haze, or low clouds

B – Light wind shear, poor visibility, haze, and light rain

C – Turbulent air, poor visibility, fog, low stratus type clouds, and showery precipitation

6-7. Answer A. GFDPP 6-17, AW

Low-level temperature inversions normally occur in stable, smooth air, with poor visibility due to trapped pollutants, which are commonly referred to as condensation nuclei. In addition, high humidity tends to cause formation of fog and low clouds.

6-8   PLT512   PA.I.C.K3c

What is meant by the term "dewpoint"?

A – The temperature at which condensation and evaporation are equal

B – The temperature at which dew always forms

C – The temperature to which air must be cooled to become saturated

6-8. Answer C. GFDPP 6-20, AW

When air is cooled to its dewpoint, it can hold no more moisture, and is said to be saturated.

6-9   PLT512   PA.I.C.K3c

The amount of water vapor which air can hold depends on the

A – dewpoint.

B – air temperature.

C – stability of the air.

6-9. Answer B. GFDPP 6-19, AW
The amount of moisture in the air primarily depends on the temperature. For example, warm air can hold more moisture than cool air.

6-10   PLT512   PA.I.C.K4j

Clouds, fog, or dew always forms when

A – water vapor condenses.

B – water vapor is present.

C – relative humidity reaches 100 percent.

6-10. Answer A. GFDPP 6-22, AW
Condensation occurs when water vapor changes to liquid form. Examples are when water vapor changes to clouds, fog, or dew.

6-11   PLT512   PA.I.C.K4j

What are the processes by which moisture is added to unsaturated air?

A – Evaporation and sublimation

B – Heating and condensation

C – Supersaturation and evaporation

6-11. Answer A. GFDPP 6-19, AW
Evaporation occurs when liquid water changes to water vapor. Sublimation is the changing of ice directly to water vapor. Both processes add moisture to the air.

6-12   PLT512   PA.I.C.K3k

Which conditions result in the formation of frost?

A – The temperature of the collecting surface is at or below freezing when small droplets of moisture fall on the surface.

B – The temperature of the collecting surface is at or below the dewpoint of the adjacent air and the dewpoint is below freezing.

C – The temperature of the surrounding air is at or below freezing when small drops of moisture fall on the collecting surface.

6-12. Answer B. GFDPP 6-20, AW
When the dewpoint of the surrounding air is below freezing, and the collecting surface is at or below the dewpoint, water vapor sublimates directly into ice crystals or frost instead of condensing into dew.

6-13   PLT512   PA.I.C.K4d

The presence of ice pellets at the surface is evidence that there

A – are thunderstorms in the area.

B – has been cold frontal passage.

C – is a temperature inversion with freezing rain at a higher altitude.

6-13. Answer C. GFDPP 6-27, AW

Due to a temperature inversion, a warm layer of air is aloft and keeps the rain in liquid form. As the rain falls through colder air, it begins to freeze, finally turning into ice pellets. Ice pellets always indicate freezing rain at a higher altitude. Ice pellets can form under various conditions, and do not necessarily indicate thunderstorms.

6-14   PLT512   PA.I.C.K4a

What measurement can be used to determine the stability of the atmosphere?

A – Atmospheric pressure

B – Actual lapse rate

C – Surface temperature

6-14. Answer B. GFDPP 6-17, AW

The stability of air refers to its resistance to displacement upward or downward; it is determined by the actual lapse rate. Lapse rate generally refers to the decrease in temperature with an increase in altitude. A high lapse rate tends to indicate unstable air, and a low lapse rate is an indicator of stability in the atmosphere.

6-15   PLT512   PA.I.C.K4a

What would decrease the stability of an air mass?

A – Warming from below

B – Cooling from below

C – Decrease in water vapor

6-15. Answer A. GFDPP 6-16, AW

Stability is affected by a change in the lapse rate of an air mass. Warming from below or cooling from above increases the lapse rate and makes the air less stable.

6-16   PLT512   PA.I.C.K4a

What is a characteristic of stable air?

A – Stratiform clouds

B – Unlimited visibility

C – Cumulus clouds

6-16. Answer A. GFDPP 6-23, AW

Very little vertical development of clouds occurs in stable air, and stratiform clouds and poor visibility are typical. Cumulus clouds and good visibility are indicators of unstable air.

6-17   PLT192   PA.I.C.K3f

When warm, moist, stable air flows upslope, it

A – produces stratus type clouds.

B – causes showers and thunderstorms.

C – develops convective turbulence.

6-17. Answer A. GFDPP 6-23, AW

Stratus clouds are produced in stable air. When moist air flows upslope it cools to its saturation point, and clouds are formed.

6-18   PLT512   PA.I.C.K3f

If an unstable air mass is forced upward, what type clouds can be expected?

A – Stratus clouds with little vertical development

B – Stratus clouds with considerable associated turbulence

C – Clouds with considerable vertical development and associated turbulence

6-19   PLT512   PA.I.C.K3c

What feature is associated with a temperature inversion?

A – A stable layer of air

B – An unstable layer of air

C – Chinook winds on mountain slopes

6-20   PLT512   PA.I.C.K3f

What is the approximate base of the cumulus clouds if the surface air temperature at 1,000 feet MSL is 70°F and the dewpoint is 48°F?

A – 4,000 feet MSL

B – 5,000 feet MSL

C – 6,000 feet MSL

6-21   PLT512   PA.I.C.K3f

At approximately what altitude above the surface would the pilot expect the base of cumuliform clouds if the surface air temperature is 82°F and the dewpoint is 38°F?

A – 9,000 feet AGL

B – 10,000 feet AGL

C – 11,000 feet AGL

6-18. Answer C. GFDPP 6-25, AW

Clouds with extensive vertical development are formed when unstable air is lifted. These cumulus type clouds are associated with moderate to severe turbulence.

6-19. Answer A. GFDPP 6-17, AW

Temperature inversions occur in stable air. Inversions cannot form in unstable air. As Chinook winds descend, the temperature rises. This phenomenon is the opposite of an inversion (cooler air under a warmer layer). In the U.S., the typical example of Chinook winds is the downslope, easterly flow from the Rocky Mountains.

6-20. Answer C. GFDPP 6-20, AW

When warm, moist air rises in a convective current, the temperature and dewpoint converge at 4.4°F per 1,000 feet. Divide the temperature/dewpoint spread at the surface (70°F – 48°F) by 4.4°F to find the approximate cloudbase in thousands of feet. In this case, the cloudbase are 5,000 (22 ÷ 4.4 × 1,000) feet above the surface. Because the surface is 1,000 feet MSL, the cloudbase should be approximately 6,000 feet MSL.

6-21. Answer B. GFDPP 6-20, AW

When warm, moist air rises in a convective current, the temperature and dewpoint converge at 4.4°F per 1,000 feet. You can estimate the cloudbase by dividing the temperature/dewpoint spread at the surface by 4.4°F per 1,000 feet.

In this case: (82°F – 38°F) ÷ 4.4°F/1,000 ft. = 10,000 feet AGL.

6-22   PLT512   PA.I.C.K4a

What are characteristics of a moist, unstable air mass?

A – Cumuliform clouds and showery precipitation

B – Poor visibility and smooth air

C – Stratiform clouds and showery precipitation

6-22. Answer A. GFDPP 6-29, AW

Cumuliform clouds are indicative of unstable air. These clouds normally produce showery, not continuous, precipitation. Poor visibility, smooth air, and stratiform clouds are characteristic of stable air.

6-23   PLT512   PA.I.C.K4a

What are characteristics of unstable air?

A – Turbulence and good surface visibility

B – Turbulence and poor surface visibility

C – Nimbostratus clouds and good surface visibility

6-23. Answer A. GFDPP 6-29, AW

The lifting motion of unstable air produces turbulence. Clouds and pollutants are not trapped as they are in stable layers of air, and good visibility is typical with unstable air. Poor surface visibility and nimbostratus clouds are typical of stable air masses.

6-24   PLT511   PA.I.C.K4a

A stable air mass is most likely to have which characteristic?

A – Showery precipitation

B – Turbulent air

C – Smooth air

6-24. Answer C. GFDPP 6-29, AW

Stable air resists the lifting motion that is associated with turbulence, and is typically smooth. Showery precipitation and turbulent air are characteristics of unstable air.

6-25   PLT192   PA.I.C.K3f

The suffix "nimbus," used in naming clouds, means

A – a cloud with extensive vertical development.

B – a rain cloud.

C – a middle cloud containing ice pellets.

6-25. Answer B. GFDPP 6-22, AW

The word "nimbus" is the Latin word for rainstorm or cloud, and is used today to designate rain clouds, such as cumulonimbus or nimbostratus.

6-26   PLT192   PA.I.C.K3f

Clouds are divided into four families according to their

A – outward shape.

B – height range.

C – composition.

6-26. Answer B. GFDPP 6-22, AW

Clouds are also grouped by families according to their altitudes (height range). The four families are low, middle, high, and clouds with extensive vertical development.

6-27 PLT511   PA.I.C.K4e

The boundary between two different air masses is referred to as a

A – frontolysis.

B – frontogenesis.

C – front.

6-27. Answer C. GFDPP 6-30, AW

The boundary area where two air masses of different properties meet is called a front.

6-28 PLT511   PA.I.C.K4e

One of the most easily recognized discontinuities across a front is

A – a change in temperature.

B – an increase in cloud coverage.

C – an increase in relative humidity.

6-28. Answer A. GFDPP 6-31, AW

Because a front is the boundary between air masses of differing temperatures, one of the easiest ways to recognize frontal passage is the change in temperature.

6-29 PLT511   PA.I.C.K4e

One weather phenomenon that always occurs when flying across a front is a change in the

A – wind direction.

B – type of precipitation.

C – stability of the air mass.

6-29. Answer A. GFDPP 6-31, AW

A shift in wind direction always occurs across a front.

6-30 PLT511   PA.I.C.K4d

Steady precipitation preceding a front is an indication of

A – stratiform clouds with moderate turbulence.

B – cumuliform clouds with little or no turbulence.

C – stratiform clouds with little or no turbulence.

6-30. Answer C. GFDPP 6-23, 32, AW

Steady precipitation, stratiform clouds, and little or no turbulence are all typical of stable air.

6-31 PLT226   PA.I.C.K4j

What situation is most conducive to the formation of radiation fog?

A – Warm, moist air over low, flatland areas on clear, calm nights

B – Moist, tropical air moving over cold, offshore water

C – The movement of cold air over much warmer water

6-31. Answer A. GFDPP 6-23, AW

On clear, calm nights in flat areas, radiation fog forms when moist air cools to its dewpoint. Ground fog is a form of radiation fog.

6-32   PLT226   PA.I.C.K4j

If the temperature/dewpoint spread is small and decreasing, and the temperature is 62°F, what type weather is most likely to develop?

A – Freezing precipitation

B – Thunderstorms

C – Fog or low clouds

6-32. Answer C. GFDPP 6-22, AW

When the temperature/dewpoint spread decreases to zero, the likely result is the condensation of water vapor into visible moisture, such as fog or low clouds.

6-33   PLT226   PA.I.C.K4j

In which situation is advection fog most likely to form?

A – A warm, moist air mass on the windward side of mountains

B – An air mass moving inland from the coast in winter

C – A light breeze blowing colder air out to sea

6-33. Answer B. GFDPP 6-23, AW

On clear, calm nights in flat areas, radiation fog forms when moist air cools to its dewpoint. Ground fog is a form of radiation fog.

When warmer air moves inland, advection fog is likely to form.

6-34   PLT226   PA.I.C.K4j

What types of fog depend upon wind to exist?

A – Radiation fog and ice fog

B – Steam fog and ground fog

C – Advection fog and upslope fog

6-34. Answer C. GFDPP 6-23, AW

On clear, calm nights in flat areas, radiation fog forms when moist air cools to its dewpoint. Ground fog is a form of radiation fog.

When warmer air moves inland, advection fog is likely to form.

6-35   PLT226   PA.I.C.K4j

Low-level turbulence can occur and icing can become hazardous in which type of fog?

A – Rain-induced fog

B – Upslope fog

C – Steam fog

6-35. Answer C. GFDPP 6-23, AW

Steam fog is formed by cold, dry air moving over warmer water. As the water particles evaporate and rise, they often freeze and fall back into the water. Icing and low-level turbulence can result.

SECTION C — WEATHER HAZARDS

As a pilot, you can combine knowledge of the weather with respect for what it can do to avoid flying in the most hazardous conditions. This section covers such hazards as thunderstorms, turbulence, icing, and restrictions to visibility.

THUNDERSTORMS

- Cumulonimbus clouds have the greatest turbulence.
- The conditions necessary for the formation of cumulonimbus clouds are a lifting action and unstable, moist air.
- Thunderstorms are formed when high humidity, lifting force, and unstable conditions combine.
- A non-frontal, narrow band of active thunderstorms that often develops ahead of a cold front is known as a squall line. Squall line thunderstorms generally produce the most intense hazard to aircraft

LIFE CYCLE

- The cumulus stage of a thunderstorm is associated with a continuous updraft.
- The mature stage of a thunderstorm begins with precipitation beginning to fall.
- Thunderstorms reach their greatest intensity during the mature stage.
- The dissipating stage is characterized predominantly by downdrafts.

HAZARDS

- If thunderstorm activity exists in the vicinity of an airport at which you plan to land, you can expect to encounter wind-shear turbulence during the landing approach.
- Lightning is always associated with thunderstorms.

TURBULENCE

- Upon encountering severe turbulence, the pilot should attempt to maintain a level flight attitude.
- Towering cumulus clouds indicate convective turbulence.

WAKE TURBULENCE

- Wingtip vortices are created only when an aircraft is developing lift.
- The greatest vortex strength occurs when the generating aircraft is heavy, clean, and slow.
- Wingtip vortices created by a large aircraft tend to sink below the aircraft that is generating the turbulence.
- When taking off or landing at an airport where heavy aircraft are operating, one should be particularly alert to the hazards of wingtip vortices because this turbulence tends to sink into the flight path of the aircraft operating below the aircraft generating the turbulence.
- The wind condition that requires maximum caution when avoiding wake turbulence on landing is a light, quartering tailwind.

MOUNTAIN WAVE TURBULENCE

- An almond or lens-shaped cloud that appears stationary, but that can contain winds of up to 50 knots or more, is referred to as a lenticular cloud.
- Crests of standing mountain waves are often marked by stationary, lens-shaped clouds known as standing lenticular clouds.
- A pilot can expect possible mountain wave turbulence when winds of 40 knots or greater blow across a mountain ridge, when the air is stable.

WIND SHEAR

- Wind shear can occur at any altitude, in any direction.
- Hazardous wind shear can be expected in areas of low-level temperature inversion, frontal zones, and clear air turbulence.
- A pilot can expect a wind shear zone in a temperature inversion whenever the wind speed at 2,000–4,000 feet above the surface is at least 25 knots.

ICING

- Visible moisture is necessary for the formation of in-flight structural icing.
- Areas of freezing rain create the environment in which structural icing is most likely to have the highest accumulation rate.
- Frost disrupts the smooth flow of air over the wing, adversely affecting its lifting capability.

6-36   PLT192   PA.I.C.K3g

An almond or lens-shaped cloud that appears stationary, but that can contain winds of 50 knots or more, is referred to as

A – an inactive frontal cloud.

B – a funnel cloud.

C – a lenticular cloud.

6-36. Answer C. GFDPP 6-50, AW
Lenticular clouds are the lens-shaped clouds that form at the crests of mountain waves.

6-37   PLT192   PA.I.C.K3g

Crests of standing mountain waves may be marked by stationary, lens-shaped clouds known as

A – mammatocumulus clouds.

B – standing lenticular clouds.

C – roll clouds.

6-37. Answer B. GFDPP 6-50, AW
Lenticular clouds are the lens-shaped clouds that form at the crests of mountain waves.

6-38   PLT192   PA.I.C.K3g

What clouds have the greatest turbulence?

A – Towering cumulus

B – Cumulonimbus

C – Nimbostratus

6-38. Answer B. GFDPP 6-42, AW
Cumulonimbus clouds, which form thunderstorms and tornadoes, produce the most severe turbulence.

6-39   PLT192   PA.I.C.K3g

What cloud types would indicate convective turbulence?

A – Cirrus clouds

B – Nimbostratus clouds

C – Towering cumulus clouds

6-40   PLT518   PA.I.C.K3g

Possible mountain wave turbulence could be anticipated when winds of 40 knots or greater blow

A – across a mountain ridge, and the air is stable.

B – down a mountain valley, and the air is unstable.

C – parallel to a mountain peak, and the air is stable.

6-41   PLT518   PA.I.C.K3g

Where does wind shear occur?

A – Only at higher altitudes

B – Only at lower altitudes

C – At all altitudes, in all directions

6-42   PLT518   PA.I.C.K3g

When may hazardous wind shear be expected?

A – When stable air crosses a mountain barrier where it tends to flow in layers forming lenticular clouds.

B – In areas of low-level temperature inversion, frontal zones, and clear air turbulence.

C – Following frontal passage when stratocumulus clouds form indicating mechanical mixing.

6-43   PLT518   PA.I.C.K3g

A pilot can expect a wind-shear zone in a temperature inversion whenever the wind speed at 2,000 to 4,000 feet above the surface is at least

A – 10 knots.

B – 15 knots.

C – 25 knots.

6-39. Answer C. GFDPP 6-45, AW

Towering cumulus clouds are formed by convective currents, caused by rising heated air. These rising air currents cause convective turbulence.

6-40. Answer A. GFDPP 6-50, AW

Mountain waves are formed when strong winds (40 knots or greater) flow across a barrier, such as a mountain ridge. When the air is stable, the flow is laminar, or layered, and creates a series of waves. Unstable air that is forced upward tends to continue rising, often creating thunderstorms.

6-41. Answer C. GFDPP 6-51, AW

Wind shear can occur at middle and high altitudes near thunderstorms or the jet stream, and near the ground in the vicinity of thunderstorms or temperature inversions. The shear can be either vertical or horizontal.

6-42. Answer B. GFDPP 6-50, 51, AW

Wind shear can be found above a temperature inversion when the surface air is cold and calm, and the warmer layer above it is moving at 25 knots or more. Because frontal zones are identified by a shift in the wind, wind shear can be expected. Clear air turbulence can be associated with either vertical or horizontal wind shear.

6-43. Answer C. GFDPP 6-51, AW

A temperature inversion with light surface winds may form near the surface on a clear night. If the winds at 2,000–4,000 feet are 25 knots or more, you can expect a shear zone in the inversion.

6-44   PLT274   PA.I.C.K3i
One in-flight condition necessary for structural icing to form is

A – small temperature/dewpoint spread.

B – stratiform clouds.

C – visible moisture.

6-44. Answer C. GFDPP 6-53, AW
Structural icing requires two conditions to form: (1) visible moisture, such as rain or cloud droplets, and (2) temperature of the aircraft surface must be at or below freezing. A small temperature/dewpoint spread may be present without visible moisture. Stratiform clouds are not the only cloud types in which icing can occur.

6-45   PLT274   PA.I.C.K3i
In which environment is aircraft structural ice most likely to have the highest accumulation rate?

A – Cumulus clouds with below freezing temperatures

B – Freezing drizzle

C – Freezing rain

6-45. Answer C. GFDPP 6-53, AW
The rate of structural ice accumulation is usually the highest in freezing rain below a frontal surface. As the rain falls through air with temperatures below freezing, it becomes supercooled. The supercooled drops freeze on impact with the large water droplets, and heavy rain accelerates the buildup.

6-46   PLT274   PA.I.C.K3k
Why is frost considered hazardous to flight?

A – Frost changes the basic aerodynamic shape of the airfoils, decreasing lift.

B – Frost slows the airflow over the airfoils, increasing control effectiveness.

C – Frost spoils the smooth flow of air over the wings, decreasing lifting capability.

6-46. Answer C. GFDPP 6-20, AW
Frost disrupts the smooth airflow over the wing and can cause early separation of the airflow, resulting in a loss of lift.

6-47   PLT274   PA.I.C.K3k
How does frost affect the lifting surfaces of an airplane on takeoff?

A – Frost may prevent the airplane from becoming airborne at normal takeoff speed.

B – Frost changes the camber of the wing, increasing lift during takeoff.

C – Frost may cause the airplane to become airborne with a lower angle of attack at a lower indicated airspeed.

6-47. Answer A. GFDPP 6-20, AW
Frost disrupts the smooth airflow over the wing and can cause early separation of the airflow, resulting in a loss of lift.

By disrupting the airflow over the wings, frost can prevent an airplane from becoming airborne at the normal takeoff speed.

6-48   PLT134   PA.I.C.K3k

How does frost on the wings of an airplane affect takeoff performance?

A – Frost disrupts the smooth flow of air over the wing, adversely affecting its lifting capability.

B – Frost changes the camber of the wing, increasing its lifting capability.

C – Frost causes the airplane to become airborne with a higher angle of attack, decreasing the stall speed.

6-48. Answer A. GFDPP 6-20, PHB

Frost disrupts the smooth airflow over the wing and can cause early separation of the airflow, resulting in a loss of lift.

6-49   PLT192   PA.I.C.K3h

The conditions necessary for the formation of cumulonimbus clouds are a lifting action and

A – unstable air containing an excess of condensation nuclei.

B – unstable, moist air.

C – either stable or unstable air.

6-49. Answer B. GFDPP 6-38,42, AW

Three conditions are normally required for the formation of cumulonimbus clouds—lifting action, instability, and moisture.

6-50   PLT495   PA.I.C.K3h

What feature is normally associated with the cumulus stage of a thunderstorm?

A – Roll cloud

B – Continuous updraft

C – Frequent lightning

6-50. Answer B. GFDPP 6-40, AW

In the early, or cumulus, stage of a thunderstorm, continuous updrafts cause the cloud to build upwards.

6-51   PLT495   PA.I.C.K3h

Which weather phenomenon signals the beginning of the mature stage of a thunderstorm?

A – The appearance of an anvil top

B – Precipitation beginning to fall

C – Maximum growth rate of the clouds

6-51. Answer B. GFDPP 6-41, AW

The mature stage of a thunderstorm begins when the rain drops grow too large to be supported by the updrafts, and precipitation begins to fall.

6-52   PLT271   PA.I.C.K3h

The destination airport has one runway, 08-26, and the wind is calm. The normal approach in calm wind is a left-hand pattern to runway 08. No other traffic is at the airport. A thunderstorm about 6 miles west is beginning its mature stage, and rain is starting to reach the ground. The pilot decides to

A – fly the pattern to runway 08 because the storm is too far away to affect the wind at the airport.

B – fly the normal pattern to runway 08 because the storm is west and moving north and any unexpected wind will be from the east or southeast toward the storm.

C – fly an approach to runway 26 because any unexpected wind due to the storm will be westerly.

6-52. Answer C. GFDPP 6C, AW

The outflow from a mature thunderstorm west of the airport could create significant winds from the west. If landing on Runway 08, the aircraft could experience a dangerous sheer to a tailwind. Landing to the west, on Runway 26, is the best choice. In addition, a Runway 26 traffic pattern is on the east side of the airport, farther away from the storm.

6-53   PLT495   PA.I.C.K3h

What conditions are necessary for the formation of thunderstorms?

A – High humidity, lifting force, and unstable conditions

B – High humidity, high temperature, and cumulus clouds

C – Lifting force, moist air, and extensive cloud cover

6-53. Answer A. GFDPP 6-38, AW

Three conditions are normally required for the formation of cumulonimbus clouds—lifting action, instability, and moisture.

As moist, unstable air is lifted, it builds cumulonimbus clouds, which form thunderstorms.

6-54   PLT495   PA.I.C.K3h

During the life cycle of a thunderstorm, which stage is characterized predominately by downdrafts?

A – Cumulus

B – Dissipating

C – Mature

6-54. Answer B. GFDPP 6-41, AW

As moist, unstable air is lifted, it builds cumulonimbus clouds, which form thunderstorms.

The mature stage of a thunderstorm begins when the rain drops grow too large to be supported by the updrafts, and precipitation begins to fall.

As a thunderstorm dissipates, updrafts weaken and downdrafts become predominate.

6-55   PLT495   PA.I.C.K3h

Thunderstorms reach their greatest intensity during the

A – mature stage.

B – downdraft stage.

C – cumulus stage.

6-55. Answer A. GFDPP 6-41, AW

Thunderstorms are most violent during the mature stage, with strong updrafts and downdrafts, severe turbulence, lightning, heavy rain, hail, strong surface winds, and gust fronts.

6-56   PLT495   PA.I.C.K3h

Thunderstorms that generally produce the most intense hazard to aircraft are

A – squall line thunderstorms.

B – steady-state thunderstorms.

C – warm front thunderstorms.

6-56. Answer A. GFDPP 6-39, AW
Squall lines often contain severe steady-state thunderstorms and present the most hazardous conditions to aircraft.

6-57   PLT495   PA.I.C.K3h

A nonfrontal, narrow band of active thunderstorms that often develop ahead of a cold front is known as a

A – prefrontal system.

B – squall line.

C – dry line.

6-57. Answer B. GFDPP 6-39, AW
Squall lines are a narrow band of thunderstorms that often develop ahead of a cold front.

6-58   PLT495   PA.I.C.K3h

If thunderstorm activity is in the vicinity of an airport at which you plan to land, which hazardous atmospheric phenomenon might be expected on the landing approach?

A – Precipitation static

B – Wind-shear turbulence

C – Steady rain

6-58. Answer B. GFDPP 6-50, AW
In the vicinity of thunderstorms, hazardous wind-shear turbulence should always be expected.

6-59   PLT501   PA.I.C.K3g

Upon encountering severe turbulence, which flight condition should the pilot attempt to maintain?

A – Constant altitude and airspeed

B – Constant angle of attack

C – Level flight attitude

6-59. Answer C. GFDPP 6-44, AW
If entering severe turbulence, the best procedure is to slow to a speed not faster than maneuvering airspeed and maintain a constant level flight attitude. Variations in airspeed and altitude should be expected and tolerated.

6-60   PLT495   PA.I.C.K3h

Which weather phenomenon is always associated with a thunderstorm?

A – Lightning

B – Heavy rain

C – Hail

6-60. Answer A. GFDPP 6-43, AW
Because lightning causes thunder, lightning is always associated with a thunderstorm.

6-61   PLT509   PA.II.F.K4

Wingtip vortices are created only when an aircraft is

A – operating at high airspeeds.

B – heavily loaded.

C – developing lift.

6-61. Answer C. GFDPP 6-47, PHB

Any time an aircraft is developing lift, air flows over the wingtip to form wingtip vortices.

6-62   PLT509   PA.IV.A.R2d

The greatest vortex strength occurs when the generating aircraft is

A – light, dirty, and fast.

B – heavy, dirty, and fast.

C – heavy, clean, and slow.

6-62. Answer C. GFDPP 6-47, PHB

Heavy aircraft, in a clean configuration, flying at low airspeeds with high angles of attack, generate the strongest vortices.

6-63   PLT509   PA.IV.A.R2d

Wingtip vortices created by large aircraft tend to

A – sink below the aircraft generating turbulence.

B – rise into the traffic pattern.

C – rise into the takeoff or landing path of a crossing runway.

6-63. Answer A. GFDPP 6-47, PHB

Wingtip vortices tend to sink below the flight path of the aircraft that generated them.

6-64   PLT509   PA.IV.A.R2d

When taking off or landing at an airport where heavy aircraft are operating, pilots should be alert to the hazards of wingtip vortices because this turbulence tends to

A – rise from a crossing runway into the takeoff or landing path.

B – rise into the traffic pattern area surrounding the airport.

C – sink into the flight path of aircraft operating below the aircraft generating the turbulence.

6-64. Answer C. GFDPP 6-47, PHB

Wingtip vortices tend to sink below the flight path of the aircraft that generated them.

6-65   PLT509   PA.IV.B.R2d

The wind condition that requires maximum caution when avoiding wake turbulence on landing is a

A – light, quartering headwind.

B – light, quartering tailwind.

C – strong headwind.

6-65. Answer B. GFDPP 6-47, AIM

A light, quartering tailwind is the most hazardous because it can move the upwind vortex over the runway and forward into the landing zone.

6-66   PLT509   PA.IV.B.R2d

When landing behind a large aircraft, the pilot should avoid wake turbulence by staying

A – above the large aircraft's final approach path and landing beyond the large aircraft's touchdown point.

B – below the large aircraft's final approach path and landing before the large aircraft's touchdown point.

C – above the large aircraft's final approach path and landing before the large aircraft's touchdown point.

6-66. Answer A. GFDPP 6-47, PHB
Because wake turbulence tends to sink, an aircraft that is a large aircraft should stay above the large aircraft's flight path and land beyond its touchdown point.

6-67   PLT509   PA.IV.A.R2d

When departing behind a heavy aircraft, the pilot should avoid wake turbulence by maneuvering the aircraft

A – below and downwind from the heavy aircraft.

B – above and upwind from the heavy aircraft.

C – below and upwind from the heavy aircraft.

6-67. Answer B. GFDPP 6-47, AIM
Because wake turbulence tends to sink and drift downwind, an aircraft should stay above and upwind of the preceding aircraft.

6-68   PLT509   PA.IV.B.R2d

When landing behind a large aircraft, which procedure should be followed for vortex avoidance?

A – Stay above its final approach flight path all the way to touchdown.

B – Stay below and to one side of its final approach flight path.

C – Stay well below its final approach flight path and land at least 2,000 feet behind.

6-68. Answer A. GFDPP 6-47, AIM
Vortices (wake turbulence) are generated at the wingtips of an airplane whenever the wings are producing lift. Wingtip vortices tend to sink below the flight path of the generating airplane. Therefore, remaining above the glide path and landing beyond the touchdown point of a large airplane is a recommended practice to avoid wake turbulence.

6-69   PLT509   PA.II.F.R3

How does the wake turbulence vortex circulate around each wingtip?

A – Inward, upward, and around each tip

B – Inward, upward, and counterclockwise

C – Outward, upward, and around each tip

6-69. Answer C. GFDPP 6-47, PHB
Wake turbulence vortices are a by-product of lift. They move outward, upward and around each wingtip.

CHAPTER 7

INTERPRETING WEATHER DATA

SECTION A — THE FORECASTING PROCESS

No FAA questions

SECTION B — PRINTED REPORTS AND FORECASTS

By learning to interpret printed weather reports and forecasts, you add to your ability to visualize the weather patterns that affect your flying.

WEATHER REPORTS
Weather reports give information about observed weather conditions.

METARS
- Winds on an aviation routine weather report are referenced to true north.
- Peak gusts on an aviation routine weather report are denoted by a number following a "G" after the wind direction and base speed.
- Cloud heights or visibility into an obscuration are reported with three digits in hundreds of feet. Visibility is reported in statute miles and is indicated by the abbreviation "SM."
- For aviation purposes, ceiling is defined as the height above the surface of the earth of the lowest broken or overcast layer or vertical visibility into an obscuration.
- The definition of VFR is visibility of at least 3 miles and a ceiling of at least 1,000 feet.
- The remarks section of a METAR is used to report weather considered significant to aircraft operations. The contraction "RMK" precedes the remarks.

PIREPS
- In a PIREP, identified by the letters "UA," sky condition is designated by the letters "SK," followed by the base and top of each cloud layer.
- The wind direction and velocity in a PIREP are shown as "WV" followed by the direction and speed, with the last digit of the wind direction dropped.
- The ceiling is the lowest cloud layer reported as broken, overcast, or obscured.
- Turbulence is reported in a PIREP as "TB" followed by an intensity designation, such as "SVR," "MDT," or "LGT." The altitude of the turbulence layer is also reported.
- Icing is reported in a PIREP after the letters "IC"—followed by the intensity of the icing, and the altitude of the layers in which it was encountered.

WEATHER FORECASTS
Weather forecasts predict future weather conditions.

TERMINAL AERODROME FORECASTS (TAFS)

- TAFs are usually valid for a 24-hour period and are scheduled four times a day (0000Z, 0600Z, 1200Z, and 1800Z). The six-digit issuance date-time group is followed by the valid date-time group.

- In a TAF, the abbreviation "SHRA" stands for rain showers.

- The abbreviation "BECMG" precedes a gradual change in the weather with the Zulu time period over which the weather is forecast to change. For example, "BECMG 1012" means that the weather change is expected to occur between 1000Z and 1200Z. The time frame is followed by the change expected, such as "3 SM" would mean the visibility is forecast to change to three statute miles.

- When rapid changes in the forecast are expected (usually within one hour), the code "FM" is used. When the abbreviation "VRB" appears before the wind speed, the wind is expected to be variable at that speed.

- A change group is used when a significant, lasting change to the weather conditions is forecast during the valid time.

- Wind blocks read as follows: wind direction comes first, followed by speed, and then any gust factor expected. Ceilings are written with the amount of coverage, followed by the cloudbase height, in hundreds of feet.

- The code "NSW" means that no significant weather change is forecast to occur.

- Cumulonimbus clouds are the only cloud type included in the TAFs.

WINDS AND TEMPERATURES ALOFT FORECASTS (FDs)

- The first two digits represent the wind direction in relation to true north. The next two digits are the speed. Temperatures follow the wind block. Temperatures are assumed to be negative above 24,000 feet MSL.

- Winds of 100 to 199 knots have 50 added to the direction. For example, when you observe a wind direction above 360, subtract 50 to get wind direction, and add 100 to the listed wind speed.

- "Light and variable" in a winds aloft forecast is coded as 9900 for forecast winds less than five knots.

SEVERE WEATHER REPORTS AND FORECASTS

Severe weather reports and forecasts alert pilots to hazardous flight conditions, both potential and actual.

AIRMETS AND SIGMETS

- An AIRMET is a warning of weather conditions that hazardous primarily to small, single-engine aircraft.

- A SIGMET is a warning of weather conditions hazardous to all aircraft.

- A SIGMET contains information on severe icing, because it is a hazard to all aircraft.

CONVECTIVE SIGMETS

- Tornadoes, embedded thunderstorms, and hail 3/4 inch or greater in diameter are all weather phenomenon contained within a convective SIGMET.

- The embedded thunderstorms forecast in a convective SIGMET are thunderstorms that are expected to be obscured by massive cloud layers.

7-1   PLT059   PA.I.C.K4l

(Refer to figure 12.)

Which of the reporting stations have VFR weather?

A – All

B – KINK, KBOI, and KJFK

C – KINK, KBOI, and KLAX

7-1. Answer C. GFDPP 7B, AWS

To answer this question, you must know that the definition of VFR is visibility of at least three statute miles and ceiling of at least 1,000 feet. KINK has 15 miles visibility with clear skies, KBOI has 30 miles visibility with a scattered layer at 15,000 feet, and KLAX has 6 miles visibility, with scattered layers at 700 feet and 25,000 feet. Remember, a scattered layer does not constitute a ceiling.

7-2   PLT026   PA.I.C.K4f

For aviation purposes, ceiling is defined as the height above the earth's surface of the

A – lowest reported obscuration and the highest layer of clouds reported as overcast.

B – lowest broken or overcast layer or vertical visibility into an obscuration.

C – lowest layer of clouds reported as scattered, broken, or thin.

7-2. Answer B. GFDPP 7B, AWS

According to Aviation Weather Services, AC 00-45, a ceiling is defined as the lowest broken or overcast layer, or vertical visibility into an obscuration.

7-3   PLT059   PA.I.C.K4l

(Refer to Figure 12.)
The wind direction and velocity at KJFK is from

A – 180° true at 4 knots.

B – 180° magnetic at 4 knots.

C – 040° true at 18 knots.

7-3. Answer A. GFDPP 7B, AWS

The wind entry for KJFK is "18004KT," meaning the wind is from 180 degrees at four knots. Winds on an aviation routine weather report are referenced to true north.

7-4   PLT059   PA.I.C.K4l

(Refer to Figure 12.) What are the wind conditions at Wink, Texas (KINK)?

A – Calm

B – 110° at 12 knots, peak gusts 18 knots

C – 111° at 2 knots, peak gusts 18 knots

7-4. Answer B. GFDPP 7B, AWS

The wind entry for KINK is "11012G18KT," meaning the wind direction is 110 degrees, and the velocity is 12 knots, with peak gusts of 18 knots.

7-5   PLT059   PA.I.C.K4l

(Refer to Figure 12.) The remarks section for KMDW has RAB35 listed. This entry means

A – blowing mist has reduced the visibility to 1-1/2 SM.

B – rain began at 1835Z.

C – the barometer has risen 0.35 inches Hg.

7-5. Answer B. GFDPP 7B, AWS

The remarks section of a METAR is used to report weather considered significant to aircraft operations. The contraction "RMK" precedes remarks, which include the beginning and ending times of certain weather phenomena. In this case, "RAB35" means that the rain began at 35 minutes past the hour, or 1835Z.

7-6   PLT059   PA.I.C.K4l
(Refer to Figure 12.) What are the current conditions depicted for Chicago Midway Airport (KMDW)?

A – Sky 700 feet overcast, visibility 1-1/2 SM, rain

B – Sky 7000 feet overcast, visibility 1-1/2 SM, heavy rain

C – Sky 700 feet overcast, visibility 11, occasionally 2SM, with rain

7-6. Answer A. GFDPP 7B, AWS
Cloud heights or the vertical visibility into an obscuration is reported with three digits in hundreds of feet. Visibility is reported in statute miles (SM). In this case, the METAR from KMDW indicates that Midway's visibility is 1-1/2 miles and the sky is overcast at 700 feet. "RA" indicates precipitation in the form of rain.

7-7   PLT061   PA.I.C.K4o
(Refer to Figure 14.) The base and tops of the overcast layer reported by a pilot are

A – 1,800 feet MSL and 5,500 feet MSL.

B – 5,500 feet AGL and 7,200 feet MSL.

C – 7,200 feet MSL and 8,900 feet MSL.

7-7. Answer C. GFDPP 7B, AWS
In the PIREP, which is identified by the letters, UA, sky cover is designated by the letters, SK, followed by the base and top of each cloud layer. The overcast layer is shown as OVC 072-TOP 089, which means the base is 7,200 feet and the tops are 8,900 feet. Altitudes are MSL unless otherwise noted.

7-8   PLT061   PA.I.C.K4o
(Refer to Figure 14.) The wind and temperature at 12,000 feet MSL as reported by a pilot are

A – 080° at 21 knots and -7°C.

B – 090° at 21 MPH and -9°F.

C – 090° at 21 knots and -9°C.

7-8. Answer A. GFDPP 7B, AWS
The ambient temperature and wind velocity appear in the part of the pilot report that says "/TA M7/WV 08021/". All temperatures aloft are given in degrees Celsius, and the "M" indicates temperatures below zero. Wind speed is reported in knots.

7-9   PLT061   PA.I.C.K4o
(Refer to Figure 14.)
If the terrain elevation is 1,295 feet MSL, what is the height above ground level of the base of the ceiling?

A – 505 feet AGL

B – 1,295 feet AGL

C – 6,586 feet AGL

7-9. Answer A. GFDPP 7B, AWS
The ceiling is the lowest cloud layer reported as broken, overcast, or obscured. In this case, the lowest layer is 1,800 feet broken (MSL). To find the AGL height, subtract the ground elevation (1,800 – 1,295 = 505 feet AGL).

7-10   PLT061   PA.I.C.K4o
(Refer to Figure 14.) The intensity of the turbulence reported at a specific altitude is

A – moderate from 5,500 feet to 7,200 feet.

B – moderate at 5,500 feet and at 7,200 feet.

C – light from 5,500 feet to 7,200 feet.

7-10. Answer C. GFDPP 7B, AWS
Turbulence is reported as "/TB LGT 055-072/", meaning light turbulence between 5,500 and 7,200 feet MSL.

7-11   PLT061   PA.I.C.K4o
(Refer to Figure 14.)
The intensity and type of icing reported by a pilot is

A – light to moderate rime.

B – light to moderate.

C – light to moderate clear.

7-11. Answer A. GFDPP 7B, AWS
Icing intensity and type is shown in this pilot report (PIREP) as "/IC LGT-MDT RIME/" or light to moderate rime.

7-12   PLT072   PA.I.C.K4l
(Refer to Figure 15.)
What is the valid period for the TAF for KMEM?

A – 1200Z to 1200Z

B – 1200Z to 1800Z

C – 1800Z to 1800Z

7-12. Answer C. GFDPP 7B, AWS
TAFs are usually valid for a 24-hour period and are scheduled four times a day (0000Z, 0600Z, 1200Z, and 1800Z). The six-digit issuance date-time group is followed by the valid date-time group. Therefore, "121720Z 121818" indicates that the KMEM TAF was issued on the 12th at 1720 Zulu. This report is valid from 1800 Zulu on the 12th until 1800 Zulu on the 13th.

7-13   PLT072   PA.I.C.K4l
(Refer to Figure 15.) In the TAF for KMEM, what does "SHRA" stand for?

A – Rain showers are expected.

B – A shift in wind direction is expected.

C – A significant change in precipitation is possible.

7-13. Answer A. GFDPP 7B, AWS
This group of the TAF, "PROB40 2202 3SM SHRA," indicates a 40-percent probability, between 2200 Zulu and 0200 Zulu, that the visibility will be 3 statute miles with showery precipitation or rain showers (SHRA). The next entry, "FM0200 35012KT OVC008" indicates, from 0200 Zulu, the wind is expected to be from 350° at 12 knots.

7-14   PLT072   PA.I.C.K4l
(Refer to Figure 15.) Between 1000Z and 1200Z, the visibility at KMEM is forecast to be?

A – 1/2 statute mile

B – 3 statute miles

C – 6 statute miles

7-14. Answer B. GFDPP 7B, AWS
During a specified time period, when changes in the weather conditions are forecast, a change group is appended to the forecast. In this case, "BECMG 1012" indicates that a change in the weather will occur between 1000Z and 1200Z. The "3SM" indicates that the visibility is forecast to become 3 statute miles.

7-15   PLT072   PA.I.C.K4l
(Refer to Figure 15.) What is the forecast wind for KMEM from 1600Z until the end of the forecast?

A – Variable in direction at 6 knots

B – No significant wind

C – Variable in direction at 4 knots

7-15. Answer A. GFDPP 7B, AWS
This part of the forecast reads, "FM1600 VRB06KT P6SM SKC=" From 1600Z until the end of forecast, the wind is variable in direction at 6 knots, with visibility greater than 6 miles.

7-16   PLT072   PA.I.C.K4l
(Refer to Figure 15.) In the TAF from KOKC, the "FM (FROM) Group" is forecast for the hours from 1600Z to 2200Z with the wind from

A – 180° at 10 knots, becoming 200° at 13 knots.

B – 160° at 10 knots.

C – 180° at 10 knots.

7-16. Answer C. GFDPP 7B, AWS
The code "FM" followed by the time, indicates a rapid change in the forecast conditions starting at that time. 18010KT indicates wind from 180 degrees at 10 knots. "BECMG 2224" means that the next change will happen gradually from 2200 to 2400Z.

7-17   PLT072   PA.I.C.K4l
(Refer to Figure 15.)
In the TAF from KOKC, the clear sky becomes

A – overcast at 2,000 feet during the forecast period between 2200Z and 2400Z.

B – overcast at 200 feet with a 40% probability of becoming overcast at 600 feet during the forecast period between 2200Z and 2400Z.

C – overcast at 200 feet with the probability of becoming overcast at 400 feet during the forecast period between 2200Z and 2400Z.

7-17. Answer A. GFDPP 7B, AWS
When a gradual change in the forecast weather is expected, the becoming (BECMG) change group is used, followed by the beginning and ending times. The TAF from KOKC, "BECMG 2224 20013G20KT 4SM SHRA OVC020" means between 2200Z and 2400Z the weather will gradually change to winds from 200° at 13 knots gusting to 20 knots, 4 miles visibility in rain showers, and overcast skies at 2,000 feet.

7-18   PLT072   PA.I.C.K4l
(Refer to Figure 15.)
During the time period from 0600Z to 0800Z, what visibility is forecast for KOKC?

A – Greater than six statute miles

B – Not forecasted

C – Possibly six statute miles

7-18. Answer A. GFDPP 7B, AWS
This section reads, "BECMG 0608 21015KT P6SM SCT040=." These abbreviations mean that between 0600-0800Z, the wind will become 210° at 15 knots, visibility is forecast to be more than (not possibly) 6 statute miles, and clouds will become scattered at 4,000 feet.

7-19   PLT072   PA.I.C.K4l
(Refer to Figure 15.)
The only cloud type forecast in TAF reports is

A – Nimbostratus.

B – Cumulonimbus.

C – Scattered cumulus.

7-19. Answer B. GFDPP 7B, AWS
If cumulonimbus clouds are expected at the airport, the contraction "CB" is appended to the height of the cloud layer to indicate the base of the cumulonimbus cloud.

7-20   PLT294   PA.I.C.K2

To determine the freezing level and areas of probable icing aloft, the pilot should refer to the

A – inflight aviation weather advisories.

B – area forecast.

C – weather depiction chart.

7-20. Answer A. GFDPP 7B, AWS

Freezing level and icing aloft are contained in in-flight weather advisories, which include SIGMETs, convective SIGMETs, AIRMETs, alert service weather watch bulletins (AWWs), center weather advisories (CWAs), and urgent PIREPs. These advisories are broadcast over hazardous in-flight weather advisory service (HIWAS) or provided by Flight Service.

7-21   PLT067   PA.I.C.K3

What is indicated when a CONVECTIVE SIGMET forecasts thunderstorms?

A – Moderate thunderstorms covering 30 percent of the area

B – Moderate or severe turbulence

C – Thunderstorms obscured by massive cloud layers

7-21. Answer C. GFDPP 7B, AIM

Convective SIGMETs forecast level 4 thunderstorms (very strong, not moderate) covering 40 percent (not 30 percent) of an area. They also are issued for embedded thunderstorms; those obscured by massive cloud layers. All convective SIGMETs imply severe or greater turbulence, not moderate turbulence.

7-22   PLT067   PA.I.C.K3

What information is contained in a CONVECTIVE SIGMET?

A – Tornadoes, embedded thunderstorms, and hail 3/4 inch or greater in diameter

B – Severe icing, severe turbulence, or widespread duststorms lowering visibility to less than 3 miles

C – Surface winds greater than 40 knots or thunderstorms equal to or greater than video integrator processor (VIP) level 4

7-22. Answer A. GFDPP 7B, AIM

Convective SIGMETs are issued for any of the following phenomena: tornadoes, lines of thunderstorms, embedded thunderstorms, areas of level 4 thunderstorms covering 40 percent of the area, and hail of 3/4 inch or greater in diameter.

7-23   PLT067   PA.I.C.K3

SIGMETs are issued as a warning of weather conditions hazardous to which aircraft?

A – Small aircraft only

B – Large aircraft only

C – All aircraft

7-23. Answer C. GFDPP 7B, AWS

SIGMETs are issued for weather potentially hazardous to all aircraft. An AIRMET advises of weather that is of operational interest to all aircraft, but that could be hazardous to aircraft with limited capabilities, such as light single-engine airplanes.

7-24   PLT290   PA.I.C.K3
Which in-flight advisory would contain information on severe icing not associated with thunderstorms?

A – Convective SIGMET

B – SIGMET

C – AIRMET

7-24. Answer B. GFDPP 7B, AWS
A SIGMET advises of weather potentially hazardous to all aircraft, which would include severe icing. A convective SIGMET is an advisory of especially hazardous thunderstorm activity.

7-25   PLT290   PA.I.C.K3
AIRMETs are advisories of significant weather phenomena but of lower intensities than SIGMETs and are intended for dissemination to

A – only IFR pilots.

B – all pilots.

C – only VFR pilots.

7-25. Answer B. GFDPP 7B, AWS
An AIRMET advises of weather that is of operational interest to all aircraft, but may be hazardous to aircraft with limited capabilities, such as light single-engine airplanes.

7-26   PLT076   PA.I.C.K3
(Refer to Figure 17.)
What wind is forecast for STL at 9,000 feet?

A – 230° true at 32 knots

B – 230° magnetic at 25 knots

C – 230° true at 25 knots

7-26. Answer A. GFDPP 7B, AWS
In the Winds and Temperatures Aloft Forecast (FD), directions are relative to TRUE NORTH and rounded to the nearest 10 degrees. The wind information is given as 2332+02. The first two digits represent the wind direction in relation to true north, 230°. The next two digits are the speed, which in this case is 32 knots. The temperature is +2°C.

7-27   PLT076   PA.I.C.K3
(Refer to Figure 17.)
What wind is forecast for STL at 12,000 feet?

A – 230° true at 56 knots

B – 230° true at 39 knots

C – 230° magnetic at 56 knots

7-27. Answer B. GFDPP 7B, AWS
In the Winds and Temperatures Aloft Forecast (FD), directions are relative to TRUE NORTH and rounded to the nearest 10 degrees. The wind entry for STL at 12,000 feet is 2339–04. The first two digits represent the wind direction, 230° true. The next two digits are the speed, 39 knots. The temperature is –4°C.

7-28   PLT076   PA.I.C.K3
What values are used for Winds Aloft Forecasts?

A – Magnetic direction and knots

B – Magnetic direction and miles per hour

C – True direction and knots

7-28. Answer C. GFDPP 7B, AWS
All forecast and ASOS/AWOS-reported winds are given in true direction, and speed is always in knots. The only time wind direction is given in magnetic is when it is provided by the Tower or ATIS.

7-29   PLT076   PA.I.C.K3

When the term "light and variable" is used in a winds aloft forecast, the coded group and wind speed is

A – 0000 and less than 7 knots.

B – 9900 and less than 5 knots.

C – 9999 and less than 10 knots.

7-29. Answer B. GFDPP 7B, AWS

The direction is shown as 99, which means the direction is variable. When the second two digits are listed as 00, the speed is less than 5 knots.

SECTION C — GRAPHIC WEATHER PRODUCTS

Graphic weather products help you grasp the overall weather picture by giving you maps of actual and forecast patterns.

GRAPHIC REPORTS

Graphic weather reports use information gathered from ground observations, weather radar, satellites, and other sources to give you a pictorial view of large-scale weather patterns and trends.

SURFACE ANALYSIS CHART

A stationary front is depicted with rounded warm front symbols on one side and triangular cold front symbols on the opposite side.

RADAR PRODUCTS

- WSR-88D (NexRad) radars continuously generate radar observations. Each radar observation, called a volume scan, consists of 5 to 14 separate elevation "tilts," and takes between 4 and 11 minutes to generate, depending on the mode of operation of the radar.
- NexRad radar reflects off precipitation and reports its intensity, but does not show clouds or fog.
- Next-gen near-real-time radar weather maps are disseminated through Flight Service (**1800wxbrief.com**), the Aviation Weather Center (**AviationWeather.gov**), and overlaid on in-cockpit moving maps in FIS-B- and XM-weather-equipped aircraft.
- Study the legends on your system to interpret the intensity on your radar display; reflectivity is normally displayed with some variations using the following colors: green—light echoes (up to 30 dbZ), yellow to orange—moderate echoes (30–45 dbZ), red to magenta—heavy echoes (50–60 dbZ and higher).
- Arrows or similar symbols can show the direction of movement of a radar echo, or many displays animate the motion (past and projected). Some displays label the height of selected echoes in hundreds of feet MSL.
- Always verify the age or the time of a radar depiction, which should be prominently shown on any active radar display, and know that the echoes depicted are often 10–20 minutes old, and often older than the time shown on the display.

GRAPHIC FORECASTS

Graphic forecasts take reported conditions and trends and extrapolate future weather from them, displaying these predictions pictorially.

SIGNIFICANT WEATHER PROGNOSTIC CHART

- The significant weather prognostic charts are best used by a pilot for determining areas to avoid, due to freezing levels and turbulence.
- Short-range surface prognostic (prog) charts provide depictions of forecast surface pressure systems, fronts, and precipitation.
- Low-level significant weather (SIGWX) charts provide depictions of forecast aviation weather hazards such as MFVR and IFR conditions, turbulence, and freezing levels.
- A dashed line represents the freezing level. Numbers on this line show the altitude of the freezing level in hundreds of feet MSL.

7-30   PLT037   PA.I.C.K2

Radar weather reports are of special interest to pilots because they indicate

A – location of precipitation along with type, intensity, and cell movement of precipitation.

B – location of precipitation along with type, intensity, and trend.

C – large areas of low ceilings and fog.

7-30. Answer A. GFDPP 7C, AWS

Radar weather reports show areas of precipitation; type, such as rain showers; intensity, such as light or heavy; and azimuth of movement.

7-31   PLT068   PA.I.C.K2

How are low-level significant weather (sigwx) prognostic charts best used by a pilot?

A – For overall planning at all altitudes

B – For determining areas to avoid (freezing levels and turbulence)

C – For analyzing current frontal activity and cloud coverage

7-31. Answer B. GFDPP 7C, AWS

Low-level SIGWX charts depict weather flying categories, turbulence, and freezing levels. In flight icing is not depicted on the low-level SIGWX chart.

7-32   PLT068   PA.I.C.K2

Short-range surface prognostic (prog) charts provide depictions of forecast

A – surface pressure systems, fronts, and precipitation.

B – aviation weather hazards such as MFVR and IFR conditions, turbulence, and freezing levels.

C – areas of probable turbulence, icing, and IFR conditions.

7-32. Answer A. GFDPP 7C, AWS

The short-range surface prognostic (prog) chart provides depictions of surface pressure systems, fronts, and precipitation. It is available in five forecast periods: 12, 18, 24, 48, and 60 hours. Each chart depicts a "snapshot" of weather elements expected at the specified valid time.

MVFR and IFR conditions, and areas of probable turbulence are shown on SIGWX, not surface prog, charts. Icing is not specifically forecast on either SIGWX or surface prog charts.

7-33   PLT068   PA.I.C.K2

Low-level significant weather (SIGWX) charts provide depictions of forecast

A – surface pressure systems and fronts.

B – aviation weather hazards such as MFVR and IFR conditions, turbulence, and freezing levels.

C – areas of probable precipitation, including ice, snow, and thunderstorms.

7-33. Answer B. GFDPP 7C, AWS

Low-level significant weather (SIGWX) charts cover altitudes up to flight level 240. They forecast aviation weather hazards to be used as guidance for pre-flight briefings, including flying categories (MFVR, IFR), turbulence, and freezing levels. They provide a "snapshot" of weather expected at the valid time, 12 or 24 hours after chart issuance.

Surface pressure systems, fronts, and areas of probable precipitation are depicted on the surface prog chart, not the low-level SIGWX chart.

7-34   PLT063   PA.I.C.K6

What considerations apply when using a cockpit display of radar data obtained from FIS-B?

A – Echoes and terrain that are close to your aircraft can shield echoes that are farther away.

B – The radar echoes that are depicted on the cockpit display can sometimes be more than 20 minutes old.

C – The in-cockpit radar display lacks the accuracy and integrity of radar mosaics obtained from Flight Service.

7-34. Answer B. GFDPP 7D, AWS

FIS-B can provide METARs, TAFs, a high-quality radar mosaic, and other information. While echoes and terrain can shield convective activity that is behind them, this shielding affects the activity as seen from NEXRAD radar antenna. They are not a factor from the airplane position because the radar signal is not transmitted from the airplane. The main concern with in-cockpit radar is that the data can be up to 20 minutes older than the age shown on the display and significant changes can occur over that time.

SECTION D — SOURCES OF WEATHER INFORMATION

PREFLIGHT WEATHER SOURCES

You can get preflight weather information from a variety of media, including television and on-line sources. Flight Service remains the primary source for aviation weather briefings.

- You can obtain an official weather briefing by calling 1-800-WX-BRIEF or by going to **1800wxbrief.com**.
- When calling a weather briefing facility for preflight weather information, state the aircraft identification or your name. Also state the intended route, destination, type of aircraft and whether you intend to fly VFR only. When using the Flight Service website, you provide this information in a flight plan form.
- To get a complete weather briefing for the planned flight, request a standard briefing.
- To supplement mass-disseminated data, or to update a previous briefing, request an abbreviated briefing.
- An outlook briefing is the weather briefing provided when the information requested is six or more hours before the proposed departure time. When requesting information for the following morning, ask for an outlook briefing.

IN-FLIGHT WEATHER SOURCES

Often, you need to receive updated information during flight. To obtain in-flight weather information, contact Flight Service.

- Obtain actual weather information and thunderstorm activity along the route from Flight Service.
- Refer to communication boxes on VFR charts or your navigation database for nearby Flight Service frequencies.
- Flight information service-broadcast (FIS-B) can provide updated weather forecasts and conditions at airports along your route, if your airplane is properly equipped.
- When using an FIS-B radar mosaic to avoid thunderstorm activity, know that the echoes you see on your screen can be up to 20 minutes old, and that significant changes can occur during that time period.

7-35   PLT513   PA.I.C.K1

When telephoning a weather briefing facility for preflight weather information, pilots should state

A – the aircraft identification or the pilot's name.

B – true airspeed.

C – fuel on board.

7-35. Answer A. GFDPP 7-44, AWS
Pilots should give their name or the aircraft number, and other information, to the weather briefer.

7-36   PLT514   PA.I.C.K1

To get a complete weather briefing for the planned flight, the pilot should request

A – a general briefing.

B – an abbreviated briefing.

C – a standard briefing.

7-36. Answer C. GFDPP 7-45, AIM
A standard briefing is the most compete type of weather briefing.

7-37   PLT514   PA.I.C.K1

Which type weather briefing should a pilot request, when departing within the hour, if no preliminary weather information has been received?

A – Outlook briefing

B – Abbreviated briefing

C – Standard briefing

7-37. Answer C. GFDPP 7-45, AIM
A standard briefing is the most compete type of weather briefing.

7-38   PLT514   PA.I.C.S1

Which type of weather briefing should a pilot request to supplement mass disseminated data?

A – An outlook briefing

B – A supplemental briefing

C – An abbreviated briefing

7-38. Answer C. GFDPP 7-46, AIM
An abbreviated briefing is appropriate for supplementing non-official weather data, or for updating the information from a previous briefing.

7-39   PLT514   PA.I.C.S1

To update a previous weather briefing, a pilot should request

A – an abbreviated briefing.

B – a standard briefing.

C – an outlook briefing.

7-39. Answer A. GFDPP 7-46, AIM

An abbreviated briefing is appropriate for supplementing non-official weather data, or for updating the information from a previous briefing.

7-40   PLT514   PA.I.C.S1

A weather briefing that is provided when the information requested is six or more hours before the proposed departure time is

A – an outlook briefing.

B – a forecast briefing.

C – a prognostic briefing.

7-40. Answer A. GFDPP 7-46, AIM

An outlook briefing is appropriate for flights that are at least six hours in the future.

7-41   PLT514   PA.I.C.S1

When requesting weather information for the following morning, a pilot should request

A – an outlook briefing.

B – a standard briefing.

C – an abbreviated briefing.

7-41. Answer A. GFDPP 7-46, AIM

Assuming the flight is six or more hours away, the pilot would request an outlook briefing.

7-42   PLT514   PA.I.C.K1

You plan to call a weather briefing facility for preflight weather information. You should

A – provide the number of occupants on board.

B – begin with your route of flight.

C – identify yourself as a pilot.

7-42. Answer C. GFDPP 7-44, AWS

You should identify yourself as a pilot or student pilot and include concise facts about your flight.

1. Type of flight VFR or IFR
2. Aircraft identification or your name
3. Aircraft type
4. Departure point
5. Route of flight
6. Destination
7. Altitude
8. Estimated time of departure
9. Estimated time enroute or estimated time of arrival

Briefers do not need to know how many hours you have flown. They also do not need to know the number of occupants on board the aircraft; this information is on the flight plan.

7-43   PLT513   PA.I.C.S1

When calling a weather briefing facility for preflight weather information, pilots should state

A – the full name and address of the formation commander.

B – that they possess a current pilot certificate.

C – whether they intend to fly VFR only.

7-43. Answer C. GFDPP 7-44, AWS

It is important that the briefer knows whether a pilot intends to fly VFR or IFR, so that the information can help the pilot make a Go/No-go decision.

7-44   PLT513   PA.I.C.S1

To obtain a Flight Service briefing over the internet, go to

A – FSS.gov and enter your pilot certificate number.

B – 1800wxbrief.com and sign up using your pilot credentials.

C – AviationWeather.gov and select Standard Briefing.

7-44. Answer B. GFDPP 7D, AWS

The site for official Flight Service briefings is 1800wxbrief.com. This website is for pilots only and you must sign up before you can use this site. You can also obtain official National Weather Service aviation products at AviationWeather.gov, but an official record is not made of those briefings, and they do not provide NOTAMs and TFRs. FSS.gov is not a valid website.

AIRPLANE PERFORMANCE

SECTION A — PREDICTING PERFORMANCE

Performance describes the effectiveness of an aircraft in doing the jobs for which it was designed. In this section, you review performance speeds, factors affecting performance, and the pilot's operating handbook (POH). The content includes typical examples of performance charts and tables.

DENSITY ALTITUDE
- If the outside air temperature at a given altitude is warmer than standard, the density altitude is higher than pressure altitude.
- High temperature, high relative humidity, and high density altitude all reduce aircraft takeoff and climb performance.
- (Refer to Figure 8.) To find the density altitude for given conditions, first find the pressure altitude, using the pressure altitude conversion factor scale and interpolating for the current pressure. Then, find the temperature on the OAT scale at the bottom of the graph and follow its line vertically to where it intersects the pressure altitude line. From this point, follow the horizontal density altitude line to the left scale to find an approximate density altitude.
- Density altitude and pressure altitude are the same value at standard temperature.

TAKEOFF AND LANDING PERFORMANCE
- (Refer to Figure 36.) To find the headwind and crosswind components, first determine the difference between the runway heading and the wind direction. Then, find the intersection of the degrees line and the wind velocity arc.
- (Refer to Figure 36.) To find a velocity at the maximum crosswind component for an aircraft, begin with the crosswind component at the bottom of the chart. Follow the line up to where it intersects the degree line representing the angle of crosswind. Then, read the wind velocity.
- (Refer to Figure 37.) To determine the total distance required to land, start at the bottom left side of the chart. Find the OAT and follow the line up to the corresponding pressure altitude. Move right to the reference line and parallel the diagonal guide line downward to intersect the weight line. Move straight across to the next reference line, and parallel the diagonal headwind guide line down to intersect the wind component line. Move straight across to the next reference line and parallel the diagonal obstacle height guide line up to the obstacle given. The landing distance is read on the right side.
- (Refer to Figure 38.) To determine the landing distance, find the table that corresponds to the temperature and pressure altitudes that most closely resemble the given conditions. To consider an obstacle, select the distance to clear an obstacle. Be sure to check additional factors listed at the bottom of the chart, including headwind, nonstandard temperature, and surface conditions.
- (Refer to Figure 40.) To determine takeoff distance, start at the bottom left of the chart, and find the temperature and pressure altitude. Move straight across to the reference line, and follow the guide line down to the given weight. Move across to the next reference line, and follow the headwind guide line down to the given value. Follow the line straight across to the next reference line, and move to the stated obstacle height. Move parallel to the guide line and read the distance from the right side of the chart. If no wind or obstacle requires consideration, move straight across the corresponding section to the next reference line.

CLIMB PERFORMANCE

- V_X is the best angle of climb speed, providing the greatest gain in altitude over the shortest distance during climb after takeoff.
- V_Y is the best rate of climb, and it provides the greatest gain in altitude over a given time.
- You can find the operating limitations for an aircraft in the current, FAA-approved flight manual, approved manual material, markings, placards, or a combination of these references.

CRUISE PERFORMANCE

- (Refer to Figure 35.) To determine the true airspeed (TAS) in given conditions, use the left-hand portion of the table, under the appropriate temperature heading. Interpolate between the given pressure altitudes, if necessary, to find the TAS.
- (Refer to Figure 35.) To determine the expected fuel consumption, first go to the table under the appropriate temperature heading. Go down to the given pressure altitude and read across to find the fuel flow and TAS. Find the time enroute by dividing the distance by the TAS. Multiply the time by the fuel flow.
- (Refer to Figure 35.) To determine the manifold pressure setting, go to the appropriate temperature heading, and go down to the pressure altitude. Read the MP from the table, noting all RPM values are the same.

8-1   PLT506   PA.I.F.K2a

Which would provide the greatest gain in altitude in the shortest distance during climb after takeoff?

A – V_Y

B – V_A

C – V_X

8-1. Answer C. GFDPP 8-16, AFH

V_X is the best angle-of-climb speed—it gives you the greatest gain in altitude for the horizontal distance traveled.

8-2   PLT506   PA.I.F.K2a

After takeoff, which airspeed would the pilot use to gain the most altitude in a given time?

A – V_Y

B – V_X

C – V_A

8-2. Answer A. GFDPP 8-16, AFH

To gain altitude in minimum time, when nearby obstacles are not a factor, use V_Y, the best *rate*-of-climb speed. To gain altitude in the minimum horizontal distance and clear obstacles, use the slower V_X, the best *angle*-of-climb speed. V_A, maneuvering speed, is not a climb speed.

8-3   PLT127   PA.I.F.K1

What effect does high density altitude, as compared to low density altitude, have on propeller efficiency and why?

A – Efficiency is increased due to less friction on the propeller blades.

B – Efficiency is reduced because the propeller exerts less force at high density altitudes than at low density altitudes.

C – Efficiency is reduced due to the increased force of the propeller in the thinner air.

8-3. Answer B. GFDPP 8-19, PHB

Because the high-density-altitude air is less dense, a smaller mass of air flows through the propeller, reducing force and efficiency.

8-4   PLT134   PA.I.F.K2a

Which combination of atmospheric conditions reduces aircraft takeoff and climb performance?

A – Low temperature, low relative humidity, and low density altitude

B – High temperature, low relative humidity, and low density altitude

C – High temperature, high relative humidity, and high density altitude

8-4. Answer C. GFDPP 8-8, PHB
High temperature increases density altitude with a resulting decrease in aircraft performance. In addition, high humidity reduces engine performance.

8-5   PLT127   PA.I.F.K2a

What effect does high density altitude have on aircraft performance?

A – It increases engine performance.

B – It reduces climb performance.

C – It increases takeoff performance.

8-5. Answer B. GFDPP 8-19, PHB
A high density altitude decreases engine performance with a resulting reduction in climb performance.

8-6   PLT127   PA.I.F.K2a

What effect, if any, does high humidity have on aircraft performance?

A – It increases performance.

B – It decreases performance.

C – It has no effect on performance.

8-6. Answer B. GFDPP 8-8, PHB
High humidity reduces engine performance by slightly increasing the density altitude of air entering the engine and retarding smooth burning of the fuel.

8-7   PLT012   PA.I.F.K1

(Refer to Figure 35.)
Approximately what true airspeed should a pilot expect with 65 percent maximum continuous power at 9,500 feet with a temperature of 36°F below standard?

A – 158 knots

B – 161 knots

C – 163 knots

8-7. Answer A. GFDPP 8-22, PHB
Use the left-hand portion of the table, under ISA −36°F. Interpolate between the TAS values for 8,000 feet (157 knots) and 10,000 feet (160 knots). The closest answer is 158 knots.

8-8   PLT012   PA.I.F.K1

(Refer to Figure 35.)
What is the expected fuel consumption for a 1,000-nautical mile flight under the following conditions?

Pressure altitude…8,000 ft

Temperature…22°C

Manifold pressure…20.8 inches Hg.

Wind…Calm

A – 60.2 gallons

B – 70.1 gallons

C – 73.2 gallons

8-8. Answer B. GFDPP 8-22, PHB

The temperature of 22°C is found on the right-hand portion of the table (ISA + 20°C) at 8,000 feet. Read across to find a fuel flow of 11.5 GPH, and TAS of 164 Knots (use knots because the distance is in nautical miles). Now, find the time enroute by dividing 1,000 NM by 164 knots (Normally you would use groundspeed, but with a calm wind, TAS equals groundspeed.) The time enroute is approximately 6.1 hours. Multiply the time by fuel flow. The total fuel consumption is 70.1 gallons.

8-9   PLT012   PA.I.F.K1

(Refer to Figure 35.) What fuel flow should a pilot expect at 11,000 feet on a standard day with 65 percent maximum continuous power?

A – 10.6 gallons per hour

B – 11.2 gallons per hour

C – 11.8 gallons per hour

8-9. Answer B. GFDPP 8-22, PHB

Use the center portion of the table for a standard day. You can interpolate to find the fuel flow for 11,000 feet, which is halfway between 12,000 feet and 10,000 feet.

   (11.5 − 10.9)/2 + 10.9

= (0.6 ÷ 2) + 10.9

= 0.3 + 10.9

= 11.2 gallons per hour

8-10   PLT012   PA.I.F.S2

(Refer to Figure 35.) Determine the approximate manifold pressure setting with 2,450 RPM to achieve 65 percent maximum continuous power at 6,500 feet with a temperature of 36°F higher than standard.

A – 19.8 inches Hg.

B – 20.8 inches Hg.

C – 21.0 inches Hg.

8-10. Answer C. GFDPP 8-22, PHB

The RPM is the same for all altitudes. Therefore, to determine what manifold pressure (MP) is required to achieve 65% maximum continuous power, enter the table under ISA + 36°F. The MP for 6,000 feet is 21.0", and for 8,000 feet it is 20.8". The interpolated MP for 6,500 feet is 20.95". The closest answer is 21.0" Hg.

8-11   PLT013

(Refer to Figure 36.) What is the headwind component for a landing on Runway 18 if the tower reports the wind as 220° at 30 knots?

A – 19 knots

B – 23 knots

C – 26 knots

8-11. Answer B. GFDPP 8-12, PHB

First, compute the difference between the runway (180°) and the wind (220°). The result is an angle of 40 degrees. Find the intersection of the 40-degree line and the 30-knot wind velocity arc, then read across to the left side to find the headwind component of 23 knots.

8-12   PLT013   PA.I.F.R1

(Refer to Figure 36.) Determine the maximum wind velocity for a 45° crosswind if the maximum crosswind component for the airplane is 25 knots.

A – 25 knots

B – 29 knots

C – 35 knots

8-12. Answer C. GFDPP 8-12, PHB

Start with the crosswind component of 25 knots at the bottom of the chart, and follow the line straight up to where it intersects the 45-degree angle line. This intersection is midway between the 30 and 40 knot wind velocity lines, or 35 knots.

8-13   PLT013   PA.I.F.R1

(Refer to Figure 36.) What is the maximum wind velocity for a 30° crosswind if the maximum crosswind component for the airplane is 12 knots?

A – 16 knots

B – 20 knots

C – 24 knots

8-13. Answer C. GFDPP 8-12, PHB

Start with the crosswind component of 12 knots at the bottom of the chart, and follow the line straight up to where it intersects the 30-degree angle line. This intersection is approximately 24 knots on the wind velocity scale.

8-14   PLT013   PA.I.F.R2

(Refer to Figure 36.) With a reported wind of north at 20 knots, which runway (6, 29, or 32) is acceptable for use for an airplane with a 13-knot maximum crosswind component?

A – Runway 6

B – Runway 29

C – Runway 32

8-14. Answer C. GFDPP 8-12, PHB

At first glance, Runway 32 is most closely aligned with north (360°). To verify, find the crosswind component for each runway. Runway 32 is 40 degrees from the wind, and because the wind speed is 20 knots, the crosswind component is slightly less than 13 knots, so Runway 32 is acceptable. Runway 6 is 60 degrees from the wind, and the crosswind component is about 17.5 knots. Runway 29 is 70 degrees from the wind, and the crosswind component is about 19 knots. Both Runways 6 and 29 exceed the 13 knot maximum crosswind component.

8-15   PLT013   PA.I.F.R2

(Refer to Figure 36.) With a reported wind of south at 20 knots, which runway (10, 14, or 24) is appropriate for an airplane with a 13-knot maximum crosswind component?

A – Runway 10

B – Runway 14

C – Runway 24

8-15. Answer B. GFDPP 8-12, PHB

Runway 14 is most closely aligned with the wind and would have the least crosswind. The crosswind angle and component for each runway is: Runway 14, 40 degrees, 12.5 knots; Runway 10, 80 degrees, 19.7 knots; Runway 24, 60 degrees, 17.5 knots. Runway 14 is the only appropriate runway because the crosswind component is less than 13 knots.

8-16   PLT013   PA.I.F.K1

(Refer to Figure 36.)
What is the crosswind component for a landing on
Runway 18 if the tower reports the wind as 220° at 30
knots?

A – 19 knots

B – 23 knots

C – 30 knots

8-16. Answer A. GFDPP 8-12, PHB
The crosswind angle is 40 degrees (220° – 180° =
40°). Find the intersection of 40 degrees and 30 knots.
Then read down to find the crosswind component of
about 19 knots.

8-17   PLT008   PA.I.F.S2

(Refer to Figure 37.)
Determine the approximate total distance required to
land over a 50-foot obstacle.

OAT...90°F

Pressure altitude...4,000 ft

Weight...2,800 lb

Headwind component...10 knots

A – 1,525 feet

B – 1,775 feet

C – 1,950 feet

8-17. Answer B. GFDPP 8-15, PHB
Start at the lower left at 90°F (32°C), and move up
to where it intersects the 4,000-foot pressure altitude
line. Go right to the weight reference line and then
down and to the right to 2,800 lb. Go straight right to
the wind component reference line, down and to the
right to the 10-knot headwind line, and straight right to
the obstacle height reference line. Move up and to the
right through the obstacle height and read the landing
distance over a 50-foot obstacle on the right-hand
scale.

8-18   PLT008   PA.I.F.S2

(Refer to Figure 38.)
Determine the approximate landing ground roll
distance.

Pressure altitude...Sea level

Headwind...4 knots

Temperature...Std

A – 356 feet

B – 401 feet

C – 490 feet

8-18. Answer B. GFDPP 8-14, 15, PHB
Use the table listed under sea level and 59°F, which
is the standard temperature. Because you need the
landing ground roll distance, do not include obstacle
clearance. The ground roll is given as 445, but
according to Note 1, you must correct for headwind
by decreasing the distance 10% for every four knots
of headwind. In this case, subtract 10% of 445 (44.5)
from 445.

8-19   PLT008   PA.I.F.S2
(Refer to Figure 38.)
Determine the total distance required to land over a
50-foot obstacle.

  Pressure altitude...7,500 ft

  Headwind...8 knots

  Temperature...32°F

  Runway...Hard surface

A – 1,004 feet

B – 1,205 feet

C – 1,506 feet

8-19. Answer A. GFDPP 8-14, 15, PHB
According to the table, the landing distance over a
50-ft obstacle is 1,255 feet at 7,500 feet MSL and
32°F. Note 1 says to decrease this distance by 10%
for every four knots of headwind, so with 8 knots
headwind, subtract 20 percent. 1,255 ft × 0.80 =
1,004 ft

8-20   PLT008   PA.I.F.S2
(Refer to Figure 38.)
Determine the total distance required to land over a
50-foot obstacle.

  Pressure altitude...5,000 ft

  Headwind...8 knots

  Temperature...41°F

  Runway...Hard surface

A – 837 feet

B – 956 feet

C – 1,076 feet

8-20. Answer B. GFDPP 8-14, 15, PHB
Use the table at 5,000 feet and 41°F. The distance
to land over a 50-ft obstacle is 1,195 feet. According
to Note 1, decrease the distance by 20% (239 ft) for
the 8-knot headwind: (1,195 ft – 239 ft = 956-ft total
landing distance).

8-21   PLT008   PA.I.F.S2
(Refer to Figure 38.)
Determine the approximate landing ground roll
distance.

  Pressure altitude...5,000 ft

  Headwind...Calm

  Temperature...101°F

A – 445 feet

B – 495 feet

C – 545 feet

8-21. Answer C. GFDPP 8-14, 15, PHB
At 5,000 feet and 41°F (ISA Standard Temperature),
the ground roll distance is 495 feet. According to
Note 2, this distance is increased 10% for every 60°F
above standard.

8-22   PLT008   PA.I.F.K1

(Refer to Figure 38.)
Determine the total distance required to land over a
50-foot obstacle.

Pressure altitude...3,750 ft

Headwind...12 knots

Temperature...Std

A – 794 feet

B – 836 feet

C – 816 feet

8-22. Answer C. GFDPP 8-14, 15, PHB

1. At 2,500 feet MSL and standard ISA temperature,
the landing distance over a 50-ft obstacle with
zero wind is 1,135 feet. At 5,000 feet MSL, this
distance is 1,195 feet. At 3,750 feet MSL, assume
that the landing distance is half way between
1,135 and 1,195 feet. (1,135 + 1,195) feet ÷ 2 =
1,165 feet.

2. Note 1 says to decrease the distance 10% for
every four knots of headwind. The headwind is 12
knots. 12 knots × 10% decrease/(4 knots) = 30%
decrease. 1,165 feet × (100% – 30%) = 816 feet.

8-23   PLT008   PA.I.

(Refer to Figure 38.) Determine the approximate
landing ground roll distance.

Pressure altitude...1,250 ft

Headwind...8 knots

Temperature...Std

A – 275 feet

B – 366 feet

C – 470 feet

8-23. Answer B. GFDPP 8-14, 15, PHB

This problem requires that you interpolate between
the ground roll distances at sea level and 2,500 feet
PA. Because 1,250 feet is midway between the two
values, the ground roll is 458-ft—(470 – 445) ÷ 2 +
445). To correct for headwind, subtract 20% of the
distance (10% for every 4 knots). 20% of 457.5 is 91.5.

The landing distance is 457.5 – 91.5 = 366 feet

8-24   PLT208   PA.I.F.K1

If an emergency situation requires a downwind
landing, pilots should expect a faster

A – airspeed at touchdown, a longer ground roll, and
better control throughout the landing roll.

B – groundspeed at touchdown, a longer ground roll,
and the likelihood of overshooting the desired
touchdown point.

C – groundspeed at touchdown, a shorter ground roll,
and the likelihood of undershooting the desired
touchdown point.

8-24. Answer B. GFDPP 8-13

Wind should be considered in all landings, whether
normal or emergency. When you fly the same
indicated airspeed for landing, a headwind lowers
the groundspeed at touchdown, resulting in a shorter
ground roll. The reverse is true for a tailwind, which is
why pilots always try to land into the wind. In addition,
the higher groundspeed produced by a tailwind
results in the aircraft traveling faster in the roundout
and flare, which can result in overshooting the desired
touchdown point.

8-25   PLT011   PA.I.F.S2
(Refer to Figure 40.) Determine the total distance required for takeoff to clear a 50-foot obstacle.

OAT...Std

Pressure altitude...4,000 ft

Takeoff weight...2,800 lb

Headwind component...Calm

A – 1,500 feet

B – 1,750 feet

C – 2,000 feet

8-25. Answer B. GFDPP 8-6, 7, PHB
Because temperature is standard, start at the intersection of the ISA and 4,000 foot pressure altitude line. Move right to the reference line and follow the guide line diagonally downward to the 2,800-pound line. Because winds are calm, move straight across to the obstacle height reference line. Follow the guide line upward to the 50 foot line, which is on the right-hand border. The takeoff distance is approximately 1,700 feet.

8-26   PLT011   PA.I.F.S2
(Refer to Figure 40.) Determine the total distance required for takeoff to clear a 50-foot obstacle.

OAT...Std

Pressure altitude...Sea level

Takeoff weight...2,700 lb

Headwind component...Calm

A – 1,000 feet

B – 1,400 feet

C – 1,700 feet

8-26. Answer B. GFDPP 8-6, 7, PHB
Because temperature is standard, start at the intersection of the ISA line and sea level (S.L.). Move right to the reference line and follow the guide line diagonally downward to the 2,700-pound line. Move straight across to the obstacle height reference line, because winds are calm. Follow the guide line upward to the 50 foot line. The takeoff distance is about 1,400 feet.

8-27   PLT011   PA.I.F.S2
(Refer to Figure 40.) Determine the approximate ground roll distance required for takeoff.

OAT...38°C

Pressure altitude...2,000 ft

Takeoff weight...2,750 lb

Headwind component...Calm

A – 1,150 feet

B – 1,300 feet

C – 1,800 feet

8-27. Answer A. GFDPP 8-6, 7, PHB
Start at 38°C, move up to the 2,000 foot pressure altitude line, then right to the reference line. Follow the guide line down to 2,750 pounds. Because winds are calm, with no obstacle, move straight across to the right-hand border. The ground roll is about 1,150 feet.

8-28   PLT011   PA.I.F.K1

(Refer to Figure 40.) Determine the approximate ground roll distance required for takeoff.

OAT...32°C

Pressure altitude...2,000 ft

Takeoff weight...2,500 lb

Headwind component...20 knots

A – 650 feet

B – 800 feet

C – 1,000 feet

8-28. Answer A. GFDPP 8-6, 7, PHB

Start at 32°C, move up to the 2,000 foot pressure altitude line, then right to the reference line. Follow the guide line down to 2,500 pounds. Move across to the next reference line, and follow the headwind guide line down to 20 knots. Because no obstacle exists, move straight across to the right-hand border. The ground roll is about 650 feet.

8-29   PLT208   PA.I.F.K1

If an emergency situation requires a downwind landing, pilots should expect a faster

A – airspeed at touchdown, a longer ground roll, and better control throughout the landing roll.

B – groundspeed at touchdown, a longer ground roll, and the likelihood of overshooting the desired touchdown point.

C – groundspeed at touchdown, a shorter ground roll, and the likelihood of undershooting the desired touchdown point.

8-29. Answer B. GFDPP 8-13, AFH

Consider the wind in every landing, whether normal or emergency. When flying the same indicated airspeed for landing, a headwind lowers the groundspeed at touchdown, resulting in a shorter ground roll. The reverse is true for a tailwind, which is why pilots always try to land into the wind. In addition, a higher groundspeed produced by a tailwind results in the aircraft traveling farther in the roundout and flare, which can result in overshooting the desired touchdown point.

SECTION B — WEIGHT AND BALANCE

Pilots must keep weight within specified limits and balance the load on board to maintain controllability of the airplane. This section covers weight and balance charts and tables, how to determine weight and balance, and how to apply the weight shift formula.

WEIGHT AND BALANCE TERMS

- Included in the basic empty weight of an aircraft are the unusable fuel and undrainable oil.
- The standard weight of gasoline is 6 pounds per gallon. To determine the amount of fuel to drain, if necessary, divide the excess weight by six.

PRINCIPLES OF WEIGHT AND BALANCE

The center of gravity (CG) is the total moment divided by the total weight. Datum is a vertical plane in the aircraft from which weight and balance distances are measured. Arm is the distance from datum of a particular station, or place in the aircraft. To calculate aircraft moment, multiply the weight at a station by the arm. Positive CG values are aft of datum, negative CG values are forward of the datum.

DETERMINING TOTAL WEIGHT AND CENTER OF GRAVITY

Several methods can aid you in calculating the center of gravity and total weight of your aircraft, and the change in CG with a shift in weight.

TABLE METHOD

- The best way to determine aircraft weight and balance is to construct a table, or spreadsheet, that lists the stations of the aircraft, the weight at each station, and the arm of each station. From here, you can find the moment at each station, and add up the total weight and moments. The CG is the total moment divided by the total weight.
- (Refer to Figures 32 and 33.) To find the arm at each station, look for the station, such as usable fuel, on the table and read the arm listed at the top. Many charts calculate moments for a specific weight range, so that you can simply read these values off the table as well.
- (Refer to Figure 34.) Other charts provide arm and moment information graphically. To read the moment from the chart, find the line that corresponds to the station, and follow it to the weight at that station. To find the moment, move down to the bottom of the graph.

WEIGHT SHIFT FORMULA

Use the weight shift formula to determine how far the center of gravity shifts when weight is added to or removed from the aircraft:

- Weight Moved ÷ Weight of Airplane = Distance CG Moves ÷ Distance between Arms
- Some weight shift questions require you to construct a table of weights and moments first.

8-30   PLT328   PA.I.F.S1

Which items are included in the empty weight of an aircraft?

A – Unusable fuel and undrainable oil

B – Only the airframe, powerplant, and optional equipment

C – Full fuel tanks and engine oil to capacity

8-30. Answer A. GFDPP 8-32, PHB

The empty weight of an aircraft includes unusable fuel. The term basic empty weight includes full engine oil.

On older airplanes, the term licensed empty weight includes only undrainable oil.

8-31   PLT328   PA.I.F.S1

An aircraft is loaded 110 pounds over maximum certificated gross weight. If fuel (gasoline) is drained to bring the aircraft weight within limits, how much fuel should be drained?

A – 15.7 gallons

B – 16.2 gallons

C – 18.4 gallons

8-31. Answer C. GFDPP 8-33, PHB

This problem requires converting the weight of fuel to gallons. Divide 110 pounds by 6 pounds per gallon, the standard weight of gasoline.

8-32   PLT328

GIVEN:

	WEIGHT (lb)	ARM (in)	MOMENT (lb-in)
Empty weight	1,495	101.4	151,593
Pilot and Pass	380	64.0	-----
Fuel (30 gal usable no reserve)	-----	96.0	-----

The CG is located how far aft of datum?

A – 92.44 inches

B – 94.01 inches

C – 119.8 inches

8-33   PLT328   PA.I.F.S1

(Refer to Figures 32 and 33.)
What is the maximum amount of baggage that can be carried when the airplane is loaded as follows?

Front seat occupants...387 lb

Rear seat occupants...293 lb

Fuel...35 gal

A – 45 pounds

B – 63 pounds

C – 220 pounds

8-32. Answer B. GFDPP 8-36, PHB

First, fill in the table by entering the fuel weight (30 gal × 6 lb/gal = 180 lb). Then, multiply each weight by the arm to find the moment.

The CG is the total moment divided by the total weight = 193,193 lb-in ÷ 2,055 lb = 94.01 in

8-33. Answer A. GFDPP 8-39, PHB

Add up all the weights to determine that the airplane is 45 lb underweight. When adding the 45 lb of baggage, be sure to verify that the resulting center of gravity (CG) is within limits.

8-34   PLT328   PA.I.F.S1

(Refer to Figures 32 and 33.)
Determine if the airplane weight and balance is within limits.

Front seat occupants...415 lb

Rear seat occupants...110 lb

Fuel, main tanks...44 gal

Fuel, aux. tanks...19 gal

Baggage...32 lb

A – 19-pounds overweight, CG within limits

B – 19-pounds overweight, CG out of limits forward

C – Weight within limits, CG out of limits

8-34. Answer C. GFDPP 8-36, 39, PHB

First, construct a weight and moment table.

	WEIGHT (lb)	ARM (in)	MOMENT (lb-in/100)
Empty weight	2,015		1,554.0
Front Seat	415	85	352.8
Rear Seat	110	121	133.1
Fuel 44 gal	264	75	198.0
Aux 19 gal	114	94	107.2
Baggage	32	140	44.8
Totals	**2,950**		**2,389.9**

The total weight is at the maximum limit. To find the CG, divide the total moment by the total weight.

CG = (2,389 lb-in × 100) ÷ 2,950 lb

The result is 81.0 inches, which is outside the limits.

8-35   PLT328   PA.I.F.S1

(Refer to Figure 34.)

What is the maximum amount of baggage that may be loaded aboard the airplane for the CG to remain within the moment envelope?

	WEIGHT (lb)	MOM/1000
Empty weight	1,350	51.5
Pilot and Front passenger	250	-----
Rear passengers	400	-----
Baggage	-----	-----
Fuel, 30 gal	-----	-----
Oil, 8 qt	-----	-0.2

A – 105 pounds

B – 110 pounds

C – 120 pounds

8-35. Answer A. GFDPP 8-40, PHB

Use Figure 34 to convert oil and fuel to pounds. Add up the known weights, for a total of 2,195 pounds. Subtract 2,195 pounds from 2,300 max weight to find the maximum baggage weight of 105 pounds. This eliminates all answers but choice A, but you still should check the CG limits. Use the LOADING GRAPH and find the moment for each weight.

	WEIGHT (lb)	MOMENT (1,000 lb-in)
Empty Weight	1,350	51.5
Front Seat	250	9.4
Rear Seat	400	29.3
Fuel 30 gal	180	8.7
Oil 8 qt	15	–0.2
Subtotal	2,195	98.7
Baggage	105	10.0
Totals	**2,300**	**108.7**

Total the moments and locate the maximum weight on the CENTER OF GRAVITY MOMENT ENVELOPE graph. The intersection of the loaded weight and moment is at the upper right-hand corner of the normal category envelope, and is barely within limits.

8-36   PLT328   PA.I.F.S1

(Refer to Figure 34.)
Calculate the moment of the airplane and determine which category is applicable.

	WEIGHT (lb)	MOM/1000
Empty weight	1,350	51.5
Pilot and Front passenger	310	-----
Rear passengers	96	-----
Fuel, 38 gal	-----	-----
Oil, 8 qt	-----	-0.2

A – 79.2, utility category

B – 80.8, utility category

C – 81.2, normal category

8-36. Answer B. GFDPP 8-40, PHB

Complete the table of weights and moments, using the LOADING GRAPH:

	WEIGHT (lb)	MOMENT (lb-in/1000)
Empty Weight	1,350	51.5
Front Seat	310	11.6
Rear Seat	96	7.0
Fuel 38 gal	228	11.0
Oil 8 qt	15	−0.2
Totals	**1,999**	**80.9**

The total moment/1,000 is 80.9 lb-in. To find the total weight and total moment, use the CENTER OF GRAVITY MOMENT ENVELOPE graph. The intersection falls within the upper right-hand corner of the utility category envelope.

8-37   PLT328   PA.I.F.S1

(Refer to Figure 34.)

If an airplane loaded as follows, what is the maximum amount of fuel that may be aboard on takeoff?

	WEIGHT (lb)	MOM/1000
Empty weight	1,350	51.5
Pilot and Front passenger	340	-----
Rear passengers	310	-----
Baggage	45	-----
Oil, 8 qt	-----	-----

A – 24 gallons

B – 32 gallons

C – 40 gallons

8-37. Answer C. GFDPP 8-40, PHB

Complete the table of weights and moments, using the LOADING GRAPH:

	WEIGHT (lb)	MOMENT (lb-in/1000)
Empty Weight	1,350	51.5
Front Seat	340	12.7
Rear Seat	310	22.6
Baggage	45	4.3
Oil 8 qt	15	–.2
Subtotal	2060	90.9
Fuel 40 gal	240	11.5
Totals	**2300**	**102.4**

The total weight without fuel is 2,060 lb. This weight is 240 lb below the maximum of 2,300 lb.

Dividing by 6 lb/gal, the maximum fuel load is 40 gallons. Check the moments as well. The total moment of 102.4 is within the CG envelope, so 40 gallons is acceptable.

8-38   PLT328   PA.I.F.S1

(Refer to Figure 34.)

Determine the moment with the following data:

	WEIGHT (lb)	MOM/1000
Empty weight	1,350	51.5
Pilot and Front passenger	340	-----
Fuel (std. tanks)	Capacity	-----
Oil, 8 qt	-----	-----

A – 69.9 pound-inches

B – 74.9 pound-inches

C – 77.6 pound-inches

8-38. Answer B. GFDPP 8-40, PHB

To determine the moment for each item, use the LOADING GRAPH. To find the total moment of 74.9, add up the individual moments.

	WEIGHT (lb)	MOMENT (lb-in/1000)
Empty Weight	1,350	51.5
Front Seat	340	12.6
Fuel 38 gal	228	11.0
Oil 8 qt.	15	–0.2
Totals	**1,933**	**74.9**

8-39   PLT328   PA.I.F.S1

(Refer to Figure 34.)

Determine the aircraft loaded moment and the aircraft category.

	WEIGHT (lb)	MOM/1000
Empty weight	1,350	51.5
Pilot and Front passenger	380	-----
Fuel, 48 gal	288	-----
Oil, 8 qt	-----	-----

A – 78.2, normal category

B – 79.2, normal category

C – 80.4, utility category

8-40   PLT328   PA.I.F.S1

(Refer to Figures 32 and 33.)

Upon landing, the front passenger (180 pounds) departs the airplane. A rear passenger (204 pounds) moves to the front passenger position. What effect does this weight shift have on the CG if the airplane weighed 2,690 pounds and the MOM/100 was 2,260 before the passenger transfer?

A – The CG moves forward approximately 3 inches.

B – The weight changes, but the CG is not affected.

C – The CG moves forward approximately 0.1 inches.

8-39. Answer B. GFDPP 8-40, PHB

Use the LOADING GRAPH to determine the moments:

	WEIGHT (lb)	MOMENT (lb-in/1000)
Empty Weight	1,350	51.5
Front Seat	380	14.2
Fuel 48 gal	288	13.7
Oil, 8 qt	15	–0.2
Totals	**2,033**	**79.2**

The total weight is 2,033 pounds, and the total moment is 79.2. Use the CENTER OF GRAVITY MOMENT ENVELOPE graph with the total weight and total moment. The intersection falls within the normal category, and outside the utility category.

8-40. Answer A. GFDPP 8-36, 41, PHB

First, calculate the effect of the front seat passenger disembarking. Use the table in Figure 32 to determine the moment of the departing 180-lb passenger.

Weight: 2,690 – 180 = 2,510 lb; CG = 84.01 in

Moment: 2260 – 153 = 2107 (100 lb-in); CG = 83.94 in

The CG from the initial deplaning decreases 0.07 in.

Then, determine the effect of the rear seat passenger moving to the front seat. Find the arms for the front and rear passenger seats in Figure 32; the difference is 121 – 85 = 36. Use the weight-shift formula to determine how far the CG shifts when the 204-lb passenger moves to the front seat.

Weight Moved ÷ Weight of Airplane = Distance CG Moves ÷ Distance Between Arms

204 ÷ 2,510 = Distance CG Moves ÷ 36 in

Distance CG Moves = 204 × 36 ÷ 2,510 = 2.93 in

The additional change in CG is 2.93 inches, so the total change in CG is 3.0 inches forward

8-41   PLT328   PA.I.F.S1

(Refer to Figures 32 and 33.) Which action can adjust the weight of the airplane to maximum gross weight and the CG to within limits for takeoff?

Front seat occupants...425 lb

Rear seat occupants...300 lb

Fuel, main tanks...44 gal

A – Drain 12 gallons of fuel.

B – Drain 9 gallons of fuel.

C – Transfer 12 gallons of fuel from the main tanks to the auxiliary tanks.

8-41. Answer B. GFDPP 8-39, PHB

Complete the weight and moment table as shown in the following table:

	WEIGHT (lb)	ARM (in)	MOMENT (lb-in/100)
Empty Weight	2,015		1,554.0
Front Seat	425	85	361.3
Rear Seat	300	121	363.0
Fuel 44 gal	264	75	198.0
Total	3,004		2,476.3
Max Weight	−2,950		
	54		

The total weight of 3,004 lb is 54 lb over maximum weight and 54 lb of fuel is 9 gallons (54 lb ÷ 6 lb/gal = 9 gallons). Now use Figure 32 to look up the new fuel moment for the 35 gallons that remain, and recalculate the total moment—2,436 (× 100) lb-in.

	WEIGHT (lb)	ARM (in)	MOMENT (lb-in/100)
Empty Weight	2,015		1,554.0
Front Seat	425	85	361.3
Rear Seat	300	121	363.0
Fuel 35 gal	210	75	157.5
Total	**2,950**		**2,435.8**

Using the table in Figure 33, determine that the total weight and total moment are within the limits.

8-42   **PLT328**   **PA.I.F.S1**

(Refer to Figures 32 and 33.)
What effect does a 35-gallon fuel burn (main tanks) have on the weight and balance if the airplane weighed 2,890 pounds and the MOM/100 was 2,452 at takeoff?

A – Weight is reduced by 210 pounds and the CG is aft of limits.

B – Weight is reduced by 210 pounds and the CG is unaffected.

C – Weight is reduced to 2,680 pounds and the CG moves forward.

8-42. Answer A. GFDPP 8-39, PHB

Use the chart in Figure 32 to find the weight and moment for 35 gallons of fuel in the main tanks, and subtract these values from the total weight and moment. The result is the total weight and moment after the fuel burn.

	WEIGHT (lb)	MOMENT (lb-in/100)
Total	2,890	2,452
Fuel 35 gal	–210	–158
Adjusted	2,680	2,294

Refer to the chart in Figure 34 for the weight of 2,680 lb. The. moment of 2,294 lb-in exceeds the maximum (aft) limit.

8-43   PLT328   PA.I.F.S1
(Refer to Figures 32 and 33.)
With the airplane loaded as follows, what action can be taken to balance the airplane?

Front seat occupants..411 lb

Rear seat occupants...100 lb

Main wing tanks...44 gal

A – Fill the auxiliary wing tanks.

B – Add a 100-pound weight to the baggage compartment.

C – Transfer 10 gallons of fuel from the main tanks to the auxiliary tanks.

8-43. Answer B. GFDPP 8-36, 39, 41, PHB
Construct a table like the following. Find the subtotal weight and moment, and use the chart in Figure 34. The subtotal moment (2,222.4) at the original weight is less than the minimum (forward) limit.

	WEIGHT (lb)	ARM (in)	MOMENT (lb-in/100)
Empty Weight	2,015		1,554.0
Front Seat	411	85	349.4
Rear Seat	100	121	121.0
Fuel 44 gal	264	75	198.0
Subtotal	2,790		2,222.4
Baggage	100		140.0
Total	**2,890**		**2,362.4**

Because the baggage compartment is in an aft location, adding weight to this part of the airplane shifts the CG aft. To find the adjusted totals, add the baggage weight and moment to the subtotals. Check the chart in Figure 33 to ensure that the moment is within limits. Answer (A) is wrong because if the auxiliary wing tanks are filled and the total weight and moment are adjusted, the moment is less than the minimum. To check answer (C), find the original CG using the subtotals:

CG = Total Moments ÷ Total Weight
     = 2,222.4 lb-in ÷ 2,790 lb

     = 79.7 in

Then use the weight shift formula:

Weight Moved ÷ Weight of Airplane
= Distance CG Moves ÷ Distance between Arms

The weight of fuel is 10 gal × 6 lb/gal = 60 lb. The distance between arms is 94 inches − 75 inches = 19 inches. Because the fuel is transferred from an arm of 75 inches to an arm of 94 inches, the CG moves aft 0.4 inches.

Distance CG Moves = 60 lb × 19 in ÷ 2,790 lb = 0.4 in

The new CG is 80.1 (79.7 + 0.4). Then, find the new moment on the chart in Figure 33. The new moment is less than the minimum.

8-44   PLT328   PA.I.F.S1
(Refer to Figure 61.)
If 50 pounds of weight is located at point X and 100 pounds at point Z, how much weight must be located at point Y to balance the plank?

A – 30 pounds

B – 50 pounds

C – 300 pounds

8-44. Answer C. GFDPP 8B
You must equalize the moments generated by the weights on each side of the fulcrum, then solve for the unknown weight as shown in the following calculations:

(50 lb × 50 in) + (Y lb × 25 in) = (100 lb × 100 in)

2,500 lb-in + 25Y lb-in = 10,000 lb-in

25Y lb-in = 7,500 lb-in

Y = 300 lb

8-45   PLT328   PA.I.F.S1
(Refer to Figure 60.)
How should the 500-pound weight be shifted to balance the plank on the fulcrum?

A – 1 inch to the left

B – 1 inch to the right

C – 4.5 inches to the right

8-45. Answer A. GFDPP 8B
The moment of the 500-lb weight on the left side of the fulcrum must equal the sum of the moments of the 250-lb weight and the unequal weight of the plank on the right side.

500 lb × L in = (250 lb × 20 in) + (200 lb × 15 in)

500 lb × L in = 5,000 lb-in + 3,000 lb-in

500 lb × L in = 8,000 lb-in

L = –16 inches

Because the 500-lb weight is now sitting at –15 inches from the fulcrum, it must be moved 1 inch to the left.

SECTION C — FLIGHT COMPUTERS

Although you will probably use an application on your computer or tablet for flight planning, it is important to first understand how these calculations are done. Flight computers—not to be confused with your laptop or tablet computer—help a pilot complete various specialized calculations. Both mechanical and electronic flight computers can provide you with "hands-on" experience in flight planning. This section considers the basic principles of flight computers, and detailed procedures for solving navigation problems.

MECHANICAL FLIGHT COMPUTERS

In some questions, you need to calculate the groundspeed and then the estimated time of arrival.

1. Determine the groundspeed of the aircraft: measure the distance between the departure point and the destination. Determine the elapsed time. Divide the distance by the time to derive the groundspeed.

2. Determine the estimated time of arrival (ETA) at the destination by adding the elapsed time to the departure time.

Some questions require you to calculate groundspeed and then complete a time-speed-distance problem.

3. Measure the distance between the departure point and the destination.

4. Determine the true course (TC).

5. Determine the groundspeed, using your flight computer: Enter the wind direction and speed. Enter the TC. Enter the true airspeed (TAS) and find the groundspeed.

6. Determine the time enroute—distance ÷ groundspeed.

7. Add departure and climbout time (if any is given). Round as needed to arrive at one of the answer selections.

8-46   PLT005   PA.VI.A.K2a

(Refer to Figure 8.)

What is the effect of a temperature increase from 25°F to 50°F on the density altitude if the pressure altitude remains at 5,000 feet?

A – 1,200-foot increase

B – 1,400-foot increase

C – 1,650-foot increase

8-46. Answer C. GFDPP 8-9, 56, PHB

Follow the line above 25°F up to where it intersects 5,000 feet pressure altitude, and read 3,750 feet density altitude on the left scale. Do the same with 50°F, up to 5,000 feet, and then left to read 5,400 feet. The difference is an increase of 1,650 feet.

8-47   PLT005   PA.I.F.K1

(Refer to Figure 8.)

Determine the pressure altitude with an indicated altitude of 1,380 feet MSL with an altimeter setting of 28.22 at standard temperature.

A – 3,010 feet

B – 2,991 feet

C – 2,913 feet

8-47. Answer B. GFDPP 8-9, 56, PHB

Using the table on the right side of the chart, interpolate between 28.2 and 28.3 to get a conversion factor of 1,611 (a value 20% of the way between 1,630 and 1,533). Add 1,611 to the indicated altitude of 1,380 for a pressure altitude of 2,991 feet.

8-48   PLT005   PA.I.F.K1

(Refer to Figure 8.)

Determine the density altitude for these conditions:

  Altimeter setting...29.25

  Runway temperature...+81°F

  Airport elevation...5,250 ft MSL

A – 4,600 feet MSL.

B – 5,877 feet MSL.

C – 8,500 feet MSL.

8-48. Answer C. GFDPP 8-9, 56, PHB

First find the pressure altitude by using the pressure altitude conversion factor scale and interpolate for 29.25. The conversion factor is 626—(673 − 579) ÷ 2 + 579. Add 626 feet to 5,250 feet to find a pressure altitude of 5,876 feet. Now, find 81°F on the OAT scale at the bottom of the graph and follow its line vertically to where it intersects with the 5,876-ft pressure altitude line. From this point, follow the horizontal density altitude line to the left scale to find an approximate density altitude of 8,500 feet.

8-49   PLT019   PA.I.F.K1

(Refer to Figure 8.)

Determine the pressure altitude at an airport that is 3,563 feet MSL with an altimeter setting of 29.96.

A – 3,527 feet MSL.

B – 3,556 feet MSL.

C – 3,639 feet MSL.

8-49. Answer A. GFDPP 8-9, 56, PHB

Find the conversion factors for 30.00 and 29.92, and interpolate to find the factor for 29.96 (−73 − 0) ÷ 2 = −36.5). Subtract 36.5 from the elevation of 3,563 feet, to find a pressure altitude of 3,526.5 feet. Round up to 3,527 feet.

8-50   PLT124   PA.I.F.K1
(Refer to Figure 8.)
What is the effect of a temperature increase from 35°F to 50°F on the density altitude if the pressure altitude remains at 3,000 feet MSL?

A – 1,000-foot increase

B – 1,100-foot decrease

C – 1,300-foot increase

8-50. Answer A. GFDPP 8-9,56, PHB
An increase in temperature increases density altitude (DA). Find the DA for 35°F—about 1,900 feet. At 50°F, the DA is about 2,900 feet, an increase of 1,000 feet.

8-51   PLT005   PA.I.F.K1
(Refer to Figure 8.)
Determine the pressure altitude at an airport that is 1,386 feet MSL with an altimeter setting of 29.97.

A – 1,341 feet

B – 1,451 feet

C – 1,562 feet

8-51. Answer A. GFDPP 8-9, 56, PHB
First you must interpolate to find the conversion factor for 29.97 (−73 − 0 = −73 ÷ 8 increments = −9 × 5 increments = −45). Subtract 45 from 1,386 to find the pressure altitude of 1,341 feet.

8-52   PLT005   PA.I.F.K1
(Refer to Figure 8.)
What is the effect of a temperature decrease and a pressure altitude increase on the density altitude from 90°F and 1,250 feet pressure altitude to 55°F and 1,750 feet pressure altitude?

A – 1,750-foot increase

B – 1,350-foot decrease

C – 1,750-foot decrease

8-52. Answer C. GFDPP 8-9, 56, PHB
1. Enter the graph at 90°F on the bottom scale. Draw a line straight up to meet the upsloping 1,250-ft pressure altitude line (visualize this line or draw it in between the 1,000-ft and 2,000-ft lines), then go left to 3,600 feet on the density altitude scale.

2. Repeat for 55°F and 1,750-ft pressure altitude to get a density altitude of 1,850 feet.

3. The difference is (1,850 − 3,600) feet = −1,750 ft.

8-53 PLT012   PA.I.D.K3a
(Refer to Figure 20.)
Enroute to First Flight Airport (area 5), your flight passes over Hampton Roads Airport (area 2) at 1456 and then over Chesapeake Municipal at 1501. At what time should your flight arrive at First Flight?

A – 1516

B – 1521

C – 1526

8-53. Answer C. GFDPP 8C, PHB
NOTE: Use scale at top of chart for distance.

This question requires you to calculate groundspeed and then estimated time of arrival.

1. Determine the actual groundspeed (GS) of the aircraft.

   a. Measure the distance between Hampton Roads Airport and Chesapeake Municipal (CPK)—10 NM.

   b. Determine the elapsed time (15:01 – 14:56 = 5 min).

   c. Determine the GS (10 NM in 5 min = 2 NM/min × 60 min = 120 knots groundspeed).

2. Determine the estimated time of arrival (ETA) at First Flight Airport.

   a. Measure the distance between Chesapeake Municipal and First Flight Airport (50 NM).

   b. Determine the time enroute between the two points (50 NM at 120 knots = approximately 25 minutes).

   c. If the aircraft was over Chesapeake Municipal at 15:01, the ETA at First Flight Airport is about 15:26. (15:01 + 25 min = 15:26).

8-54   PLT012   PA.I.D.K3a
(Refer to Figure 21.)
What is the estimated time enroute from Mercer County Regional Airport (area 3) to Minot International (area 1)? The wind is from 330° at 25 knots and the true airspeed is 100 knots. Add 3-1/2 minutes for departure and climbout.

A – 44 minutes

B – 48 minutes

C – 52 minutes

8-54. Answer B. GFDPP 8C, PHB
This question requires you to calculate groundspeed and then complete a time-speed-distance problem.

1. Measure the distance between Mercer County Regional Airport and Minot International—59 NM

2. Determine the True Course (TC)—012°

3. Determine the groundspeed using your flight computer:

    a. Enter the wind direction and speed (330° True at 25 knots)

    b. Enter the TC—012°

    c. Enter the true airspeed (TAS)—100 knots

    d. GS = 80 knots

4. Determine the time enroute using your flight computer: (59 NM at 80 NM/hr = 44 min 15 sec)

5. Add departure and climbout time: (3 min 30 sec + 44 min 15 sec = 47 min 45 sec)

Round up to 48 minutes.

8-55   PLT012   PA.I.D.K3a
(Refer to Figure 22.)
What is the estimated time enroute from Sandpoint Airport (area 1) to St. Maries Airport (area 4)? The wind is from 215° at 25 knots and the true airspeed is 125 knots.

A – 38 minutes

B – 34 minutes

C – 30 minutes

8-55. Answer B. GFDPP 08C, PHB
This question requires you to calculate groundspeed and then complete a time-speed-distance problem.

1. Measure the distance from Sandpoint Airport Maries Airport (approximately 58 NM).

2. Determine the true course (TC = 181°).

3. Determine groundspeed using the flight computer.

    a. Enter the wind direction and speed (215° True at 25 knots).

    b. Enter the TC (181°).

    c. Enter the True Airspeed (125 knots).

    d. GS=103 knots

4. Determine the time enroute using the flight computer (58 NM at 103 NM/hr = 34 min).

8-56   PLT012   PA.I.D.K3a
(Refer to Figure 22.)
Determine the estimated time enroute for a flight from Priest River Airport (area 1) to Shoshone County Airport (area 3). The wind is from 030 at 12 knots and the true airspeed is 95 knots. Add 2 minutes for climbout.

A – 27 minutes

B – 29 minutes

C – 31 minutes

8-56. Answer C. GFDPP 8C, PHB
This question requires you to calculate groundspeed and then complete a time-speed-distance problem.

1. Measure the distance from Priest River Airport to Shoshone County Airport (48 NM).

2. Determine the true course (TC = 143°).

3. Determine groundspeed using the flight computer.

   a. Enter the wind direction and speed (030° True at 12 knots).

   b. Enter the TC (143°).

   c. Enter the True Airspeed (95 knots).

   d. GS=99 knots

4. Determine the time enroute using the flight computer (48 NM at 99 NM/hr = 29 min).

5. Add 2 min for departure and climbout (2 min+ 29 min = 31 min).

8-57   PLT012   PA.I.D.K3a
(Refer to Figure 22.)
What is the estimated time enroute for a flight from St. Maries Airport (area 4) to Priest River Airport (area 1)? The wind is from 300° at 14 knots and the true airspeed is 90 knots. Add 3 minutes for climbout.

A – 38 minutes

B – 43 minutes

C – 48 minutes

8-57. Answer B. GFDPP 8C, PHB
This question requires you to calculate groundspeed and then complete a time-speed-distance problem.

1. Measure the distance from St. Maries Airport to Priest River Airport (53 NM).

2. Determine the True Course (345°).

3. Determine groundspeed using your flight computer.

   a. Enter the wind direction and speed (300° at 14 knots).

   b. Enter the True Course (345°).

   c. Enter the TAS (90 knots).

   d. GS = 80 knots

4. Determine the time enroute using your flight computer (53 NM at 80 NM/hr = 39 min 45 sec).

5. Add 3 min for departure and climbout (3 min + 39 min 45 sec = 42 min 45 sec). Round up to 43 minutes.

8-58   PLT012   PA.I.D.K3a
(Refer to Figure 23.)
What is the estimated time enroute for a flight from Allendale County Airport (area 1) to Claxton-Evans County Airport (area 2)? The wind is from 100° at 18 knots and the true airspeed is 115 knots. Add 2 minutes for climbout.

A – 33 minutes

B – 27 minutes

C – 30 minutes

8-58. Answer C. GFDPP 8C, PHB
This question requires you to calculate groundspeed and then complete a time-speed-distance problem.

1. Measure the distance from Allendale County to Claxton-Evans County Airport (57 NM).

2. Determine the true course (TC = 212°).

3. Determine groundspeed using the flight computer.

    a. Enter the wind direction and speed (100° True at 18 knots).

    b. Enter the TC (212°).

    c. Enter the True Airspeed (115 knots).

    d. GS = 121 knots

4. Determine the time enroute using the flight computer (57 NM ÷ 121 NM/hr = 28 min 15 sec).

5. Add 2 min for departure and climbout (2 min + 28 min 15 sec = 30 min 15 sec).

8-59   PLT012   PA.I.D.K3a
(Refer to Figure 23.)
What is the estimated time enroute for a flight from Claxton-Evans County Airport (area 2) to Hampton Varnville Airport (area 1)? The wind is from 290° at 18 knots and the true airspeed is 85 knots. Add 2 minutes for climbout.

A – 35 minutes

B – 39 minutes

C – 44 minutes

8-59. Answer B. GFDPP 8C, PHB
This question requires you to calculate groundspeed and then complete a Time-Speed-Distance problem.

1. Measure the distance from Claxton-Evans County Airport to Hampton Varnville Airport (57 NM).

2. Determine the True Course (045°).

3. Determine the groundspeed using your flight computer.

    a. Enter the wind direction and speed (290° at 18 knots).

    b. Enter the True Course (045°).

    c. Enter the TAS (85 knots).

    d. GS = 91 knots

4. Determine the time enroute using your flight computer (57 NM ÷ 91 NM/hr = 37 min 30 sec).

5. Add 2 minutes for departure and climbout (2 min + 37 min 30 sec = 39 min 30 sec).

8-60   PLT012   PA.VI.A.K7
(Refer to Figure 23.)
While enroute on Victor 185, a flight crosses the 248°
radial of Allendale VOR at 0953 and then crosses the
216° radial of Allendale VOR at 1000. What is the
estimated time of arrival at Savannah VORTAC?

A – 1023

B – 1027

C – 1036

8-60. Answer B. GFDPP 8C, PHB
This question requires you to calculate groundspeed
and then estimated time of arrival.

1. Determine the groundspeed of the aircraft.

    a. Measure the distance along Victor 185 where
        it crosses the 248° radial and the 216° radial of
        Allendale VOR (10 NM).

    b. Determine the elapsed time. (10:00 – 09:53 =
        7 min).

    c. Determine the groundspeed (10 NM ÷ 7 min =
        86 knots).

2. Determine the estimated time of arrival (ETA)
    over the Savannah VORTAC.

    a. Measure the distance along Victor 185 from
        the 216° radial of Allendale VORTAC to the
        Savannah VORTAC (39 NM).

    b. Determine time enroute (GS is 86 knots)
        (39 NM ÷ 86 NM/hr = 27 min)

    c. Determine estimated time of arrival (10:00 +
        27 min = 10:27).

8-61   PLT012   PA.I.D.K3a
(Refer to Figure 25.)
What is the estimated time enroute for a flight from
Denton Muni (area 1) to Addison (area 2)? The wind
is from 200° at 20 knots, the true airspeed is 110
knots, and the magnetic variation is 7° east.

A – 13 minutes

B – 16 minutes

C – 19 minutes

8-61. Answer A. GFDPP 8C, PHB
This question requires you to calculate groundspeed,
then complete a time-speed-distance problem.

1. Measure the distance from Denton Muni to
    Addison Airport (23 NM).

2. Determine True Course (128°).

3. Determine the groundspeed using your flight
    computer.

    a. Enter the wind direction and speed (200° at 20
        knots).

    b. Enter the True Course (128°).

    c. Enter the TAS (110 knots).

    d. GS = 102 knots

4. Determine time enroute (23 NM ÷ 102 NM/hr = 13
    min 30 sec). The closest answer is 13 minutes.

8-62   PLT012   PA.I.D.K3a
(Refer to Figure 25.)
Estimate the time enroute from Addison (area 2) to
Dallas Executive (area 3). The wind is from 300°
at 15 knots, the true airspeed is 120 knots, and the
magnetic variation is 4° east.

A – 8 minutes

B – 11 minutes

C – 14 minutes

8-62. Answer A. GFDPP 8C, PHB
This question requires you to calculate groundspeed,
then complete a time-speed-distance problem.

1. Measure the distance from Addison Airport to
   Dallas Executive (RBD) Airport (17 NM).

2. Determine the true course (186°).

3. Determine the groundspeed using your flight
   computer.

   a. Enter the wind direction and speed (300° at 15
      knots).

   b. Enter the TC (186°).

   c. Enter the TAS (120 knots).

   d. GS = 125 knots

4. Determine time enroute:
   17 NM ÷ 125 NM/hr × 60 min/hr = 8 min

8-63   PLT012   PA.I.D.K3a
If a true heading of 135° results in a ground track
of 130° and a true airspeed of 135 knots results in a
groundspeed of 140 knots, the wind would be from

A – 019° and 12 knots

B – 200° and 13 knots

C – 246° and 13 knots

8-63. Answer C. GFDPP 8C
Use a flight computer to solve for wind direction and
velocity. This calculation is essentially the reverse of
predicting groundspeed from forecast winds aloft.

8-64   PLT012   PA.V.B.K3
(Refer to Figure 62.)
In flying the rectangular course, when would the
aircraft be turned less than 90°?

A – Corners 1 and 4

B – Corners 1 and 2

C – Corners 2 and 4

8-64. Answer A. GFDPP 8C, AFH
To maintain the rectangular ground track at turn 1,
the aircraft is turned less than 90 degrees to establish
a right crab into the wind. Approaching turn 4, the
aircraft is crabbed left into the wind and is therefore
turned less than 90 degrees into the direct headwind.

8-65   PLT219   PA.V.B.K3
(Refer to Figure 66.)
While practicing S-turns, a consistently smaller half-circle is made on one side of the road than on the other, and this turn is not completed before crossing the road or reference line. This would most likely occur in turn

A – 1-2-3 because the bank is decreased too rapidly during the latter part of the turn.

B – 4-5-6 because the bank is increased too rapidly during the early part of the turn.

C – 4-5-6 because the bank is increased too slowly during the latter part of the turn.

8-65. Answer B. AFH
Turn 4-5-6 begins with an upwind leg (traveling into a headwind), resulting in a slower groundspeed. The slower groundspeed requires the pilot to add bank more slowly than on the downwind leg, so the aircraft has more time to travel equidistant from the "road" as it did on the other side, helping to create semicircles with the same radii.

8-66   PLT012   PA.I.D.K3a
How far will an aircraft travel in 2-1/2 minutes with a groundspeed of 98 knots?

A – 2.45 NM

B – 3.35 NM

C – 4.08 NM

8-66. Answer C. GFDPP 8C
You can solve this problem using a flight computer or mathematically. The basic formula for calculating time, speed, and distance is:

Distance = Groundspeed × Time

Distance = 98 NM/hr × 2.5 min ÷ 60 min/hr

8-67   PLT012   PA.I.D.K3a
How far will an aircraft travel in 7.5 minutes with a groundspeed of 114 knots?

A – 14.25 NM

B – 15.00 NM

C – 14.50 NM

8-67. Answer A. GFDPP 8C, PHB
You can calculate this distance on a flight computer or do the basic math:

114 NM/hr × 7.5 min ÷ 60 min/hr = 14.25 NM

8-68   PLT012   PA.VI.A.K7

On a cross-country flight, point A is crossed at 1500 hours and the plan is to reach point B at 1530 hours. Use the following information to determine the indicated airspeed required to reach point B on schedule.

Distance between A and B: 70 NM

Forecast wind: 310° at 15 knots

Pressure altitude: 8,000 ft

Ambient temperature: -10°C

True course: 270°

The required indicated airspeed would be approximately

A – 126 knots.

B – 137 knots.

C – 152 knots.

8-68. Answer B. GFDPP 8C, PHB

1. Determine the groundspeed required to reach point B by 1530. Use a flight computer or calculate mathematically:
    70 NM ÷ 30 min × 60 min/hr = 140 knots

2. Use the Winds function of your flight computer to determine the required TAS with the given right quartering headwind: 152 knots

3. Use the airspeed function of your flight computer to determine the indicated airspeed (or calibrated airspeed): 137 knots

CHAPTER 9

NAVIGATION

SECTION A — PILOTAGE AND DEAD RECKONING

Pilotage and dead reckoning allow pilots to navigate over unfamiliar terrain. The two systems are used to cross check each other, and together they enable pilots to create a course and stay on that course. This section covers pilotage, which is navigating by using checkpoints; and dead reckoning, which enables you to determine and adjust your course. Using a navigation log and filling out a flight plan form are also covered.

DEAD RECKONING

- Dead reckoning involves calculating distance, speed, time, and direction as a means of navigating from your departure to your destination.

- To determine a magnetic course, you must first find the true course, using a plotter. Then, find the nearest isogonic line to the course. Add, or subtract, the variation. When the variation listed is west, add it to the true course to derive the magnetic course. If the variation is east, you must subtract it.

- To determine the magnetic heading, you must first determine the true heading by correcting the true course for winds. Use the wind side of your flight computer. Then, correct true heading for magnetic variation.

VFR CRUISING ALTITUDES

- On an eastbound course (0° to 179°) above 3,000 feet AGL, VFR cruising altitudes are odd thousands plus 500 feet.

- On a westbound course (180° to 359°), VFR cruising altitudes are even thousands plus 500 feet.

FUEL REQUIREMENTS

- For a VFR night flight in an airplane, there must be enough fuel, considering wind and forecast weather conditions, to fly to the first point of intended landing, and, assuming normal cruising speed, 45 minutes beyond that point.

- For VFR day flight in an airplane, there must be enough fuel to fly to the first point of intended landing, and to fly for 30 minutes after that, assuming normal cruising speed.

9-1   PLT467   PA.VI.A.K12
Which cruising altitude is appropriate for a VFR flight on a magnetic course of 135°?

A – Even thousands

B – Even thousands plus 500 feet

C – Odd thousands plus 500 feet

9-1. Answer C. GFDPP 9A, FAR 91.159
On an easterly magnetic course (0° to 179°) above 3,000 feet AGL, VFR cruising altitudes are odd thousands plus 500 feet.

9-2   PLT467   PA.VI.A.K12

Which VFR cruising altitude is acceptable for a flight on a Victor Airway with a magnetic course of 175°? The terrain is less than 1,000 feet.

A – 4,500 feet

B – 5,000 feet

C – 5,500 feet

9-2. Answer C. GFDPP 9A, FAR 91.159

On a westerly magnetic course (180° to 359°) above 3,000 feet AGL, VFR cruising altitudes are even thousands plus 500 feet.

9-3   PLT467   PA.VI.A.K12

Which VFR cruising altitude is appropriate when flying above 3,000 feet AGL on a magnetic course of 185°?

A – 4,000 feet

B – 4,500 feet

C – 5,000 feet

9-3. Answer B. GFDPP 9A, FAR 91.159

On a westerly magnetic course (180° to 359°) above 3,000 feet AGL, VFR cruising altitudes are even thousands plus 500 feet.

9-4   PLT467   PA.VI.A.K12

Each person operating an aircraft at a VFR cruising altitude shall maintain an odd-thousand plus 500-foot altitude while on a

A – magnetic heading of 0° through 179°.

B – magnetic course of 0° through 179°.

C – true course of 0° through 179°.

9-4. Answer B. GFDPP 9A, FAR 91.159

On an easterly magnetic course (0° to 179°) above 3,000 feet AGL, VFR cruising altitudes are even thousands plus 500 feet.

9-5   PLT012   PA.VI.A.K2

(Refer to Figure 20.)
Determine the magnetic course from First Flight Airport (area 5) to Hampton Roads Airport (area 2).

A – 141°

B – 321°

C – 331°

9-5. Answer C. GFDPP 9A, PHB

This question requires finding the magnetic course by determining true course, then correcting for magnetic variation.

1. Determine the True Course with a plotter (321°).

2. Locate the nearest isogonic line (10° West).

3. Convert TC to MC by adding west variation (321° + 10° = 331°).

9-6   PLT012   PA.VI.A.K5

(Refer to Figure 21.) Determine the magnetic heading for a flight from Mercer County Regional Airport (area 3) to Minot International (area 1). The wind is from 330° at 25 knots, the true airspeed is 100 knots, and the magnetic variation is 10° east.

A – 002°

B – 012°

C – 352°

9-6. Answer C. GFDPP 9A, PHB

This question requires you to find magnetic heading. First, determine the true heading by correcting true course for winds. Then, correct true heading for magnetic variation.

1. Use the plotter to measure true course (012°).

2. Use the flight computer to determine true heading.

    a. Enter wind direction and speed (330° at 25 knots).

    b. Enter the true course (012°).

    c. Enter the TAS (100 knots).

    d. TH = 002°.

3. Convert TH to MH by correcting for magnetic variation (10°E). (Because this is an east variation, you must subtract it from the true heading.)

    TH ± Variation = MH (002° – 10° = 352°)

9-7   PLT012   PA.VI.A.K5

(Refer to Figure 22.) Determine the magnetic heading for a flight from Sandpoint Airport (area 1) to St. Maries Airport (area 4). The wind is from 215° at 25 knots, and the true airspeed is 125 knots.

A – 171°

B – 187°

C – 351°

9-7. Answer A. GFDPP 9A, PHB

This question requires you to find magnetic heading. First, determine the true heading by correcting true course for winds. Then, correct true heading for magnetic variation.

1. Use the plotter to measure true course (181°).

2. Use the flight computer to determine true heading.

    a. Enter the wind direction and speed (215° at 25 knots).

    b. Enter the true course (181°).

    c. Enter the TAS (125 knots).

    d. Determine true heading (TH = 187°).

3. Convert TH to MH by correcting for magnetic variation (round to 16°E). Because this is an east variation, you must subtract it from the true heading.)

    TH ± Variation = MH (187° – 16° = 171°).

9-8   PLT012   PA.VI.A.K5
(Refer to Figure 22.)
What is the magnetic heading for a flight from Priest River Airport (area 1) to Shoshone County Airport (area 3)? The wind is from 030° at 12 knots and the true airspeed is 95 knots.

A – 120°

B – 136°

C – 143°

9-8. Answer A. GFDPP 9A, PHB
This question requires you to find magnetic heading. First, determine the true heading by correcting true course for winds. Then, correct true heading for magnetic variation.

1. Use the plotter to measure true course (143°).

2. Use the flight computer to calculate true heading.

   a. Enter the wind direction and speed (030° at 12 knots).

   b. Enter the true course (143°).

   c. Enter the TAS (95 knots).

   d. TH = 136°

3. Convert TH to MH by correcting for magnetic variation (round to 16°E). Because this is an east variation, you must subtract it from the true heading.)
      TH ± Variation = MH (136° – 16° = 120°).

9-9   PLT012   PA.VI.A.K5
(Refer to Figure 22.)
Determine the magnetic heading for a flight from St. Maries Airport (area 4) to Priest River Airport (area 1). The wind is from 340° at 10 knots and the true airspeed is 90 knots.

A – 320°

B – 329°

C – 345°

9-9. Answer B. GFDPP 9A, PHB
This question requires you to find magnetic heading. First, determine the true heading by correcting true course for winds. Then, correct true heading for magnetic variation.

1. Use the plotter to measure true course (345°).

2. Use the flight computer to calculate true heading.

   a. Enter the wind direction and speed (340° at 10 knots).

   b. Enter the true course (345°).

   c. Enter the TAS (90 knots).

   d. TH = 345°

3. Convert TH to MH by correcting for magnetic variation (round to 16°E). Because this is an east variation, you must subtract it from the true heading.)
      TH± Variation = MH (345° – 16° = 329°).

9-10   PLT012   PA.VI.A.K5
(Refer to Figure 23.)
Determine the magnetic heading for a flight from
Allendale County Airport (area 1) to Claxton-Evans
County Airport (area 2). The wind is from 090° at
16 knots and the true airspeed is 90 knots and the
magnetic variation is 6°W.

A – 209°

B – 215°

C – 230°

9-10. Answer A. GFDPP 9A, PHB
This question requires you to find magnetic heading.
First, determine the true heading by correcting true
course for winds. Then, correct true heading for
magnetic variation.

1. Use the plotter to measure true course (212°).

2. Use the flight computer to calculate true heading.

   a. Enter the wind direction and speed (090° at 16
      knots).

   b. Enter the true course (212°).

   c. Enter the TAS (90 knots).

   d. TH = 203°

3. Convert TH to MH by correcting for magnetic
   variation (6°W). Because this is a west variation,
   you must add it from the true heading.)
   TH ± Variation = MH (203° + 6° = 209°).

9-11   PLT012   PA.VI.A.K10
(Refer to Figure 23 and 58.)
Determine the compass heading for a flight from
Claxton-Evans County Airport (area 2) to Hampton
Varnville Airport (area 1). The wind is from 280° at
08 knots, and the true airspeed is 85 knots, and the
magnetic variation is 6°W.

A – 033°

B – 038°

C – 044°

9-11. Answer C. GFDPP 9A, PHB
This question requires you to find the heading, then
correct for variation and deviation to achieve compass
heading.

1. Use the plotter to measure true course (045°).

2. Use the flight computer to calculate true heading
   (041°).

3. Add variation (6°W) to TH to get magnetic heading
   (047°).

4. Adjust per compass card (–3°) to determine
   compass heading (044°).

9-12   PLT012   PA.VI.A.K2
(Refer to Figure 24.)
Determine the magnetic course from Airpark East
Airport (area 1) to Winnsboro Airport (area 2).
Magnetic variation is 3°E.

A – 079°

B – 082°

C – 091°

9-12. Answer B. GFDPP 9A, PHB
This question requires you find the magnetic course
by determining true course, then correcting it for
magnetic variation.

1. Use the plotter to measure true course (085°).

2. Convert TC to MC by correcting for variation.
   (Because this is an east variation, you must
   subtract it from true course.)
   TC ± Variation = MC (085° – 3° = 082°

9-13   PLT012   PA.VI.A.K5

(Refer to Figure 25.)
Determine the magnetic heading for a flight from Fort Worth Meacham (area 4) to Denton Muni (area 1). The wind is from 330° at 25 knots, the true airspeed is 110 knots, and the magnetic variation is 4° east.

A – 007°

B – 017°

C – 023°

9-13. Answer A. GFDPP 9A, PHB

This question requires you to find magnetic heading. First, determine the true heading by correcting true course for winds. Then, correct true heading for magnetic variation.

1. Use your plotter to determine true course (021°).

2. Use your flight computer to calculate true heading.

    a. Enter the wind direction and speed (330° at 25 knots).

    b. Enter the true course (021°).

    c. Enter the TAS (110 knots).

    d. TH = 011°

3. Convert TH to MH by correcting for magnetic variation (4°E). (Because this is an east variation, you must subtract it from the true heading.)
TH ± Variation = MH (011° − 4° = 007°)

9-14   PLT012   PA.VI.A.K2

(Refer to Figure 27.)
Determine the magnetic course from BRYN (Pvt) Airport (area 2) to Jamestown Airport (area 4).

A – 228°

B – 233°

C – 360°

9-14. Answer A. GFDPP 9A, PHB

The true course, as measured with a plotter, is 233°. The isogonic line down the middle of the figure indicates a 5° east magnetic variation.

Subtract easterly variation to get magnetic course (233° − 5° = 228°).

9-15   PLT455   PA.I.D.K5

How should a VFR flight plan be closed at the completion of the flight at a controlled airport?

A – The tower automatically closes the flight plan when the airplane turns off the runway.

B – The pilot must close the flight plan with Flight Service or by using EasyClose from 1800wxbrief.com.

C – The tower relays the instructions to Flight Service when the aircraft contacts the tower for landing.

9-15. Answer B. GFDPP 9A, PHB

To close a VFR flight plan, you must notify Flight Service by radio or telephone, or click the link in EasyClose email or text message you get if you register with Flight Service.

SECTION B — VOR NAVIGATION

This section covers the components of the VOR system, including distance measuring equipment (DME), and how to use this equipment in the airplane.

NAVIGATION PROCEDURES

- To find your position relative to a VOR on the sectional chart, draw a line along a radial until it intersects your position, or the position of the object you wish to locate. Determine the radial using the compass rose depicted on the chart. Measure the distance from the VOR using a plotter.

- To determine your course to a VOR, find your position along a radial, and find the reciprocal by adding or subtracting 180° from the radial.

- The magnetic course can be determined by plotting a line from your position or departure point to the VOR. Remember that the radial you read from the compass rose is the reciprocal of what you would select on the OBS to fly TO the station.

- You can find your position by triangulation, using two or more VORs. Determine the radial you are on from one VOR, and draw a line from the VOR through the compass rose on that radial. Repeat the procedure with another VOR facility. The intersection point is your location.

- Your position is reflected on the VOR receiver by the position of the CDI needle. If the needle is vertical, you are on the radial selected on the OBS. If the needle shows a left or right deflection, you are left or right of course. If the needle is centered with a FROM indication, the heading tuned in on the OBS reflects the radial you are on. Make sure that you have the correct radial selected on the OBS; if you have tuned in the reciprocal, the CDI reverse senses.

- If the TO-FROM indicator is blank, you are over the cone of confusion, and the aircraft is either over the station, or on a radial offset 90 degrees from the radial selected on the OBS.

- When the CDI needle is centered during an omnireceiver check using a VOR test signal (VOT), the OBS and the TO-FROM indicator should read 0° FROM or 180° TO, regardless of the position of the aircraft from the VOT.

9-16   PLT090   PA.VI.B.K1
(Refer to Figure 20, area 3 and Figure 28.)
The VOR is tuned to Elizabeth City VOR, and the aircraft is positioned over Shawboro, a small town 3 NM west of Currituck County Regional (ONX). Which VOR indication is correct?

A – 2

B – 5

C – 8

9-16. Answer B. GFDPP 9-23, PHB
Shawboro is on the 030° radial of Elizabeth City VOR. A VOR needle would be centered on 030° with a FROM indication (VOR #9) or 210° with a TO indication (VOR #5).

9-17   PLT014   PA.VI.B.K1
(Refer to Figure 21.)
What course should be selected on the omnibearing selector (OBS) to make a direct flight from Mercer County Regional Airport (area 3) to the Minot VORTAC (area 1) with a TO indication?

A – 357°

B – 177°

C – 001°

9-17. Answer A. GFDPP 9B, PHB
The magnetic course can be determined by plotting a line from Mercer County Regional Airport to the Minot VORTAC. The line intersects the Minot VORTAC compass rose at 177°. The reciprocal of 177° is 357°, which is what you would set in the OBS.

9-18   PLT012   PA.VI.B.K1
(Refer to Figure 23.)
What is the approximate position of the aircraft if the VOR receivers indicate the 341° radial of Savannah VORTAC (area 3) and the 184° radial of Allendale VOR (area 1)?

A – Town of Guyton

B – Town of Springfield

C – 3 miles east of Marlow

9-18. Answer B. GFDPP 9B, PHB
The intersection of these two radials places the aircraft near the town of Springfield. The town of Guyton is west of both of these radials.

9-19   PLT014   PA.VI.B.K1
(Refer to Figure 23.)
On what course should the VOR receiver (OBS) be set to navigate direct from Hampton Varnville Airport (area 1) to Savannah VORTAC (area 3)?

A – 015°

B – 195°

C – 220°

9-19. Answer B. GFDPP 9B, PHB
If you draw a line from Hampton Varnville Airport to Savannah VORTAC, which is on the field at Savannah Hilton Head International airport, it crosses the Savannah compass rose at 015°. To navigate inbound with a "TO" indication would require the reciprocal of 015°, or 195°, to be set in the course selector.

9-20   PLT014   PA.VI.B.K1
(Refer to Figure 24.)
What is the approximate position of the aircraft if the VOR receivers indicate the 245° radial of Sulphur Springs VOR-DME (area 5) and the 144° radial of Bonham VORTAC (area 3)?

A – The town of Lone Oak

B – Glenmar Airport

C – Majors Airport

9-20. Answer B. GFDPP 9-23, PHB
Draw the radials from these VORs. The intersection of these two radials puts the aircraft near the Glenmar private airport. Majors Airport and the town of Lone Oak are both west of the Bonham 144° radial.

9-21   PLT014   PA.VI.B.K1
(Refer to Figure 24.)
On what course should the VOR receiver (OBS) be set to navigate direct from Majors Airport (area 1) to Quitman VOR (area 2)?

A – 100°

B – 108°

C – 280°

9-21. Answer A. GFDPP 9B, PHB
A direct course from Majors Airport to Quitman VOR crosses the compass rose at 280°. The inbound course to be set in the OBS is the reciprocal of 280°, or 100°.

9-22   PLT014   PA.VI.B.K1
(Refer to Figure 24 and 28.)
The VOR is tuned to Bonham VORTAC (area 3), and the aircraft is positioned over the Sulphur Springs airport (area 5). Which VOR indication is correct?

A – 1

B – 3 or 7

C – 8

9-22. Answer B. GFDPP 9B, PHB
Sulfur Springs airport is on the 120° radial of the Bonham VORTAC. Because all the VOR indicators in the figure have either 030° or 210° set in the OBS, you must determine the position of the aircraft in relation to these settings and the VOR station. Because the 120° radial is perpendicular to the 030°/210° radials, the TO-FROM indicator indicates "OFF".

With the OBS set to 030°, the CDI is deflected to the left, which is the display on VOR indicator #7.

With the OBS set to 210°, the CDI is deflected to the right, which is the display on VOR indicator #3.

VOR indicators #1 and #8 are incorrect because the TO-FROM indicators indicate "TO" instead of "OFF".

9-23   PLT014   PA.VI.B.K1
(Refer to Figure 25, area 5.)
The VOR is tuned to the Maverick VOR, which is just south of DFW. The omnibearing selector (OBS) is set on 253°, with a TO indication, and a left course deviation indicator (CDI) deflection. What is the aircraft's position from the VORTAC?

A – East-northeast

B – East-southeast

C – West-southwest

9-23. Answer A. GFDPP 9B, PHB
A course of 253° with a TO indication takes the aircraft to the station. This means that the aircraft is generally on the east side of the station. A CDI deflection to the left means the aircraft to the right (north) of the 253° inbound course.

9-24   PLT014   PA.VI.B.K1
(Refer to Figure 26, areas 2 and 4, and Figure 28.)
The VOR is tuned to Jamestown VOR, and the
aircraft is positioned over Cooperstown Airport.
Which VOR indication is correct?

A – 1

B – 6

C – 9

9-24. Answer C. GFDPP 9B, PHB
Jamestown VOR is in area 4 and the aircraft is
positioned over Cooperstown Airport in area 2, which
is on the JMS 030° radial. With the OBS set to 030°,
the TO-FROM indicator reads "FROM", and the CDI
shows the aircraft centered on course as in OBS
number 9. If the OBS is set to 210°, the TO-FROM
indicator would indicate "TO", so OBS number 5 would
also be correct.

9-25   PLT014   PA.VI.B.K1
(Refer to Figure 28, illustration 1.)
The VOR receiver has the indications shown. What is
the aircraft's position relative to the station?

A – North

B – East

C – South

9-25. Answer B. GFDPP 9B, PHB
With the 210° course selected and a "TO" indication,
if the needle were centered, the aircraft would be on
the 030° radial and a 210° course would take it to
the station. With a right CDI deflection, as shown on
illustration 1, the aircraft is left of course, between
the 030° and 120° radials. That places it east of the
station.

9-26   PLT014   PA.VI.B.K1
(Refer to Figure 28, illustration 3.)
The VOR receiver has the indications shown. What is
the aircraft's position relative to the station?

A – East

B – Southeast

C – West

9-26. Answer B. GFDPP 9B, PHB
The TO-FROM indicator indicates OFF, which means
the aircraft is somewhere on the 120° or 300° radial,
90° from the 210° course. The right CDI deflection
puts the aircraft left of the 210° course, which would
be southeast of the station.

9-27   PLT014   PA.VI.B.K1
(Refer to Figure 28, illustration 8.)
The VOR receiver has the indications shown. What
radial is the aircraft on?

A – 030°

B – 210°

C – 300°

9-27. Answer B. GFDPP 9B, PHB
The aircraft is on the centerline of the selected
course. A 030° course takes the aircraft to the station,
as indicated by a "TO" in the TO-FROM window. That
means the aircraft is on the reciprocal radial of 030°,
the 210° radial.

9-28   PLT014   PA.VI.B.K1

When the course deviation indicator (CDI) needle is centered using a VOR test signal (VOT), the omnibearing selector (OBS) and the TO-FROM indicator should read

A – 180° FROM, only if the pilot is due north of the VOT

B – 0° TO or 180° FROM, regardless of the position from the VOT

C – 0° FROM or 180° TO, regardless of the pilot's position from the VOT

9-28. Answer C. GFDPP 9B, AIM

No matter where the aircraft is located in relation to the VOT, the VOR should always read 180° with a "TO" indication or 0° with a "FROM"

SECTION C — SATELLITE NAVIGATION — GPS

THE GPS SYSTEM

- Global navigation satellite system (GNSS) is the standard generic term for satellite navigation systems. The United States Global Positioning System (GPS) is a primary satellite navigation system that is globally available.
- GPS consists of three segments—the space segment contains a minimum of 24 GPS satellites in orbits that ensure users can view at least four satellites from virtually any point on the earth; the control segment, a network of ground facilities that manages the GPS satellites; and the user segment, the GPS receivers themselves
- By using trilateration, a GPS receiver calculates its distance from three satellites to determine its general position for latitude, longitude, and altitude. A fourth satellite is necessary to determine an accurate position—small timing errors from all four satellites are adjusted to determine the exact location of the airplane.
- Using receiver autonomous integrity monitoring (RAIM), a fifth satellite monitors the position provided by the other four satellites and alerts you of any discrepancy.
- The accuracy of GPS is enhanced with the use of a satellite-based augmentation system (SBAS) known as the Wide Area Augmentation System (WAAS)—a series of ground stations generate a corrective message that is transmitted to aircraft by a geostationary satellite.

AIRBORNE GPS NAVIGATION SYSTEMS

- RNAV equipment computes the aircraft position, actual track, and groundspeed and then displays distance and time estimates relative to the selected course or waypoint.
- GPS equipment installed in the airplane includes panel-mounted units that might also include navigation and communication radios and integrated systems that include digital instrument displays.
- A flight management system (FMS) is a computer system containing a database that enables programming of routes, approaches, and departures. The FMS can supply navigation data to a flight director or autopilot from various sources, and can calculate flight data such as fuel consumption and time remaining.
- Manufacturers divide information into categories, such as NAV, WPT, AUX, and NRST, each of which might contain several pages of information on the GPS display.

NAVIGATING WITH GPS

- Before flight, verify that the navigation database and other databases are current. Database information might include the database type, cycle number, and valid operating dates.
- GPS equipment installed in the airplane normally displays a course deviation indicator (CDI) on an analog indicator or HSI display, and on the GPS unit.
- When the navigation source is GPS, the CDI displays cross-track error in nautical miles. The CDI has three different sensitivities: enroute, terminal, and approach.
- A GPS moving map provides a pictorial view of the present position of the aircraft, the programmed route, the surrounding airspace, and topographical features.

9-29   PLT354   PA.VI.B.K2

If receiver autonomous integrity monitoring (RAIM) capability is lost in-flight,

A – the pilot may still rely on GPS derived altitude for vertical information.

B – the pilot has no assurance of the accuracy of the GPS position.

C – GPS position is reliable provided at least 3 GPS satellites are available.

9-29. Answer B. GFDPPT 9-51, PHB

Receiver autonomous integrity monitoring (RAIM) verifies that enough satellites are in view by your aircraft that if a satellite goes out of view or if the information from a satellite is corrupt, the information from the remaining satellites still provides an accurate position. RAIM provides the degree of reliability necessary for IFR operations. Without RAIM, the accuracy of the GPS position solution is questionable.

9-30   PA.VI.B.K2

What is RAIM?

A – A method by which the GPS receiver uses a fifth satellite to continuously verify the integrity of the signals received from the GPS constellation and then alert you of a discrepancy

B – A series of ground stations that generate a corrective message to improve navigational accuracy by accounting for positional drift of the satellites and signal delays caused by the ionosphere and other atmospheric factors

C – A method by which the GPS receiver computes the aircraft position, track, and groundspeed and displays distance and time estimates relative to the selected course or waypoint

9-30. Answer A. GFDPP 9C

Receiver autonomous integrity monitoring (RAIM) is a method by which the GPS receiver uses a fifth satellite to verify the integrity of the signals received from the GPS constellation and then alert you of any discrepancy.

9-31   **PA.VI.B.K2**

Select the true statement regarding the CDI used for GPS navigation.

A – The CDI displays the lateral distance from the course.

B – The CDI displays the angular deviation from the course.

C – The CDI has three different sensitivities that you must select based on your phase of flight.

9-31. Answer A. GFDPP 9C

Unlike the course deviation indicator (CDI) on a VOR, which displays angular deviation from course, an RNAV CDI displays distance (in NM) off course. GPS CDIs have three different sensitivities based on your phase of flight (enroute, terminal, or approach), but they are not pilot selectable.

9-32   **PA.VI.B.K2**

What is a common error using a GPS moving map?

A – Using the moving map to enhance situational awareness and cross check primary navigation

B – Overreliance on the moving map leading to complacency

C – Incorrectly setting the scale and level of detail on the moving map

9-32. Answer B. GFDPP 9C

Two common errors associated with using a moving map are: using the moving map as a primary navigation instrument and overreliance on the moving map leading to complacency.

9-33   **PA.VI.B.K2**

Select the true statement regarding GPS navigation.

A – Direct-To navigation enables you create a route using several waypoints.

B – The desired track to the next waypoint is the active leg and is normally shown in magenta on a moving map.

C – To check the currency of the navigation database, you must select the valid operating dates to be displayed with other navigation data, such as track and groundspeed.

9-33. Answer B. GFDPP 9C

The desired track for your current (active) leg is shown in magenta by convention. A Direct-To route, contains only a destination waypoint; you navigate there from your present position or along a specific course you designate. To determine the currency of your navigation database, you normally view a message when turning on the system; it is not displayed with other navigation data.

9-34   **PA.VI.B.K2**

What is cross-track error?

A – The distance from your present position to the desired track, measured in nautical miles

B – The difference between your heading and the course caused by a crosswind

C – The difference in direction between the desired track and the aircraft's actual track in degrees

9-34. Answer A. GFDPP 9C

Cross-track error is your deviation from course, or desired track (DTK), in nautical miles—it is what is shown on your course deviation indicator.

The difference in direction between the desired track and the aircraft's actual track is called track angle error (TKE).

APPLYING HUMAN FACTORS PRINCIPLES

SECTION A — AVIATION PHYSIOLOGY

Humans are earthbound creatures, but we possess a remarkable ability to adapt to our surroundings. Our bodies can adjust to the demands of aviation to a certain extent, but you should be aware of the limitations to what humans can cope with in the air. This section covers the role that vision plays in flight, and the dangers of spatial disorientation, carbon monoxide poisoning, hypoxia and hyperventilation.

VISION IN FLIGHT

Understanding how your eyes work under different conditions is crucial to safe flying. Night flying brings on specific issues of which you should be aware.

NIGHT VISION

- The most effective way to look for traffic during night flight is to scan slowly, to permit off-center viewing. Look to the side of an object for the clearest focus.
- During a night flight, you observe a steady red light and a flashing red light ahead and at the same altitude. The other aircraft is crossing to the left.
- During a night flight, you observe a steady white light and a flashing red light ahead and at the same altitude. The other aircraft is flying away from you.
- During a night flight, you observe steady red and green lights ahead and at the same altitude. The other aircraft is approaching head-on.
- VFR approaches to land at night should be accomplished the same as during the daytime.
- To adapt the eyes for night flying, the pilot should avoid bright white lights for at least 30 minutes before the flight.

DISORIENTATION

- A lack of orientation regarding the position, attitude, or movement of the aircraft in space is defined as spatial disorientation.
- You can reduce the danger of spatial disorientation during flight in poor visual conditions by trusting in the instruments rather than taking a chance on your kinesthetic senses. Pilots are more subject to spatial disorientation if using body signals to interpret flight attitude.
- If experiencing spatial disorientation during flight in restricted visibility, the best way to overcome the effect is to rely on the aircraft instrument indications.

RESPIRATION AND ALTITUDE

As humans, we depend on oxygen for our survival. During flight, you can climb to altitudes where oxygen is scarce. Be familiar with the effects that decreased oxygen can have on your ability to perform.

HYPOXIA

Hypoxia is a state of oxygen deficiency in the body.

CARBON MONOXIDE POISONING

- Large accumulations of carbon monoxide in the body result in the loss of muscular power.
- Susceptibility to carbon monoxide poisoning increases as altitude increases.

SUPPLEMENTAL OXYGEN

- When operating an aircraft at cabin pressure altitudes above 12,500 feet MSL up to and including 14,000 feet MSL, supplemental oxygen shall be used, by required crewmembers, during that flight time more than 30 minutes at those altitudes.

- Unless each person is provided with supplemental oxygen, no person may operate a civil aircraft of US registry above a maximum cabin pressure altitude of 15,000 feet MSL.

HYPERVENTILATION

- Rapid or extra deep breathing while using oxygen can cause a condition known as hyperventilation.

- Emotional tension, anxiety, or fear can also lead to hyperventilation.

- A pilot can overcome the symptoms, or avoid future occurrences of hyperventilation, by slowing the breathing rate, breathing into a bag or talking aloud.

10-1   PLT099   PA.XI.A.K1

What is the most effective way to use the eyes during night flight?

A – Look only at far away, dim lights.

B – Scan slowly to permit off-center viewing.

C – Concentrate directly on each object for a few seconds.

10-1. Answer B. GFDPP 10-4, AFH

The rods in the retina are used for night vision. Because they are not located directly behind the pupil, you must use off-center viewing. Also, in dim light, you might need to move your eyes more slowly to prevent blurring of images than during the day.

10-2   PLT099   PA.XI.A.K1

The best method to use when looking for other traffic at night is to

A – look to the side of the object and scan slowly.

B – scan the visual field very rapidly.

C – look to the side of the object and scan rapidly.

10-2. Answer A. GFDPP 10-4, AFH

The most effective method of night scanning is to use off center vision, which means looking to the side of an object, and to scan slowly to prevent blurring.

10-3   PLT099   PA.XI.A.K1

The most effective method of scanning for other aircraft for collision avoidance during nighttime hours is to use

A – regularly spaced concentration on the 3-, 9-, and 12-o'clock positions.

B – a series of short, regularly spaced eye movements to search each 30-degree sector.

C – peripheral vision by scanning small sectors and utilizing off-center viewing.

10-3. Answer C. GFDPP 10-4, FTH

Scanning should be done slowly, in small sectors, using off-center (peripheral) vision.

10-4 PLT333 PA.XI.A.K5
During a night flight, you observe a steady red light and a flashing red light ahead and at the same altitude. What is the general direction of movement of the other aircraft?

A – The other aircraft is crossing to the left.

B – The other aircraft is crossing to the right.

C – The other aircraft is approaching head-on.

10-4. Answer A. GFDPP 10-5, AFH
The steady red light is a position light on the left wing and the flashing red light is an anticollision beacon. If you are looking at the left wingtip, the other aircraft would be crossing to the left.

10-5 PLT119 PA.XI.A.K5
During a night flight, you observe a steady white light and a flashing red light ahead and at the same altitude. What is the general direction of movement of the other aircraft?

A – The other aircraft is flying away from you.

B – The other aircraft is crossing to the left.

C – The other aircraft is crossing to the right.

10-5. Answer A. GFDPP 10-5, AFH
The white position light is on the tail and the flashing red light is the anticollision light. Therefore, you would be looking at the rear of the aircraft, which indicates it is flying away from you.

10-6 PLT119 PA.XI.A.K5
During a night flight, you observe steady red and green lights ahead and at the same altitude. What is the general direction of movement of the other aircraft?

A – The other aircraft is crossing to the left.

B – The other aircraft is flying away from you.

C – The other aircraft is approaching head-on.

10-6. Answer C. GFDPP 10-5, AFH
In this case, you are seeing both wingtip lights. Without a white tail light in between them, you would most likely be looking head-on at the aircraft. In this situation, the green light is on the left and the red light is on the right.

10-7 PLT333 PA.XI.A.K5
VFR approaches to land at night should be accomplished

A – at a higher airspeed.

B – with a steeper descent.

C – the same as during daytime.

10-7. Answer C. GFDPP 10-8, AFH
Try to make night VFR approaches the same as day approaches.

10-8   PLT330   PA.I.H.K1f

Large accumulations of carbon monoxide in the human body result in

A – tightness across the forehead.

B – loss of muscular power.

C – an increased sense of well-being.

10-8. Answer B. GFDPP 10-15, AC 20-32
The key word in this question is "large" accumulations. This condition can produce a loss of muscle power.

10-9   PLt330   PA.I.H.K1a

Which statement best defines hypoxia?

A – A state of oxygen deficiency in the body

B – An abnormal increase in the volume of air breathed

C – A condition of gas bubble formation around the joints or muscles

10-9. Answer A. GFDPP 10-13, AIM
Hypoxia occurs when the body tissues do not receive enough oxygen.

10-10   PLT332   PA.I.H.K1b

When a stressful situation is encountered in flight, an abnormal increase in the volume of air breathed in and out can cause a condition known as

A – hyperventilation.

B – aerosinusitis.

C – aerotitis.

10-10. Answer A. GFDPP 10-18, AIM
Hyperventilation occurs when the breathing rate is too rapid or too deep. It usually occurs with stress and can occur with or without the use of supplemental oxygen. Aerosinusitis is an inflammation of the sinuses and aerotitis is an inflammation of the middle ear. Both problems are caused by changes in air pressure.

10-11   PLT332   PA.I.H.K1b

Which would most likely result in hyperventilation?

A – Emotional tension, anxiety, or fear

B – The excessive consumption of alcohol

C – An extremely slow rate of breathing and insufficient oxygen

10-11. Answer A. GFDPP 10-18, AIM
Emotional tension, anxiety, and fear can cause the rapid, deep breathing associated with hyperventilation.

10-12   PLT332   PA.I.H.K1b

A pilot experiencing the effects of hyperventilation should be able to restore the proper carbon dioxide level in the body by

A – slowing the breathing rate, breathing into a paper bag, or talking aloud.

B – breathing spontaneously and deeply or gaining mental control of the situation.

C – increasing the breathing rate in order to increase lung ventilation.

10-12. Answer A. GFDPP 10-18, AIM
Slowing the breathing rate is one of the best ways to stop hyperventilation. Breathing into a bag and talking aloud are also helpful.

10-13   PLT097   PA.I.H.K1f

Susceptibility to carbon monoxide poisoning increases as

A – altitude increases.

B – altitude decreases.

C – air pressure increases.

10-13. Answer A. GFDPP 10-14, 15, AC 20-32
Because carbon monoxide poisoning is a form of hypoxia, its effects are increased with altitude, where less oxygen is available.

10-14   PLT333   PA.I.H.K1j

What preparation should a pilot make to adapt the eyes for night flying?

A – Wear sunglasses after sunset until ready for flight.

B – Avoid red lights at least 30 minutes before the flight.

C – Avoid bright white lights at least 30 minutes before the flight.

10-14. Answer C. GFDPP 10-5, AIM
The rods in the human eye can take up to 30 minutes to adapt fully to the dark. Bright lights must be avoided for this amount of time.

10-15   PLT334   PA.I.H.K1d

The danger of spatial disorientation during flight in poor visual conditions can be reduced by

A – shifting the eyes quickly between the exterior visual field and the instrument panel.

B – having faith in the instruments rather than taking a chance on the sensory organs.

C – leaning the body in the opposite direction of the motion of the aircraft.

10-15. Answer B. GFDPP 10-9, AIM
To avoid spatial disorientation, a pilot must rely on the instruments in the cockpit and not the feelings from the sensory organs.

10-16   PLT334   PA.I.H.K1d

A lack of orientation regarding the position, attitude, or movement of the aircraft in space is defined as

A – spatial disorientation.

B – hyperventilation.

C – hypoxia.

10-16. Answer A. GFDPP 10-8, PHB

Spatial disorientation occurs when visual cues are removed and the vestibular system in the inner ear and the somatosensory system (nerves and hearing) provide conflicting information to the brain.

10-17   PLT334   PA.I.H.K1d

Pilots are more subject to spatial disorientation if

A – they ignore the sensations of muscles and inner ear.

B – visual cues are taken away, as they are in instrument meteorological conditions (IMC).

C – eyes are moved often in the process of cross-checking the flight instruments.

10-17. Answer B. GFDPP 10-9, PHB

During flight in visual meteorological conditions (VMC), the eyes are the major orientation source and usually prevail over false sensations from other sensory systems. When these visual cues are taken away, as they are in instrument meteorological conditions (IMC), false sensations can quickly cause a pilot to become disoriented. Pilots can overcome spatial disorientation if they ignore the sensations of muscles and inner ear and focus on the flight instruments. Moving the eyes often to cross check the flight instruments is a proper scanning technique that helps prevent spatial disorientation.

10-18   PLT334   PA.I.H.K1d

If a pilot experiences spatial disorientation during flight in a restricted visibility condition, the best way to overcome the effect is to

A – rely upon the aircraft instrument indications.

B – concentrate on yaw, pitch, and roll sensations.

C – consciously slow the breathing rate until symptoms clear and then resume normal breathing rate.

10-18. Answer A. GFDPP 10-9, AIM

Because the brain receives confusing messages from the senses, the pilot must rely on the flight instruments.

SECTION B — SINGLE-PILOT RESOURCE MANAGEMENT

- Single-pilot resource management (SRM) is the art and science of managing all available resources (both on board the airplane and from outside sources) prior and during flight to ensure the successful completion of a flight.
- Five hazardous attitudes that can interfere with a pilot's ability to make effective decisions are: antiauthority, macho, impulsivity, invulnerability, and resignation.

10-19   PLT104   PA.I.H.R2
What is the antidote when a pilot has a hazardous attitude, such as "Macho"?

A – I can do it.

B – Taking chances is foolish.

C – Nothing will happen.

10-19. Answer B. GFDPP 10B, AC 60-22
The antidote for the hazardous attitude, "Macho" is: Taking chances is foolish. "I can do it" and "Nothing will happen" are not antidotes to any of the hazardous attitudes.

10-20   PLT104   PA.I.H.R2
What is the antidote when a pilot has a hazardous attitude, such as "Resignation"?

A – What is the use?

B – Someone else is responsible.

C – I am not helpless.

10-20. Answer C. GFDPP 10B, AC 60-22
The antidote for the hazardous attitude, "Resignation" is: I am not helpless. "What is the use" and "Someone else is responsible" are not antidotes to any of the hazardous attitudes.

10-21   PLT104   PA.I.H.R2
Who is responsible for determining whether a pilot is fit to fly for a particular flight, even with a current medical certificate?

A – The FAA

B – The medical examiner

C – The pilot

10-21. Answer C. GFDPP 10B, AC 60-22
You, the pilot, are always responsible for determining if you are fit to fly for a particular flight. The FAA and medical examiners determine if you are fit to hold a medical certificate.

10-22   PLT104   PA.I.H.K4
Which is the most common factor in preventable accidents?

A – Structural failure

B – Mechanical malfunction

C – Human error

10-22. Answer C. GFDPP 10B, AC 60-22
Most preventable accidents involve human error. Even when a mechanical malfunction or structural failure did occur, human error was a contributing or aggravating factor in many of these accidents.

10-23   PLT103   PA.I.H.K1d
What often leads to spatial disorientation or collision with ground or obstacles when flying under visual flight rules (VFR)?

A – Continued flight into instrument conditions

B – Getting behind the aircraft

C – Duck-under syndrome

10-23. Answer A. GFDPP 10B, AC 60-22
Continuing flight under VFR into instrument conditions often leads to spatial disorientation or collision with ground or obstacles. Getting behind the aircraft does not normally result in spatial disorientation or collision with the ground. Although duck-under syndrome often leads to impact with the ground, it normally does not result in spatial disorientation.

10-24   PLT104   PA.II.B.K2

What is one of the neglected items when a pilot relies on short and long-term memory for repetitive tasks?

A – Checklists

B – Situational awareness

C – Flying outside the envelope

10-24. Answer A. AC 60-22

Pilots who rely on their memory for repetitive tasks often neglect the use of checklists.

10-25   PLT103   PA.I.H.R2

Hazardous attitudes occur to every pilot to some degree at some time. What are some of these hazardous attitudes?

A – Poor risk management and lack of stress management

B – Antiauthority, impulsivity, macho, resignation, and invulnerability

C – Poor situational awareness, snap judgments, and lack of a decision-making process

10-25. Answer B. GFDPP 10B, PHB

The commonly listed hazardous attitudes are antiauthority, impulsivity, macho, resignation, and invulnerability. Each has its own "antidote," as indicated in the following list:

Antiauthority—Follow the rules, they are usually right.

Impulsivity—Not so fast. Think first.

Macho—Taking chances is foolish.

Resignation—I'm not helpless, I can make a difference.

Invulnerability—It *could* happen to me.

10-26   PLT103   PA.I.H.R2

In the aeronautical decision making (ADM) process, what is the first step in neutralizing a hazardous attitude?

A – Making a rational judgment

B – Recognizing hazardous thoughts

C – Recognizing the invulnerability of the situation

10-26. Answer B. GFDPP 10B, PHB

To prevent hazardous attitudes from endangering a flight, pilots must recognize a hazardous attitude, correctly label the thought, and recall its antidote.

10-27   PLT104

Risk management, as part of the aeronautical decision making (ADM) process, relies on which features to reduce the risks associated with each flight?

A – Application of stress management and risk element procedures

B – Situational awareness, problem recognition, and good judgment

C – The mental process of analyzing all information in a particular situation and making a timely decision on what action to take

10-27. Answer B. GFDPP 10B, PHB

As defined by the FAA, Risk Management is the part of the decision-making process that relies on situational awareness, problem recognition, and good judgment to reduce risks associated with each flight.

10-28 PLT011   PA.I.H.K4

A pilot and two passengers landed on a 2,100-foot east-west gravel strip with an elevation of 1,800 feet. The temperature is warmer than expected and after computing the density altitude it is determined the takeoff distance over a 50 foot obstacle is 1,980 feet. The airplane is 75 pounds under gross weight. What would be the best choice?

A – Take off to the west because the headwind will give the extra climbout time needed.

B – Try a takeoff without the passengers to make sure the climb is adequate.

C – Wait until the temperature decreases, and recalculate the takeoff performance.

10-28. 10B. Answer C. AOPA ASI SA18

ADM and risk management questions often do not have a clear-cut answer. Technically, if no obstacles were present, the airplane could take off under the conditions given. However, the safety margin is not as much as planned (which you can infer from the warmer-than-expected temperature in the scenario). The AOPA Air Safety Institute 50/50 solution, a widely accepted safety recommendation, is to add 50 percent to the takeoff distance over a 50-foot obstacle. In this case, the required runway length would be 1,980 × 1.50 = 2,970 feet. Therefore, waiting for the temperature to decrease is the most prudent option.

Nothing in the scenario suggests that taking off to the west would provide a more favorable headwind. Taking off without passengers to "test" the performance might seem like a good option, but it does not provide conclusive performance data by which to risk subsequently taking off with the passengers.

FLYING CROSS-COUNTRY

SECTION A — THE FLIGHT PLANNING PROCESS

This section covers aspects of preflight protocol, including airworthiness, preflight inspection, route selection, weather considerations, completing a navigation log and cockpit management.

- A flight overview includes ensuring that the flight is feasible, selecting the date and time, gathering your flight planning materials, and reviewing your training and experience.

- When you develop the route, you must consider terrain and obstacles, airspace requirements, special use airspace, navaids, and diversion options.

- Select easily identifiable checkpoints, such as prominent landmarks and navaids, to track your position, monitor your progress, and provide references for contacting ATC.

- Obtain your FAA-approved weather briefing by phone or online. You can fill out a preliminary flight plan and select Standard Briefing at 1800wxbrief.com or call a Flight Service briefer at 1-800-WX-BRIEF (1-800-992-7433).

- Complete a navigation log, including true airspeed, headings, leg distances, groundspeed and estimated time enroute, and fuel consumption to record the flight data and to monitor your progress during the cross-country flight.

- After completing your navigation log modify your preliminary flight plan form as necessary.

- File your flight plan with Flight Service online or by phone so that SAR organizations can locate you if you do not reach your destination and close your flight plan.

- The last step in the flight planning process is to perform preflight tasks—assess your condition and the airworthiness of the airplane.

PREFLIGHT INSPECTION

- Each pilot in command shall, before beginning a flight, become familiar with all available information concerning that flight.

- Preflight action, as required for all flights away from the vicinity of an airport, shall include an alternate course of action if the flight cannot be completed as planned.

- In addition to the other preflight actions for a VFR flight away from the vicinity of the departure airport, regulations specifically require the pilot in command to determine runway lengths at airports of intended use and the takeoff and landing distance data for the aircraft.

AIRWORTHINESS

- The airworthiness certificate of an airplane remains valid as long as the aircraft is maintained and operated as required by Federal Aviation Regulations.

- The owner or operator of an aircraft is responsible for ensuring that an aircraft is maintained in an airworthy condition.

WALK-AROUND INSPECTION

- The pilot in command is responsible for determining that an aircraft is in condition for safe flight.
- Concerning preflighting an aircraft, the minimum expected of a pilot prior to every flight is to perform a walk-around inspection.
- The use of a written checklist is recommended for preflight inspection and engine start to ensure that all necessary items are completed in a logical sequence.
- After an aircraft has been stored for an extended time, the pilot should make a special check for damage or obstructions caused by animals, birds, or insects.

11-1   PLT377   PA.I.B.K1

How long does the airworthiness certificate of an aircraft remain valid?

A – As long as the aircraft has a current Registration Certificate

B – Indefinitely, unless the aircraft suffers major damage

C – As long as the aircraft is maintained and operated as required by Federal Aviation Regulations

11-1. Answer C. GFDPP 11A, PHB
The Airworthiness Certificate remains valid only as long as the aircraft is maintained and operated in accordance with the FARs.

11-2   PA.I.C.K1

You planned a route and obtained preliminary weather information to determine the feasibility of your flight. On the morning of your flight, an FAA-approved briefing consists of

A – obtaining a standard briefing at 1800wxbrief.com.

B – obtaining recorded weather by telephone at 1-800-WX-BRIEF (1-800-992-7433).

C – viewing official weather reports, forecasts, and charts at AviationWeather.gov.

11-2. Answer A. GFDPP 11A, PHB
Obtain your FAA-approved weather briefing by telephone or online. You can fill out a preliminary flight plan and select Standard Briefing at 1800wxbrief.com or call a Flight Service briefer at 1-800-WX-BRIEF (1-800-992-7433). While you can obtain official weather service information by listening to recorded weather at 1-800-WX-BRIEF or online at AviationWeather.gov, these methods are not substitutes for an approved briefing, and do not include temporary flight restrictions (TFRs) or other essential NOTAMs.

11-3   PLT444   PA.I.B.S2

During the preflight inspection who is responsible for determining the aircraft is safe for flight?

A – The owner or operator

B – The certificated mechanic who performed the annual inspection

C – The pilot in command

11-3. Answer C. GFDPP 11A, PHB

The owner or operator is responsible to make sure that the required maintenance and inspections are performed. These tasks may be assigned to a certificated maintenance technician, but the responsibility for compliance remains with the owner or operator. Preflight inspection is the responsibility of the pilot in command (PIC). Before every flight, the PIC is required to accomplish a thorough and systematic preflight to ensure that the aircraft is safe for flight. The preflight inspection should be completed according to procedures recommended by the manufacturer. Normally, this means the PIC should use a checklist for the preflight inspection.

11-4   PLT444   PA.I.B.S2

How should an aircraft preflight inspection be accomplished for the first flight of the day?

A – Thorough and systematic means recommended by the manufacturer

B – Quick walk around with a check of gas and oil

C – Any sequence as determined by the pilot-in-command

11-4. Answer A. GFDPP 11-11, 12, PHB

The owner or operator is responsible to make sure that the required maintenance and inspections are performed. These tasks may be assigned to a certificated maintenance technician, but the responsibility for compliance remains with the owner or operator. Preflight inspection is the responsibility of the pilot in command (PIC). Before every flight, the PIC is required to accomplish a thorough and systematic preflight to ensure that the aircraft is safe for flight. The preflight inspection should be completed according to procedures recommended by the manufacturer. Normally, this means the PIC should use a checklist for the preflight inspection.

11-5   PLT377   PA.I.B.K1

Who is primarily responsible for maintaining an aircraft in airworthy condition?

A – Pilot-in-command

B – Owner or operator

C – Mechanic

11-5. Answer B. GFDPP 11-11, PHB

The owner or operator is responsible to make sure that the required maintenance and inspections are performed. These tasks may be assigned to a certificated maintenance technician, but the responsibility for compliance remains with the owner or operator. Preflight inspection is the responsibility of the pilot in command (PIC). Before every flight, the PIC is required to accomplish a thorough and systematic preflight to ensure that the aircraft is safe for flight. The preflight inspection should be completed according to procedures recommended by the manufacturer. Normally, this means the PIC should use a checklist for the preflight inspection.

SECTION B — THE FLIGHT

- As pilot in command, you are expected, before beginning a flight, to become familiar with all available information concerning that flight.
- For day VFR flight in an airplane, you must carry enough fuel (considering wind and forecast weather conditions) to fly to the first point of intended landing, and, assuming normal cruising speed, 30 minutes thereafter. For night VFR flight, you must carry a 45-minute fuel reserve.
- To increase forward visibility during a climb, lower the nose periodically and clear the area, and then transition to cruise climb when altitude permits.

11-6   PLT440   PA.I.D.S1

Which preflight action is specifically required of the pilot before each flight?

A – Check the aircraft logbooks for appropriate entries.

B – Become familiar with all available information concerning the flight.

C – Review wake turbulence avoidance procedures.

11-6. Answer B. GFDPP 11B, FAR 91.103
Each pilot in command shall, before beginning a flight, become familiar with all available information concerning that flight. Checking the aircraft logbooks is an appropriate action, but that is not the most direct or complete answer.

11-7   PLT440   PA.I.D.S1

Preflight action, as required for all flights away from the vicinity of an airport, shall include

A – the designation of an alternate airport.

B – a study of arrival procedures at airports/heliports of intended use.

C – an alternate course of action if the flight cannot be completed as planned.

11-7. Answer C. GFDPP 11B, FAR 91.103
The preflight action for flights away from the vicinity of an airport include checking weather reports and forecasts, fuel requirements, alternatives available if the flight cannot be completed as planned, and any known traffic delays.

11-8   PLT413   PA.I.D.K3c

What is the specific fuel requirement for flight under VFR during daylight hours in an airplane?

A – Enough to complete the flight at normal cruising speed with adverse wind conditions

B – Enough to fly to the first point of intended landing and to fly after that for 30 minutes at normal cruising speed

C – Enough to fly to the first point of intended landing and to fly after that for 45 minutes at normal cruising speed

11-8. Answer B. FAR 91.151
For day VFR flight in an airplane, you must carry enough fuel (considering wind and forecast weather conditions) to fly to the first point of intended landing, and, assuming normal cruising speed, 30 minutes thereafter.

11-9   PLT413   PA.I.D.K3c
What is the specific fuel requirement for flight under VFR at night in an airplane?

A – Enough to complete the flight at normal cruising speed with adverse wind conditions

B – Enough to fly to the first point of intended landing and to fly after that for 30 minutes at normal cruising speed

C – Enough to fly to the first point of intended landing and to fly after that for 45 minutes at normal cruising speed

11-9. Answer C. FAR 91.151
For night VFR flight in an airplane, you must carry enough fuel (considering wind and forecast weather conditions) to fly to the first point of intended landing, and assuming normal cruising speed, 45 minutes thereafter.

11-10   PA.VI.A.R1
What is an effective way to scan for traffic in front of your airplane during climb?

A – Perform 90 degree turns every 1–2 miles to check for traffic along your flight path.

B – Use your cockpit display of traffic information (CDTI) to avoid aircraft that cannot be seen in a nose-high attitude.

C – Lower the nose periodically and clear the area, and then transition to cruise climb when altitude permits.

11-10. Answer C. GFDPP 11B, PHB
Your forward visibility is reduced in the climb. To clear the area, lower the nose periodically for just a moment, and then return to the climb attitude. Another method is to perform small S-turns (not 90-degree turns) to check for traffic along your flight path. Transition to a cruise climb when altitude permits in order to improve forward visibility and engine cooling, and to increase your groundspeed. A CDTI should be used as a back-up, not a replacement, for your scanning technique.

11-11   PA.VI.A.K7
While flying enroute, you arrive at a checkpoint 15 minutes later than the time you calculated in your flight plan. What actions should you take next?

A – Recalculate your ETA and plan to use your fuel reserve as required.

B – Determine the reason for the deviation, add a fuel stop if needed, and notify Flight Service of your revised ETA.

C – Reduce power to increase fuel economy and notify Flight Service of your revised ETA.

11-11. Answer D. GFDPP 11B, PHB
After recognizing a change—the deviation from your ETA at the checkpoint—the next steps are to define the problem and choose a course of action.

If you brought a large fuel reserve, you might be able to use part of it, although you should plan a fuel stop any time the fuel reserve drops below your personal minimums. You could also reduce power to extend your range, if you know that will be sufficient. However, neither of these actions is appropriate before determining the cause of the deviation and the actions needed to manage it successfully.

11-12   PA.VI.C.S2

A passenger is experiencing medical problems and you decide to divert. What are the appropriate techniques to handle the diversion?

A – Perform precise measurements and calculations before turning toward your new destination to ensure that you do not miss it.

B – Prioritize tasks and avoid using the autopilot, so that you can maintain situational awareness enroute to the alternate airport.

C – Immediately turn the airplane in the general direction of the new landing point and then use rule-of-thumb computations, or the Nearest and Direct-To functions of your GPS, to navigate there.

11-12. Answer C. GFDPP 11B, PHB

First, fly the airplane. Stay calm and avoid letting anxiety impair your flying skills. Use the autopilot if you have one. Turn the airplane toward the airport of intended landing and then complete flight planning details to navigate to the new destination. Take advantage of all possible shortcuts, such as rule-of-thumb computations, and the Nearest and Direct-To navigation functions of your GPS equipment.

CHAPTER 12

FEDERAL AVIATION REGULATIONS

SECTION A — 14 CFR PART 1— DEFINITIONS AND ABBREVIATIONS

As a private pilot, you should have a working knowledge of 14 CFR Parts 1, 61, and 91 (also referred to as federal aviation regulations (FARs). You also must know the accident reporting requirements of 49 CFR (NTSB) 830 and understand the TSA regulations in 49 CFR 1540-1562 that apply to private pilots. You can find most of the information about applicable regulations in the Private Pilot textbook, in the operational sections most related to those regulations. The test questions on those regulations is in the same chapter and section of this test guide.

However, you also need to study a current publication of the regulations as part of your test preparation, because you are expected to learn all appropriate flight regulations. You can obtain a FAR/AIM printed manual or e-Book from Jeppesen with other private pilot training materials.

NIGHT

The definition of nighttime is the time between the end of evening civil twilight and the beginning of morning civil twilight.

12-1 PLT383 PA.XI.A.K5

The definition of nighttime is

A – sunset to sunrise.

B – 1 hour after sunset to 1 hour before sunrise.

C – the time between the end of evening civil twilight and the beginning of morning civil twilight.

12-1. Answer C. FAR 1.1

Night is the time between the end of evening civil twilight and the beginning of morning civil twilight. One hour after sunset to one hour before sunrise is used for night currency, because it approximately corresponds to nighttime.

SECTION B — 14 CFR PART 61 — CERTIFICATION: PILOTS, FLIGHT INSTRUCTORS, AND GROUND INSTRUCTORS

As a pilot, you need to know the Part 61 requirements for obtaining certificates and ratings, and the privileges and limitations associated with your license.

PILOT DOCUMENTS

- While operating an aircraft as pilot in command, you must have both your medical certificate and your pilot certificate in your personal possession.
- Each person who holds a pilot certificate or a medical certificate shall present it for inspection upon the request of the Administrator, the National Transportation Safety Board, or any federal, state, or local law enforcement officer.
- To act as pilot in command of an aircraft, a pilot must show by logbook endorsement the satisfactory completion of a flight review or completion of a pilot proficiency check within the preceding 24 calendar months.
- A certificated pilot may not act as pilot in command of an aircraft towing a glider unless a minimum of 100 hours of pilot flight time in powered aircraft is entered in the pilot's logbook.
- To act as pilot in command of an aircraft towing a glider, a person is required to have made within the preceding 12 months at least three actual or simulated glider tows while accompanied by a qualified pilot.

PRIVATE PILOT LIMITATIONS

- If a pilot changes permanent mailing address and fails to notify the FAA Airmen Certification Branch of the new address, the pilot is entitled to exercise the privileges of the pilot certificate for a period of only 30 days after the date of the move.
- A private pilot may share the pro rata share of the operating expenses of a flight with passengers.
- A private pilot may act as pilot in command of an aircraft used in a passenger-carrying airlift sponsored by a charitable organization, and for which the passengers make a donation to the organization.

12-2　　PLT399　　　　PA.I.A.K2

What documents must be in your personal possession or readily accessible in the aircraft while operating as pilot in command of an aircraft?

A – A pilot certificate with an endorsement showing accomplishment of an annual flight review and a pilot logbook showing recency of experience

B – Certificates showing accomplishment of a checkout in the aircraft and a current biennial flight review

C – An appropriate pilot certificate and an appropriate current medical certificate if required

12-2. Answer C. FAR 61.3
Both an appropriate pilot certificate and an appropriate medical certificate if required, must be in your personal possession or readily accessible in the aircraft in order to act as pilot in command of an aircraft.

12-3   PLT399   PA.I.A.K2

When must a current pilot certificate be in the pilot's personal possession or readily accessible in the aircraft?

A – When acting as a crew chief during launch and recovery

B – Only when passengers are carried

C – Anytime when acting as pilot in command or as a required crewmember

12-3. Answer C. FAR 61.3

You must have a current pilot certificate in your personal possession or readily accessible in the aircraft whenever you are pilot in command or acting as a required pilot flight crewmember.

12-4   PLT399   PA.I.A.K4

Each person who holds a pilot certificate or a medical certificate shall present it for inspection upon the request of any

A – authorized representative of the Department of Transportation

B – person in a position of authority

C – Federal, state, or local law enforcement officer

12-4. Answer C. FAR 61.3

By regulation you, as the pilot, are required to present your pilot certificate upon request of the Administrator, an authorized representative of the National Transportation Safety Board (NTSB) or any federal, state, or local law enforcement officer. "Authorized representative of the Department of Transportation" does not mean the same thing as "the Administrator." Generally, FAA inspectors are the ones who represent the Administrator. Not every person "in a position of authority" is entitled to examine your certificates.

12-5   PLT399   PA.I.A.K2

A private pilot acting as pilot in command, or in any other capacity as a required pilot flight crewmember, must have their personal possession or readily accessible in the aircraft a current

A – endorsement on the pilot certificate to show that a flight review has been satisfactorily accomplished

B – medical certificate if required and an appropriate pilot certificate

C – logbook endorsement to show that a flight review has been satisfactorily accomplished

12-5. Answer B. FAR 61.3

To act as PIC or as a required crewmember, you must have an appropriate medical certificate, if required, and an appropriate pilot certificate. Although you must have a logbook (not pilot certificate) endorsement of completing a flight review within the preceding 24 calendar months, you are not required to carry the logbook that contains this endorsement.

12-6   PLT387   PA.I.A.K1

If a certificated pilot changes permanent mailing address and fails to notify the FAA Airmen Certification Branch of the new address, the pilot is entitled to exercise the privileges of the pilot certificate for a period of only

A – 30 days after the date of the move.

B – 60 days after the date of the move.

C – 90 days after the date of the move.

12-6. Answer A. FAR 61.60

As a pilot, you may not exercise the privileges of your certificate after 30 days from the date of your permanent mailing address change unless you notify the FAA's Airman Certificate Branch in writing of the new address.

12-7   PLT444   PA.I.A.K1

A certificated private pilot may not act as pilot in command of an aircraft towing a glider unless there is entered in the pilot's logbook a minimum of

A – 100 hours of pilot-in-command time in the aircraft category, class, and type, if required, that the pilot is using to tow a glider.

B – 200 hours of pilot-in-command time in the aircraft category, class, and type, if required, that the pilot is using to tow a glider.

C – 100 hours of pilot flight time in any aircraft, that the pilot is using to tow a glider.

12-7. Answer A. FAR 61.69

No person may act as pilot in command for towing a glider unless that person has logged at least 100 hours of pilot-in-command time in the aircraft category, class, and type, if required, that the pilot is using to tow a glider.

12-8   PLT444   PA.I.A.K1

To act as pilot in command of an aircraft towing a glider, a pilot is required to have made within the preceding 12 months

A – at least three flights in a powered glider.

B – at least three flights as observer in a glider being towed by an aircraft.

C – at least three actual or simulated glider tows while accompanied by a qualified pilot.

12-8. Answer C. FAR 61.69

The pilot in command of an aircraft towing a glider must have, within the preceding 12 months, made at least three actual, or simulated glider tows while accompanied by a qualified pilot, or made at least three flights as PIC of a glider towed by an aircraft.

SECTION C — 14 CFR PART 91 — GENERAL OPERATING AND FLIGHT RULES

As a pilot, you must be familiar with the "rules of the sky" to operate safely in the National Airspace System. The regulations covered in this section are an important part of your aeronautical knowledge.

PILOT IN COMMAND

- The pilot in command is the final authority as to the operation of an aircraft.
- The pilot in command is directly responsible for the pre-launch briefing of the passengers for a flight.
- If an in-flight emergency requires immediate action, the pilot in command may deviate from the FARs to the extent required to meet that emergency. A written report is not required unless requested by the FAA.

DROPPING OBJECTS

Objects may be dropped from an aircraft if precautions are taken to avoid injury or damage to persons or property on the surface.

SAFETY BELTS

- Flight crewmembers are required to keep their safety belts and shoulder harnesses fastened during takeoffs and landings. Safety belts must stay fastened while enroute.
- The pilot in command must brief the passengers on the use of safety belts and notify them to fasten their safety belts during taxi, takeoff, and landing. Passengers must have their safety belts fastened during taxi, takeoffs, and landings.

FORMATION FLIGHT

No person may operate an aircraft in formation flight except by prior arrangement with the pilot in command of each aircraft.

POSITION LIGHTS

During sunset to sunrise, except in Alaska, lighted position lights must be displayed on an aircraft.

AEROBATIC FLIGHT

- No person may operate an aircraft in aerobatic flight when over any congested area of a city, town, or settlement.
- Aerobatic flight is prohibited in Class D airspace, and Class E airspace designated for Federal Airways.
- The lowest altitude permitted for aerobatic flight is 1500 feet AGL. In-flight visibility must be at least 3 miles.

PARACHUTES

- A parachute with natural canopy, shroud, and harness components must have been packed by a certificated and appropriately rated parachute rigger within the preceding 60 days.
- A parachute with synthetic canopy, shroud, and harness components must have been packed by a certificated and appropriately rated parachute rigger within the preceding 180 days.

RESTRICTED AND EXPERIMENTAL AIRCRAFT

- Flight over densely populated areas is prohibited in restricted category aircraft.
- Unless specifically authorized, no person may operate an aircraft that has an experimental certificate over a densely populated area or in a congested airway.

12-9   PLT444   PA.I.A.K2

The final authority as to the operation of an aircraft is the

A – Federal Aviation Administration.

B – pilot in command.

C – aircraft manufacturer.

12-9. Answer B. FAR 91.3

As clearly indicated in the regulation, the pilot in command of an aircraft is directly responsible for, and is the final authority as to, the operation of that aircraft.

12-10   PLT444   PA.II.B.K1

Pre-takeoff briefing of passengers for a flight is the responsibility of

A – all passengers.

B – the pilot.

C – a crewmember.

12-10. Answer B. FAR 91.107, 91.519

Even if nonpilot crewmembers deliver the passenger briefings, the pilot in command is responsible for ensuring that these briefings are completed.

12-11   PLT444   PA.I.A.K2

If an in-flight emergency requires immediate action, the pilot in command may

A – deviate from the FARs to the extent required to meet the emergency, but must submit a written report to the Administrator within 24 hours.

B – deviate from the FARs to the extent required to meet that emergency.

C – not deviate from the FARs unless prior approval for the deviation is granted by the Administrator.

12-11. Answer B. FAR 91.3

In an in-flight emergency requiring immediate action, the pilot in command may deviate from any rule to the extent required to meet that emergency.

12-12   PLT444   PA.I.A.K2

When must a pilot who deviates from a regulation during an emergency send a written report of that deviation to the Administrator?

A – Within 7 days

B – Within 10 days

C – Upon request

12-12. Answer C. FAR 91.3

The regulations clearly indicate that a written report is not required, unless a report is requested from the FAA.

12-13   PLT401   PA.I.A.S1*

Under what conditions may objects be dropped from an aircraft?

A – Only in an emergency

B – If precautions are taken to avoid injury or damage to persons or property on the surface

C – If prior permission is received from the Federal Aviation Administration

12-13. Answer B. FAR 91.15

Objects can be dropped from an aircraft in flight, if reasonable precautions are taken to avoid injury or damage to persons or property.

12-14   PLT440   PA.I.D.R3

In addition to other preflight actions for a VFR flight away from the vicinity of the departure airport, regulations specifically require the pilot in command to

A – review traffic control light signal procedures.

B – check the accuracy of the navigation equipment and the emergency locator transmitter (ELT).

C – determine runway lengths at airports of intended use and the takeoff and landing distance data for the aircraft.

12-14. Answer C. FAR 91.103

For any flight, a pilot must determine runway lengths at airports of use and the takeoff and landing distance data.

12-15   PLT465   PA.II.B.K1

Flight crewmembers are required to keep their safety belts and shoulder harnesses fastened during

A – takeoffs and landings.

B – all flight conditions.

C – flight in turbulent air.

12-15. Answer A. FAR 91.105

According to the regulation, safety belts are required during takeoff and landing and while enroute. In addition, shoulder harnesses are required during takeoff and landing, unless the seat of the crewmembers' stations are not equipped with shoulder harnesses, or the crewmembers are not able to perform their duties with the shoulder harness fastened.

12-16   PLT465   PA.II.B.K1

Which best describes the flight conditions under which flight crewmembers are specifically required to keep their safety belts and shoulder harnesses fastened?

A – Safety belts during takeoff and landing; shoulder harnesses during takeoff and landing

B – Safety belts during takeoff and landing; shoulder harnesses during takeoff and landing and while enroute

C – Safety belts during takeoff and landing and while enroute; shoulder harnesses during takeoff and landing

12-16. Answer C. FAR 91.105

During takeoff and landing, and while enroute, each required flight crewmember shall keep the safety belt fastened while at the crewmember station. In addition, each required flight crewmember shall, during takeoff and landing, keep the shoulder harness fastened while at the crewmember station.

12-17   PLT465   PA.II.B.K1

Regarding passengers, what obligation, if any, does a pilot in command have concerning the use of safety belts?

A – The pilot in command must instruct the passengers to keep safety belts fastened for the entire flight.

B – The pilot in command must brief the passengers on the use of safety belts and notify them to fasten their safety belts during taxi, takeoff, and landing.

C – The pilot in command has no obligation concerning passengers' use of safety belts.

12-17. Answer B. FAR 91.107

The pilot in command must ensure that each person on board is briefed on how to fasten and unfasten the safety belt and shoulder harness, as well as ensure that all persons on board are notified to fasten their safety belt (and shoulder harness, if installed) during taxi, takeoff, or landing.

12-18   PLT465   PA.II.B.K1

With certain exceptions, safety belts are required to be secured about passengers during

A – taxi, takeoffs, and landings.

B – all flight conditions.

C – flight in turbulent air.

12-18. Answer A. FAR 91.107
Passengers are only required to have safety belts (and shoulder harnesses, if installed) fastened during taxi, takeoff, and landing.

12-19   PLT465   PA.II.B.K1

Safety belts are required to be properly secured about which persons in an aircraft and when?

A – Pilots only, during takeoffs and landings

B – Passengers, during taxi, takeoffs, and landings only

C – Each person on board the aircraft during the entire flight

12-19. Answer B. FAR 91.107
Passengers are required to have safety belts (and shoulder harnesses, if installed) fastened during taxi, takeoff, and landing.

12-20   PLT444   PA.II.B.S2*

No person may operate an aircraft in formation flight

A – over a densely populated area.

B – in Class D Airspace under special VFR.

C – except by prior arrangement with the pilot in command of each aircraft.

12-20. Answer C. FAR 91.111
No person may operate an aircraft in formation flight except by arrangement with the pilot in command of each aircraft in the formation.

12-21   PLT370   PA.VI.C.K2

When would a pilot be required to submit a detailed report of an emergency that caused the pilot to deviate from an ATC clearance?

A – When requested by ATC

B – Immediately

C – Within 7 days

12-21. Answer A. FAR 91.3, FAR 91.123
A pilot in command who deviates from a clearance and then is given priority by ATC because of that emergency, shall submit a detailed report of that emergency within 48 hours to the manager of that ATC facility, if requested by ATC.

12-22 PLT403 PA.VI.C.K2

What action, if any, is appropriate if the pilot deviates from an ATC instruction during an emergency and is given priority?

A – Take no special action because you are pilot in command.

B – File a detailed report within 48 hours to the chief of the appropriate ATC facility, if requested.

C – File a report to the FAA Administrator, as soon as possible.

12-22. Answer B. FAR 91.123
A pilot in command who is given priority by ATC because of an emergency, shall submit a detailed report of that emergency within 48 hours to the manager of that ATC facility, if requested by ATC.

12-23 PLT400 PA.I.A.K1

In addition to a valid Airworthiness Certificate, what documents or records must be aboard an aircraft during flight?

A – Aircraft engine and airframe logbooks, and owner's manual

B – Radio operator's permit, and repair and alteration forms

C – Operating limitations and Registration Certificate

12-23. Answer C. FAR 91.203, FAR 91.9
An acronym commonly used by pilots for remembering the required certificates and documents is ARROW. The ARROW acronym means AIRWORTHINESS certificate; aircraft REGISTRATION; RADIO station permit; OPERATING limitations; and WEIGHT and balance.

12-24 PLT461 PA.I.B.K3

Except in Alaska, during what time period should lighted position lights be displayed on an aircraft?

A – End of evening civil twilight to the beginning of morning civil twilight

B – 1 hour after sunset to 1 hour before sunrise

C – Sunset to sunrise

12-24. Answer C. FAR 91.209
No person may, during the period from sunset to sunrise, operate an aircraft unless it has lighted position lights.

12-25 PLT438 PA.I.G.K11

When operating an aircraft at cabin pressure altitudes above 12,500 feet MSL up to and including 14,000 feet MSL, supplemental oxygen shall be used during

A – the entire flight time at those altitudes.

B – that flight time more than 10 minutes at those altitudes.

C – that flight time more than 30 minutes at those altitudes.

12-25. Answer C. FAR 91.211
Between cabin pressure altitudes of 12,500 feet MSL and 14,000 feet MSL, the required minimum flight crew is required to use supplemental oxygen for any duration of the flight past 30 minutes.

12-26 PLT438   PA.I.G.K1l
Unless each occupant is provided with supplemental oxygen, no person may operate a civil aircraft of U.S. registry above a maximum cabin pressure altitude of

A – 12,500 feet MSL.

B – 14,000 feet MSL.

C – 15,000 feet MSL.

12-26. Answer C. FAR 91.211
At cabin pressure altitudes above 15,000 feet MSL, each occupant of the aircraft must be provided with supplemental oxygen.

12-27 PLT369   PA.I.E.K1
No person may operate an aircraft in aerobatic flight when

A – flight visibility is less than 5 miles.

B – over any congested area of a city, town, or settlement.

C – less than 2,500 feet AGL.

12-27. Answer B. FAR 91.303
No person may operate an aircraft in aerobatic flight over any congested area of a city, town, or settlement.

12-28 PLT369   PA.I.E.K1
In which class of airspace is aerobatic flight prohibited?

A – Class E airspace not designated for Federal Airways above 1,500 feet AGL

B – Class E airspace below 1,500 feet AGL

C – Class G airspace above 1,500 feet AGL

12-28. Answer B. FAR 91.303
No person may operate an aircraft in aerobatic flight within class B, C, or D airspace, class E airspace designated for an airport, or within 4 NM of the centerline of any Federal Airway. Aerobatic flight is also prohibited below 1,500 feet AGL and when the flight visibility is less than 3 statute miles.

12-29 PLT369   PA.I.E.K1
What is the lowest altitude permitted for aerobatic flight?

A – 1,000 feet AGL

B – 1,500 feet AGL

C – 2,000 feet AGL

12-29. Answer B. FAR 91.303
No person may operate an aircraft in aerobatic flight below an altitude of 1,500 feet above the surface.

12-30 PLT369   PA.I.E.K1
No person may operate an aircraft in aerobatic flight when the flight visibility is less than

A – 3 miles.

B – 5 miles.

C – 7 miles.

12-30. Answer A. FAR 91.303
No person may operate an aircraft in aerobatic flight when flight visibility is less than three statute miles.

12-31   PLT405   PA.I.B.K3

An approved parachute constructed of natural materials must have been packed by a certificated and appropriately rated parachute rigger within the preceding

A – 60 days.

B – 90 days.

C – 120 days.

12-31. Answer A. FAR 91.307
Parachutes must be repacked periodically to satisfy regulations. The materials used determine the interval. No pilot of a civil aircraft may allow an emergency parachute to be carried in that aircraft unless it is an approved type and has been packed by a certificated and appropriately rated parachute rigger within the preceding 60 days if its canopy, shrouds, and harness are composed exclusively of natural fiber or materials.

12-32   PLT405   PA.I.B.K3

An approved synthetic parachute may be carried in an aircraft for emergency use if it has been packed by an appropriately rated parachute rigger within the preceding

A – 120 days.

B – 180 days.

C – 365 days.

12-32. Answer B. FAR 91.307
Parachutes must be repacked periodically to satisfy regulations. The materials used determine the interval. No pilot of a civil aircraft may allow an emergency parachute to be carried in that aircraft unless it is an approved type and has been packed by a certificated and appropriately rated parachute rigger within the preceding 180 days if its canopy, shrouds, and harness are composed exclusively of nylon, rayon, or other similar synthetic fiber or materials.

12-33   PLT405   PA.I.B.K3

With certain exceptions, when must each occupant of an aircraft wear an approved parachute?

A – When a door is removed from the aircraft to facilitate parachute jumpers

B – When intentionally pitching the nose of the aircraft up or down 30° or more

C – When intentionally banking in excess of 30°

12-33. Answer B. FAR 91.307
Unless each occupant of the aircraft is wearing an approved parachute, no pilot of a civil aircraft, carrying any person (other than a crewmember) may carry out any intentional maneuver that exceeds a nose-up or nose-down attitude of 30 degrees relative to the horizon.

12-34   PLT373   PA.I.B.K1c

Which is normally prohibited when operating a restricted category civil aircraft?

A – Flight under instrument flight rules

B – Flight over a densely populated area

C – Flight within Class D airspace

12-34. Answer B. FAR 91.313
No person may operate a restricted category civil aircraft within the United States over a densely populated area.

12-35   PLT375   PA.I.B.K7

If an alteration or repair substantially affects the operation of an aircraft in flight, that aircraft must be test flown by an appropriately rated pilot and approved for return to service before being operated

A – by any private pilot.

B – with passengers aboard.

C – for compensation or hire.

12-35. Answer B. FAR 91.407

Before any person (other than a crewmember) can fly in an aircraft that has been maintained, rebuilt, or altered in a manner that may have appreciably changed its flight characteristics or substantially affected the operation in flight, an appropriately rated pilot with at least a private pilot certificate must first conduct a test flight and log the flight in aircraft records.

12-36   PLT375   PA.I.B.K7

Before passengers may be carried in an aircraft that has been altered in a manner that could have appreciably changed its flight characteristics, it must be flight tested by an appropriately rated pilot who holds at least a

A – Commercial Pilot Certificate with an instrument rating.

B – Private Pilot Certificate.

C – Commercial Pilot Certificate and a mechanic's certificate.

12-36. Answer B. FAR 91.407

An appropriately rated pilot with at least a private pilot certificate is authorized to flight test the aircraft.

SECTION D — NTSB 830 — AIRCRAFT ACCIDENT AND INCIDENT REPORTING

Pilots must know the procedures and requirements for reporting aircraft accidents, incidents, and overdue aircraft to the National Transportation Safety Board (NTSB).

ACCIDENTS

- If an aircraft is involved in an accident that results in substantial damage to the aircraft, the nearest NTSB field office must be notified immediately.
- Aircraft wreckage may be moved prior to the time the NTSB takes custody only to protect the wreckage from further damage.
- The owner of an aircraft that has been involved in an accident is required to file an accident report within ten days.

INCIDENTS

- A flight control system malfunction or failure, and an in flight fire are two incidents that require immediate notification to the nearest NTSB field office.
- An overdue aircraft that is believed to be involved in an accident must be immediately reported to the nearest NTSB field office.
- The operator of an aircraft that has been involved in an incident is required to submit a report to the nearest NTSB field office when requested.

12-37   PLT366   PA.III.A.K8

If an aircraft is involved in an accident that results in substantial damage to the aircraft, the nearest NTSB field office should be notified

A – immediately.

B – within 48 hours.

C – within 7 days.

12-37. Answer A. NTSB 830.5

The operator of an aircraft shall immediately, and by the most expeditious means available, notify the nearest National Transportation Safety Board field office when an aircraft accident occurs.

12-38   PLT366   PA.III.A.K8

Which incident requires an immediate notification to the nearest NTSB field office?

A – A forced landing due to engine failure

B – Landing gear damage, due to a hard landing

C – Flight control system malfunction or failure

12-38. Answer C. NTSB 830.5

The operator of an aircraft shall immediately, and by the most expeditious means available, notify the nearest National Transportation Safety Board field office when a flight control system malfunction or failure occurs.

12-39   PLT366   PA.III.A.K8

Which incident would require an immediate notification to the nearest NTSB field office?

A – An in-flight generator or alternator failure

B – An in-flight fire

C – An in-flight loss of VOR receiver capability

12-39. Answer B. NTSB 830.5

The operator of an aircraft shall immediately, and by the most expeditious means available, notify the nearest National Transportation Safety Board field office when a fire in flight occurs.

12-40   PLT366   PA.III.A.K8

Which incident requires an immediate notification be made to the nearest NTSB field office?

A – An overdue aircraft that is believed to be involved in an accident

B – An in-flight radio communication failure

C – An in-flight generator or alternator failure

12-40. Answer A. NTSB 830.5

The operator of an aircraft shall immediately, and by the most expeditious means available, notify the nearest National Transportation Safety Board field office when an overdue aircraft is believed to be involved in an accident.

12-41   PLT366   PA.III.A.K8

May aircraft wreckage be moved prior to the time the NTSB takes custody?

A – Yes, but only if moved by a federal, state, or local law enforcement officer.

B – Yes, but only to protect the wreckage from further damage.

C – No, it may not be moved under any circumstances.

12-41. Answer B. NTSB 830.10

Before the Board or its authorized representative takes custody of aircraft wreckage, mail, or cargo, such wreckage may not be disturbed or moved except to the extent necessary to protect the wreckage from further damage.

12-42   PLT366   PA.III.A.K8

The operator of an aircraft that has been involved in an accident is required to file an accident report within how many days?

A – 5

B – 7

C – 10

12-42. Answer C. NTSB 830.15

The operator of an aircraft shall file a report within 10 days after an accident, or after 7 days if an overdue aircraft is still missing.

12-43   PLT366   PA.III.A.K8

The operator of an aircraft that has been involved in an incident is required to submit a report to the nearest field office of the NTSB

A – within 7 days.

B – within 10 days.

C – when requested.

12-43. Answer C. NTSB 830.15

A report on an incident for which notification is required by 830.5(a) shall be filed only when requested by an authorized representative of the Board.

APPENDIX

1

FAA LEGENDS

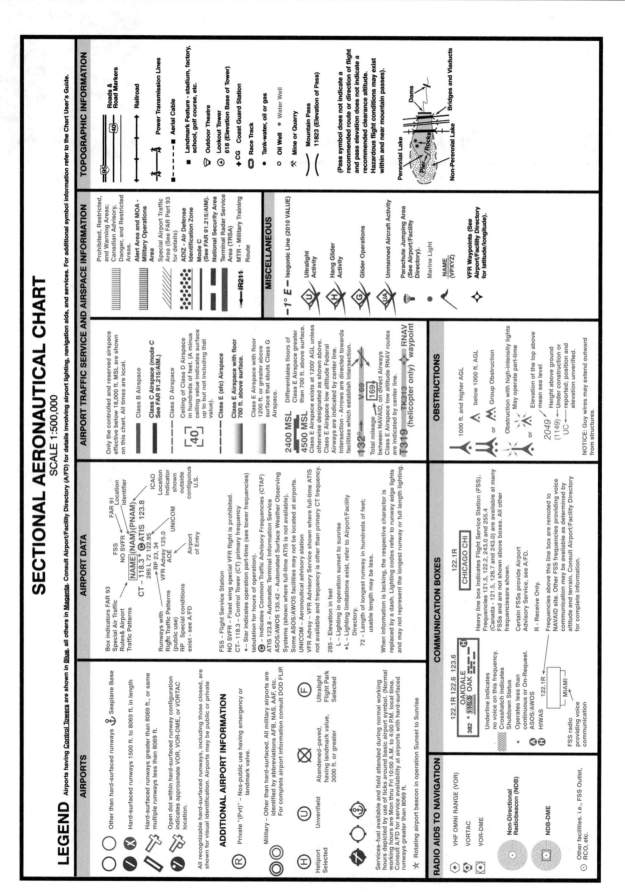

LEGEND 1.—Sectional Aeronautical Chart.

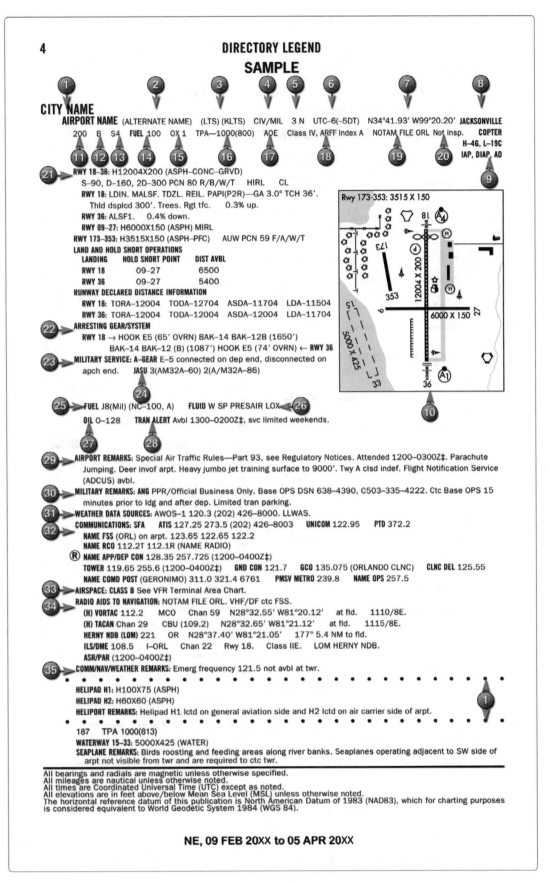

4

DIRECTORY LEGEND
SAMPLE

CITY NAME
AIRPORT NAME (ALTERNATE NAME)   (LTS) (KLTS)   CIV/MIL   3 N   UTC-6(-5DT)   N34°41.93' W99°20.20'   JACKSONVILLE
200   B   S4   FUEL 100   OX 1   TPA—1000(800)   AOE   Class IV, ARFF Index A   NOTAM FILE ORL   Not insp.   COPTER
                                                                                                            H–4G, L–19C
                                                                                                            IAP, DIAP, AD

RWY 18–36: H12004X200 (ASPH–CONC–GRVD)
    S–90, D–160, 2D–300 PCN 80 R/B/W/T   HIRL   CL
    RWY 18: LDIN. MALSF. TDZL. REIL. PAPI(P2R)—GA 3.0° TCH 36'.
        Thld dsplcd 300'. Trees. Rgt tfc.   0.3% up.
    RWY 36: ALSF1.   0.4% down.
    RWY 09–27: H6000X150 (ASPH) MIRL
    RWY 173–353: H3515X150 (ASPH–PFC)   AUW PCN 59 F/A/W/T
    LAND AND HOLD SHORT OPERATIONS

LANDING	HOLD SHORT POINT	DIST AVBL
RWY 18	09–27	6500
RWY 36	09–27	5400

    RUNWAY DECLARED DISTANCE INFORMATION
    RWY 18: TORA–12004   TODA–12704   ASDA–11704   LDA–11504
    RWY 36: TORA–12004   TODA–12004   ASDA–12004   LDA–11704
ARRESTING GEAR/SYSTEM
    RWY 18 → HOOK E5 (65' OVRN) BAK–14 BAK–12B (1650')
        BAK–14 BAK–12 (B) (1087') HOOK E5 (74' OVRN) ← RWY 36
MILITARY SERVICE: A–GEAR E–5 connected on dep end, disconnected on
    apch end.   JASU 3(AM32A–60) 2(A/M32A–86)

FUEL J8(Mil) (NC–100, A)   FLUID W SP PRESAIR LOX
OIL O–128   TRAN ALERT Avbl 1300–0200Z‡, svc limited weekends.

AIRPORT REMARKS: Special Air Traffic Rules—Part 93, see Regulatory Notices. Attended 1200–0300Z‡. Parachute
    Jumping. Deer invof arpt. Heavy jumbo jet training surface to 9000'. Twy A clsd indef. Flight Notification Service
    (ADCUS) avbl.
MILITARY REMARKS: ANG PPR/Official Business Only. Base OPS DSN 638–4390, C503–335–4222. Ctc Base OPS 15
    minutes prior to ldg and after dep. Limited tran parking.
WEATHER DATA SOURCES: AWOS–1 120.3 (202) 426–8000. LLWAS.
COMMUNICATIONS: SFA   ATIS 127.25 273.5 (202) 426–8003   UNICOM 122.95   PTD 372.2
    NAME FSS (ORL) on arpt. 123.65 122.65 122.2
    NAME RCO 112.2T 112.1R (NAME RADIO)
Ⓡ NAME APP/DEP CON 128.35 257.725 (1200–0400Z‡)
    TOWER 119.65 255.6 (1200–0400Z‡)   GND CON 121.7   GCO 135.075 (ORLANDO CLNC)   CLNC DEL 125.55
    NAME COMD POST (GERONIMO) 311.0 321.4 6761   PMSV METRO 239.8   NAME OPS 257.5
AIRSPACE: CLASS B See VFR Terminal Area Chart.
RADIO AIDS TO NAVIGATION: NOTAM FILE ORL. VHF/DF ctc FSS.
    (H) VORTAC 112.2   MCO   Chan 59   N28°32.55' W81°20.12'   at fld.   1110/8E.
    (H) TACAN Chan 29   CBU (109.2)   N28°32.65' W81°21.12'   at fld.   1115/8E.
    HERNY NDB (LOM) 221   OR   N28°37.40' W81°21.05'   177° 5.4 NM to fld.
    ILS/DME 108.5   I–ORL   Chan 22   Rwy 18.   Class IIE.   LOM HERNY NDB.
    ASR/PAR (1200–0400Z‡)
COMM/NAV/WEATHER REMARKS: Emerg frequency 121.5 not avbl at twr.

· ·
HELIPAD H1: H100X75 (ASPH)
HELIPAD H2: H60X60 (ASPH)
HELIPORT REMARKS: Helipad H1 lctd on general aviation side and H2 lctd on air carrier side of arpt.
· ·
187   TPA 1000(813)
WATERWAY 15–33: 5000X425 (WATER)
SEAPLANE REMARKS: Birds roosting and feeding areas along river banks. Seaplanes operating adjacent to SW side of
    arpt not visible from twr and are required to ctc twr.

All bearings and radials are magnetic unless otherwise specified.
All mileages are nautical unless otherwise noted.
All times are Coordinated Universal Time (UTC) except as noted.
All elevations are in feet above/below Mean Sea Level (MSL) unless otherwise noted.
The horizontal reference datum of this publication is North American Datum of 1983 (NAD83), which for charting purposes
is considered equivalent to World Geodetic System 1984 (WGS 84).

NE, 09 FEB 20XX to 05 APR 20XX

Inset (airport diagram): Rwy 173-353: 3515 X 150; 12004 X 200; 6000 X 150; 5000 X 425

LEGEND 2.—Chart Supplements U.S. (formerly Airport/Facility Directory).

DIRECTORY LEGEND 5

(10) SKETCH LEGEND

RUNWAYS/LANDING AREAS

Hard Surfaced . . . .

Metal Surface . . . .

Sod, Gravel, etc. . . . .

Light Plane, ...
Ski Landing Area or Water

Under Construction . . . . .

Closed . . . . ⊠

Helicopter Landings Area . . . . (H)

Displaced Threshold . . . .

Taxiway, Apron and Stopways . .

RADIO AIDS TO NAVIGATION

VORTAC . . . ⬡   VOR . . . . ⬡

VOR/DME . . ⬡   NDB . . . .

TACAN . . . . ⬠   NDB/DME . . . .

MISCELLANEOUS AERONAUTICAL FEATURES

Airport Beacon . . . . ☆ ✪

Wind Cone . . . .

Landing Tee . . . .

Tetrahedron . . . .

Control Tower . . . . or TWR

When control tower and rotating beacon
are co-located beacon symbol will be
used and further identified as TWR.

MISCELLANEOUS BASE AND CULTURAL FEATURES

Buildings . . . .

Power Lines . . . . —T—T—

Fence . . . . ×××××××

Towers . . . .

Tanks . . . .

Oil Well . . . .

Smoke Stack . . . .

Obstruction . . . . 5812 ∧

Controlling Obstruction . . . . +5812

Trees . . . .

Populated Places . . . .

Cuts and Fills . . . . . . Cut   Fill

Cliffs and Depressions . .

Ditch . . . .

Hill . . . .

APPROACH LIGHTING SYSTEMS

A dot '•' portrayed with approach lighting
letter identifier indicates sequenced flashing
lights (F) installed with the approach lighting
system e.g. (A) Negative symbology, e.g., (A1)
(V) indicates Pilot Controlled Lighting (PCL).

Runway Centerline Lighting . . . . .

(A) Approach Lighting System ALSF–2 . .

(A1) Approach Lighting System ALSF–1 . .

(A2) Short Approach Lighting System SALS/SALSF . . . .

(A3) Simplified Short Approach Lighting System (SSALR) with RAIL . . . . .

(A4) Medium Intensity Approach Lighting System (MALS and MALSF)/(SSALS and SSALF)

(A5) Medium Intensity Approach Lighting System (MALSR) and RAIL . . . . . .

(⊕) Omnidirectional Approach Lighting System (ODALS) . . . .

(D) Navy Parallel Row and Cross Bar . . .

(✝) Air Force Overrun . . . .

(V) Visual Approach Slope Indicator with Standard Threshold Clearance provided

(V2) Pulsating Visual Approach Slope Indicator (PVASI)

(V3) Visual Approach Slope Indicator with a threshold crossing height to accomodate long bodied or jumbo aircraft

(V4) Tri-color Visual Approach Slope Indicator (TRCV)

(V5) Approach Path Alignment Panel (APAP)

(P) Precision Approach Path Indicator (PAPI)

NE, 09 FEB 20XX to 05 APR 20XX

LEGEND 3.—Chart Supplements U.S. (formerly Airport/Facility Directory).

6   **DIRECTORY LEGEND**

LEGEND

This directory is a listing of data on record with the FAA on all open to the public airports, military facilities and selected private use facilities specifically requested by the Department of Defense (DoD) for which a DoD Instrument Approach Procedure has been published in the U.S. Terminal Procedures Publication. Additionally this listing contains data for associated terminal control facilities, air route traffic control centers, and radio aids to navigation within the conterminous United States, Puerto Rico and the Virgin Islands. Joint civil/military and civil airports are listed alphabetically by state, associated city and airport name and cross-referenced by airport name. Military facilities are listed alphabetically by state and official airport name and cross-referenced by associated city name. Navaids, flight service stations and remote communication outlets that are associated with an airport, but with a different name, are listed alphabetically under their own name, as well as under the airport with which they are associated.

The listing of an open to the public airport in this directory merely indicates the airport operator's willingness to accommodate transient aircraft, and does not represent that the facility conforms with any Federal or local standards, or that it has been approved for use on the part of the general public. Military and private use facilities published in this directory are open to civil pilots only in an emergency or with prior permission. See Special Notice Section, Civil Use of Military Fields.

The information on obstructions is taken from reports submitted to the FAA. Obstruction data has not been verified in all cases. Pilots are cautioned that objects not indicated in this tabulation (or on the airports sketches and/or charts) may exist which can create a hazard to flight operation. Detailed specifics concerning services and facilities tabulated within this directory are contained in the Aeronautical Information Manual, Basic Flight Information and ATC Procedures.

The legend items that follow explain in detail the contents of this Directory and are keyed to the circled numbers on the sample on the preceding pages.

 CITY/AIRPORT NAME

Civil and joint civil/military airports and facilities in this directory are listed alphabetically by state and associated city. Where the city name is different from the airport name the city name will appear on the line above the airport name. Airports with the same associated city name will be listed alphabetically by airport name and will be separated by a dashed rule line. A solid rule line will separate all others. FAA approved helipads and seaplane landing areas associated with a land airport will be separated by a dotted line. Military airports are listed alphabetically by state and official airport name.

 ALTERNATE NAME

Alternate names, if any, will be shown in parentheses.

 LOCATION IDENTIFIER

The location identifier is a three or four character FAA code followed by a four-character ICAO code assigned to airports. ICAO codes will only be published at joint civil/military, and military facilities. If two different military codes are assigned, both codes will be shown with the primary operating agency's code listed first. These identifiers are used by ATC in lieu of the airport name in flight plans, flight strips and other written records and computer operations. Zeros will appear with a slash to differentiate them from the letter "O".

 OPERATING AGENCY

Airports within this directory are classified into two categories, Military/Federal Government and Civil airports open to the general public, plus selected private use airports. The operating agency is shown for military, private use and joint civil/military airports. The operating agency is shown by an abbreviation as listed below. When an organization is a tenant, the abbreviation is enclosed in parenthesis. No classification indicates the airport is open to the general public with no military tenant.

A	US Army	MC	Marine Corps
AFRC	Air Force Reserve Command	N	Navy
AF	US Air Force	NAF	Naval Air Facility
ANG	Air National Guard	NAS	Naval Air Station
AR	US Army Reserve	NASA	National Air and Space Administration
ARNG	US Army National Guard	P	US Civil Airport Wherein Permit Covers
CG	US Coast Guard		Use by Transient Military Aircraft
CIV/MIL	Joint Use Civil/Military	PVT	Private Use Only (Closed to the Public)
DND	Department of National Defense Canada		

 AIRPORT LOCATION

Airport location is expressed as distance and direction from the center of the associated city in nautical miles and cardinal points, e.g., 4 NE.

 TIME CONVERSION

Hours of operation of all facilities are expressed in Coordinated Universal Time (UTC) and shown as "Z" time. The directory indicates the number of hours to be subtracted from UTC to obtain local standard time and local daylight saving time UTC–5(–4DT). The symbol ‡ indicates that during periods of Daylight Saving Time effective hours will be one hour earlier than shown. In those areas where daylight saving time is not observed the (–4DT) and ‡ will not be shown. Daylight saving time is in effect from 0200 local time the second Sunday in March to 0200 local time the first Sunday in November. Canada and all U.S. Conterminous States observe daylight saving time except Arizona and Puerto Rico, and the Virgin Islands. If the state observes daylight saving time and the operating times are other than daylight saving times, the operating hours will include the dates, times and no ‡ symbol will be shown, i.e., April 15–Aug 31 0630–1700Z, Sep 1–Apr 14 0600–1700Z.

NE, 09 FEB 20XX to 05 APR 20XX

LEGEND 4.—Chart Supplements U.S. (formerly Airport/Facility Directory).

DIRECTORY LEGEND   7

 GEOGRAPHIC POSITION OF AIRPORT—AIRPORT REFERENCE POINT (ARP)

Positions are shown as hemisphere, degrees, minutes and hundredths of a minute and represent the approximate geometric center of all usable runway surfaces.

 CHARTS

Charts refer to the Sectional Chart and Low and High Altitude Enroute Chart and panel on which the airport or facility is located. Helicopter Chart locations will be indicated as COPTER. IFR Gulf of Mexico West and IFR Gulf of Mexico Central will be depicted as GOMW and GOMC.

 INSTRUMENT APPROACH PROCEDURES, AIRPORT DIAGRAMS

IAP indicates an airport for which a prescribed (Public Use) FAA Instrument Approach Procedure has been published. DIAP indicates an airport for which a prescribed DoD Instrument Approach Procedure has been published in the U.S. Terminal Procedures. See the Special Notice Section of this directory, Civil Use of Military Fields and the Aeronautical Information Manual 5–4–5 Instrument Approach Procedure Charts for additional information. AD indicates an airport for which an airport diagram has been published. Airport diagrams are located in the back of each A/FD volume alphabetically by associated city and airport name.

 AIRPORT SKETCH

The airport sketch, when provided, depicts the airport and related topographical information as seen from the air and should be used in conjunction with the text. It is intended as a guide for pilots in VFR conditions. Symbology that is not self-explanatory will be reflected in the sketch legend. The airport sketch will be oriented with True North at the top. Airport sketches will be added incrementally.

 ELEVATION

The highest point of an airport's usable runways measured in feet from mean sea level. When elevation is sea level it will be indicated as ''00''. When elevation is below sea level a minus ''−'' sign will precede the figure.

 ROTATING LIGHT BEACON

B indicates rotating beacon is available. Rotating beacons operate sunset to sunrise unless otherwise indicated in the AIRPORT REMARKS or MILITARY REMARKS segment of the airport entry.

 SERVICING—CIVIL

S1:	Minor airframe repairs.	S5:	Major airframe repairs.
S2:	Minor airframe and minor powerplant repairs.	S6:	Minor airframe and major powerplant repairs.
S3:	Major airframe and minor powerplant repairs.	S7:	Major powerplant repairs.
S4:	Major airframe and major powerplant repairs.	S8:	Minor powerplant repairs.

 FUEL

CODE	FUEL	CODE	FUEL
80	Grade 80 gasoline (Red)	B+	Jet B, Wide-cut, turbine fuel with FS–II*, FP** minus 50° C.
100	Grade 100 gasoline (Green)		
100LL	100LL gasoline (low lead) (Blue)	J4 (JP4)	(JP–4 military specification) FP** minus 58° C.
115	Grade 115 gasoline (115/145 military specification) (Purple)		
		J5 (JP5)	(JP–5 military specification) Kerosene with FS–11, FP** minus 46°C.
A	Jet A, Kerosene, without FS–II*, FP** minus 40° C.		
		J8 (JP8)	(JP–8 military specification) Jet A–1, Kerosene with FS–II*, FP** minus 47°C.
A+	Jet A, Kerosene, with FS–II*, FP** minus 40°C.		
A1	Jet A–1, Kerosene, without FS–II*, FP** minus 47°C.	J8+100	(JP–8 military specification) Jet A–1, Kerosene with FS–II*, FP** minus 47°C, with-fuel additive package that improves thermo stability characteristics of JP-8.
A1+	Jet A–1, Kerosene with FS–II*, FP** minus 47° C.		
		J	(Jet Fuel Type Unknown)
B	Jet B, Wide-cut, turbine fuel without FS–II*, FP** minus 50° C.	MOGAS	Automobile gasoline which is to be used as aircraft fuel.

*(Fuel System Icing Inhibitor)
**(Freeze Point)

<u>NOTE:</u>   Certain automobile gasoline may be used in specific aircraft engines if a FAA supplemental type certificate has been obtained. Automobile gasoline, which is to be used in aircraft engines, will be identified as ''MOGAS'', however, the grade/type and other octane rating will not be published.

Data shown on fuel availability represents the most recent information the publisher has been able to acquire. Because of a variety of factors, the fuel listed may not always be obtainable by transient civil pilots. Confirmation of availability of fuel should be made directly with fuel suppliers at locations where refueling is planned.

 OXYGEN—CIVIL

OX 1	High Pressure	OX 3	High Pressure—Replacement Bottles
OX 2	Low Pressure	OX 4	Low Pressure—Replacement Bottles

TRAFFIC PATTERN ALTITUDE

Traffic Pattern Altitude (TPA)—The first figure shown is TPA above mean sea level. The second figure in parentheses is TPA above airport elevation. Multiple TPA shall be shown as ''TPA—See Remarks'' and detailed information shall be shown in the Airport or Military Remarks Section. Traffic pattern data for USAF bases, USN facilities, and U.S. Army airports (including those on which ACC or U.S. Army is a tenant) that deviate from standard pattern altitudes shall be shown in Military Remarks.

NE, 09 FEB 20XX to 05 APR 20XX

LEGEND 5.—Chart Supplements U.S. (formerly Airport/Facility Directory).

8 **DIRECTORY LEGEND**

 AIRPORT OF ENTRY, LANDING RIGHTS, AND CUSTOMS USER FEE AIRPORTS

U.S. CUSTOMS USER FEE AIRPORT—Private Aircraft operators are frequently required to pay the costs associated with customs processing.

AOE—Airport of Entry. A customs Airport of Entry where permission from U.S. Customs is not required to land. However, at least one hour advance notice of arrival is required.

LRA—Landing Rights Airport. Application for permission to land must be submitted in advance to U.S. Customs. At least one hour advance notice of arrival is required.

NOTE: Advance notice of arrival at both an AOE and LRA airport may be included in the flight plan when filed in Canada or Mexico. Where Flight Notification Service (ADCUS) is available the airport remark will indicate this service. This notice will also be treated as an application for permission to land in the case of an LRA. Although advance notice of arrival may be relayed to Customs through Mexico, Canada, and U.S. Communications facilities by flight plan, the aircraft operator is solely responsible for ensuring that Customs receives the notification. (See Customs, Immigration and Naturalization, Public Health and Agriculture Department requirements in the International Flight Information Manual for further details.)

US Customs Air and Sea Ports, Inspectors and Agents

Northeast Sector (New England and Atlantic States—ME to MD)	407–975–1740
Southeast Sector (Atlantic States—DC, WV, VA to FL)	407–975–1780
Central Sector (Interior of the US, including Gulf states—MS, AL, LA)	407–975–1760
Southwest East Sector (OK and eastern TX)	407–975–1840
Southwest West Sector (Western TX, NM and AZ)	407–975–1820
Pacific Sector (WA, OR, CA, HI and AK)	407–975–1800

 CERTIFICATED AIRPORT (14 CFR PART 139)

Airports serving Department of Transportation certified carriers and certified under 14 CFR part 139 are indicated by the Class and the ARFF Index; e.g. Class I, ARFF Index A, which relates to the availability of crash, fire, rescue equipment. Class I airports can have an ARFF Index A through E, depending on the aircraft length and scheduled departures. Class II, III, and IV will always carry an Index A.

14 CFR PART 139 CERTIFICATED AIRPORTS
AIRPORT CLASSIFICATIONS

Type of Air Carrier Operation	Class I	Class II	Class III	Class IV
Scheduled Air Carrier Aircraft with 31 or more passenger seats	X			
Unscheduled Air Carrier Aircraft with 31 or more passengers seats	X	X		X
Scheduled Air Carrier Aircraft with 10 to 30 passenger seats	X	X	X	

14 CFR–PART 139 CERTIFICATED AIRPORTS
INDICES AND AIRCRAFT RESCUE AND FIRE FIGHTING EQUIPMENT REQUIREMENTS

Airport Index	Required No. Vehicles	Aircraft Length	Scheduled Departures	Agent + Water for Foam
A	1	<90'	≥1	500#DC or HALON 1211 or 450#DC + 100 gal H$_2$O
B	1 or 2	≥90', <126'	≥5	Index A + 1500 gal H$_2$O
		≥126', <159'	<5	
C	2 or 3	≥126', <159'	≥5	Index A + 3000 gal H$_2$O
		≥159', <200'	<5	
D	3	≥159', <200'		Index A + 4000 gal H$_2$O
		>200'	<5	
E	3	≥200'	≥5	Index A + 6000 gal H$_2$O

> Greater Than; < Less Than; ≥ Equal or Greater Than; ≤ Equal or Less Than; H$_2$O–Water; DC–Dry Chemical.

NOTE: The listing of ARFF index does not necessarily assure coverage for non-air carrier operations or at other than prescribed times for air carrier. ARFF Index Ltd.—indicates ARFF coverage may or may not be available, for information contact airport manager prior to flight.

 NOTAM SERVICE

All public use landing areas are provided NOTAM service. A NOTAM FILE identifier is shown for individual langing areas, e.g., "NOTAM FILE BNA". See the AIM, Basic Flight Information and ATC Procedures for a detailed description of NOTAMs.

NE, 09 FEB 20XX to 05 APR 20XX

LEGEND 6.—Chart Supplements U.S. (formerly Airport/Facility Directory).

DIRECTORY LEGEND   9

Current NOTAMs are available from flight service stations at 1–800–WX–BRIEF (992–7433) or online through the FAA PilotWeb at https://pilotweb.nas.faa.gov. Military NOTAMs are available using the Defense Internet NOTAM Service (DINS) at https://www.notams.jcs.mil.

Pilots flying to or from airports not available through the FAA PilotWeb or DINS can obtain assistance from Flight Service.

20 FAA INSPECTION

All airports not inspected by FAA will be identified by the note: Not insp. This indicates that the airport information has been provided by the owner or operator of the field.

21 RUNWAY DATA

Runway information is shown on two lines. That information common to the entire runway is shown on the first line while information concerning the runway ends is shown on the second or following line. Runway direction, surface, length, width, weight bearing capacity, lighting, and slope, when available are shown for each runway. Multiple runways are shown with the longest runway first. Direction, length, width, and lighting are shown for sea-lanes. The full dimensions of helipads are shown, e.g., 50X150. Runway data that requires clarification will be placed in the remarks section.

RUNWAY DESIGNATION

Runways are normally numbered in relation to their magnetic orientation rounded off to the nearest 10 degrees. Parallel runways can be designated L (left)/R (right)/C (center). Runways may be designated as Ultralight or assault strips. Assault strips are shown by magnetic bearing.

RUNWAY DIMENSIONS

Runway length and width are shown in feet. Length shown is runway end to end including displaced thresholds, but excluding those areas designed as overruns.

RUNWAY SURFACE AND LENGTH

Runway lengths prefixed by the letter "H" indicate that the runways are hard surfaced (concrete, asphalt, or part asphalt–concrete). If the runway length is not prefixed, the surface is sod, clay, etc. The runway surface composition is indicated in parentheses after runway length as follows:

(AFSC)—Aggregate friction seal coat	(GRVD)—Grooved	(PSP)—Pierced steel plank
(AMS)—Temporary metal planks coated	(GRVL)—Gravel, or cinders	(RFSC)—Rubberized friction seal coat
with nonskid material	(MATS)—Pierced steel planking,	(TURF)—Turf
(ASPH)—Asphalt	landing mats, membranes	(TRTD)—Treated
(CONC)—Concrete	(PEM)—Part concrete, part asphalt	(WC)—Wire combed
(DIRT)—Dirt	(PFC)—Porous friction courses	

RUNWAY WEIGHT BEARING CAPACITY

Runway strength data shown in this publication is derived from available information and is a realistic estimate of capability at an average level of activity. It is not intended as a maximum allowable weight or as an operating limitation. Many airport pavements are capable of supporting limited operations with gross weights in excess of the published figures. Permissible operating weights, insofar as runway strengths are concerned, are a matter of agreement between the owner and user. When desiring to operate into any airport at weights in excess of those published in the publication, users should contact the airport management for permission. Runway strength figures are shown in thousand of pounds, with the last three figures being omitted. Add 000 to figure following S, D, 2S, 2T, AUW, SWL, etc., for gross weight capacity. A blank space following the letter designator is used to indicate the runway can sustain aircraft with this type landing gear, although definite runway weight bearing capacity figures are not available, e.g., S, D. Applicable codes for typical gear configurations with S=Single, D=Dual, T=Triple and Q=Quadruple:

CURRENT	NEW	NEW DESCRIPTION
S	S	Single wheel type landing gear (DC3), (C47), (F15), etc.
D	D	Dual wheel type landing gear (BE1900), (B737), (A319), etc.
T	D	Dual wheel type landing gear (P3, C9).
ST	2S	Two single wheels in tandem type landing gear (C130).
TRT	2T	Two triple wheels in tandem type landing gear (C17), etc.
DT	2D	Two dual wheels in tandem type landing gear (B707), etc.
TT	2D	Two dual wheels in tandem type landing gear (B757, KC135).
SBTT	2D/D1	Two dual wheels in tandem/dual wheel body gear type landing gear (KC10).
None	2D/2D1	Two dual wheels in tandem/two dual wheels in tandem body gear type landing gear (A340–600).
DDT	2D/2D2	Two dual wheels in tandem/two dual wheels in double tandem body gear type landing gear (B747, E4).
TTT	3D	Three dual wheels in tandem type landing gear (B777), etc.
TT	D2	Dual wheel gear two struts per side main gear type landing gear (B52).
TDT	C5	Complex dual wheel and quadruple wheel combination landing gear (C5).

NE, 09 FEB 20XX to 05 APR 20XX

LEGEND 7.—Chart Supplements U.S. (formerly Airport/Facility Directory).

10   **DIRECTORY LEGEND**

AUW—All up weight. Maximum weight bearing capacity for any aircraft irrespective of landing gear configuration.

SWL—Single Wheel Loading. (This includes information submitted in terms of Equivalent Single Wheel Loading (ESWL) and Single Isolated Wheel Loading).

PSI—Pounds per square inch. PSI is the actual figure expressing maximum pounds per square inch runway will support, e.g., (SWL 000/PSI 535).

Omission of weight bearing capacity indicates information unknown.

The ACN/PCN System is the ICAO standard method of reporting pavement strength for pavements with bearing strengths greater than 12,500 pounds. The Pavement Classification Number (PCN) is established by an engineering assessment of the runway. The PCN is for use in conjunction with an Aircraft Classification Number (ACN). Consult the Aircraft Flight Manual, Flight Information Handbook, or other appropriate source for ACN tables or charts. Currently, ACN data may not be available for all aircraft. If an ACN table or chart is available, the ACN can be calculated by taking into account the aircraft weight, the pavement type, and the subgrade category. For runways that have been evaluated under the ACN/PCN system, the PCN will be shown as a five-part code (e.g. PCN 80 R/B/W/T). Details of the coded format are as follows:

(1) The PCN NUMBER—The reported PCN indicates that an aircraft with an ACN equal or less than the reported PCN can operate on the pavement subject to any limitation on the tire pressure.

(2) The type of pavement:
R — Rigid
F — Flexible

(3) The pavement subgrade category:
A — High
B — Medium
C — Low
D — Ultra-low

(4) The maximum tire pressure authorized for the pavement:
W — High, no limit
X — Medium, limited to 217 psi
Y — Low, limited to 145 psi
Z — Very low, limited to 73 psi

(5) Pavement evaluation method:
T — Technical evaluation
U — By experience of aircraft using the pavement

NOTE: Prior permission from the airport controlling authority is required when the ACN of the aircraft exceeds the published PCN or aircraft tire pressure exceeds the published limits.

RUNWAY LIGHTING

Lights are in operation sunset to sunrise. Lighting available by prior arrangement only or operating part of the night and/or pilot controlled lighting with specific operating hours are indicated under airport or military remarks. At USN/USMC facilities lights are available only during airport hours of operation. Since obstructions are usually lighted, obstruction lighting is not included in this code. Unlighted obstructions on or surrounding an airport will be noted in airport or military remarks. Runway lights nonstandard (NSTD) are systems for which the light fixtures are not FAA approved L-800 series: color, intensity, or spacing does not meet FAA standards. Nonstandard runway lights, VASI, or any other system not listed below will be shown in airport remarks or military service. Temporary, emergency or limited runway edge lighting such as flares, smudge pots, lanterns or portable runway lights will also be shown in airport remarks or military service. Types of lighting are shown with the runway or runway end they serve.

NSTD—Light system fails to meet FAA standards.
LIRL—Low Intensity Runway Lights.
MIRL—Medium Intensity Runway Lights.
HIRL—High Intensity Runway Lights.
RAIL—Runway Alignment Indicator Lights.
REIL—Runway End Identifier Lights.
CL—Centerline Lights.
TDZL—Touchdown Zone Lights.
ODALS—Omni Directional Approach Lighting System.
AF OVRN—Air Force Overrun 1000' Standard Approach Lighting System.
LDIN—Lead-In Lighting System.
MALS—Medium Intensity Approach Lighting System.
MALSF—Medium Intensity Approach Lighting System with Sequenced Flashing Lights.
MALSR—Medium Intensity Approach Lighting System with Runway Alignment Indicator Lights.

SALS—Short Approach Lighting System.
SALSF—Short Approach Lighting System with Sequenced Flashing Lights.
SSALS—Simplified Short Approach Lighting System.
SSALF—Simplified Short Approach Lighting System with Sequenced Flashing Lights.
SSALR—Simplified Short Approach Lighting System with Runway Alignment Indicator Lights.
ALSAF—High Intensity Approach Lighting System with Sequenced Flashing Lights.
ALSF1—High Intensity Approach Lighting System with Sequenced Flashing Lights, Category I, Configuration.
ALSF2—High Intensity Approach Lighting System with Sequenced Flashing Lights, Category II, Configuration.
SF—Sequenced Flashing Lights.
OLS—Optical Landing System.
WAVE–OFF.

NOTE: Civil ALSF2 may be operated as SSALR during favorable weather conditions. When runway edge lights are positioned more than 10 feet from the edge of the usable runway surface a remark will be added in the "Remarks" portion of the airport entry. This is applicable to Air Force, Air National Guard and Air Force Reserve Bases, and those joint civil/military airfields on which they are tenants.

NE, 09 FEB 20XX to 05 APR 20XX

LEGEND 8.—Chart Supplements U.S. (formerly Airport/Facility Directory).

DIRECTORY LEGEND   11

VISUAL GLIDESLOPE INDICATORS

APAP—A system of panels, which may or may not be lighted, used for alignment of approach path.

PNIL	APAP on left side of runway	PNIR	APAP on right side of runway

PAPI—Precision Approach Path Indicator

P2L	2-identical light units placed on left side of runway	P4L	4-identical light units placed on left side of runway
P2R	2-identical light units placed on right side of runway	P4R	4-identical light units placed on right side of runway

PVASI—Pulsating/steady burning visual approach slope indicator, normally a single light unit projecting two colors.

PSIL	PVASI on left side of runway	PSIR	PVASI on right side of runway

SAVASI—Simplified Abbreviated Visual Approach Slope Indicator

S2L	2-box SAVASI on left side of runway	S2R	2-box SAVASI on right side of runway

TRCV—Tri-color visual approach slope indicator, normally a single light unit projecting three colors.

TRIL	TRCV on left side of runway	TRIR	TRCV on right side of runway

VASI—Visual Approach Slope Indicator

V2L	2-box VASI on left side of runway	V6L	6-box VASI on left side of runway
V2R	2-box VASI on right side of runway	V6R	6-box VASI on right side of runway
V4L	4-box VASI on left side of runway	V12	12-box VASI on both sides of runway
V4R	4-box VASI on right side of runway	V16	16-box VASI on both sides of runway

NOTE: Approach slope angle and threshold crossing height will be shown when available; i.e., –GA 3.5° TCH 37′.

PILOT CONTROL OF AIRPORT LIGHTING

Key Mike	Function
7 times within 5 seconds	Highest intensity available
5 times within 5 seconds	Medium or lower intensity (Lower REIL or REIL-Off)
3 times within 5 seconds	Lowest intensity available (Lower REIL or REIL-Off)

Available systems will be indicated in the airport or military remarks, e.g., ACTIVATE HIRL Rwy 07–25, MALSR Rwy 07, and VASI Rwy 07—122.8.

Where the airport is not served by an instrument approach procedure and/or has an independent type system of different specification installed by the airport sponsor, descriptions of the type lights, method of control, and operating frequency will be explained in clear text. See AIM, "Basic Flight Information and ATC Procedures," for detailed description of pilot control of airport lighting.

RUNWAY SLOPE

When available, runway slope data will only be provided for those airports with an approved FAA instrument approach procedure. Runway slope will be shown only when it is 0.3 percent or greater. On runways less than 8000 feet, the direction of the slope up will be indicated, e.g., 0.3% up NW. On runways 8000 feet or greater, the slope will be shown (up or down) on the runway end line, e.g., RWY 13: 0.3% up., RWY 21: Pole. Rgt tfc. 0.4% down.

RUNWAY END DATA

Information pertaining to the runway approach end such as approach lights, touchdown zone lights, runway end identification lights, visual glideslope indicators, displaced thresholds, controlling obstruction, and right hand traffic pattern, will be shown on the specific runway end. "Rgt tfc"—Right traffic indicates right turns should be made on landing and takeoff for specified runway end.

LAND AND HOLD SHORT OPERATIONS (LAHSO)

LAHSO is an acronym for "Land and Hold Short Operations." These operations include landing and holding short of an intersection runway, an intersecting taxiway, or other predetermined points on the runway other than a runway or taxiway. Measured distance represents the available landing distance on the landing runway, in feet.

Specific questions regarding these distances should be referred to the air traffic manager of the facility concerned. The Aeronautical Information Manual contains specific details on hold–short operations and markings.

RUNWAY DECLARED DISTANCE INFORMATION

TORA—Take-off Run Available. The length of runway declared available and suitable for the ground run of an aeroplane take–off.

TODA—Take-off Distance Available. The length of the take–off run available plus the length of the clearway, if provided.

ASDA—Accelerate-Stop Distance Available. The length of the take–off run available plus the length of the stopway, if provided.

LDA—Landing Distance Available. The length of runway which is declared available and suitable for the ground run of an aeroplane landing.

22 ARRESTING GEAR/SYSTEMS

Arresting gear is shown as it is located on the runway. The a–gear distance from the end of the appropriate runway (or into the overrun) is indicated in parentheses. A–Gear which has a bi–direction capability and can be utilized for emergency approach end engagement is indicated by a (B). The direction of engaging device is indicated by an arrow. Up to 15 minutes advance notice may be required for rigging A–Gear for approach and engagement. Airport listing may show availability of other than US Systems. This information is provided for emergency requirements only. Refer to current aircraft operating manuals for specific engagement weight and speed criteria based on aircraft structural restrictions and arresting system limitations.

Following is a list of current systems referenced in this publication identified by both Air Force and Navy terminology:

NE, 09 FEB 20XX to 05 APR 20XX

LEGEND 9.—Chart Supplements U.S. (formerly Airport/Facility Directory).

12   DIRECTORY LEGEND

BI–DIRECTIONAL CABLE (B)

TYPE	DESCRIPTION
BAK–9	Rotary friction brake.
BAK–12A	Standard BAK–12 with 950 foot run out, 1–inch cable and 40,000 pound weight setting. Rotary friction brake.
BAK–12B	Extended BAK–12 with 1200 foot run, 1¼ inch Cable and 50,000 pounds weight setting. Rotary friction brake.
E28	Rotary Hydraulic (Water Brake).
M21	Rotary Hydraulic (Water Brake) Mobile.

The following device is used in conjunction with some aircraft arresting systems:

BAK–14	A device that raises a hook cable out of a slot in the runway surface and is remotely positioned for engagement by the tower on request. (In addition to personnel reaction time, the system requires up to five seconds to fully raise the cable.)
H	A device that raises a hook cable out of a slot in the runway surface and is remotely positioned for engagement by the tower on request. (In addition to personnel reaction time, the system requires up to one and one–half seconds to fully raise the cable.)

UNI–DIRECTIONAL CABLE

TYPE	DESCRIPTION
MB60	Textile brake—an emergency one–time use, modular braking system employing the tearing of specially woven textile straps to absorb the kinetic energy.
E5/E5–1/E5–3	Chain Type. At USN/USMC stations E–5 A–GEAR systems are rated, e.g., E–5 RATING–13R–1100 HW (DRY), 31L/R–1200 STD (WET). This rating is a function of the A–GEAR chain weight and length and is used to determine the maximum aircraft engaging speed. A dry rating applies to a stabilized surface (dry or wet) while a wet rating takes into account the amount (if any) of wet overrun that is not capable of withstanding the aircraft weight. These ratings are published under Military Service.

FOREIGN CABLE

TYPE	DESCRIPTION	US EQUIVALENT
44B–3H	Rotary Hydraulic) (Water Brake)	
CHAG	Chain	E–5

UNI–DIRECTIONAL BARRIER

TYPE	DESCRIPTION
MA–1A	Web barrier between stanchions attached to a chain energy absorber.
BAK–15	Web barrier between stanchions attached to an energy absorber (water squeezer, rotary friction, chain). Designed for wing engagement.

NOTE: Landing short of the runway threshold on a runway with a BAK–15 in the underrun is a significant hazard. The barrier in the down position still protrudes several inches above the underrun. Aircraft contact with the barrier short of the runway threshold can cause damage to the barrier and substantial damage to the aircraft.

OTHER

TYPE	DESCRIPTION
EMAS	Engineered Material Arresting System, located beyond the departure end of the runway, consisting of high energy absorbing materials which will crush under the weight of an aircraft.

㉓ MILITARY SERVICE

Specific military services available at the airport are listed under this general heading. Remarks applicable to any military service are shown in the individual service listing.

㉔ JET AIRCRAFT STARTING UNITS (JASU)

The numeral preceding the type of unit indicates the number of units available. The absence of the numeral indicates ten or more units available. If the number of units is unknown, the number one will be shown. Absence of JASU designation indicates non–availability.

The following is a list of current JASU systems referenced in this publication:

USAF JASU (For variations in technical data, refer to T.O. 35–1–7.)

ELECTRICAL STARTING UNITS:

A/M32A–86	AC: 115/200v, 3 phase, 90 kva, 0.8 pf, 4 wire DC: 28v, 1500 amp, 72 kw (with TR pack)
MC–1A	AC: 115/208v, 400 cycle, 3 phase, 37.5 kva, 0.8 pf, 108 amp, 4 wire DC: 28v, 500 amp, 14 kw
MD–3	AC: 115/208v, 400 cycle, 3 phase, 60 kva, 0.75 pf, 4 wire DC: 28v, 1500 amp, 45 kw, split bus
MD–3A	AC: 115/208v, 400 cycle, 3 phase, 60 kva, 0.75 pf, 4 wire DC: 28v, 1500 amp, 45 kw, split bus
MD–3M	AC: 115/208v, 400 cycle, 3 phase, 60 kva, 0.75 pf, 4 wire DC: 28v, 500 amp, 15 kw

NE, 09 FEB 20XX to 05 APR 20XX

LEGEND 10.—Chart Supplements U.S. (formerly Airport/Facility Directory).

DIRECTORY LEGEND   13

MD–4	AC: 120/208v, 400 cycle, 3 phase, 62.5 kva, 0.8 pf, 175 amp, "WYE" neutral ground, 4 wire, 120v, 400 cycle, 3 phase, 62.5 kva, 0.8 pf, 303 amp, "DELTA" 3 wire, 120v, 400 cycle, 1 phase, 62.5 kva, 0.8 pf, 520 amp, 2 wire

AIR STARTING UNITS

AM32–95	150 +/– 5 lb/min (2055 +/– 68 cfm) at 51 +/– 2 psia
AM32A–95	150 +/– 5 lb/min @ 49 +/– 2 psia (35 +/– 2 psig)
LASS	150 +/– 5 lb/min @ 49 +/– 2 psia
MA–1A	82 lb/min (1123 cfm) at 130° air inlet temp, 45 psia (min) air outlet press
MC–1	15 cfm, 3500 psia
MC–1A	15 cfm, 3500 psia
MC–2A	15 cfm, 200 psia
MC–11	8,000 cu in cap, 4000 psig, 15 cfm

COMBINED AIR AND ELECTRICAL STARTING UNITS:

AGPU	AC: 115/200v, 400 cycle, 3 phase, 30 kw gen
	DC: 28v, 700 amp
	AIR: 60 lb/min @ 40 psig @ sea level
AM32A–60*	AIR: 120 +/– 4 lb/min (1644 +/– 55 cfm) at 49 +/– 2 psia
	AC: 120/208v, 400 cycle, 3 phase, 75 kva, 0.75 pf, 4 wire, 120v, 1 phase, 25 kva
	DC: 28v, 500 amp, 15 kw
AM32A–60A	AIR: 150 +/– 5 lb/min (2055 +/– 68 cfm at 51 +/– psia
	AC: 120/208v, 400 cycle, 3 phase, 75 kva, 0.75 pf, 4 wire
	DC: 28v, 200 amp, 5.6 kw
AM32A–60B*	AIR: 130 lb/min, 50 psia
	AC: 120/208v, 400 cycle, 3 phase, 75 kva, 0.75 pf, 4 wire
	DC: 28v, 200 amp, 5.6 kw

*NOTE: During combined air and electrical loads, the pneumatic circuitry takes preference and will limit the amount of electrical power available.

USN JASU

ELECTRICAL STARTING UNITS:

NC–8A/A1	DC: 500 amp constant, 750 amp intermittent, 28v;
	AC: 60 kva @ .8 pf, 115/200v, 3 phase, 400 Hz.
NC–10A/A1/B/C	DC: 750 amp constant, 1000 amp intermittent, 28v;
	AC: 90 kva, 115/200v, 3 phase, 400 Hz.

AIR STARTING UNITS:

GTC–85/GTE–85	120 lbs/min @ 45 psi.
MSU–200NAV/A/U47A–5	204 lbs/min @ 56 psia.
WELLS AIR START SYSTEM	180 lbs/min @ 75 psi or 120 lbs/min @ 45 psi. Simultaneous multiple start capability.

COMBINED AIR AND ELECTRICAL STARTING UNITS:

NCPP–105/RCPT	180 lbs/min @ 75 psi or 120 lbs/min @ 45 psi. 700 amp, 28v DC. 120/208v, 400 Hz AC, 30 kva.

JASU (ARMY)

59B2–1B	28v, 7.5 kw, 280 amp.

OTHER JASU

ELECTRICAL STARTING UNITS (DND):

CE12	AC 115/200v, 140 kva, 400 Hz, 3 phase
CE13	AC 115/200v, 60 kva, 400 Hz, 3 phase
CE14	AC/DC 115/200v, 140 kva, 400 Hz, 3 phase, 28vDC, 1500 amp
CE15	DC 22–35v, 500 amp continuous 1100 amp intermittent
CE16	DC 22–35v, 500 amp continuous 1100 amp intermittent soft start

AIR STARTING UNITS (DND):

CA2	ASA 45.5 psig, 116.4 lb/min

COMBINED AIR AND ELECTRICAL STARTING UNITS (DND)

CEA1	AC 120/208v, 60 kva, 400 Hz, 3 phase DC 28v, 75 amp
	AIR 112.5 lb/min, 47 psig

ELECTRICAL STARTING UNITS (OTHER)

C–26	28v 45kw 115–200v 15kw 380–800 Hz 1 phase 2 wire
C–26–B, C–26–C	28v 45kw: Split Bus: 115–200v 15kw 380–800 Hz 1 phase 2 wire
E3	DC 28v/10kw

AIR STARTING UNITS (OTHER):

A4	40 psi/2 lb/sec (LPAS Mk12, Mk12L, Mk12A, Mk1, Mk2B)
MA–1	150 Air HP, 115 lb/min 50 psia
MA–2	250 Air HP, 150 lb/min 75 psia

CARTRIDGE:

MXU–4A	USAF

NE, 09 FEB 20XX to 05 APR 20XX

LEGEND 11.—Chart Supplements U.S. (formerly Airport/Facility Directory).

14   DIRECTORY LEGEND

 FUEL—MILITARY

Fuel available through US Military Base supply, DESC Into–Plane Contracts and/or reciprocal agreement is listed first and is followed by (Mil). At commercial airports where Into–Plane contracts are in place, the name of the refueling agent is shown. Military fuel should be used first if it is available. When military fuel cannot be obtained but Into–Plane contract fuel is available, Government aircraft must refuel with the contract fuel and applicable refueling agent to avoid any breach in contract terms and conditions. Fuel not available through the above is shown preceded by NC (no contract). When fuel is obtained from NC sources, local purchase procedures must be followed. The US Military Aircraft Identaplates DD Form 1896 (Jet Fuel), DD Form 1897 (Avgas) and AF Form 1245 (Avgas) are used at military installations only. The US Government Aviation Into–Plane Reimbursement (AIR) Card (currently issued by AVCARD) is the instrument to be used to obtain fuel under a DESC Into–Plane Contract and for NC purchases if the refueling agent at the commercial airport accepts the AVCARD. A current list of contract fuel locations is available online at www.desc.dla.mil/Static/ProductsAndServices.asp; click on the Commercial Airports button.

See legend item 14 for fuel code and description.

26 SUPPORTING FLUIDS AND SYSTEMS—MILITARY

CODE
ADI	Anti–Detonation Injection Fluid—Reciprocating Engine Aircraft.
W	Water Thrust Augmentation—Jet Aircraft.
WAI	Water–Alcohol Injection Type, Thrust Augmentation—Jet Aircraft.
SP	Single Point Refueling.
PRESAIR	Air Compressors rated 3,000 PSI or more.
De–Ice	Anti–icing/De–icing/Defrosting Fluid (MIL–A–8243).

OXYGEN:
LPOX	Low pressure oxygen servicing.
HPOX	High pressure oxygen servicing.
LHOX	Low and high pressure oxygen servicing.
LOX	Liquid oxygen servicing.
OXRB	Oxygen replacement bottles. (Maintained primarily at Naval stations for use in acft where oxygen can be replenished only by replacement of cylinders.)
OX	Indicates oxygen servicing when type of servicing is unknown.

NOTE: Combinations of above items is used to indicate complete oxygen servicing available;

LHOXRB	Low and high pressure oxygen servicing and replacement bottles;
LPOXRB	Low pressure oxygen replacement bottles only, etc.

NOTE: Aircraft will be serviced with oxygen procured under military specifications only. Aircraft will not be serviced with medical oxygen.

NITROGEN:

LPNIT — Low pressure nitrogen servicing.
HPNIT — High pressure nitrogen servicing.
LHNIT — Low and high pressure nitrogen servicing.

27 OIL—MILITARY

US AVIATION OILS (MIL SPECS):

CODE	GRADE, TYPE
O–113	1065, Reciprocating Engine Oil (MIL–L–6082)
O–117	1100, Reciprocating Engine Oil (MIL–L–6082)
O–117+	1100, O–117 plus cyclohexanone (MIL–L–6082)
O–123	1065, (Dispersant), Reciprocating Engine Oil (MIL–L–22851 Type III)
O–128	1100, (Dispersant), Reciprocating Engine Oil (MIL–L–22851 Type II)
O–132	1005, Jet Engine Oil (MIL–L–6081)
O–133	1010, Jet Engine Oil (MIL–L–6081)
O–147	None, MIL–L–6085A Lubricating Oil, Instrument, Synthetic
O–148	None, MIL–L–7808 (Synthetic Base) Turbine Engine Oil
O–149	None, Aircraft Turbine Engine Synthetic, 7.5c St
O–155	None, MIL–L–6086C, Aircraft, Medium Grade
O–156	None, MIL–L–23699 (Synthetic Base), Turboprop and Turboshaft Engines
JOAP/SOAP	Joint Oil Analysis Program. JOAP support is furnished during normal duty hours, other times on request. (JOAP and SOAP programs provide essentially the same service, JOAP is now the standard joint service supported program.)

28 TRANSIENT ALERT (TRAN ALERT)—MILITARY

Tran Alert service is considered to include all services required for normal aircraft turn–around, e.g., servicing (fuel, oil, oxygen, etc.), debriefing to determine requirements for maintenance, minor maintenance, inspection and parking assistance of transient aircraft. Drag chute repack, specialized maintenance, or extensive repairs will be provided within the capabilities and priorities of the base. Delays can be anticipated after normal duty hours/holidays/weekends regardless of the hours of transient maintenance operation. Pilots should not expect aircraft to be serviced for TURN–AROUNDS during time periods when servicing or maintenance manpower is not available. In the case of airports not operated exclusively by US military, the servicing indicated by the remarks will not always be available for US military

NE, 09 FEB 20XX to 05 APR 20XX

LEGEND 12.—Chart Supplements U.S. (formerly Airport/Facility Directory).

DIRECTORY LEGEND   15

aircraft. When transient alert services are not shown, facilities are unknown. NO PRIORITY BASIS—means that transient alert services will be provided only after all the requirements for mission/tactical assigned aircraft have been accomplished.

 AIRPORT REMARKS

The Attendance Schedule is the months, days and hours the airport is actually attended. Airport attendance does not mean watchman duties or telephone accessibility, but rather an attendant or operator on duty to provide at least minimum services (e.g., repairs, fuel, transportation).

Airport Remarks have been grouped in order of applicability. Airport remarks are limited to those items of information that are determined essential for operational use, i.e., conditions of a permanent or indefinite nature and conditions that will remain in effect for more than 30 days concerning aeronautical facilities, services, maintenance available, procedures or hazards, knowledge of which is essential for safe and efficient operation of aircraft. Information concerning permanent closing of a runway or taxiway will not be shown. A note "See Special Notices" shall be applied within this remarks section when a special notice applicable to the entry is contained in the Special Notices section of this publication.

Parachute Jumping indicates parachute jumping areas associated with the airport. See Parachute Jumping Area section of this publication for additional information.

Landing Fee indicates landing charges for private or non-revenue producing aircraft. In addition, fees may be charged for planes that remain over a couple of hours and buy no services, or at major airline terminals for all aircraft.

Note: Unless otherwise stated, remarks including runway ends refer to the runway's approach end.

 MILITARY REMARKS

Military Remarks published at a joint Civil/Military facility are remarks that are applicable to the Military. At Military Facilities all remarks will be published under the heading Military Remarks. Remarks contained in this section may not be applicable to civil users. The first group of remarks is applicable to the primary operator of the airport. Remarks applicable to a tenant on the airport are shown preceded by the tenant organization, i.e., (A) (AF) (N) (ANG), etc. Military airports operate 24 hours unless otherwise specified. Airport operating hours are listed first (airport operating hours will only be listed if they are different than the airport attended hours or if the attended hours are unavailable) followed by pertinent remarks in order of applicability. Remarks will include information on restrictions, hazards, traffic pattern, noise abatement, customs/agriculture/immigration, and miscellaneous information applicable to the Military.

Type of restrictions:

CLOSED: When designated closed, the airport is restricted from use by all aircraft unless stated otherwise. Any closure applying to specific type of aircraft or operation will be so stated. USN/USMC/USAF airports are considered closed during non–operating hours. Closed airports may be utilized during an emergency provided there is a safe landing area.

OFFICIAL BUSINESS ONLY: The airfield closed to all transient military aircraft for obtaining routine services such as fueling, passenger drop off or pickup, practice approaches, parking, etc. The airfield may be used by aircrews and aircraft if official government business (including civilian) must be conducted on or near the airfield and prior permission is received from the airfield manager.

AF OFFICIAL BUSINESS ONLY OR NAVY OFFICIAL BUSINESS ONLY: Indicates that the restriction applies only to service indicated.

PRIOR PERMISSION REQUIRED (PPR): Airport is closed to transient aircraft unless approval for operation is obtained from the appropriate commander through Chief, Airfield Management or Airfield Operations Officer. Official Business or PPR does not preclude the use of US Military airports as an alternate for IFR flights. If a non–US military airport is used as a weather alternate and requires a PPR, the PPR must be requested and confirmed before the flight departs. The purpose of PPR is to control volume and flow of traffic rather than to prohibit it. Prior permission is required for all aircraft requiring transient alert service outside the published transient alert duty hours. All aircraft carrying hazardous materials must obtain prior permission as outlined in AFJI 11–204, AR 95–27, OPNAVINST 3710.7.

Note: OFFICIAL BUSINESS ONLY AND PPR restrictions are not applicable to Special Air Mission (SAM) or Special Air Resource (SPAR) aircraft providing person or persons on aboard are designated Code 6 or higher as explained in AFJMAN 11–213, AR 95–11, OPNAVINST 3722–8J. Official Business Only or PPR do not preclude the use of the airport as an alternate for IFR flights.

 WEATHER DATA SOURCES

Weather data sources will be listed alphabetically followed by their assigned frequencies and/or telephone number and hours of operation.

ASOS—Automated Surface Observing System. Reports the same as an AWOS–3 plus precipitation identification and intensity, and freezing rain occurrence;

AWOS—Automated Weather Observing System

  AWOS–A—reports altimeter setting (all other information is advisory only).

  AWOS–AV—reports altimeter and visibility.

  AWOS–1—reports altimeter setting, wind data and usually temperature, dew point and density altitude.

  AWOS–2—reports the same as AWOS–1 plus visibility.

  AWOS–3—reports the same as AWOS–1 plus visibility and cloud/ceiling data.

  AWOS–3P reports the same as the AWOS–3 system, plus a precipitation identification sensor.

  AWOS–3PT reports the same as the AWOS–3 system, plus precipitation identification sensor and a thunderstorm/lightning reporting capability.

  AWOS–3T reports the same as AWOS–3 system and includes a thunderstorm/lightning reporting capability.

NE, 09 FEB 20XX to 05 APR 20XX

LEGEND 13.—Chart Supplements U.S. (formerly Airport/Facility Directory).

16   **DIRECTORY LEGEND**

See AIM, Basic Flight Information and ATC Procedures for detailed description of Weather Data Sources.

AWOS–4—reports same as AWOS–3 system, plus precipitation occurence, type and accumulation, freezing rain, thunderstorm, and runway surface sensors.

HIWAS—See RADIO AIDS TO NAVIGATION

LAWRS—Limited Aviation Weather Reporting Station where observers report cloud height, weather, obstructions to vision, temperature and dewpoint (in most cases), surface wind, altimeter and pertinent remarks.

LLWAS—indicates a Low Level Wind Shear Alert System consisting of a center field and several field perimeter anemometers.

SAWRS—identifies airports that have a Supplemental Aviation Weather Reporting Station available to pilots for current weather information.

SWSL—Supplemental Weather Service Location providing current local weather information via radio and telephone.

TDWR—indicates airports that have Terminal Doppler Weather Radar.

WSP—indicates airports that have Weather System Processor.

When the automated weather source is broadcast over an associated airport NAVAID frequency (see NAVAID line), it shall be indicated by a bold ASOS, AWOS, or HIWAS followed by the frequency, identifier and phone number, if available.

③② COMMUNICATIONS

Airport terminal control facilities and radio communications associated with the airport shall be shown. When the call sign is not the same as the airport name the call sign will be shown. Frequencies shall normally be shown in descending order with the primary frequency listed first. Frequencies will be listed, together with sectorization indicated by outbound radials, and hours of operation. Communications will be listed in sequence as follows:

Single Frequency Approach (SFA), Common Traffic Advisory Frequency (CTAF), Automatic Terminal Information Service (ATIS) and Aeronautical Advisory Stations (UNICOM) or (AUNICOM) along with their frequency is shown, where available, on the line following the heading ''COMMUNICATIONS.'' When the CTAF and UNICOM frequencies are the same, the frequency will be shown as CTAF/UNICOM 122.8.

The FSS telephone nationwide is toll free 1–800–WX–BRIEF (1–800–992–7433). When the FSS is located on the field it will be indicated as ''on arpt''. Frequencies available at the FSS will follow in descending order. Remote Communications Outlet (RCO) providing service to the airport followed by the frequency and FSS RADIO name will be shown when available.

FSS's provide information on airport conditions, radio aids and other facilities, and process flight plans. Airport Advisory Service (AAS) is provided on the CTAF by FSS's for select non-tower airports or airports where the tower is not in operation.

(See AIM, Para 4–1–9 Traffic Advisory Practices at Airports Without Operating Control Towers or AC 90–42C.)

Aviation weather briefing service is provided by FSS specialists. Flight and weather briefing services are also available by calling the telephone numbers listed.

Remote Communications Outlet (RCO)—An unmanned air/ground communications facility that is remotely controlled and provides UHF or VHF communications capability to extend the service range of an FSS.

Civil Communications Frequencies-Civil communications frequencies used in the FSS air/ground system are operated on 122.0, 122.2, 123.6; emergency 121.5; plus receive-only on 122.1.

    a. 122.0 is assigned as the Enroute Flight Advisory Service frequency at selected FSS RADIO outlets.

    b. 122.2 is assigned as a common enroute frequency.

    c. 123.6 is assigned as the airport advisory frequency at select non-tower locations. At airports with a tower, FSS may provide airport advisories on the tower frequency when tower is closed.

    d. 122.1 is the primary receive-only frequency at VOR's.

    e. Some FSS's are assigned 50 kHz frequencies in the 122–126 MHz band (eg. 122.45). Pilots using the FSS A/G system should refer to this directory or appropriate charts to determine frequencies available at the FSS or remoted facility through which they wish to communicate.

Emergency frequency 121.5 and 243.0 are available at all Flight Service Stations, most Towers, Approach Control and RADAR facilities.

Frequencies published followed by the letter ''T'' or ''R'', indicate that the facility will only transmit or receive respectively on that frequency. All radio aids to navigation (NAVAID) frequencies are transmit only.

TERMINAL SERVICES

SFA—Single Frequency Approach.

CTAF—A program designed to get all vehicles and aircraft at airports without an operating control tower on a common frequency.

ATIS—A continuous broadcast of recorded non-control information in selected terminal areas.

D–ATIS—Digital ATIS provides ATIS information in text form outside the standard reception range of conventional ATIS via landline & data link communications and voice message within range of existing transmitters.

AUNICOM—Automated UNICOM is a computerized, command response system that provides automated weather, radio check capability and airport advisory information selected from an automated menu by microphone clicks.

UNICOM—A non-government air/ground radio communications facility which may provide airport information.

PTD—Pilot to Dispatcher.

APP CON—Approach Control. The symbol Ⓡ indicates radar approach control.

TOWER—Control tower.

GCA—Ground Control Approach System.

GND CON—Ground Control.

GCO—Ground Communication Outlet—An unstaffed, remotely controlled, ground/ground communications facility. Pilots at

NE, 09 FEB 20XX to 05 APR 20XX

LEGEND 14.—Chart Supplements U.S. (formerly Airport/Facility Directory).

DIRECTORY LEGEND   17

uncontrolled airports may contact ATC and FSS via VHF to a telephone connection to obtain an instrument clearance or close a VFR or IFR flight plan. They may also get an updated weather briefing prior to takeoff. Pilots will use four "key clicks" on the VHF radio to contact the appropriate ATC facility or six "key clicks" to contact the FSS. The GCO system is intended to be used only on the ground.

DEP CON—Departure Control. The symbol ⓡ indicates radar departure control.

CLNC DEL—Clearance Delivery.

PRE TAXI CLNC—Pre taxi clearance.

VFR ADVSY SVC—VFR Advisory Service. Service provided by Non-Radar Approach Control.
   Advisory Service for VFR aircraft (upon a workload basis) ctc APP CON.

COMD POST—Command Post followed by the operator call sign in parenthesis.

PMSV—Pilot–to–Metro Service call sign, frequency and hours of operation, when full service is other than continuous. PMSV installations at which weather observation service is available shall be indicated, following the frequency and/or hours of operation as "Wx obsn svc 1900–0000Z‡" or "other times" may be used when no specific time is given. PMSV facilities manned by forecasters are considered "Full Service". PMSV facilities manned by weather observers are listed as "Limited Service".

OPS—Operations followed by the operator call sign in parenthesis.

CON

RANGE

FLT FLW—Flight Following

MEDIVAC

NOTE: Communication frequencies followed by the letter "X" indicate frequency available on request.

 AIRSPACE

Information concerning Class B, C, and part–time D and E surface area airspace shall be published with effective times. Class D and E surface area airspace that is continuous as established by Rulemaking Docket will not be shown.

CLASS B—Radar Sequencing and Separation Service for all aircraft in CLASS B airspace.

CLASS C—Separation between IFR and VFR aircraft and sequencing of VFR arrivals to the primary airport.

TRSA—Radar Sequencing and Separation Service for participating VFR Aircraft within a Terminal Radar Service Area.

Class C, D, and E airspace described in this publication is that airspace usually consisting of a 5 NM radius core surface area that begins at the surface and extends upward to an altitude above the airport elevation (charted in MSL for Class C and Class D). Class E surface airspace normally extends from the surface up to but not including the overlying controlled airspace.

When part–time Class C or Class D airspace defaults to Class E, the core surface area becomes Class E. This will be formatted as:

AIRSPACE: CLASS C svc "times" ctc **APP CON** other times CLASS E:

or

AIRSPACE: CLASS D svc "times" other times CLASS E.

When a part–time Class C, Class D or Class E surface area defaults to Class G, the core surface area becomes Class G up to, but not including, the overlying controlled airspace. Normally, the overlying controlled airspace is Class E airspace beginning at either 700' or 1200' AGL and may be determined by consulting the relevant VFR Sectional or Terminal Area Charts. This will be formatted as:

AIRSPACE: CLASS C svc "times" ctc **APP CON** other times CLASS G, with CLASS E 700' (or 1200') AGL & abv:

or

AIRSPACE: CLASS D svc "times" other times CLASS G with CLASS E 700' (or 1200') AGL & abv:

or

AIRSPACE: CLASS E svc "times" other times CLASS G with CLASS E 700' (or 1200') AGL & abv.

NOTE: AIRSPACE SVC "TIMES" INCLUDE ALL ASSOCIATED ARRIVAL EXTENSIONS. Surface area arrival extensions for instrument approach procedures become part of the primary core surface area. These extensions may be either Class D or Class E airspace and are effective concurrent with the times of the primary core surface area. For example, when a part–time Class C, Class D or Class E surface area defaults to Class G, the associated arrival extensions will default to Class G at the same time. When a part–time Class C or Class D surface area defaults to Class E, the arrival extensions will remain in effect as Class E airspace.

NOTE: CLASS E AIRSPACE EXTENDING UPWARD FROM 700 FEET OR MORE ABOVE THE SURFACE, DESIGNATED IN CONJUNCTION WITH AN AIRPORT WITH AN APPROVED INSTRUMENT PROCEDURE.

Class E 700' AGL (shown as magenta vignette on sectional charts) and 1200' AGL (blue vignette) areas are designated when necessary to provide controlled airspace for transitioning to/from the terminal and enroute environments. Unless otherwise specified, these 700'/1200' AGL Class E airspace areas remain in effect continuously, regardless of airport operating hours or surface area status. These transition areas should not be confused with surface areas or arrival extensions.

(See Chapter 3, AIRSPACE, in the Aeronautical Information Manual for further details)

NE, 09 FEB 20XX to 05 APR 20XX

Legend 15.—Chart Supplements U.S. (formerly Airport/Facility Directory).

18   **DIRECTORY LEGEND**

🔵34 RADIO AIDS TO NAVIGATION

The Airport/Facility Directory lists, by facility name, all Radio Aids to Navigation that appear on FAA, AeroNav Products Visual or IFR Aeronautical Charts and those upon which the FAA has approved an Instrument Approach Procedure, with exception of selected TACANs. Military TACAN information will be published for Military facilities contained in this publication. All VOR, VORTAC, TACAN, ILS and MLS equipment in the National Airspace System has an automatic monitoring and shutdown feature in the event of malfunction. Unmonitored, as used in this publication, for any navigational aid, means that monitoring personnel cannot observe the malfunction or shutdown signal. The NAVAID NOTAM file identifier will be shown as ''NOTAM FILE IAD'' and will be listed on the Radio Aids to Navigation line. When two or more NAVAIDS are listed and the NOTAM file identifier is different from that shown on the Radio Aids to Navigation line, it will be shown with the NAVAID listing. NOTAM file identifiers for ILSs and its components (e.g., NDB (LOM) are the same as the associated airports and are not repeated. Automated Surface Observing System (ASOS), Automated Weather Observing System (AWOS), and Hazardous Inflight Weather Advisory Service (HIWAS) will be shown when this service is broadcast over selected NAVAIDs.

NAVAID information is tabulated as indicated in the following sample:

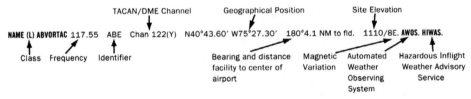

VOR unusable 020°–060° byd 26 NM blo 3,500′

Restriction within the normal altitude/range of the navigational aid (See primary alphabetical listing for restrictions on VORTAC and VOR/DME).

Note: Those DME channel numbers with a (Y) suffix require TACAN to be placed in the ''Y'' mode to receive distance information.

HIWAS—Hazardous Inflight Weather Advisory Service is a continuous broadcast of inflight weather advisories including summarized SIGMETs, convective SIGMETs, AIRMETs and urgent PIREPs. HIWAS is presently broadcast over selected VOR's throughout the U.S.

ASR/PAR—Indicates that Surveillance (ASR) or Precision (PAR) radar instrument approach minimums are published in the U.S. Terminal Procedures. Only part-time hours of operation will be shown.

RADIO CLASS DESIGNATIONS

VOR/DME/TACAN Standard Service Volume (SSV) Classifications

SSV Class	Altitudes	Distance (NM)
(T) Terminal	1000′ to 12,000′	25
(L) Low Altitude	1000′ to 18,000′	40
(H) High Altitude	1000′ to 14,500′	40
	14,500′ to 18,000′	100
	18,000′ to 45,000′	130
	45,000′ to 60,000′	100

NOTE: Additionally, (H) facilities provide (L) and (T) service volume and (L) facilities provide (T) service. Altitudes are with respect to the station's site elevation. Coverage is not available in a cone of airspace directly above the facility.

CONTINUED ON NEXT PAGE

NE, 09 FEB 20XX to 05 APR 20XX

LEGEND 16.—Chart Supplements U.S. (formerly Airport/Facility Directory).

DIRECTORY LEGEND   19
CONTINUED FROM PRECEDING PAGE

The term VOR is, operationally, a general term covering the VHF omnidirectional bearing type of facility without regard to the fact that the power, the frequency protected service volume, the equipment configuration, and operational requirements may vary between facilities at different locations.

AB	Automatic Weather Broadcast.
DF	Direction Finding Service.
DME	UHF standard (TACAN compatible) distance measuring equipment.
DME(Y)	UHF standard (TACAN compatible) distance measuring equipment that require TACAN to be placed in the ''Y'' mode to receive DME.
GS	Glide slope.
H	Non-directional radio beacon (homing), power 50 watts to less than 2,000 watts (50 NM at all altitudes).
HH	Non-directional radio beacon (homing), power 2,000 watts or more (75 NM at all altitudes).
H-SAB	Non-directional radio beacons providing automatic transcribed weather service.
ILS	Instrument Landing System (voice, where available, on localizer channel).
IM	Inner marker.
ISMLS	Interim Standard Microwave Landing System.
LDA	Localizer Directional Aid.
LMM	Compass locator station when installed at middle marker site (15 NM at all altitudes).
LOM	Compass locator station when installed at outer marker site (15 NM at all altitudes).
MH	Non-directional radio beacon (homing) power less than 50 watts (25 NM at all altitudes).
MLS	Microwave Landing System.
MM	Middle marker.
OM	Outer marker.
S	Simultaneous range homing signal and/or voice.
SABH	Non-directional radio beacon not authorized for IFR or ATC. Provides automatic weather broadcasts.
SDF	Simplified Direction Facility.
TACAN	UHF navigational facility-omnidirectional course and distance information.
VOR	VHF navigational facility-omnidirectional course only.
VOR/DME	Collocated VOR navigational facility and UHF standard distance measuring equipment.
VORTAC	Collocated VOR and TACAN navigational facilities.
W	Without voice on radio facility frequency.
Z	VHF station location marker at a LF radio facility.

NE, 09 FEB 20XX to 05 APR 20XX

LEGEND 17.—Chart Supplements U.S. (formerly Airport/Facility Directory).

20   **DIRECTORY LEGEND**

ILS FACILITY PEFORMANCE CLASSIFICATION CODES

Codes define the ability of an ILS to support autoland operations. The two portions of the code represent Official Category and farthest point along a Category I, II, or III approach that the Localizer meets Category III structure tolerances.

Official Category: I, II, or III; the lowest minima on published or unpublished procedures supported by the ILS.

Farthest point of satisfactory Category III Localizer performance for Category I, II, or III approaches: A – 4 NM prior to runway threshold, B – 3500 ft prior to runway threshold, C – glide angle dependent but generally 750–1000 ft prior to threshold, T – runway threshold, D – 3000 ft after runway threshold, and E – 2000 ft prior to stop end of runway.

ILS information is tabulated as indicated in the following sample:

    ILS/DME   108.5   I–ORL   Chan 22   Rwy 18.   Class IIE.   LOM HERNY NDB.

               ILS Facility Performance
               Classification Code

FREQUENCY PAIRING PLAN AND MLS CHANNELING

MLS CHANNEL	VHF FREQUENCY	TACAN CHANNEL	MLS CHANNEL	VHF FREQUENCY	TACAN CHANNEL	MLS CHANNEL	VHF FREQUENCY	TACAN CHANNEL
500	108.10	18X	568	109.45	31Y	636	114.15	88Y
502	108.30	20X	570	109.55	32Y	638	114.25	89Y
504	108.50	22X	572	109.65	33Y	640	114.35	90Y
506	108.70	24X	574	109.75	34Y	642	114.45	91Y
508	108.90	26X	576	109.85	35Y	644	114.55	92Y
510	109.10	28X	578	109.95	36Y	646	114.65	93Y
512	109.30	30X	580	110.05	37Y	648	114.75	94Y
514	109.50	32X	582	110.15	38Y	650	114.85	95Y
516	109.70	34X	584	110.25	39Y	652	114.95	96Y
518	109.90	36X	586	110.35	40Y	654	115.05	97Y
520	110.10	38X	588	110.45	41Y	656	115.15	98Y
522	110.30	40X	590	110.55	42Y	658	115.25	99Y
524	110.50	42X	592	110.65	43Y	660	115.35	100Y
526	110.70	44X	594	110.75	44Y	662	115.45	101Y
528	110.90	46X	596	110.85	45Y	664	115.55	102Y
530	111.10	48X	598	110.95	46Y	666	115.65	103Y
532	111.30	50X	600	111.05	47Y	668	115.75	104Y
534	111.50	52X	602	111.15	48Y	670	115.85	105Y
536	111.70	54X	604	111.25	49Y	672	115.95	106Y
538	111.90	56X	606	111.35	50Y	674	116.05	107Y
540	108.05	17Y	608	111.45	51Y	676	116.15	108Y
542	108.15	18Y	610	111.55	52Y	678	116.25	109Y
544	108.25	19Y	612	111.65	53Y	680	116.35	110Y
546	108.35	20Y	614	111.75	54Y	682	116.45	111Y
548	108.45	21Y	616	111.85	55Y	684	116.55	112Y
550	108.55	22Y	618	111.95	56Y	686	116.65	113Y
552	108.65	23Y	620	113.35	80Y	688	116.75	114Y
554	108.75	24Y	622	113.45	81Y	690	116.85	115Y
556	108.85	25Y	624	113.55	82Y	692	116.95	116Y
558	108.95	26Y	626	113.65	83Y	694	117.05	117Y
560	109.05	27Y	628	113.75	84Y	696	117.15	118Y
562	109.15	28Y	630	113.85	85Y	698	117.25	119Y
564	109.25	29Y	632	113.95	86Y			
566	109.35	30Y	634	114.05	87Y			

FREQUENCY PAIRING PLAN AND MLS CHANNELING

The following is a list of paired VOR/ILS VHF frequencies with TACAN channels and MLS channels.

TACAN CHANNEL	VHF FREQUENCY	MLS CHANNEL	TACAN CHANNEL	VHF FREQUENCY	MLS CHANNEL	TACAN CHANNEL	VHF FREQUENCY	MLS CHANNEL
2X	134.5	-	19Y	108.25	544	25X	108.80	-
2Y	134.55	-	20X	108.30	502	25Y	108.85	556
11X	135.4	-	20Y	108.35	546	26X	108.90	508
11Y	135.45	-	21X	108.40	-	26Y	108.95	558
12X	135.5	-	21Y	108.45	548	27X	109.00	-
12Y	135.55	-	22X	108.50	504	27Y	109.05	560
17X	108.00	-	22Y	108.55	550	28X	109.10	510
17Y	108.05	540	23X	108.60	-	28Y	109.15	562
18X	108.10	500	23Y	108.65	552	29X	109.20	-
18Y	108.15	542	24X	108.70	506	29Y	109.25	564
19X	108.20	-	24Y	108.75	554	30X	109.30	512

NE, 09 FEB 20XX to 05 APR 20XX

LEGEND 18.—Chart Supplements U.S. (formerly Airport/Facility Directory).

DIRECTORY LEGEND 21

TACAN CHANNEL	VHF FREQUENCY	MLS CHANNEL	TACAN CHANNEL	VHF FREQUENCY	MLS CHANNEL	TACAN CHANNEL	VHF FREQUENCY	MLS CHANNEL
30Y	109.35	566	63X	133.60	-	95Y	114.85	650
31X	109.40	·	63Y	133.65	-	96X	114.90	-
31Y	109.45	568	64X	133.70	-	96Y	114.95	652
32X	109.50	514	64Y	133.75	-	97X	115.00	-
32Y	109.55	570	65X	133.80	-	97Y	115.05	654
33X	109.60	·	65Y	133.85	-	98X	115.10	-
33Y	109.65	572	66X	133.90	-	98Y	115.15	656
34X	109.70	516	66Y	133.95	-	99X	115.20	-
34Y	109.75	574	67X	134.00	-	99Y	115.25	658
35X	109.80	·	67Y	134.05	-	100X	115.30	-
35Y	109.85	576	68X	134.10	-	100Y	115.35	660
36X	109.90	518	68Y	134.15	-	101X	115.40	-
36Y	109.95	578	69X	134.20	-	101Y	115.45	662
37X	110.00	·	69Y	134.25	-	102X	115.50	-
37Y	110.05	580	70X	112.30	-	102Y	115.55	664
38X	110.10	520	70Y	112.35	-	103X	115.60	-
38Y	110.15	582	71X	112.40	-	103Y	115.65	666
39X	110.20	·	71Y	112.45	-	104X	115.70	-
39Y	110.25	584	72X	112.50	-	104Y	115.75	668
40X	110.30	522	72Y	112.55	-	105X	115.80	-
40Y	110.35	586	73X	112.60	-	105Y	115.85	670
41X	110.40	·	73Y	112.65	-	106X	115.90	-
41Y	110.45	588	74X	112.70	-	106Y	115.95	672
42X	110.50	524	74Y	112.75	-	107X	116.00	-
42Y	110.55	590	75X	112.80	-	107Y	116.05	674
43X	110.60	·	75Y	112.85	-	108X	116.10	-
43Y	110.65	592	76X	112.90	-	108Y	116.15	676
44X	110.70	526	76Y	112.95	-	109X	116.20	-
44Y	110.75	594	77X	113.00	-	109Y	116.25	678
45X	110.80	·	77Y	113.05	-	110X	116.30	-
45Y	110.85	596	78X	113.10	-	110Y	116.35	680
46X	110.90	528	78Y	113.15	-	111X	116.40	-
46Y	110.95	598	79X	113.20	-	111Y	116.45	682
47X	111.00	·	79Y	113.25	-	112X	116.50	-
47Y	111.05	600	80X	113.30	-	112Y	116.55	684
48X	111.10	530	80Y	113.35	620	113X	116.60	-
48Y	111.15	602	81X	113.40	-	113Y	116.65	686
49X	111.20	·	81Y	113.45	622	114X	116.70	-
49Y	111.25	604	82X	113.50	-	114Y	116.75	688
50X	111.30	532	82Y	113.55	624	115X	116.80	-
50Y	111.35	606	83X	113.60	-	115Y	116.85	690
51X	111.40	·	83Y	113.65	626	116X	116.90	-
51Y	111.45	608	84X	113.70	-	116Y	116.95	692
52X	111.50	534	84Y	113.75	628	117X	117.00	-
52Y	111.55	610	85X	113.80	-	117Y	117.05	694
53X	111.60	·	85Y	113.85	630	118X	117.10	-
53Y	111.65	612	86X	113.90	-	118Y	117.15	696
54X	111.70	536	86Y	113.95	632	119X	117.20	-
54Y	111.75	614	87X	114.00	-	119Y	117.25	698
55X	111.80	·	87Y	114.05	634	120X	117.30	-
55Y	111.85	616	88X	114.10	-	120Y	117.35	·
56X	111.90	538	88Y	114.15	636	121X	117.40	·
56Y	111.95	618	89X	114.20	-	121Y	117.45	·
57X	112.00	·	89Y	114.25	638	122X	117.50	·
57Y	112.05	·	90X	114.30	-	122Y	117.55	·
58X	112.10	·	90Y	114.35	640	123X	117.60	·
58Y	112.15	·	91X	114.40	-	123Y	117.65	·
59X	112.20	·	91Y	114.45	642	124X	117.70	·
59Y	112.25	·	92X	114.50	-	124Y	117.75	·
60X	133.30	·	92Y	114.55	644	125X	117.80	·
60Y	133.35	·	93X	114.60	-	125Y	117.85	·
61X	133.40	·	93Y	114.65	646	126X	117.90	·
61Y	133.45	·	94X	114.70	-	126Y	117.95	·
62X	133.50	·	94Y	114.75	648			
62Y	133.55	·	95X	114.80	·			

35 COMM/NAV/WEATHER REMARKS:
These remarks consist of pertinent information affecting the current status of communications, NAVAIDs and weather.

NE, 09 FEB 20XX to 05 APR 20XX

LEGEND 19.—Chart Supplements U.S. (formerly Airport/Facility Directory).

FAA FIGURES

NOTE:

Some figure numbers are skipped in this appendix. Figures that are not used on the Private Pilot Airplane (PAR) test are not included here.

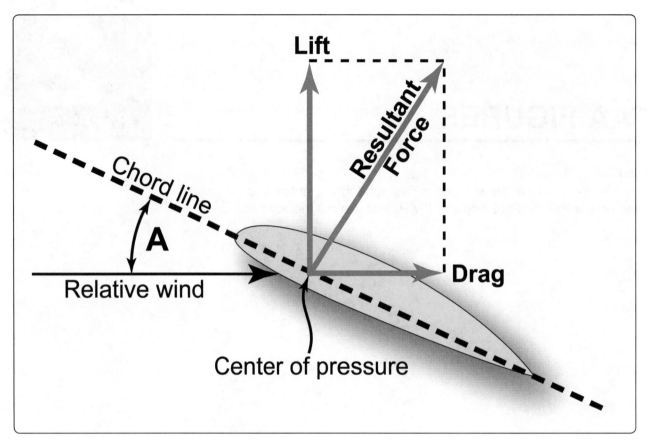

Figure 1.—Lift Vector.

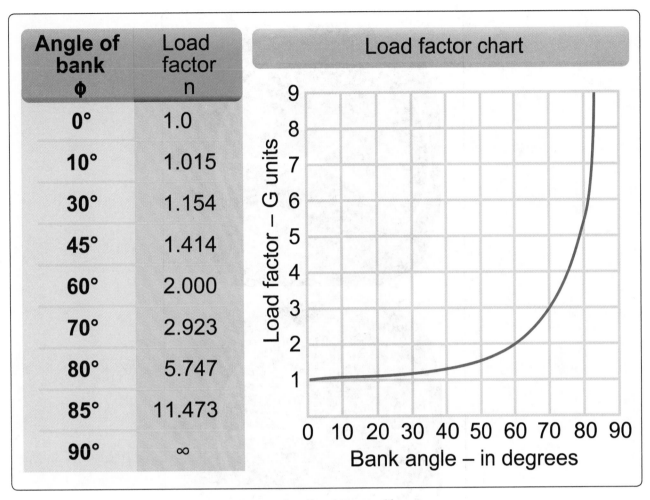

Angle of bank ϕ	Load factor n
0°	1.0
10°	1.015
30°	1.154
45°	1.414
60°	2.000
70°	2.923
80°	5.747
85°	11.473
90°	∞

FIGURE 2.—Load Factor Chart.

Figure 3.—Altimeter.

FIGURE 4.—Airspeed Indicator.

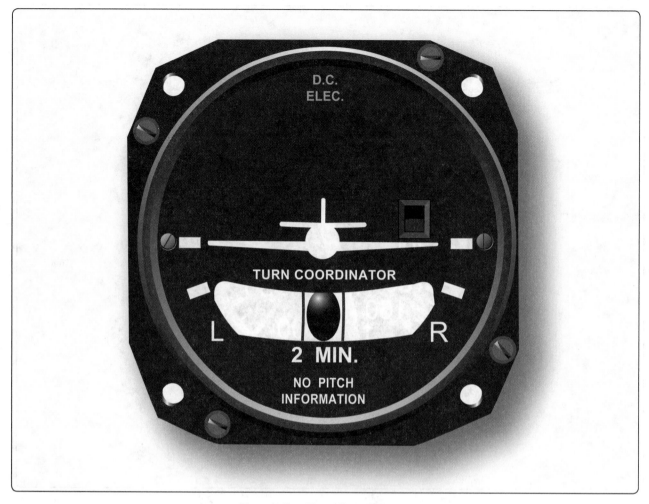

FIGURE 5.—Turn Coordinator.

FIGURE 6.—Heading Indicator.

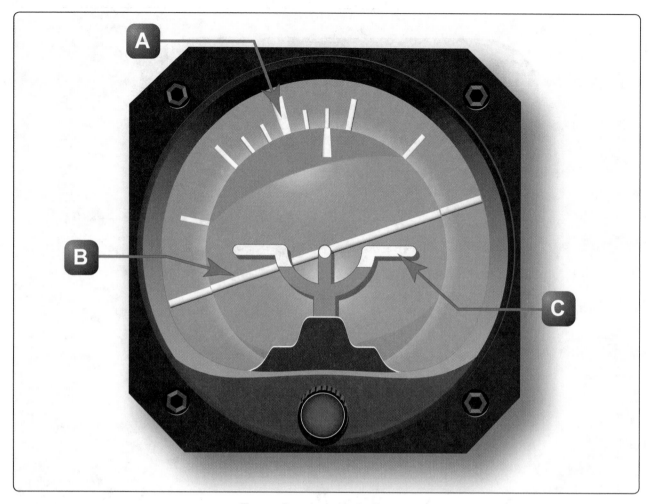

Figure 7.—Attitude Indicator.

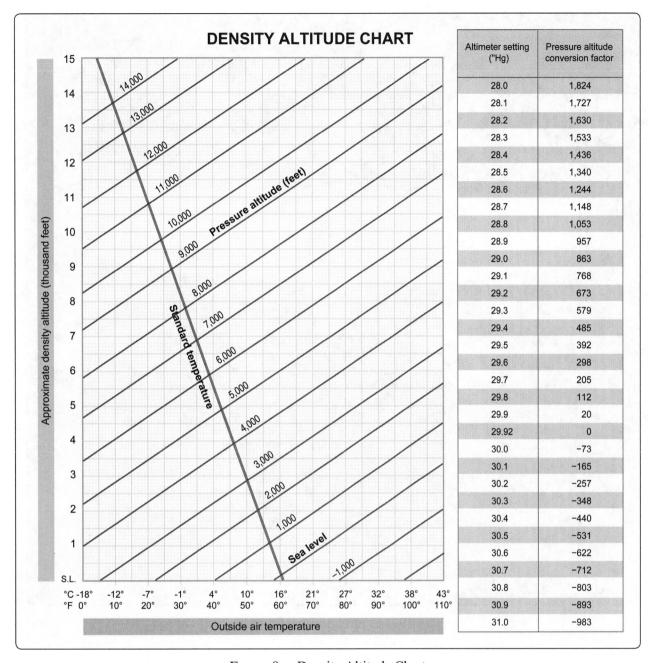

FIGURE 8.—Density Altitude Chart.

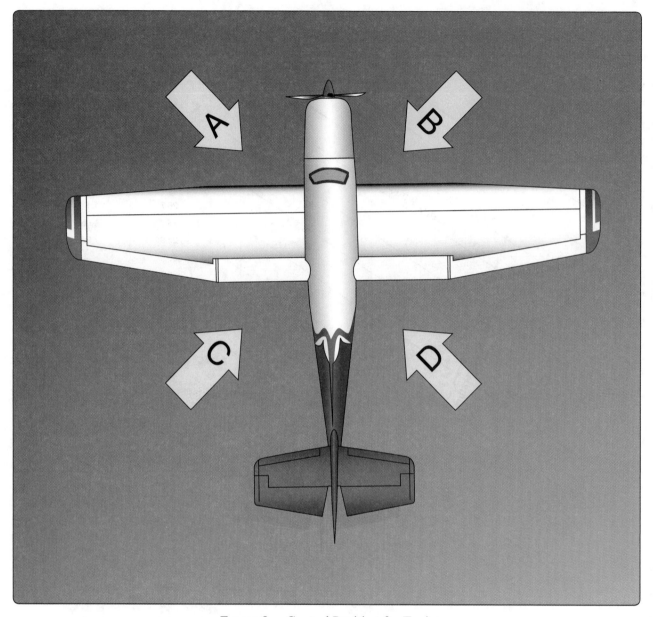

Figure 9.—Control Position for Taxi.

METAR KINK 121845Z 11012G18KT 15SM SKC 25/17 A3000

METAR KBOI 121854Z 13004KT 30SM SCT150 17/6 A3015

METAR KLAX 121852Z 25004KT 6SM BR SCT007 SCT250 16/15 A2991

SPECI KMDW 121856Z 32005KT 1 1/2SM RA OVC007 17/16 A2980 RMK RAB35

SPECI KJFK 121853Z 18004KT 1/2SM FG R04/2200 OVC005 20/18 A3006

FIGURE 12.—Aviation Routine Weather Reports (METAR).

This is a telephone weather briefing from the Dallas FSS for local operation of gliders and lighter-than-air at Caddo Mills, Texas (about 30 miles east of Dallas). The briefing is at 13Z.

"There are no adverse conditions reported or forecast for today."

"A weak low pressure over the Texas Panhandle and eastern New Mexico is causing a weak southerly flow over the area."

"Current weather here at Dallas is wind south 5 knots, visibility 12 miles, clear, temperature 21, dewpoint 9, altimeter 29 point 78."

"By 15Z, we should have a few scattered cumuliform clouds at 5 thousand AGL, with higher scattered cirrus at 25 thousand MSL. After 20Z, the wind should pick up to about 15 knots from the south."

"The winds aloft are: 3 thousand 170 at 7, temperature 20; 6 thousand 200 at 18, temperature 14; 9 thousand 210 at 22, temperature 8; 12 thousand 225 at 27, temperature 0; 18 thousand 240 at 30, temperature −7."

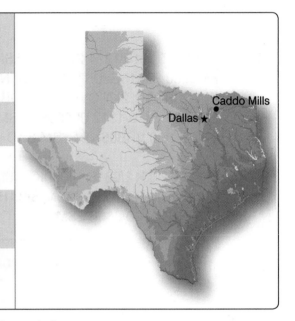

FIGURE 13.—Telephone Weather Briefing.

UA/OV KOKC-KTUL/TM 1800/FL 120/TP BE90//SK BKN018-TOP055/OVC072-TOP089/CLR ABV/TA M7/WV 08021/TB LGT 055-072/IC LGT-MOD RIME 072-089

FIGURE 14.—Pilot Weather Report.

TAF

KMEM 121720Z 1218/1324 20012KT 5SM HZ BKN030 PROB40 2022 1SM TSRA OVC008CB
      FM2200 33015G20KT P6SM BKN015 OVC025 PROB40 2202 3SM SHRA
      FM0200 35012KT OVC008 PROB40 0205 2SM-RASN BECMG 0608 02008KT BKN012
      BECMG 1310/1312 00000KT 3SM BR SKC TEMPO 1212/1214 1/2SM FG
      FM131600 VRB06KT P6SM SKC=

KOKC 051130Z 0512/0618 14008KT 5SM BR BKN030 TEMPO 0513/0516 1 1/2SM BR
      FM051600 18010KT P6SM SKC BECMG 0522/0524 20013G20KT 4SM SHRA OVC020
      PROB40 0600/0606 2SM TSRA OVC008CB BECMG 0606/0608 21015KT P6SM SCT040=

FIGURE 15.—Terminal Aerodrome Forecasts (TAF).

FB WBC 151745
DATA BASED ON 151200Z
VALID 1600Z FOR USE 1800-0300Z. TEMPS NEG ABV 24000

FT	3000	6000	9000	12000	18000	24000	30000	34000	39000
ALS			2420	2635-08	2535-18	2444-30	245945	246755	246862
AMA		2714	2725+00	2625-04	2531-15	2542-27	265842	256352	256762
DEN			2321-04	2532-08	2434-19	2441-31	235347	236056	236262
HLC		1707-01	2113-03	2219-07	2330-17	2435-30	244145	244854	245561
MKC	0507	2006+03	2215-01	2322-06	2338-17	2348-29	236143	237252	238160
STL	2113	2325+07	2332+02	2339-04	2356-16	2373-27	239440	730649	731960

FIGURE 17.—Winds and Temperatures Aloft Forecast.

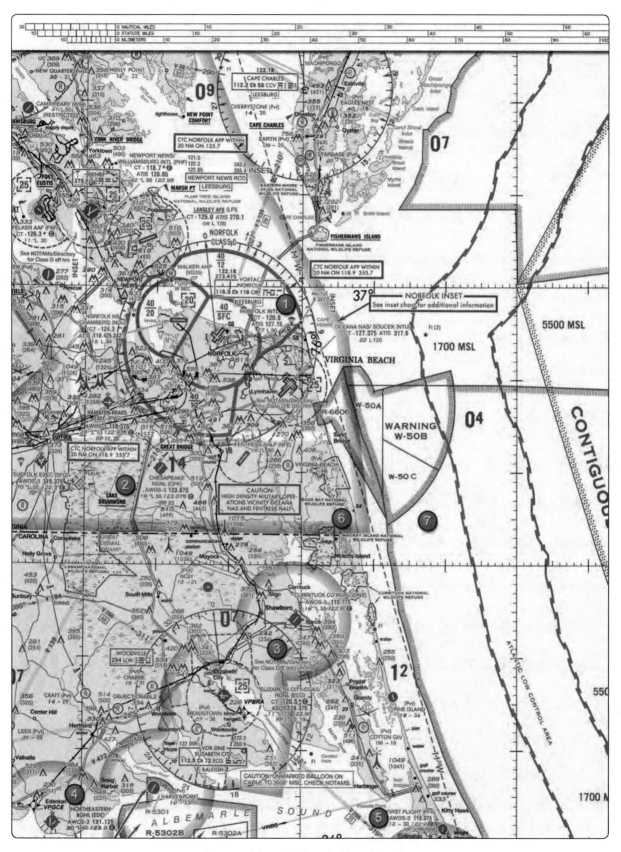

FIGURE 20.—Sectional Chart Excerpt.

NOTE: Chart is not to scale and should not be used for navigation. Use associated scale.

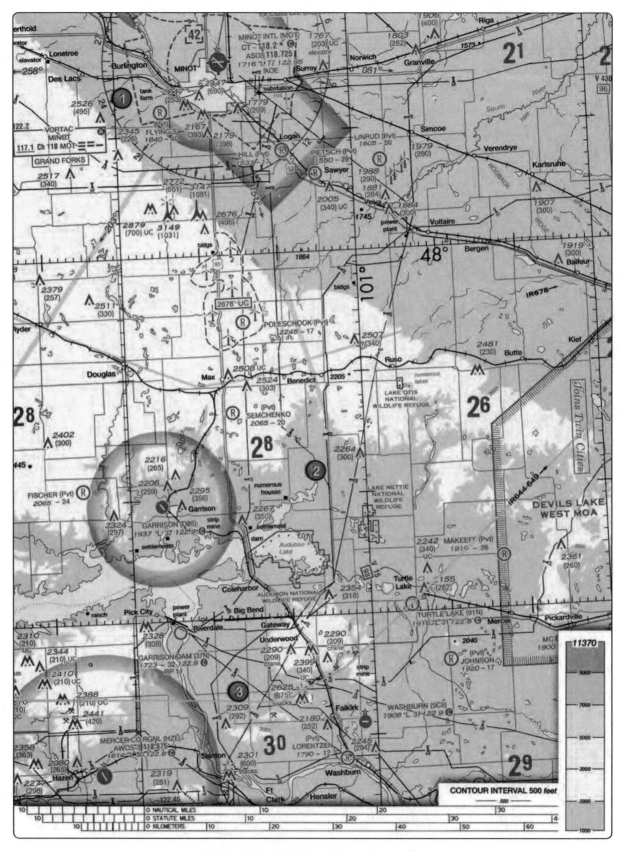

FIGURE 21.—Sectional Chart Excerpt.
NOTE: Chart is not to scale and should not be used for navigation. Use associated scale.

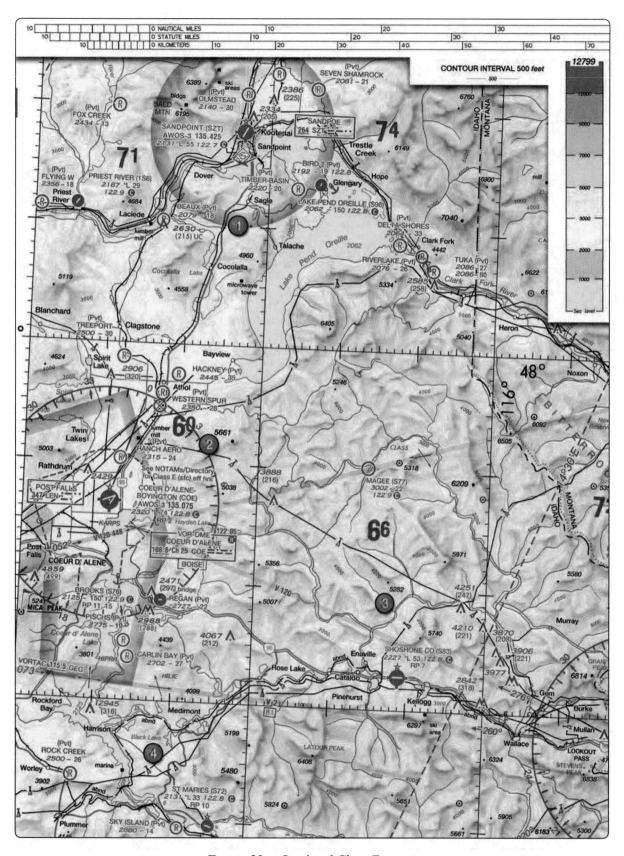

FIGURE 22.—Sectional Chart Excerpt.
NOTE: *Chart is not to scale and should not be used for navigation. Use associated scale.*

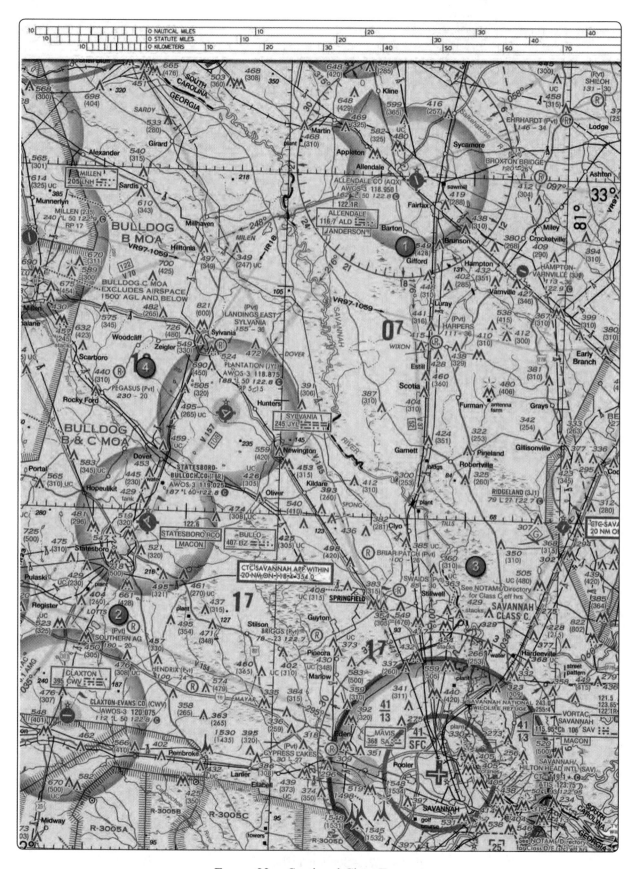

FIGURE 23.—Sectional Chart Excerpt.
NOTE: Chart is not to scale and should not be used for navigation. Use associated scale.

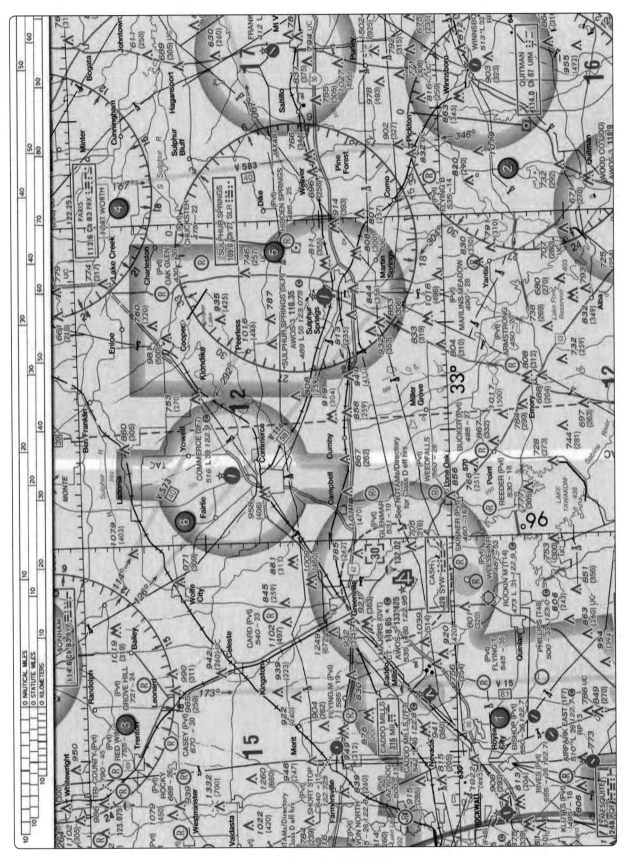

FIGURE 24.—Sectional Chart Excerpt.
NOTE: Chart is not to scale and should not be used for navigation. Use associated scale.

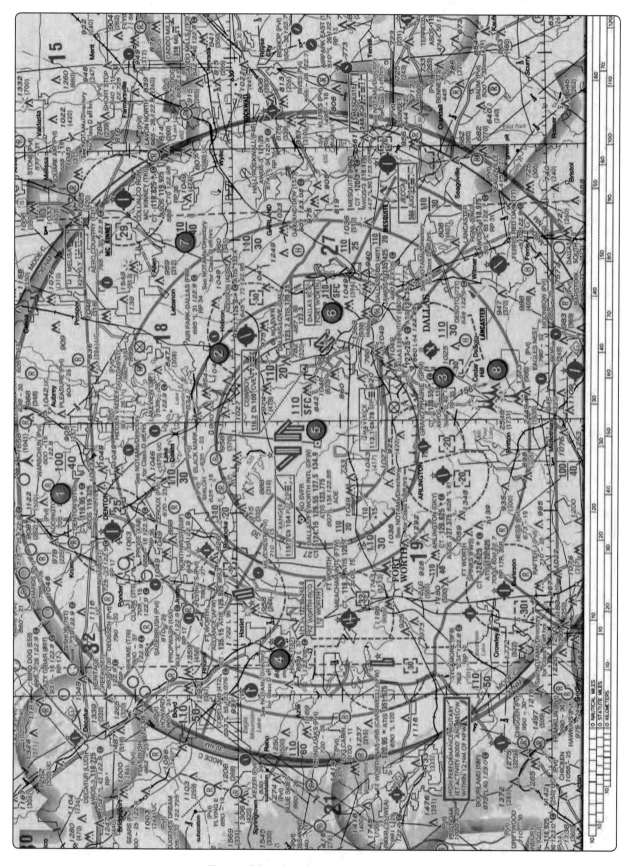

FIGURE 25.—Sectional Chart Excerpt.
NOTE: *Chart is not to scale and should not be used for navigation. Use associated scale.*

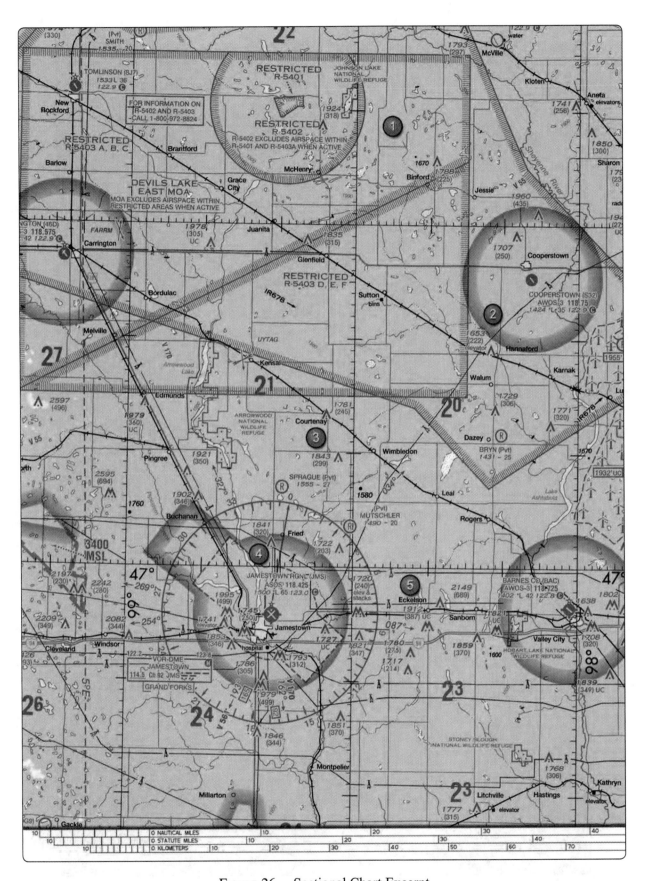

FIGURE 26.—Sectional Chart Excerpt.
NOTE: Chart is not to scale and should not be used for navigation. Use associated scale.

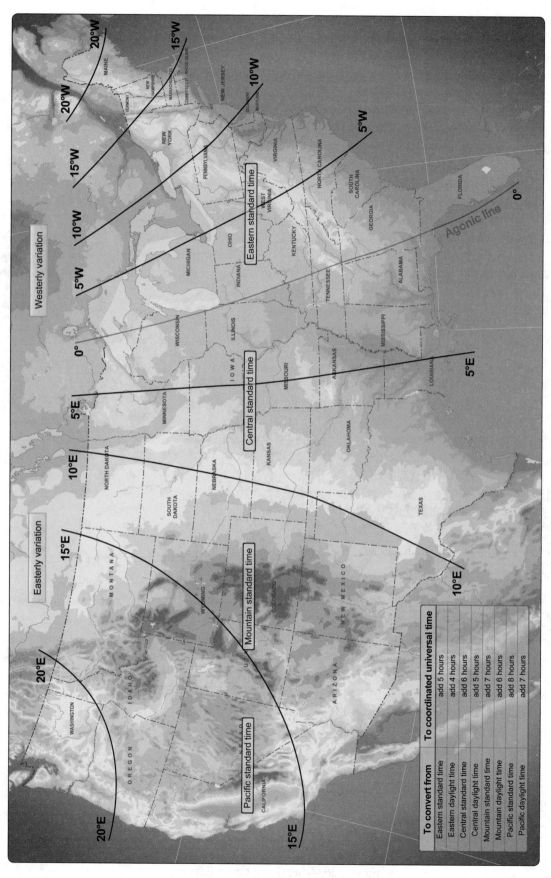

To convert from	To coordinated universal time
Eastern standard time	add 5 hours
Eastern daylight time	add 4 hours
Central standard time	add 6 hours
Central daylight time	add 5 hours
Mountain standard time	add 7 hours
Mountain daylight time	add 6 hours
Pacific standard time	add 8 hours
Pacific daylight time	add 7 hours

FIGURE 27.—Time Conversion Table.

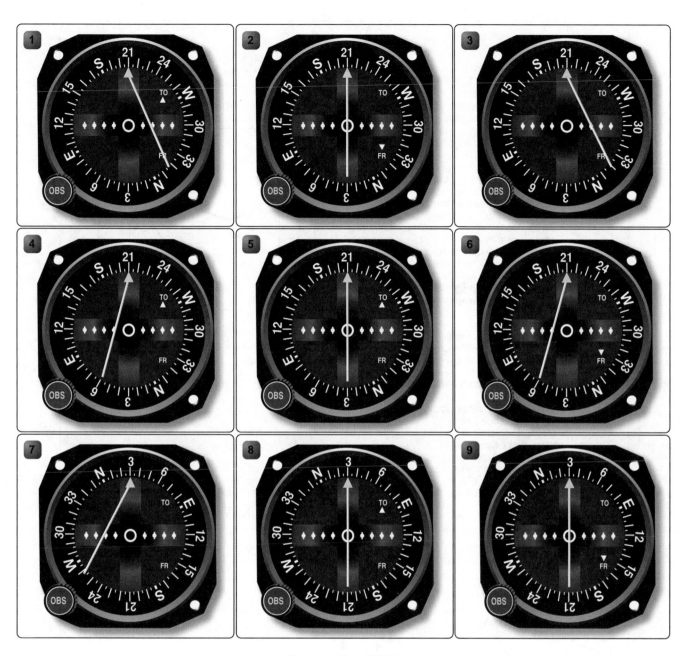

FIGURE 28.—VOR.

IDAHO   31

COEUR D'ALENE–PAPPY BOYINGTON FLD   (COE)   9 NW   UTC−8(−7DT)
         N47°46.46′ W116°49.18′   **GREAT FALLS**
  2320   B   S4   **FUEL** 100, JET A   OX 1, 2, 3, 4   Class IV, ARFF Index A   NOTAM FILE COE   H–1C, L–13B
  RWY 05–23: H7400X100 (ASPH–GRVD)   S–57, D–95, 2S–121, 2D–165   HIRL   0.6% up NE   **IAP** 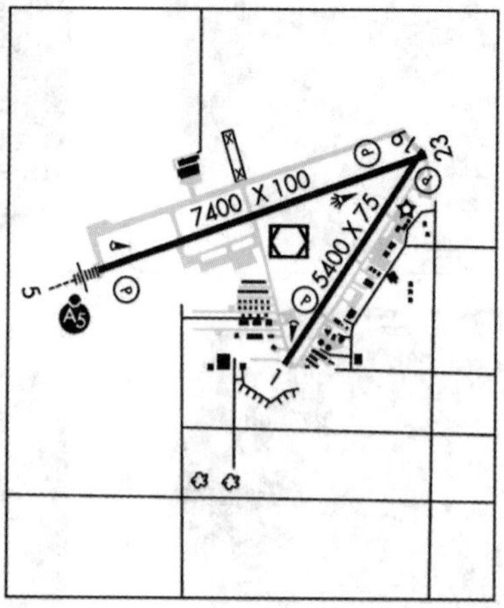
    RWY 05: MALSR (NSTD). PAPI(P4R)—GA 3.0° TCH 56′.
    RWY 23: REIL. PAPI(P4R)—GA 3.0° TCH 50′.
  RWY 01–19: H5400X75 (ASPH)   S–50, D–83, 2S–105, 2D–150
    MIRL   0.3% up N
    RWY 01: REIL. PAPI(P2L)—GA 3.0° TCH 39′. Rgt tfc.
    RWY 19: PAPI(P2L)—GA 3.0° TCH 41′.
  RUNWAY DECLARED DISTANCE INFORMATION
    RWY 01:   TORA–5400   TODA–5400   ASDA–5400   LDA–5400
    RWY 05:   TORA–7400   TODA–7400   ASDA–7400   LDA–7400
    RWY 19:   TORA–5400   TODA–5400   ASDA–5400   LDA–5400
    RWY 23:   TORA–7400   TODA–7400   ASDA–7400   LDA–7400
  AIRPORT REMARKS: Attended Mon–Fri 1500–0100Z‡. For after hrs
    fuel-self svc avbl or call 208-772-6404, 208-661-4174,
    208-661-7449, 208-699-5433. Self svc fuel avbl with credit
    card. 48 hr PPR for unscheduled ops with more than
    30 passenger seats call arpt manager 208-446-1860. Migratory
    birds on and invof arpt Oct–Nov. Remote cntl airstrip is 2.3 miles
    west AER 05. Arpt conditions avbl on AWOS. Rwy 05 NSTD
    MALSR, thld bar extends 5′ byd rwy edge lgts each side. ACTIVATE
    MIRL Rwy 01–19, HIRL Rwy 05–23, REIL Rwy 01 and Rwy 23, MALSR Rwy 05—CTAF. PAPI Rwy 01, Rwy 19, Rwy
    05, and Rwy 23 opr continuously.
  WEATHER DATA SOURCES: AWOS–3 135.075 (208) 772–8215.
    HIWAS 108.8 COE.
  COMMUNICATIONS: CTAF/UNICOM 122.8
    RCO 122.05 (BOISE RADIO)
  ® **SPOKANE APP/DEP CON** 132.1
  AIRSPACE: CLASS E svc continuous.
  RADIO AIDS TO NAVIGATION: NOTAM FILE COE.
    (T) VORW/DME 108.8   COE   Chan 25   N47°46.42′ W116°49.24′   at fld. 2320/19E.   **HIWAS.**
      DME portion unusable:
        220°–240° byd 15 NM   280°–315° byd 15 NM blo 11,000′.
    POST FALLS NDB (MHW) 347   LEN   N47°44.57′ W116°57.66′   053° 6.0 NM to fld.
    ILS 110.7   I–COE   Rwy 05   Class ID.   Localizer unusable 25° left and right of course.

Figure 31.—Chart Supplements U.S. (formerly Airport/Facility Directory).

Useful load weights and moments

Baggage or 5th seat occupant

ARM 140

Weight	Moment/100
10	14
20	28
30	42
40	56
50	70
60	84
70	98
80	112
90	126
100	140
110	154
120	168
130	182
140	196
150	210
160	224
170	238
180	252
190	266
200	280
210	294
220	308
230	322
240	336
250	350
260	364
270	378

Occupants

Front seats ARM 85		Rear seats ARM 121	
Weight	Moment/100	Weight	Moment/100
120	102	120	145
130	110	130	157
140	119	140	169
150	128	150	182
160	136	160	194
170	144	170	206
180	153	180	218
190	162	190	230
200	170	200	242

Usable fuel

Main wing tanks ARM 75

Gallons	Weight	Moment/100
5	30	22
10	60	45
15	90	68
20	120	90
25	150	112
30	180	135
35	210	158
40	240	180
44	264	198

Auxiliary wing tanks ARM 94

Gallons	Weight	Moment/100
5	30	28
10	60	56
15	90	85
19	114	107

Empty weight~2,015

MOM/100~1,554

Moment limits vs weight

Moment limits are based on the following weight and center of gravity limit data (landing gear down).

*Oil		
Quarts	Weight	Moment/100
10	19	5

*Included in basic empty weight.

Weight condition	Forward CG limit	AFT CG limit
2,950 lb (takeoff or landing)	82.1	84.7
2,525 lb	77.5	85.7
2,475 lb or less	77.0	85.7

FIGURE 32.—Airplane Weight and Balance Tables.

Moment limits vs weight (continued)						
Weight	Minimum Moment 100	Maximum Moment 100		Weight	Minimum Moment 100	Maximum Moment 100
2,100	1,617	1,800		2,500	1,932	2,143
2,110	1,625	1,808		2,510	1,942	2,151
2,120	1,632	1,817		2,520	1,953	2,160
2,130	1,640	1,825		2,530	1,963	2,168
2,140	1,648	1,834		2,540	1,974	2,176
2,150	1,656	1,843		2,550	1,984	2,184
2,160	1,663	1,851		2,560	1,995	2,192
2,170	1,671	1,860		2,570	2,005	2,200
2,180	1,679	1,868		2,580	2,016	2,208
2,190	1,686	1,877		2,590	2,026	2,216
2,200	1,694	1,885		2,600	2,037	2,224
2,210	1,702	1,894		2,610	2,048	2,232
2,220	1,709	1,903		2,620	2,058	2,239
2,230	1,717	1,911		2,630	2,069	2,247
2,240	1,725	1,920		2,640	2,080	2,255
2,250	1,733	1,928		2,650	2,090	2,263
2,260	1,740	1,937		2,660	2,101	2,271
2,270	1,748	1,945		2,670	2,112	2,279
2,280	1,756	1,954		2,680	2,123	2,287
2,290	1,763	1,963		2,690	2,133	2,295
2,300	1,771	1,971		2,700	2,144	2,303
2,310	1,779	1,980		2,710	2,155	2,311
2,320	1,786	1,988		2,720	2,166	2,319
2,330	1,794	1,997		2,730	2,177	2,326
2,340	1,802	2,005		2,740	2,188	2,334
2,350	1,810	2,014		2,750	2,199	2,342
2,360	1,817	2,023		2,760	2,210	2,350
2,370	1,825	2,031		2,770	2,221	2,358
2,380	1,833	2,040		2,780	2,232	2,366
2,390	1,840	2,048		2,790	2,243	2,374
2,400	1,848	2,057		2,800	2,254	2,381
2,410	1,856	2,065		2,810	2,265	2,389
2,420	1,863	2,074		2,820	2,276	2,397
2,430	1,871	2,083		2,830	2,287	2,405
2,440	1,879	2,091		2,840	2,298	2,413
2,450	1,887	2,100		2,850	2,309	2,421
2,460	1,894	2,108		2,860	2,320	2,428
2,470	1,902	2,117		2,870	2,332	2,436
2,480	1,911	2,125		2,880	2,343	2,444
2,490	1,921	2,134		2,890	2,354	2,452
				2,900	2,365	2,460
				2,910	2,377	2,468
				2,920	2,388	2,475
				2,930	2,399	2,483
				2,940	2,411	2,491
				2,950	2,422	2,499

FIGURE 33.—Airplane Weight and Balance Tables.

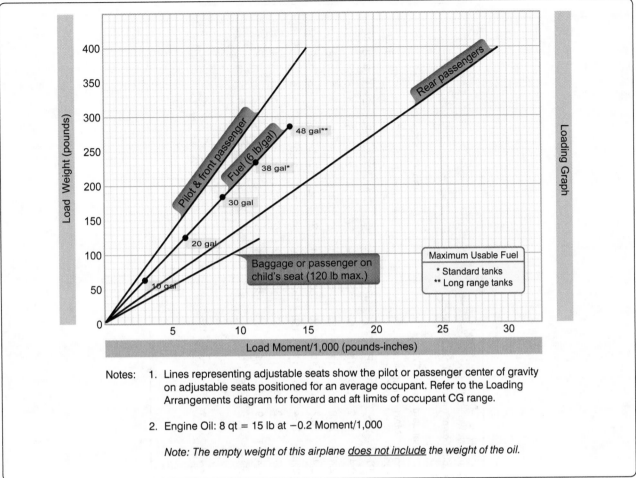

Notes: 1. Lines representing adjustable seats show the pilot or passenger center of gravity on adjustable seats positioned for an average occupant. Refer to the Loading Arrangements diagram for forward and aft limits of occupant CG range.

2. Engine Oil: 8 qt = 15 lb at −0.2 Moment/1,000

Note: The empty weight of this airplane <u>does not include</u> the weight of the oil.

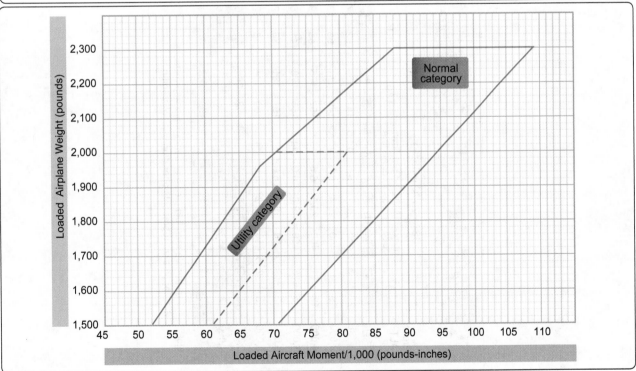

FIGURE 34.—Airplane Weight and Balance Graphs.

Cruise power settings
65% Maximum continuous power (or full throttle 2,800 pounds)

ISA −20 °C (−36 °F)

Press ALT. Feet	IOAT °F	IOAT °C	Engine speed RPM	MAN. press IN HG	Fuel flow per engine PSI	Fuel flow per engine GPH	TAS KTS	TAS MPH
SL	27	−3	2,450	20.7	6.6	11.5	147	169
2,000	19	−7	2,450	20.4	6.6	11.5	149	171
4,000	12	−11	2,450	20.1	6.6	11.5	152	175
6,000	5	−15	2,450	19.8	6.6	11.5	155	178
8,000	−2	−19	2,450	19.5	6.6	11.5	157	181
10,000	−8	−22	2,450	19.2	6.6	11.5	160	184
12,000	−15	−26	2,450	18.8	6.4	11.5	162	186
14,000	−22	−30	2,450	17.4	5.8	10.5	159	183
16,000	−29	−34	2,450	16.1	5.3	9.7	156	180

Standard day (ISA)

Press ALT. Feet	IOAT °F	IOAT °C	Engine speed RPM	MAN. press IN HG	Fuel flow per engine PSI	Fuel flow per engine GPH	TAS KTS	TAS MPH
SL	63	17	2,450	21.2	6.6	11.5	150	173
2,000	55	13	2,450	21.0	6.6	11.5	153	176
4,000	48	9	2,450	20.7	6.6	11.5	156	180
6,000	41	5	2,450	20.4	6.6	11.5	158	182
8,000	36	2	2,450	20.2	6.6	11.5	161	185
10,000	28	−2	2,450	19.9	6.6	11.5	163	188
12,000	21	−6	2,450	18.8	6.1	10.9	163	188
14,000	14	−10	2,450	17.4	5.6	10.1	160	184
16,000	7	−14	2,450	16.1	5.1	9.4	156	180

ISA +20 °C (+36 °F)

Press ALT. Feet	IOAT °F	IOAT °C	Engine speed RPM	MAN. press IN HG	Fuel flow per engine PSI	Fuel flow per engine GPH	TAS KTS	TAS MPH
SL	99	37	2,450	21.8	6.6	11.5	153	176
2,000	91	33	2,450	21.5	6.6	11.5	156	180
4,000	84	29	2,450	21.3	6.6	11.5	159	183
6,000	79	26	2,450	21.0	6.6	11.5	161	185
8,000	72	22	2,450	20.8	6.6	11.5	164	189
10,000	64	18	2,450	20.3	6.5	11.4	166	191
12,000	57	14	2,450	18.8	5.9	10.6	163	188
14,000	50	10	2,450	17.4	5.4	9.8	160	184
16,000	43	6	2,450	16.1	4.9	9.1	155	178

Note: 1. Full throttle manifold pressure settings are approximate.
2. Shaded area represents operation with full throttle.

FIGURE 35.—Airplane Power Setting Table.

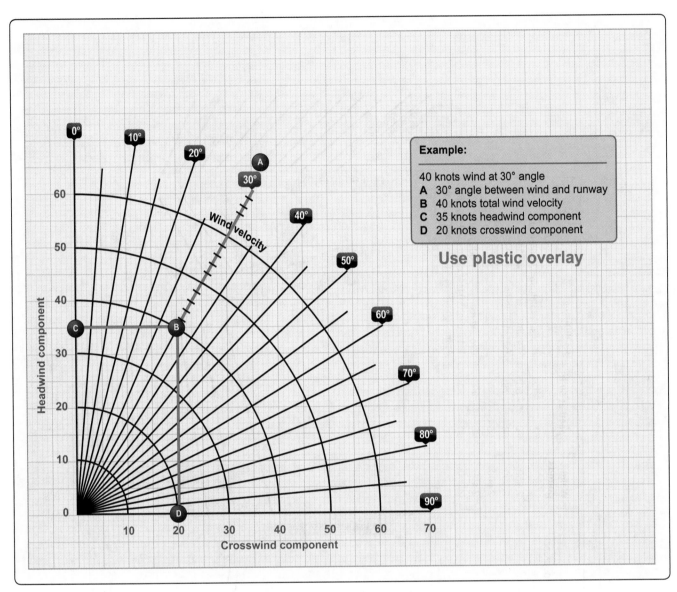

FIGURE 36.—Crosswind Component Graph.

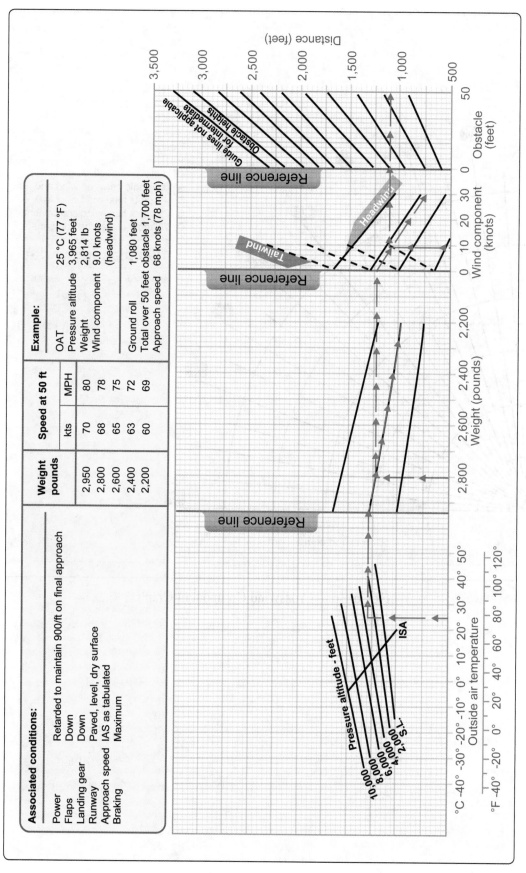

FIGURE 37.—Airplane Landing Distance Graph.

Landing distance

Flaps lowered to 40° – Power off – Hard surface runway – Zero wind

Gross weight lb	Approach speed, IAS, MPH	At sea level & 59 °F		At 2,500 feet & 50 °F		At 5,000 feet & 41 °F		At 7,500 feet & 32 °F	
		Ground roll	Total to clear 50 feet OBS	Ground roll	Total to clear 50 feet OBS	Ground roll	Total to clear 50 feet OBS	Ground roll	Total to clear 50 feet OBS
1,600	60	445	1,075	470	1,135	495	1,195	520	1,255

NOTE:

1. Decrease the distances shown by 10% for each 4 knots of headwind.
2. Increase the distance by 10% for each 60 °F temperature increase above standard.
3. For operation on a dry, grass runway, increase distance (both "ground roll" and "total to clear 50 feet obstacle") by 20% of the "total to clear 50 feet obstacle" figure.

FIGURE 38.—Airplane Landing Distance Table.

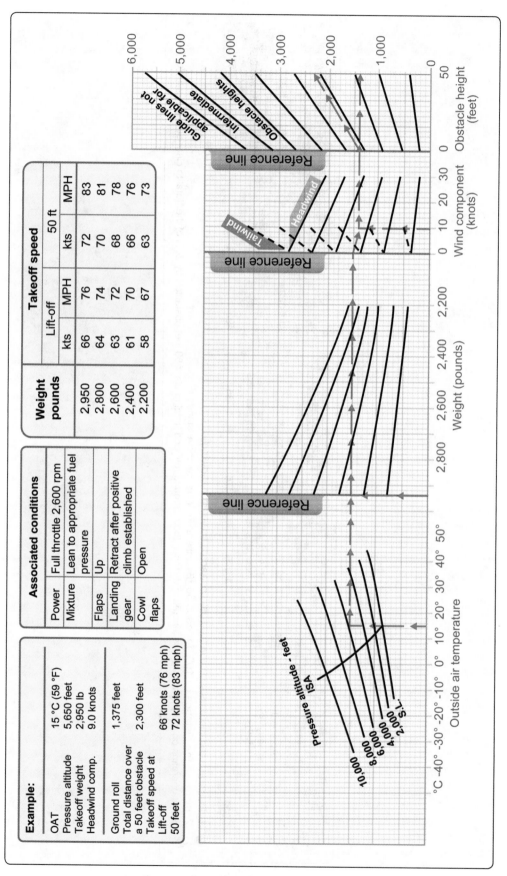

FIGURE 40.—Airplane Takeoff Distance Graph.

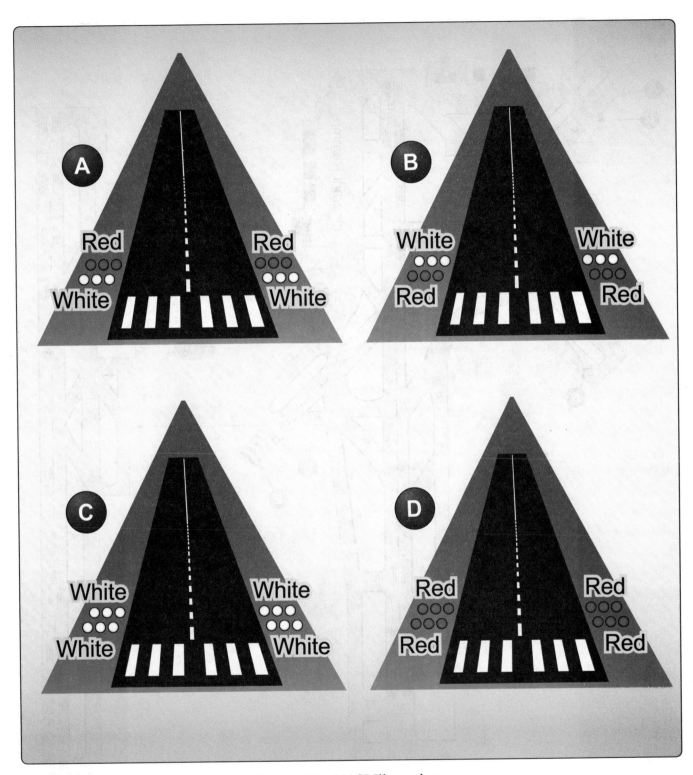

FIGURE 47.—VASI Illustrations.

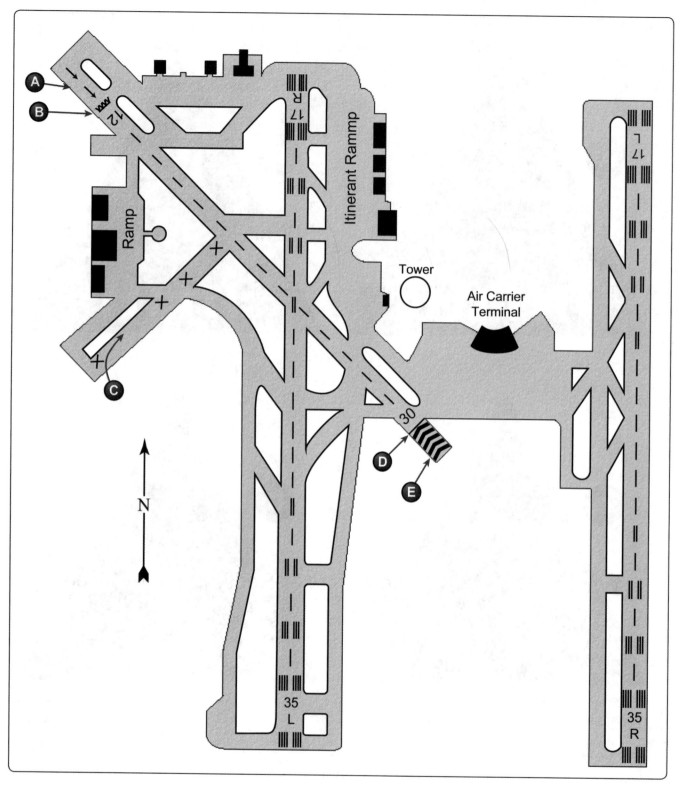

Figure 48.—Airport Diagram.

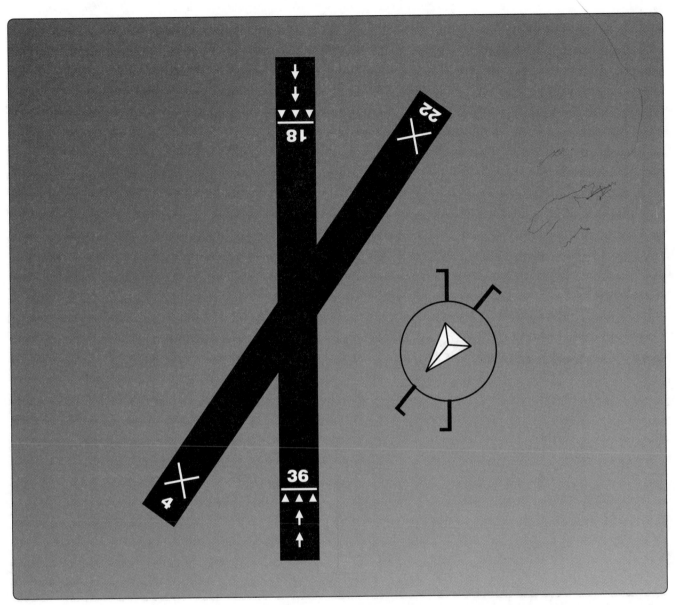

FIGURE 49.—Airport Diagram.

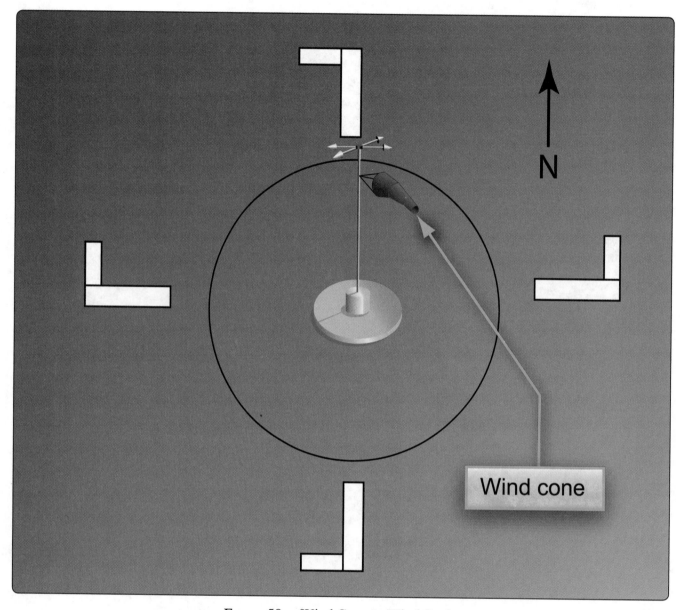

FIGURE 50.—Wind Cone to Wind Sock.

Form Approved OMB No. 2120-0026

U.S. DEPARTMENT OF TRANSPORTATION FEDERAL AVIATION ADMINISTRATION **FLIGHT PLAN**	(FAA USE ONLY) ☐ PILOT BRIEFING ☐ VNR ☐ STOPOVER		TIME STARTED	SPECIALIST INITIALS

1. TYPE	2. AIRCRAFT IDENTIFICATION	3. AIRCRAFT TYPE/ SPECIAL EQUIPMENT	4. TRUE AIRSPEED	5. DEPARTURE POINT	6. DEPARTURE TIME		7. CRUISING ALTITUDE
VFR					PROPOSED (Z)	ACTUAL (Z)	
IFR							
DVFR			KTS				

8. ROUTE OF FLIGHT

9. DESTINATION (Name of airport and city)	10. EST. TIME ENROUTE		11. REMARKS
	HOURS	MINUTES	

12. FUEL ON BOARD		13. ALTERNATE AIRPORT(S)	14. PILOT'S NAME, ADDRESS & TELEPHONE NUMBER & AIRCRAFT HOME BASE	15. NUMBER ABOARD
HOURS	MINUTES			
			17. DESTINATION CONTACT/TELEPHONE (OPTIONAL)	

16. COLOR OF AIRCRAFT	CIVIL AIRCRAFT PILOTS. 14 CFR Part 91 requires you file an IFR flight plan to operate under instrument flight rules in controlled airspace. Failure to file could result in a civil penalty not to exceed $1,000 for each violation (Section 901 of the Federal Aviation Act of 1958, as amended). Filing of a VFR flight plan is recommended as a good operating practice. See also Part 99 for requirements concerning DVFR flight plans.

FAA Form 7233-1 (8-82)   CLOSE VFR FLIGHT PLAN WITH _____ FSS ON ARRIVAL

FIGURE 51.—Flight Plan Form.

NEBRASKA   271

LINCOLN (LNK)   4 NW   UTC−6(−5DT)   N40°51.05′ W96°45.55′   OMAHA
  1219   B   S4   **FUEL** 100LL, JET A   TPA—See Remarks   ARFF Index—See Remarks   H−5C, L−10I
      NOTAM FILE LNK   IAP, AD 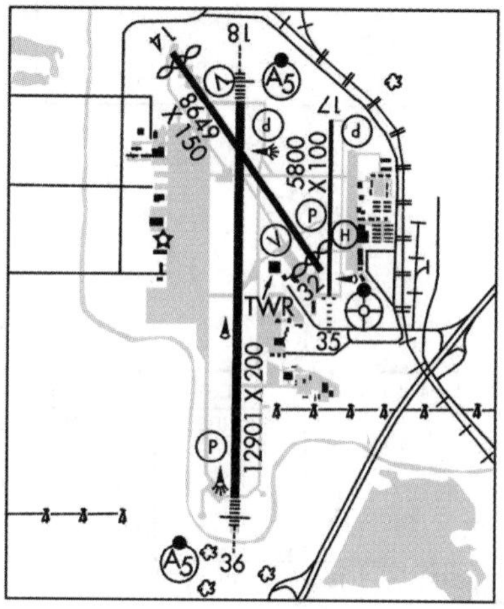
  RWY 18–36: H12901X200 (ASPH–CONC–GRVD)   S–100, D–200,
      2S–175, 2D–400   HIRL
      RWY 18: MALSR. PAPI(P4L)—GA 3.0° TCH 55′. Rgt tfc.   0.4%
        down.
      RWY 36: MALSR. PAPI(P4L)—GA 3.0° TCH 57′.
  RWY 14–32: H8649X150 (ASPH–CONC–GRVD)   S–80, D–170,
      2S–175, 2D–280   MIRL
      RWY 14: REIL. VASI(V4L)—GA 3.0° TCH 48′. Thld dsplcd 363′.
      RWY 32: VASI(V4L)—GA 3.0° TCH 50′. Thld dsplcd 470′.
        Pole.   0.3% up.
  RWY 17–35: H5800X100 (ASPH–CONC–AFSC)   S–49, D–60
        HIRL   0.8% up S
      RWY 17: REIL. PAPI(P4L)—GA 3.0° TCH 44′.
      RWY 35: ODALS. PAPI(P4L)—GA 3.0° TCH 30′. Rgt tfc.
  RUNWAY DECLARED DISTANCE INFORMATION
      RWY 14: TORA–8649   TODA–8649   ASDA–8649   LDA–8286
      RWY 18: TORA–5800   TODA–5800   ASDA–5400   LDA–5400
      RWY 18: TORA–12901 TODA–12901 ASDA–12901 LDA–12901
      RWY 32: TORA–8649   TODA–8649   ASDA–8286   LDA–7816
      RWY 35: TORA–5800   TODA–5800   ASDA–5800   LDA–5800
      RWY 36: TORA–12901 TODA–12901 ASDA–12901 LDA–12901

AIRPORT REMARKS: Attended continuously. Birds invof arpt. Rwy 18 designated calm wind rwy. Rwy 32 apch holdline
    on South A twy. TPA–2219 (1000), heavy military jet 3000 (1781). Class I, ARFF Index B. ARFF Index C level
    equipment provided. Rwy 18–36 touchdown and rollout rwy visual range avbl. When twr clsd MIRL Rwy 14–32
    preset on low ints, HIRL Rwy 18–36 and Rwy 17–35 preset on med ints, ODALS Rwy 35 operate continuously on
    med ints, MALSR Rwy 18 and Rwy 36 operate continuously and REIL Rwy 14 and Rwy 17 operate continuously
    on low ints. VASI Rwy 14 and Rwy 32, PAPI Rwy 17, Rwy 35, Rwy 18 and Rwy 36 on continuously.
WEATHER DATA SOURCES: ASOS (402) 474–9214. LLWAS
COMMUNICATIONS: CTAF 118.5   **ATIS** 118.05   **UNICOM** 122.95
    RCO 122.65 (COLUMBUS RADIO)
Ⓡ **APP/DEP CON** 124.0 (180°–359°) 124.8 (360°–179°)
    TOWER 118.5 125.7 (1130–0600Z‡)   **GND CON** 121.9   **CLNC DEL** 120.7
AIRSPACE: CLASS C svc 1130–0600Z‡ ctc **APP CON** other times CLASS E.
RADIO AIDS TO NAVIGATION: NOTAM FILE LNK.
    (H) VORTACW 116.1   LNK   Chan 108   N40°55.43′ W96°44.52′   181° 4.4 NM to fld. 1370/9E
    POTTS NDB (MHW/LOM) 385   LN   N40°44.83′ W96°45.75′   355° 6.2 NM to fld. Unmonitored when twr clsd.
    ILS 111.1   I–OCZ   Rwy 18.   Class IB   OM unmonitored.
    ILS 109.9   I–LNK   Rwy 36   Class IA   LOM POTTS NDB. MM unmonitored. LOM unmonitored when twr
      clsd.
COMM/NAV/WEATHER REMARKS: Emerg frequency 121.5 not available at twr.

LOUP CITY MUNI (0F4)   1 NW   UTC−6(−5DT)   N41°17.20′ W98°59.41′   OMAHA
  2071   B   **FUEL** 100LL   NOTAM FILE OLU   L−10H, 12H
  RWY 16–34: H3200X60 (CONC)   S–12.5   MIRL
      RWY 34: Trees.
  RWY 04–22: 2040X100 (TURF)
      RWY 04: Tree.   **RWY 22:** Road.
AIRPORT REMARKS: Unattended. For svc call 308–745–1344/1244/0664.
COMMUNICATIONS: CTAF 122.9
RADIO AIDS TO NAVIGATION: NOTAM FILE OLU.
    WOLBACH (H) VORTAC 114.8   OBH   Chan 95   N41°22.54′ W98°21.22′   253° 29.3 NM to fld. 2010/7E.

MARTIN FLD   (See SO SIOUX CITY)

FIGURE 52.—Chart Supplements U.S. (formerly Airport/Facility Directory).

For	N	30	60	E	120	150
Steer	0	27	56	85	116	148
For	S	210	240	W	300	330
Steer	181	214	244	274	303	332

FIGURE 58.—Compass Card.

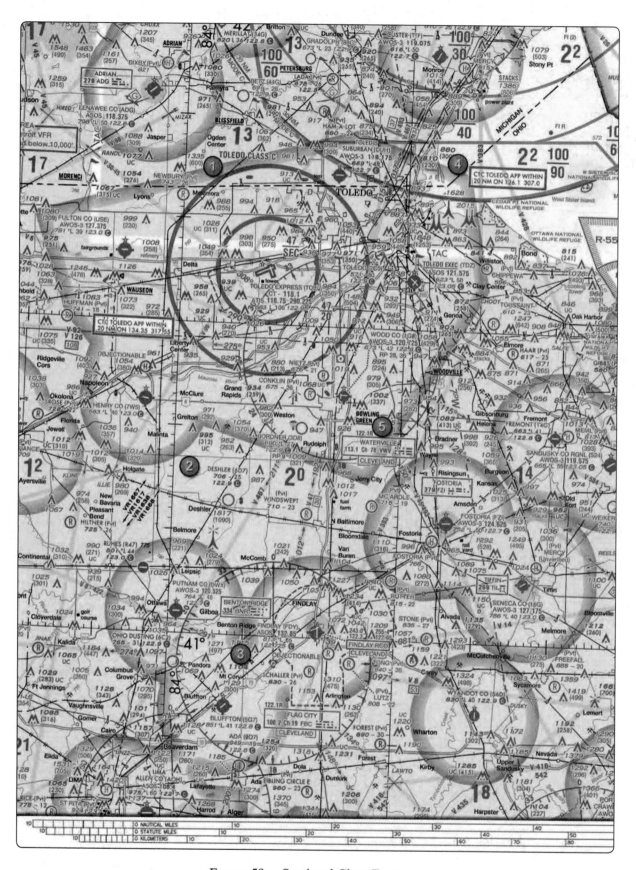

FIGURE 59.—Sectional Chart Excerpt.

NOTE: Chart is not to scale and should not be used for navigation. Use associated scale.

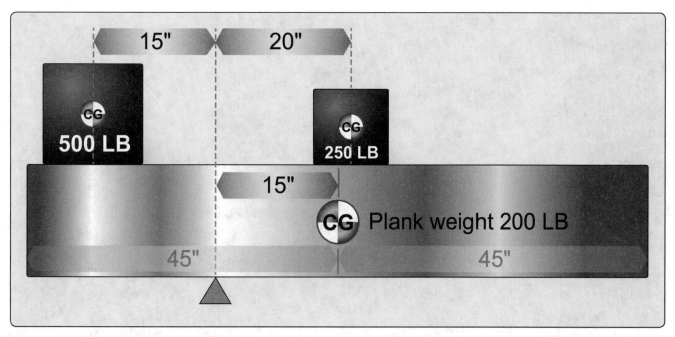

FIGURE 60.—Weight and Balance Diagram.

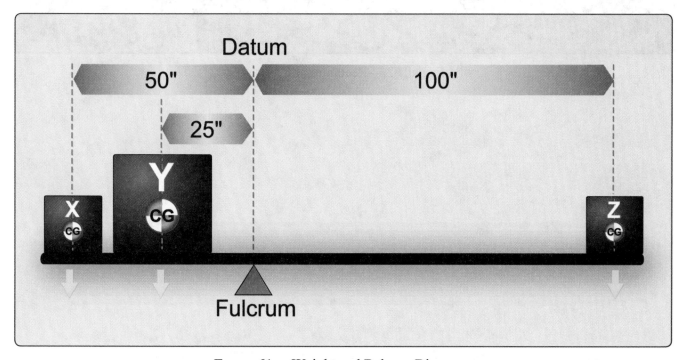

FIGURE 61.—Weight and Balance Diagram.

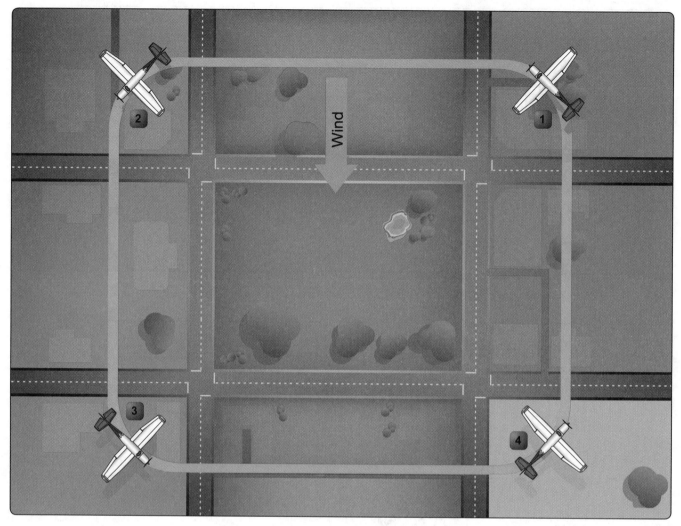

Figure 62.—Rectangular Course.

OHIO
263

TOLEDO

TOLEDO EXECUTIVE (TDZ)   6 SE   UTC–5(–4DT)   N41°33.90' W83°28.93'   DETROIT
623   B   S4   **FUEL** 100LL, JET A   OX 1, 3   NOTAM FILE TDZ   H–10G, L–28J
RWY 14–32: H5829X100 (ASPH–GRVD)   S–63, D–85, 2S–107   MIRL   IAP
  RWY 14: REIL. PAPI(P4L)—GA 3.0° TCH 34'. Thld dsplcd 225'.
  Tower.
  RWY 32: VASI(V4L)—GA 3.0° TCH 43'. Thld dsplcd 351'. Road.
RWY 04–22: H3799X75 (ASPH)   S–63, D–85, 2S–107   MIRL
  RWY 04: REIL. PAPI(P4L)—GA 3.5° TCH 35'. Thld dsplcd 100'.
  Road.
  RWY 22: REIL. PAPI(P4L)—GA 3.0° TCH 25'. Thld dsplcd 380'.
  Railroad.
AIRPORT REMARKS: Attended Mon–Fri continuously, Sat–Sun
  1300–0100Z‡. Parallel twy Rwy 04–22 and Rwy 14–32 35' wide.
  Seagulls on and invof arpt. Ldg fee. ACTIVATE MIRL Rwy 04–22
  and Rwy 14–32, REIL and PAPI Rwy 04, Rwy 22, Rwy 14 and VASI
  Rwy 32—CTAF.
WEATHER DATA SOURCES: ASOS 121.575 (419) 838–5034.
COMMUNICATIONS: CTAF/UNICOM 123.05
Ⓡ **APP/DEP CON** 126.1   **CLNC DEL** 125.6
RADIO AIDS TO NAVIGATION: NOTAM FILE CLE.
  WATERVILLE (L) VOR/DME 113.1   VWV   Chan 78   N41°27.09'
    W83°38.32'   048° 9.8 NM to fld. 664/2W.

- -

TOLEDO EXPRESS (TOL)   10 W   UTC–5(–4DT)   N41°35.21' W83°48.47'   DETROIT
683   B   S4   **FUEL** 100LL, JET A   OX 3   LRA   Class I, ARFF Index B   NOTAM FILE TOL   H–10G, L–28J
RWY 07–25: H10599X150 (ASPH–GRVD)   S–100, D–174, 2S–175, 2D–300, 2D/2D2–550   IAP, AD
  HIRL   CL
  RWY 07: ALSF2. TDZL. Trees.
  RWY 25: MALSR. VASI(V4L)—GA 3.0° TCH 51'. Trees.   0.3% up.
RWY 16–34: H5599X150 (ASPH–GRVD)   S–100, D–174, 2S–175,
  2D–300   MIRL
  RWY 16: REIL. PAPI(P4L)—GA 3.0° TCH 48'. Trees.
  RWY 34: REIL.
RUNWAY DECLARED DISTANCE INFORMATION
  RWY 07:   TORA 10599   TODA 10599   ASDA 10599   LDA 10599
  RWY 16:   TORA 5599   TODA 5599   ASDA 5599   LDA 5599
  RWY 25:   TORA 10599   TODA 10599   ASDA 10599   LDA 10599
  RWY 34:   TORA 5599   TODA 5599   ASDA 5599   LDA 5599
ARRESTING GEAR/SYSTEM
  RWY 07 ←BAK–12   BAK–12 →RWY 25
AIRPORT REMARKS: Attended continuously. Fuel and svc avbl
  1300–0500Z‡. Birds on and invof arpt. Twy A west of Rwy 16 and
  the ramp between Twy B9 and B13 not visible from twr. Twy D
  intersection of Twy D1, heavy acft use minimal power to reduce
  foreign object damage on Air National Guard ramp. Customs:
  Sat–Sun req must be made prior to 2200Z‡ on Fri, phone 419–259–6424.
WEATHER DATA SOURCES: ASOS (419) 865–8351.
COMMUNICATIONS: ATIS 118.75   UNICOM 122.95
Ⓡ **APP/DEP CON** 126.1 (360°–179°) 134.35 (180°–359°) 123.975
  TOWER 118.1   **GND CON** 121.9   **CLNC DEL** 121.75
AIRSPACE: CLASS C svc continuous ctc **APP CON**
RADIO AIDS TO NAVIGATION: NOTAM FILE CLE.
  WATERVILLE (L) VOR/DME 113.1   VWV   Chan 78   N41°27.09' W83°38.32'   319° 11.1 NM to fld. 664/2W.
  TOPHR NDB (LOM) 219   TO   N41°33.21' W83°55.27'   074° 5.5 NM to fld. Unmonitored. NOTAM FILE TOL.
  ILS 109.7.   I–TOL   Rwy 07.   Class IE.   LOM TOPHR NDB.
  ILS 108.7   I–BQE   Rwy 25.   Class IA.   LOC unusable 0.4 NM inbound. ILS unmonitored when twr clsd.
  ASR

- -

SEAGATE HELISTOP (6T2)   00 N   UTC–5(–4DT)   N41°39.25' W83°31.88'   DETROIT
650   NOTAM FILE CLE
HELIPAD H1: H50X50 (CONC)
HELIPORT REMARKS: Unattended. ACTIVATE orange perimeter lgts—CTAF. Helipad H1 NSTD 1–box (2 VASIS). Helipad
  H1 not marked with "H." Helipad H1 perimeter lgts.
COMMUNICATIONS: CTAF/UNICOM 123.05

FIGURE 63.—Chart Supplements U.S. (formerly Airport/Facility Directory).

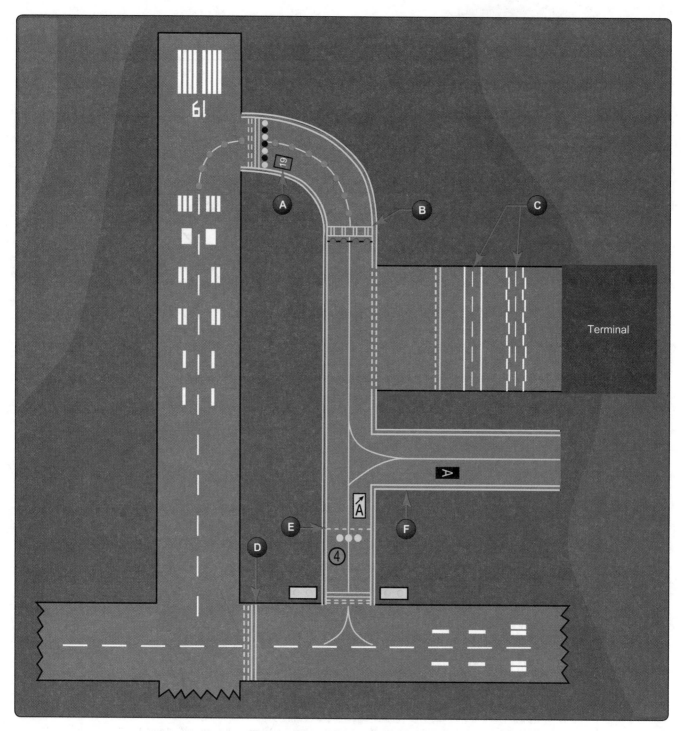

FIGURE 64.—Airport Markings.

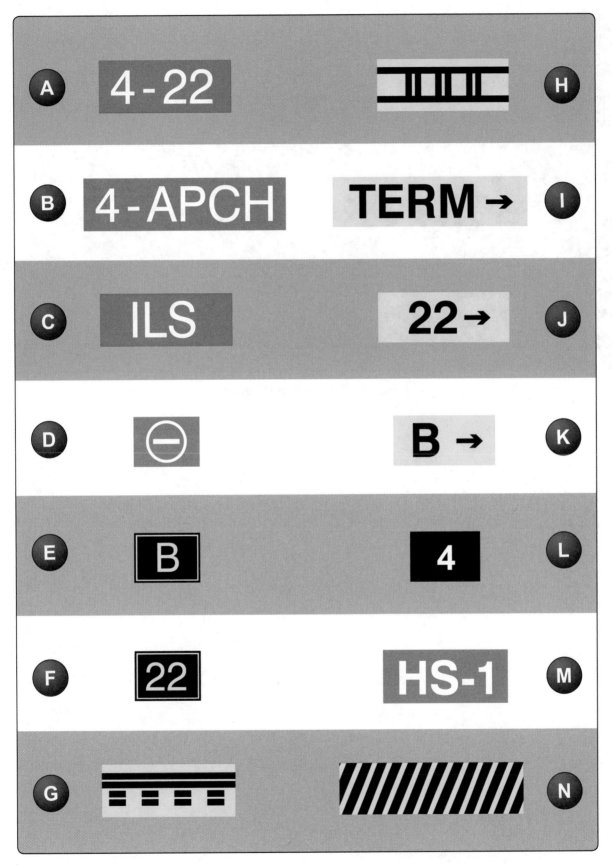

FIGURE 65.—U.S. Airport Signs.

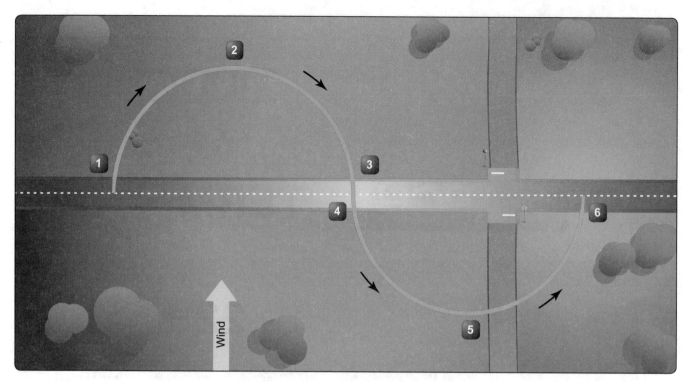

FIGURE 66.—S-Turn Diagram.

Empty Weight Data

*Oil is included in empty weight	Empty Weight (pountds)	Empty Weight Moment (/100)
Certificated Weight	2,110	1,652

Occupants

Front seats		Rear seats		
ARM 85 inches			Fwd Position ARM 111 inches	Alt Position ARM 136 inches
Weight (pounds)	Moment (in-lb)	Weight (pounds)	Moment (in-lb)	Moment (in-lb)
120	102	120	133	163
130	111	130	144	177
140	119	140	155	190
150	128	150	167	204
160	136	160	178	218
170	145	170	189	231
180	153	180	200	245
190	162	190	211	258
200	170	200	222	273

Fuel

ARM 75 inches

Gallons	Weight (pounds)	Moment (in-ib)	Gallons	Weight (pounds)	Moment (in-lb)
5	30	23	45	270	203
10	60	45	49	294	221
15	90	68	55	330	248
20	120	90	60	360	270
25	150	113	65	390	293
30	180	135	70	420	315
35	210	158	75	450	338
40	240	180	80	480	360

Baggage

ARM 150

Weight (pounds)	Moment (in-lb)
10	15
20	30
30	45
40	60
50	75
60	90
70	105
80	120
90	135
100	150
110	165
120	180
130	195
140	210
150	225
160	240
170	255
180	270
190	285
200	300
210	315
220	330
230	345
240	360
250	375
260	390
270	405

NOTE: All moments are equal to

$$\frac{weight \times arm}{100}$$

Gross Weight Moment Limits

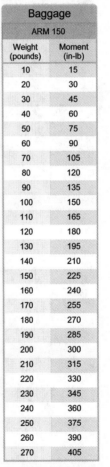

FIGURE 67.—Weight and Balance Chart.

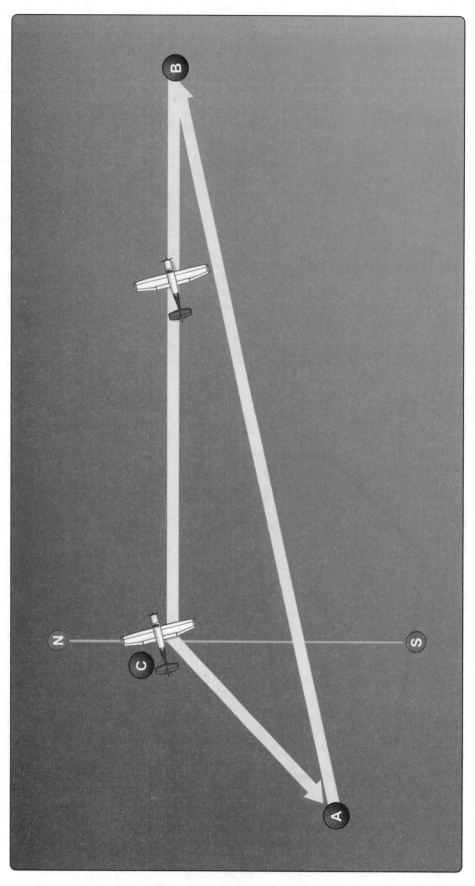

FIGURE 68.—Wind Triangle.

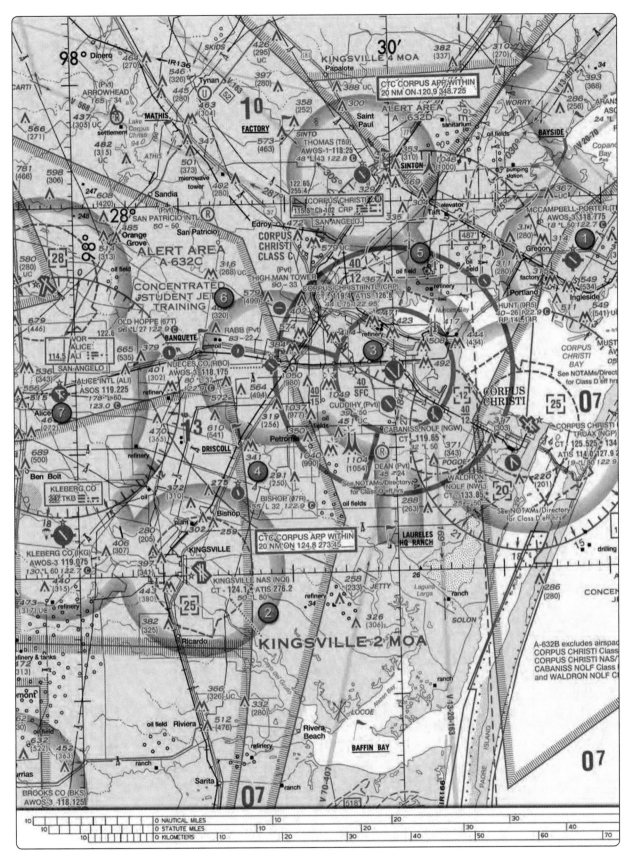

FIGURE 69.—Sectional Chart Excerpt.

NOTE: Chart is not to scale and should not be used for navigation. Use associated scale.

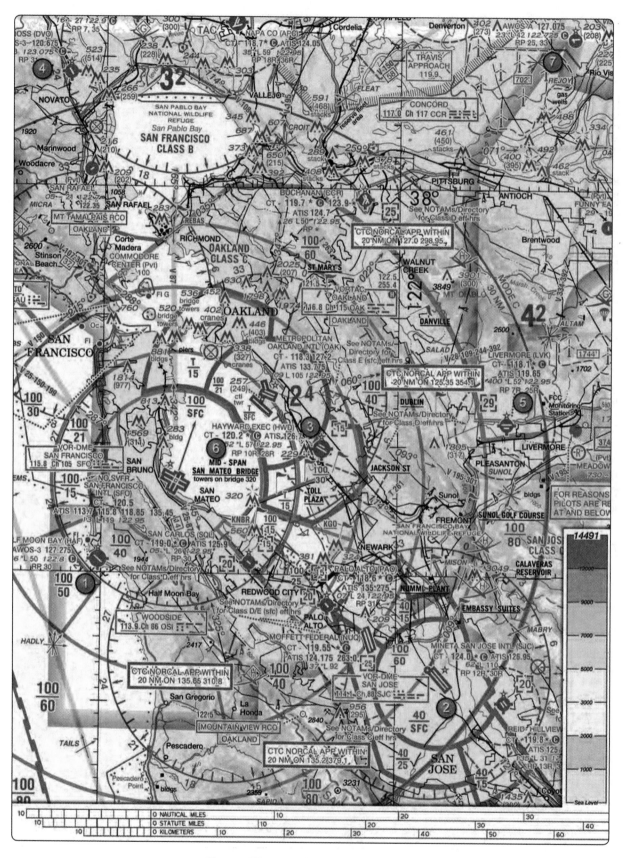

FIGURE 70.—Sectional Chart Excerpt.
NOTE: Chart is not to scale and should not be used for navigation. Use associated scale.

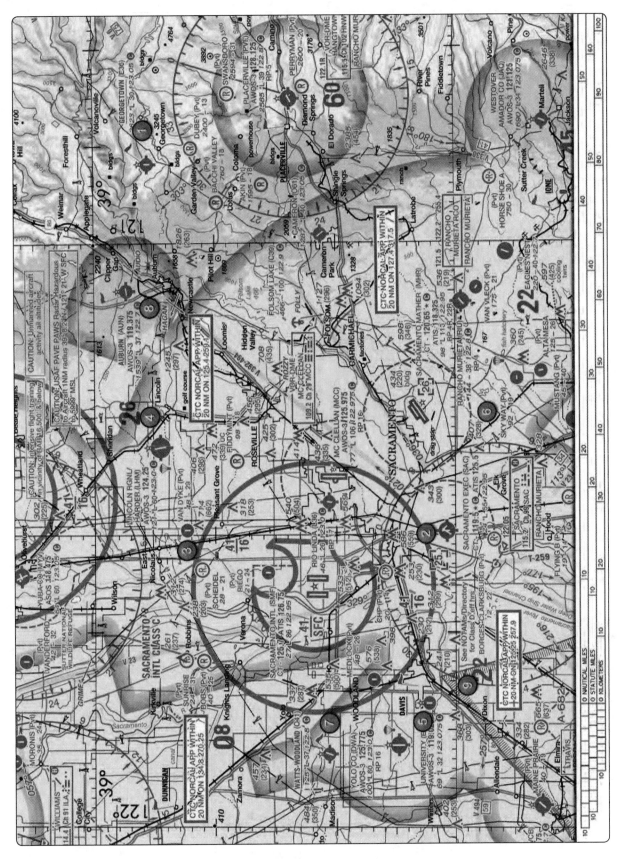

Figure 71.—Sectional Chart Excerpt.

NOTE: Chart is not to scale and should not be used for navigation. Use associated scale.

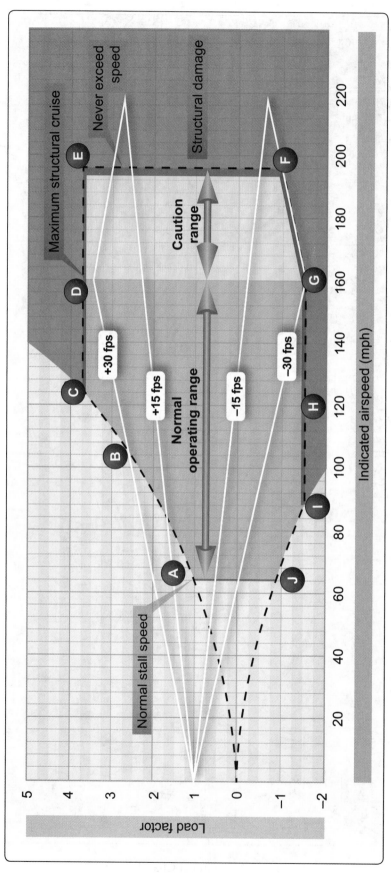

Figure 72.—Velocity vs. G-Loads.

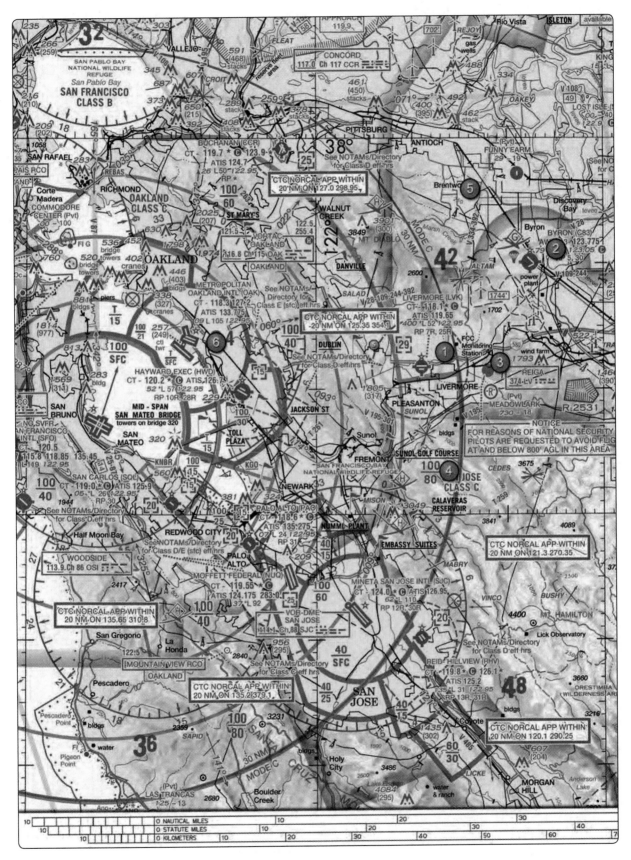

FIGURE 74.—Sectional Chart Excerpt.
NOTE: Chart is not to scale and should not be used for navigation. Use associated scale.

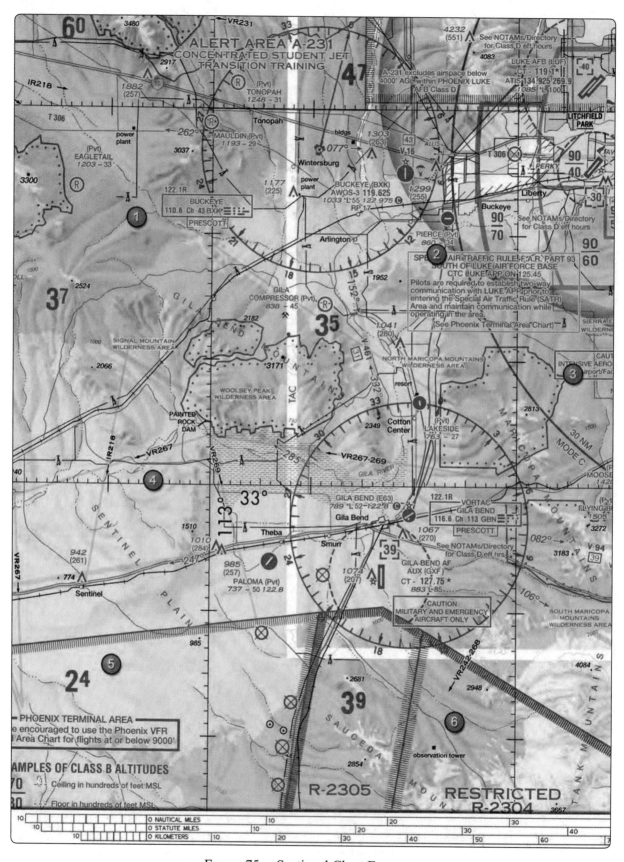

FIGURE 75.—Sectional Chart Excerpt.
NOTE: Chart is not to scale and should not be used for navigation. Use associated scale.

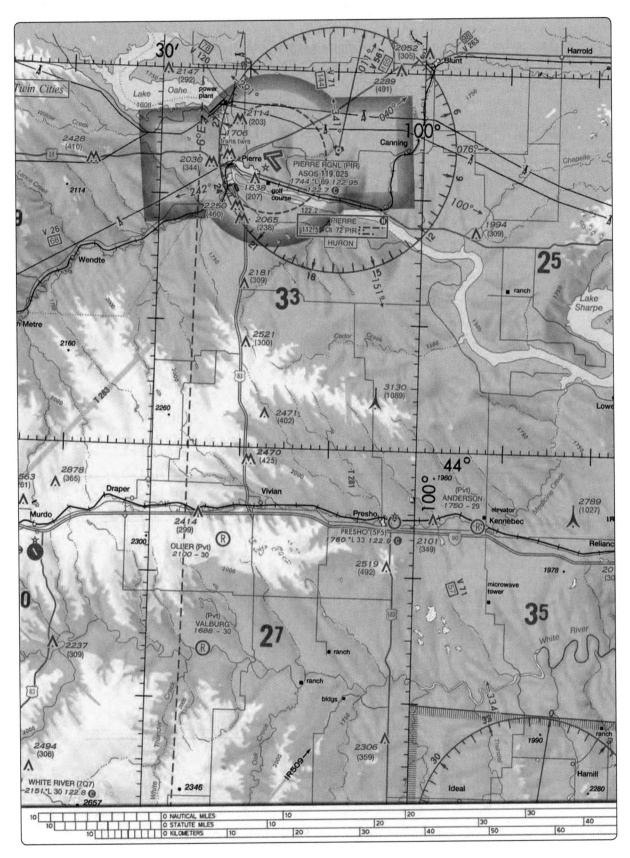

FIGURE 76.—Sectional Chart Excerpt.
NOTE: Chart is not to scale and should not be used for navigation. Use associated scale.

340   **SOUTH DAKOTA**

PIERRE RGNL   (PIR)   3 E   UTC −6(−5DT)   N44°22.96′ W100°17.16′   **OMAHA**
 1744   B   S4   **FUEL** 100LL, JET A   OX 1, 2, 3, 4   Class I, ARFF Index A   NOTAM FILE PIR   **H−2I, L−12H**
 RWY 13−31: H6900X100 (ASPH−GRVD)   S−91, D−108, 2S−137, 2D−168   HIRL   **IAP**
  RWY 13: REIL. PAPI(P4L)—GA 3.0 ° TCH 52′.
  RWY 31: MALSR. PAPI(P4L)—GA 3.0 ° TCH 52′.
 RWY 07−25: H6881X150 (ASPH−GRVD)   S−91, D−114, 2S−145,
  2D−180   HIRL   0.6% up W
  RWY 07: REIL. PAPI(P4L)—GA 3.0 ° TCH 47′. Tank.
  RWY 25: REIL. PAPI(P4L)—GA 3.0 ° TCH 54′.
 RUNWAY DECLARED DISTANCE INFORMATION
  RWY 07:   TORA−6881   TODA−6881   ASDA−6830   LDA−6830
  RWY 13:   TORA−6900   TODA−6900   ASDA−6900   LDA−6900
  RWY 25:   TORA−6881   TODA−6881   ASDA−6881   LDA−6881
  RWY 31:   TORA−6900   TODA−6900   ASDA−6900   LDA−6900
 AIRPORT REMARKS: Attended Mon−Fri 1100−0600Z‡, Sat−Sun

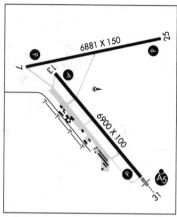

 1100−0400Z‡. For attendant other times call
 605−224−9000/8621. Arpt conditions unmonitored during
 0530−1000Z‡. Numerous non−radio acft operating in area. Birds
 on and invof arpt and within a 25 NM radius. No line of sight
 between rwy ends of Rwy 07−25. ARFF provided for part 121 air
 carrier ops only. 48 hr PPR for unscheduled acr ops involving acft
 designed for 31 or more passenger seats call 605−773−7447 or
 605−773−7405. Taxiway C is 50′ wide and restricted to acft 75,000 pounds or less. ACTIVATE HIRL Rwy 13−31
 and Rwy 07−25, MALSR Rwy 31, REIL Rwy 07, Rwy 13 and Rwy 25, PAPI Rwy 07, Rwy 25, Rwy 13 and Rwy
 31—CTAF 122.7. NOTE: See Special Notices Section—
 Aerobatic Practice Areas.
 WEATHER DATA SOURCES: ASOS 119.025 (605) 224−6087. **HIWAS** 112.5 PIR.
 COMMUNICATIONS: CTAF 122.7   UNICOM 122.95
  RCO 122.2 (HURON RADIO)
 ⓡ **MINNEAPOLIS CENTER APP/DEP CON** 125.1
 RADIO AIDS TO NAVIGATION: NOTAM FILE PIR.
  (L) VORTACW 112.5   PIR   Chan 72   N44°23.67′ W100°09.77′   251° 5.3 NM to fld. 1789/11E.   **HIWAS.**
  ILS/DME 111.9   I−PIR   Chan 56   Rwy 31.   Class IA   ILS GS unusable for coupled apch blo 2,255′. GS
   unusable blo 2135′.

PINE RIDGE   (IEN)   2 E   UTC −7(−6DT)   N43°01.35′ W102°30.66′   **CHEYENNE**
 3333   B   NOTAM FILE IEN   **H−5B, L−12G**
 RWY 12−30: H5000X60 (ASPH)   S−12   MIRL   0.7% up SE   **IAP**
  RWY 12: P−line.
  RWY 30: PAPI(P2L)—GA 3.0 ° TCH 26′. Fence.
 RWY 06−24: H3003X50 (ASPH)   S−12   0.7% up NE
  RWY 24: Fence.
 AIRPORT REMARKS: Unattended. Rwy 06−24 CLOSED indef. MIRL Rwy
  12−30 and PAPI Rwy 30 opr dusk−0530Z‡, after 0530Z‡
  ACTIVATE—CTAF.
 WEATHER DATA SOURCES: ASOS 126.775 (605) 867−1584.
 COMMUNICATIONS: CTAF 122.9
  DENVER CENTER APP/DEP CON 127.95
 RADIO AIDS TO NAVIGATION: NOTAM FILE RAP.
  RAPID CITY (H) VORTAC 112.3   RAP   Chan 70   N43°58.56′
   W103°00.74′   146° 61.3 NM to fld. 3160/13E.

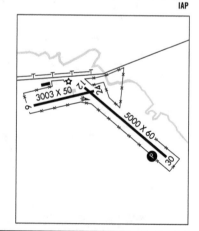

FⅼGURE 77.—Chart Supplements U.S. (formerly Airport/Facility Directory).

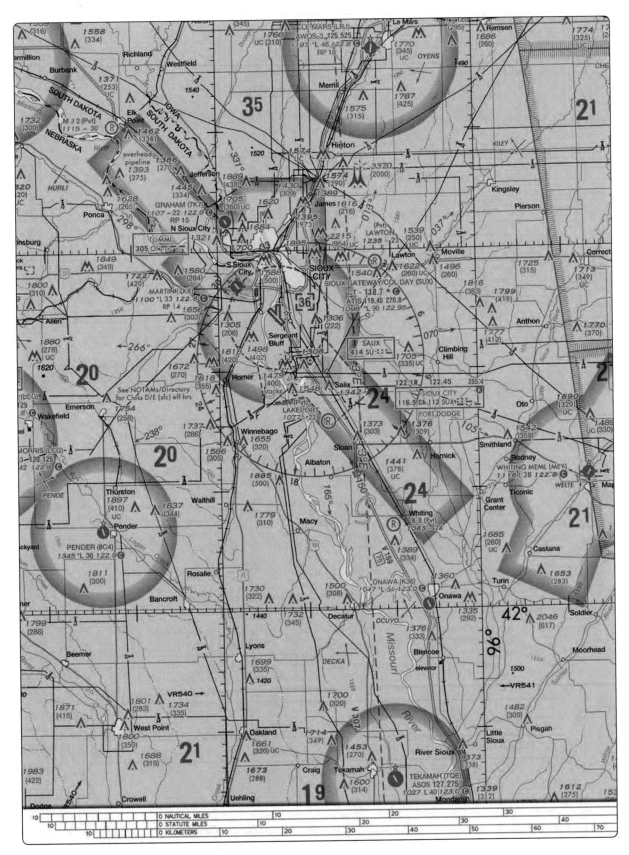

FIGURE 78.—Sectional Chart Excerpt.

NOTE: Chart is not to scale and should not be used for navigation. Use associated scale.

64   **IOWA**

SIOUX CITY   N42°20.67′ W96°19.42′   NOTAM FILE SUX   **OMAHA**
   (L) **VORTAC** 116.5   SUX   Chan 112   313 ° 4.4 NM to Sioux Gateway/Col Bud Day Fld. 1087/9E.   **HIWAS.**   **L–12I**
      VOR unusable:
         280°–292° byd 25 NM
         293°–305° byd 20 NM blo 4,500′   306°–350° byd 20 NM blo 3,000′
         293°–305° byd 35 NM   350°–280° byd 30 NM blo 3,000′
   RCO 122.45 122.1R 116.5T (FORT DODGE RADIO)

SIOUX CITY
SIOUX GATEWAY/COL BUD DAY FLD   (SUX)   6 S   UTC –6(–5DT)   N42°24.16′ W96°23.06′   **OMAHA**
   1098   B   S4   **FUEL** 100LL, 115, JET A   OX 1, 2, 3, 4   Class I, ARFF Index—See Remarks   **H–5C, L–12I**
      NOTAM FILE SUX   **IAP, AD**
   RWY 13–31: H9002X150 (CONC–GRVD)   S–100, D–120, 2S–152,
      2D–220   HIRL
      RWY 13: MALS. VASI(V4L)—GA 3.0 ° TCH 49′. Tree.
      RWY 31: MALSR. VASI(V4L)—GA 3.0 ° TCH 50′.
   RWY 17–35: H6600X150 (ASPH–PFC)   S–65, D–80, 2S–102,
      2D–130   MIRL
      RWY 17: REIL. VASI(V4R)—GA 3.0 ° TCH 50′. Trees.
      RWY 35: PAPI(P4L)—GA 3.0 ° TCH 54′. Pole.
   LAND AND HOLD SHORT OPERATIONS

LANDING	HOLD SHORT POINT	DIST AVBL
RWY 13	17–35	5400
RWY 17	13–31	5650

   ARRESTING GEAR/SYSTEM
      RWY 13 ←BAK–14 BAK–12B(B) (1392′)
                           BAK–14 BAK–12B(B) (1492′) →RWY 31
   AIRPORT REMARKS: Attended continuously. PAEW 0330–1200Z ‡ during
      inclement weather Nov–Apr. AER 31–BAK–12/14 located (1492′)
      from thld. Airfield surface conditions not monitored by arpt
      management between 0600–1000Z ‡ daily. Rwy 13–BAK–12/14
      located (1392′) from thld. All A–gear avbl only during ANG flying ops. Twr has limited visibility southeast of
      ramp near ARFF bldg and northeast of Rwy 31 touchdown zone. Rwy 31 is calm wind rwy. Class I, ARFF Index
      B. ARFF Index E fire fighting equipment avbl on request. Twy F unlit, retro–reflective markers in place. Portions
      of Twy A SE of Twy B not visible by twr and is designated a non–movement area. Rwy 13–31 touchdown and
      rollout rwy visual range avbl. When twr clsd, ACTIVATE HIRL Rwy 13–31; MIRL Rwy 17–35; MALS Rwy 13;
      MALSR Rwy 31; and REIL Rwy 17–CTAF.
   WEATHER DATA SOURCES: ASOS (712) 255–6474.   **HIWAS** 116.5 SUX. LAWRS.
   COMMUNICATIONS: CTAF 118.7   **ATIS** 119.45   **UNICOM** 122.95
      SIOUX CITY RCO 122.45 122.1R 116.5T (FORT DODGE RADIO)
   Ⓡ **SIOUX CITY APP/DEP CON** 124.6 (1200–0330Z ‡)
   Ⓡ **MINNEAPOLIS CENTER APP/DEP CON** 124.1 (0330–1200Z ‡)
      SIOUX CITY TOWER 118.7 (1200–0330Z ‡)   **GND CON** 121.9
   AIRSPACE: CLASS D svc 1200–0330Z ‡ other times CLASS E.
   RADIO AIDS TO NAVIGATION: NOTAM FILE SUX.
      SIOUX CITY (L) VORTAC 116.5   SUX   Chan 112   N42 °20.67′ W96°19.42′   313° 4.4 NM to fld. 1087/9E.
         HIWAS.
      NDB (MHW) 233   GAK   N42°24.49′ W96°23.16′   at fld.
      SALIX NDB (MHW/LOM) 414   SU   N42°19.65′ W96°17.43′   311° 6.1 NM to fld. Unmonitored.
      TOMMI NDB (MHW/LOM) 305   OI   N42°27.61′ W96°27.73′   128° 4.9 NM to fld. Unmonitored.
      ILS 109.3   I–SUX   Rwy 31   Class IT.   LOM SALIX NDB. ILS Unmonitored when twr clsd. Glide path
         unusable coupled approach (CPD) blo 1805 ′.
      ILS 111.3   I–OIQ   Rwy 13   LOM TOMMI NDB. Localizer shutdown when twr clsd.
      ASR (1200–0330Z‡)

SNORE   N43°13.96′ W95°19.66′   NOTAM FILE SPW.   **OMAHA**
   NDB (LOM) 394   SP   121° 6.8 NM to Spencer Muni.

SOUTHEAST IOWA RGNL   (See BURLINGTON)

FIGURE 79.—Chart Supplements U.S. (formerly Airport/Facility Directory).

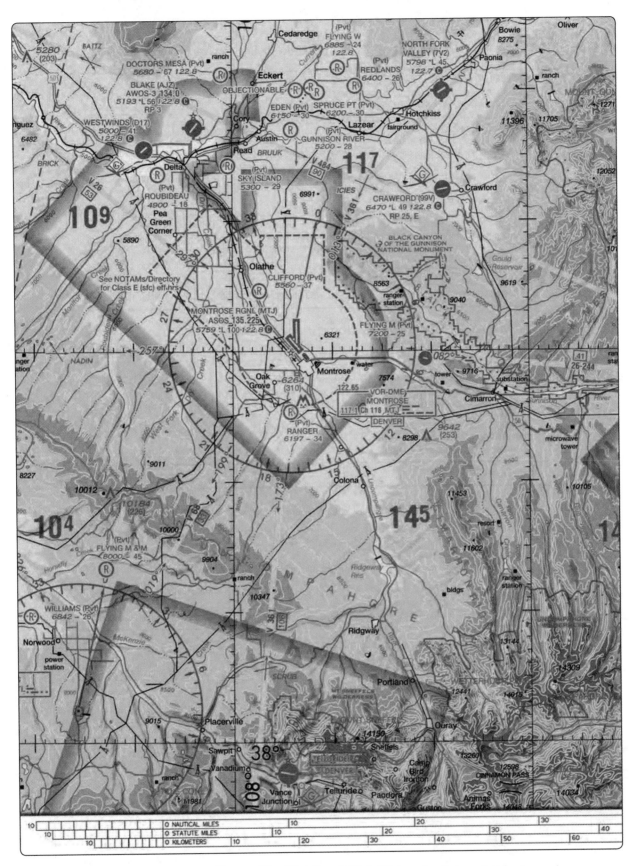

FIGURE 80.—Sectional Chart Excerpt.
NOTE: Chart is not to scale and should not be used for navigation. Use associated scale.

216   **COLORADO**

CRAWFORD   (99V)   2 W   UTC −7(−6DT)   N38°42.25′ W107°38.62′   DENVER
  6470   S2   OX 4   TPA—7470(1000)   NOTAM FILE DEN   L—9E
  RWY 07–25: H4900X20 (ASPH)   LIRL (NSTD)
    RWY 07: VASI (NSTD). Trees.   **RWY 25:** VASI (NSTD) Tank. Rgt tfc.
  RWY E–W: 2500X125 (TURF)
    RWY E: Rgt tfc.   **RWY W:** Trees.
  AIRPORT REMARKS: Attended continuously. Rwy 07–25 west 1300 ′ only 25′ wide. Heavy glider ops at arpt. Land to the
    east tkf to the west winds permitting. 100LL fuel avbl for emergency use only. Pedestrians, motor vehicles, deer
    and wildlife on and invof arpt. Unlimited vehicle use on arpt. Rwy West has +15 ′ building 170′ from thld 30′ left,
    +10′ road 100′ from thld centerline. +45′ tree 100′ L of Rwy 07 extended centerline 414 ′ from rwy end. −8′ to
    −20′ terrain off both sides of first 674 ′ of Rwy 25 end. E–W rwy occasionally has 6 inch diameter irrigation
    pipes crossing rwy width in various places. Rwy 07 has 20 ′ trees and −10′ to 20′ terrain 20′ right of rwy first
    150′. E–W rwy consists of +12 inch alfalfa vegetation during various times of the year. Arpt lgts opr
    dusk–0800Z‡. Rwy 07 1 box VASI left side for local operators only or PPR call 970–921–7700 or
    970–921–3018. Rwy 07–25 LIRL on N side from Rwy 25 end W 3800 ′. Rwy 07 1300 ′ from end E 300′. No thld
    lgts Rwy 07–25 3800′ usable for ngt ops.
  COMMUNICATIONS: CTAF/UNICOM 122.8
  RADIO AIDS TO NAVIGATION: NOTAM FILE MTJ.
    MONTROSE (H) VORW/DME 117.1   MTJ   Chan 118   N38 °30.39′ W107°53.96′   033° 16.9 NM to fld. 5713/12E.

CREEDE
  MINERAL CO MEM   (C24)   2 E   UTC −7(−6DT)   N37°49.33′ W106°55.79′   DENVER
    8680   NOTAM FILE DEN   H–3E, L–9E
  RWY 07–25: H6880X60 (ASPH)   S–12.5, D–70, 2D–110
    RWY 07: Thld dsplcd 188 ′.   **RWY 25:** Road.
  AIRPORT REMARKS: Unattended. Elk and deer on and invof arpt. Glider and hang glider activity on and in vicinity of
    arpt. Mountains in all directions. Departure to NE avoid over flight of trailers and resident homes, climb to 200 ′
    above ground level on centerline extended prior to turn. Acft stay to right of valley on apch and/or departure
    route. 2′ cable fence around apron.
  COMMUNICATIONS: CTAF 122.9
  RADIO AIDS TO NAVIGATION: NOTAM FILE DEN.
    BLUE MESA (H) VORW/DME 114.9   HBU   Chan 96   N38 °27.13′ W107°02.39′   158° 38.1 NM to fld. 8730/14E.

  CUCHARA VALLEY AT LA VETA   (See LA VETA)

DEL NORTE
  ASTRONAUT KENT ROMINGER   (8V1)   3 N   UTC −7(−6DT)   N37°42.83′ W106°21.11′   DENVER
    7949   NOTAM FILE DEN   H–3E, L–9E
  RWY 06–24: 6050X75 (ASPH)   1.1% up SW
  RWY 03–21: 4670X60 (TURF–DIRT)
    RWY 21: Mountain.
  AIRPORT REMARKS: Unattended. Wildlife on and invof arpt. Unlimited vehicle access on arpt. Mountainous terrain
    surrounds arpt in all directions.
  COMMUNICATIONS: CTAF 122.9
  RADIO AIDS TO NAVIGATION: NOTAM FILE ALS.
    ALAMOSA (H) VORTACW 113.9   ALS   Chan 86   N37 °20.95′ W105°48.93′   298° 33.7 NM to fld. 7535/13E.

FIGURE 81.—Chart Supplements U.S. (formerly Airport/Facility Directory).

FIGURE 82.—Altimeter.

LEARNING STATEMENT CODES AND LEARNING STATEMENTS

To determine the knowledge area in which a particular question was incorrectly answered, compare the learning statement code(s) on the FAA airmen knowledge test report to the following learning statement outline. The total number of test items missed may differ from the number of learning statement codes shown on the test report, since you may have missed more than one question in a specific learning statement code.

Learning Statement Codes and Learning Statements for Pilots, Instructors, Flight Engineers, Dispatchers, Navigators, and Pilot Examiners Exams (June 12, 2017)

Code	Learning Statement
PLT001	Calculate a course intercept
PLT002	Calculate aircraft performance – airspeed
PLT003	Calculate aircraft performance - center of gravity
PLT004	Calculate aircraft performance - climb / descent / maneuvering
PLT005	Calculate aircraft performance - density altitude
PLT006	Calculate aircraft performance – glide
PLT007	Calculate aircraft performance – IAS
PLT008	Calculate aircraft performance – landing
PLT009	Calculate aircraft performance - turbine temperatures (MGT, EGT, ITT, T4, etc) / torque / horsepower
PLT010	Calculate aircraft performance - STAB TRIM
PLT011	Calculate aircraft performance – takeoff
PLT012	Calculate aircraft performance - time/speed/distance/course/fuel/wind
PLT013	Calculate crosswind / headwind components
PLT014	Calculate distance / bearing to a station
PLT015	Calculate flight performance / planning – range
PLT016	Calculate fuel - dump time / weight / volume / quantity / consumption
PLT017	Calculate L/D ratio
PLT018	Calculate load factor / stall speed / velocity / angle of attack
PLT019	Calculate pressure altitude
PLT020	Calculate turbulent air penetration
PLT021	Calculate weight and balance
PLT022	Define Aeronautical Decision Making (ADM)
PLT023	Define altitude - absolute / true / indicated / density / pressure
PLT024	Define atmospheric adiabatic process
PLT025	Define Bernoulli`s principle
PLT026	Define ceiling
PLT027	Define coning

PLT028	Define crewmember
PLT029	Define critical phase of flight
PLT030	Define false lift
PLT031	Define isobars / associated winds
PLT032	Define MACH speed regimes
PLT033	Define MEA / MOCA / MRA
PLT034	Define stopway / clearway
PLT035	Define Vne / Vno
PLT036	Interpret a MACH meter reading
PLT037	Interpret a Radar Weather Report / National Convective Weather Forecast
PLT038	Interpret aircraft Power Schedule Chart
PLT039	Interpret airport landing indicator
PLT040	Interpret airspace classes - charts / diagrams
PLT041	Interpret altimeter - readings / settings
PLT042	Interpret Constant Pressure charts / Isotachs Chart
PLT043	Interpret Analysis Heights / Temperature Chart
PLT044	Interpret ATC communications / instructions / terminology
PLT045	Interpret Descent Performance Chart
PLT046	Interpret drag ratio from charts
PLT047	Interpret/Program Flight Director/FMS/Automation - modes / operation / indications / errors
PLT048	Interpret Hovering Ceiling Chart
PLT049	Interpret ILS - charts / RMI / CDI / indications
PLT050	Interpret information on a Brake Energy Limit Chart
PLT051	Interpret information on a Convective Outlook
PLT052	Interpret information on a Departure Procedure Chart
PLT053	Interpret information on a Flight Plan
PLT054	Interpret information on a Glider Performance Graph
PLT055	Interpret information on a High Altitude Chart
PLT056	Interpret information on a Horizontal Situation Indicator (HSI)
PLT057	Interpret information on a Hot Air Balloon Performance Graph
PLT058	Interpret information on a Low Altitude Chart
PLT059	Interpret information on a METAR / SPECI report
PLT060	Interpret information on a Performance Curve Chart
PLT061	Interpret information on a PIREP
PLT062	Interpret information on a Pseudo-Adiabatic Chart / K Index / Lifted Index
PLT063	Deleted
PLT064	Interpret information on a Sectional Chart
PLT065	Interpret information on a Service Ceiling Engine Inoperative Chart
PLT066	Interpret information on a Convective Outlook Chart
PLT067	Interpret information on a SIGMET
PLT068	Interpret information on a Significant Weather Prognostic Chart
PLT069	Interpret information on a Slush/Standing Water Takeoff Chart
PLT070	Interpret information on a Stability Chart
PLT071	Interpret information on a Surface Analysis Chart
PLT072	Interpret information on a Terminal Aerodrome Forecast (TAF)
PLT073	Interpret information on a Tower Enroute Control (TEC)

PLT074	Interpret information on a Velocity/Load Factor Chart
PLT075	Interpret information on a Weather Depiction Chart (DELETED 6/12/2017)
PLT076	Interpret information on a Winds and Temperatures Aloft Forecast (FB)
PLT077	Interpret information on an Airport Diagram
PLT078	Interpret information in a Chart Supplements U.S.
PLT079	Interpret information on an Airways Chart
PLT080	Interpret information on an Arrival Chart
PLT081	Interpret information on an Aviation Area Forecast (FA) (DELETED 6/12/2017)
PLT082	Interpret information on an IFR Alternate Airport Minimums Chart
PLT083	Interpret information on an Instrument Approach Procedures (IAP)
PLT084	Interpret information on an Observed Winds Aloft Chart
PLT085	Interpret information on Takeoff Obstacle / Field / Climb Limit Charts
PLT086	Interpret readings on a Turn and Slip Indicator
PLT087	Interpret readings on an Aircraft Course and DME Indicator
PLT088	Interpret speed indicator readings
PLT089	Interpret Takeoff Speeds Chart
PLT090	Interpret VOR - charts / indications / CDI / NAV
PLT091	Interpret VOR / CDI - illustrations / indications / procedures
PLT092	Interpret weight and balance - diagram
PLT093	Recall administration of medical oxygen
PLT094	Recall aerodynamics - airfoil design / pressure distribution / effects of altitude
PLT095	Recall aerodynamics - longitudinal axis / lateral axis
PLT096	Recall aeromedical factors - effects of altitude
PLT097	Recall aeromedical factors - effects of carbon monoxide poisoning
PLT098	Recall aeromedical factors - fitness for flight
PLT099	Recall aeromedical factors - scanning procedures
PLT100	Recall aeronautical charts - IFR En Route Low Altitude
PLT101	Recall aeronautical charts - pilotage
PLT102	Recall aeronautical charts - terminal procedures
PLT103	Recall Aeronautical Decision Making (ADM) - hazardous attitudes
PLT104	Recall Aeronautical Decision Making (ADM) - human factors / CRM
PLT105	Recall airborne radar / thunderstorm detection equipment - use / limitations
PLT106	Recall aircraft air-cycle machine
PLT107	Recall aircraft alternator / generator system
PLT108	Recall aircraft anti-icing / deicing - methods / fluids
PLT109	Recall aircraft batteries - capacity / charging / types / storage / rating / precautions
PLT110	Recall aircraft brake system
PLT111	Recall aircraft circuitry - series / parallel
PLT112	Recall aircraft controls - proper use / techniques
PLT113	Recall aircraft design - categories / limitation factors
PLT114	Recall aircraft design - construction / function
PLT115	Recall aircraft engine - detonation/backfiring/after firing, cause/characteristics
PLT116	Recall aircraft general knowledge / publications / AIM / navigational aids
PLT117	Recall aircraft heated windshields
PLT118	Recall aircraft instruments - gyroscopic
PLT119	Recall aircraft lighting - anti-collision / landing / navigation

PLT120   Recall aircraft limitations - turbulent air penetration
PLT121   Recall aircraft loading - computations
PLT122   Recall aircraft operations - checklist usage
PLT123   Recall aircraft performance - airspeed
PLT124   Recall aircraft performance - atmospheric effects
PLT125   Recall aircraft performance - climb / descent
PLT126   Recall aircraft performance - cold weather operations
PLT127   Recall aircraft performance - density altitude
PLT128   Recall aircraft performance - effects of icing
PLT129   Recall aircraft performance - effects of runway slope / slope landing
PLT130   Recall aircraft performance - fuel
PLT131   Recall aircraft performance - ground effect
PLT132   Recall aircraft performance - instrument markings / airspeed / definitions / indications
PLT133   Recall aircraft performance - normal climb / descent rates
PLT134   Recall aircraft performance - takeoff
PLT135   Recall aircraft pressurization - system / operation
PLT136   Recall aircraft systems - anti-icing / deicing
PLT137   Recall aircraft systems - environmental control
PLT138   Recall aircraft landing gear/tires - types / characteristics
PLT139   Recall aircraft warning systems - stall / fire / retractable gear / terrain awareness
PLT140   Recall airport operations - LAHSO
PLT141   Recall airport operations - markings / signs / lighting
PLT142   Recall airport operations - noise avoidance routes
PLT143   Recall airport operations - rescue / fire fighting vehicles and types of agents
PLT144   Recall airport operations - runway conditions
PLT145   Recall airport operations - runway lighting
PLT146   Recall airport operations - traffic pattern procedures / communication procedures
PLT147   Recall airport operations - visual glide path indicators
PLT148   Recall airport operations lighting - MALS / ALSF / RCLS / TDZL
PLT149   Recall airport preflight / taxi operations - procedures
PLT150   Recall airport traffic patterns - entry procedures
PLT151   Recall airship - buoyancy
PLT152   Recall airship - flight characteristics / controllability
PLT153   Recall airship - flight operations
PLT154   Recall airship - ground weight-off / static / trim condition
PLT155   Recall airship - maintaining pressure
PLT156   Recall airship - maximum headway / flight at equilibrium
PLT157   Recall airship - pressure height / dampers / position
PLT158   Recall airship - pressure height / manometers
PLT159   Recall airship - pressure height / super heat / valving gas
PLT160   Recall airship - stability / control / positive superheat
PLT161   Recall airspace classes - limits / requirements / restrictions / airspeeds / equipment
PLT162   Recall airspace requirements - operations
PLT163   Recall airspace requirements - visibility / cloud clearance
PLT164   Recall airspeed - effects during a turn
PLT165   Recall altimeter - effect of temperature changes

PLT166	Recall altimeter - settings / setting procedures
PLT167	Recall altimeters - characteristics / accuracy
PLT168	Recall angle of attack - characteristics / forces / principles
PLT169	Recall antitorque system - components / functions
PLT170	Recall approach / landing / taxiing techniques
PLT171	Recall ATC - reporting
PLT172	Recall ATC - system / services
PLT173	Recall atmospheric conditions - measurements / pressure / stability
PLT174	Recall autopilot/yaw damper components, operating principles, characteristics, failure modes
PLT175	Recall autorotation
PLT176	Recall balance tab - purpose / operation
PLT177	Recall balloon - flight operations
PLT178	Recall balloon - flight operations / gas
PLT179	Recall balloon - ground weight-off / static equilibrium / load
PLT180	Recall balloon gas/hot air - lift / false lift / characteristics
PLT181	Recall balloon - hot air / physics
PLT182	Recall balloon - inspecting the fabric
PLT183	Recall balloon flight operations - ascent / descent
PLT184	Recall balloon flight operations - launch / landing
PLT185	Recall basic instrument flying - fundamental skills
PLT186	Recall basic instrument flying - pitch instruments
PLT187	Recall basic instrument flying - turn coordinator / turn and slip indicator
PLT188	Recall cabin atmosphere control
PLT189	Recall carburetor - effects of carburetor heat / heat control
PLT190	Recall carburetor ice - factors affecting / causing
PLT191	Recall carburetors - types / components / operating principles / characteristics
PLT192	Recall clouds - types / formation / resulting weather
PLT193	Recall cockpit voice recorder (CVR) - operating principles / characteristics / testing
PLT194	Recall collision avoidance - scanning techniques
PLT195	Recall collision avoidance - TCAS
PLT196	Recall communications - ATIS broadcasts
PLT197	Recall Coriolis effect
PLT198	Recall course / heading - effects of wind
PLT199	Recall cyclic control pressure - characteristics
PLT200	Recall dead reckoning - calculations / charts
PLT201	Recall departure procedures - ODP / SID
PLT202	Recall DME - characteristics / accuracy / indications / Arc
PLT203	Recall earth's atmosphere - layers / characteristics / solar energy
PLT204	Recall effective communication - basic elements
PLT205	Recall effects of alcohol on the body
PLT206	Recall effects of temperature - density altitude / icing
PLT207	Recall electrical system - components / operating principles / characteristics / static bonding and shielding
PLT208	Recall emergency conditions / procedures
PLT210	Recall engine shutdown - normal / abnormal / emergency / precautions
PLT211	Recall evaluation testing characteristics

PLT212	Recall fire extinguishing systems - components / operating principles / characteristics
PLT213	Recall flight characteristics - longitudinal stability / instability
PLT214	Recall flight characteristics - structural / wing design
PLT215	Recall flight instruments - magnetic compass
PLT216	Recall flight instruments - total energy compensators
PLT217	Recall flight maneuvers - quick stop
PLT218	Recall flight operations - common student errors
PLT219	Recall flight operations - maneuvers
PLT220	Recall flight operations - night and high altitude operations
PLT221	Recall flight operations - takeoff / landing maneuvers
PLT222	Recall flight operations - takeoff procedures
PLT223	Recall flight operations multiengine - engine inoperative procedures
PLT224	Recall flight plan - IFR
PLT225	Recall flight plan - requirements
PLT226	Recall fog - types / formation / resulting weather
PLT227	Recall FOI techniques - integrated flight instruction
PLT228	Recall FOI techniques - lesson plans
PLT229	Recall FOI techniques - professionalism
PLT230	Recall FOI techniques - responsibilities
PLT231	Recall FOI techniques / human behavior - anxiety / fear / stress
PLT232	Recall FOI techniques / human behavior - dangerous tendencies
PLT233	Recall FOI techniques / human behavior - defense mechanisms
PLT234	Recall forces acting on aircraft - 3 axis intersect
PLT235	Recall forces acting on aircraft - aerodynamics
PLT236	Recall forces acting on aircraft - airfoil / center of pressure / mean camber line
PLT237	Recall forces acting on aircraft - airspeed / air density / lift / drag
PLT238	Recall forces acting on aircraft - aspect ratio
PLT239	Recall forces acting on aircraft - buoyancy / drag / gravity / thrust
PLT240	Recall forces acting on aircraft - CG / flight characteristics
PLT241	Recall forces acting on aircraft - drag / gravity / thrust / lift
PLT242	Recall forces acting on aircraft - lift / drag / thrust / weight / stall / limitations
PLT243	Recall forces acting on aircraft - propeller / torque
PLT244	Recall forces acting on aircraft - stability / controllability
PLT245	Recall forces acting on aircraft - stalls / spins
PLT246	Recall forces acting on aircraft - steady state climb / flight
PLT247	Recall forces acting on aircraft - thrust / drag / weight / lift
PLT248	Recall forces acting on aircraft - turns
PLT249	Recall fuel - air mixture
PLT250	Recall fuel - types / characteristics / contamination / fueling / defueling / precautions
PLT251	Recall fuel characteristics / contaminants / additives
PLT252	Recall fuel dump system - components / methods
PLT253	Recall fuel system - components / operating principles / characteristics / leaks
PLT254	Recall fuel tank - components / operating principles / characteristics
PLT255	Recall fueling procedures - safety / grounding / calculating volume
PLT256	Recall glider performance - effect of loading
PLT257	Recall glider performance - speed / distance / ballast / lift / drag

PLT258	Recall ground reference maneuvers - ground track diagram
PLT259	Recall ground resonance - conditions to occur
PLT260	Recall gyroplane - aerodynamics / rotor systems
PLT261	Recall hail - characteristics / hazards
PLT262	Recall helicopter hazards - dynamic rollover / Low G / LTE
PLT263	Recall hazardous weather - fog / icing / turbulence / visibility restriction
PLT264	Recall helicopter approach - settling with power
PLT265	Recall helicopter takeoff / landing - ground resonance action required
PLT266	Recall high lift devices - characteristics / functions
PLT267	Recall hot air balloon - weight-off procedure
PLT268	Recall hovering - aircraft performance / tendencies
PLT269	Recall human behavior - defense mechanism
PLT270	Recall human behavior - social / self-fulfillment / physical
PLT271	Recall human factors (ADM) - judgment
PLT272	Recall human factors - stress management
PLT273	Recall hydraulic systems - components / operating principles / characteristics
PLT274	Recall icing - formation / characteristics
PLT275	Recall ILS - indications / HSI
PLT276	Recall ILS - indications / OBS / CDI
PLT277	Recall ILS - marker beacon / indicator lights / codes
PLT278	Recall indicating systems - airspeed / angle of attack / attitude / heading / manifold pressure / synchro / EGT
PLT279	Recall Inertial/Doppler Navigation System principles / regulations / requirements / limitations
PLT280	Recall inflight illusions - causes / sources
PLT281	Recall information in a Chart Supplements U.S.
PLT282	Recall information in the certificate holder`s manual
PLT283	Recall information on a Constant Pressure Analysis Chart
PLT284	Recall information on a Forecast Winds and Temperatures Aloft (FB)
PLT285	Recall information on a Height Velocity Diagram
PLT286	Recall information on a Significant Weather Prognostic Chart
PLT287	Recall information on a Surface Analysis Chart
PLT288	Recall information on a Terminal Aerodrome Forecast (TAF)
PLT289	Recall information on a Weather Depiction Chart
PLT290	Recall information on AIRMETS / SIGMETS
PLT291	Recall information on an Aviation Area Forecast (FA) (DELETED 6/12/2017)
PLT292	Recall information on an Instrument Approach Procedures (IAP)
PLT293	Recall information on an Instrument Departure Procedure Chart
PLT294	Recall information on Inflight Aviation Weather Advisories
PLT295	Recall instructor techniques - obstacles / planning / activities / outcome
PLT296	Recall instrument procedures - holding / circling
PLT297	Recall instrument procedures - unusual attitude / unusual attitude recovery
PLT298	Recall instrument procedures - VFR on top
PLT300	Recall instrument/navigation system checks/inspections - limits / tuning / identifying / logging
PLT301	Recall inversion layer - characteristics
PLT302	Recall jet stream - types / characteristics
PLT303	Recall L/D ratio

PLT304	Recall launch / aero-tow procedures
PLT305	Recall leading edge devices - types / effect / purpose / operation
PLT306	Recall learning process - levels of learning / transfer of learning / incidental learning
PLT307	Recall learning process - memory / fact / recall
PLT308	Recall learning process - laws of learning elements
PLT309	Recall load factor - angle of bank
PLT310	Recall load factor - characteristics
PLT311	Recall load factor - effect of airspeed
PLT312	Recall load factor - maneuvering / stall speed
PLT313	Recall loading – limitations / terminology
PLT314	Recall longitudinal axis - aerodynamics / center of gravity / direction of motion
PLT315	Recall Machmeter - principles / functions
PLT316	Recall meteorology - severe weather watch (WW)
PLT317	Recall microburst - characteristics / hazards
PLT318	Recall minimum fuel advisory
PLT319	Recall navigation – celestial / navigation chart / characteristics
PLT320	Recall navigation - true north / magnetic north
PLT321	Recall navigation - types of landing systems
PLT322	Recall navigation - VOR / NAV system
PLT323	Recall NOTAMS - classes / information / distribution
PLT324	Recall oil system - types / components / functions / oil specifications
PLT325	Recall operations manual - transportation of prisoner
PLT326	Recall oxygen system - components / operating principles / characteristics
PLT327	Recall oxygen system - install / inspect / repair / service / precautions / leaks
PLT328	Recall performance planning - aircraft loading
PLT329	Recall physiological factors - cabin pressure
PLT330	Recall physiological factors - cause / effects of hypoxia
PLT331	Recall physiological factors - effects of scuba diving / smoking
PLT332	Recall physiological factors – hyperventilation / stress / fatigue
PLT333	Recall physiological factors - night vision
PLT334	Recall physiological factors - spatial disorientation
PLT335	Recall pilotage - calculations
PLT336	Recall pitch control - collective / cyclic
PLT337	Recall pitot-static system - components / operating principles / characteristics
PLT338	Recall pneumatic system - operation
PLT340	Recall positive exchange of flight controls
PLT341	Recall power settling - characteristics
PLT342	Recall powerplant - controlling engine temperature
PLT343	Recall powerplant - operating principles / operational characteristics / inspecting
PLT344	Recall precipitation - types / characteristics
PLT345	Recall pressure altitude
PLT346	Recall primary / secondary flight controls - types / purpose / functionality / operation
PLT347	Recall principles of flight - critical engine
PLT348	Recall principles of flight - turns
PLT349	Recall procedures for confined areas
PLT350	Recall propeller operations - constant / variable speed

PLT351 Recall propeller system - types / components / operating principles / characteristics
PLT352 Recall purpose / operation of a stabilizer
PLT353 Recall Radar Summary Chart
PLT354 Recall radio - GPS / RNAV / RAIM
PLT355 Recall radio - HSI
PLT356 Recall radio - ILS / compass locator
PLT357 Recall radio - ILS
PLT358 Recall radio - LOC / ILS
PLT363 Recall radio - VOR / VOT
PLT364 Recall radio system - license requirements / frequencies
PLT365 Recall reciprocating engine - components / operating principles / characteristics
PLT366 Recall regulations - accident / incident reporting and preserving wreckage
PLT367 Recall regulations - additional equipment/operating requirements large transport aircraft
PLT368 Recall regulations - admission to flight deck
PLT369 Recall regulations - aerobatic flight requirements
PLT370 Recall regulations - Air Traffic Control authorization / clearances
PLT371 Recall regulations - Aircraft Category / Class
PLT372 Recall regulations - aircraft inspection / records / expiration
PLT373 Recall regulations - aircraft operating limitations
PLT374 Recall regulations - aircraft owner / operator responsibilities
PLT375 Recall regulations - aircraft return to service
PLT376 Recall regulations - airspace, other, special use / TFRS
PLT377 Recall regulations - airworthiness certificates / requirements / responsibilities
PLT378 Recall regulations - Airworthiness Directives
PLT379 Recall regulations - alternate airport requirements
PLT380 Recall regulations - alternate airport weather minima
PLT381 Recall regulations - altimeter settings
PLT382 Recall regulations - approach minima
PLT383 Recall regulations - basic flight rules
PLT384 Recall regulations - briefing of passengers
PLT385 Recall regulations - cargo in passenger compartment
PLT386 Recall regulations - certificate issuance / renewal
PLT387 Recall regulations - change of address
PLT388 Recall regulations - cockpit voice / flight data recorder(s)
PLT389 Recall regulations - commercial operation requirements / conditions / OpSpecs
PLT390 Recall regulations - communications en route
PLT391 Recall regulations - communications failure
PLT392 Recall regulations - compliance with local regulations
PLT393 Recall regulations - controlled / restricted airspace - requirements
PLT394 Recall regulations - declaration of an emergency
PLT395 Recall regulations - definitions
PLT396 Recall regulations - departure alternate airport
PLT397 Recall regulations - destination airport visibility
PLT398 Recall regulations - dispatch
PLT399 Recall regulations - display / inspection of licenses and certificates
PLT400 Recall regulations - documents to be carried on aircraft during flight

PLT401   Recall regulations - dropping / aerial application / towing restrictions
PLT402   Recall regulations - ELT requirements
PLT403   Recall regulations - emergency deviation from regulations
PLT404   Recall regulations - emergency equipment
PLT405   Recall regulations - equipment / instrument / certificate requirements
PLT406   Recall regulations - equipment failure
PLT407   Recall regulations - experience / training requirements
PLT408   Recall regulations - fire extinguisher requirements
PLT409   Recall regulations - flight / duty time
PLT410   Recall regulations - flight engineer qualifications / privileges / responsibilities
PLT411   Recall regulations - flight instructor limitations / qualifications
PLT412   Recall regulations - flight release
PLT413   Recall regulations - fuel requirements
PLT414   Recall regulations - general right-of-way rules
PLT415   Recall regulations - IFR flying
PLT416   Recall regulations - immediate notification
PLT417   Recall regulations - individual flotation devices
PLT418   Recall regulations - instructor demonstrations / authorizations
PLT419   Recall regulations - instructor requirements / responsibilities
PLT420   Recall regulations - instrument approach procedures
PLT421   Recall regulations - instrument flight rules
PLT422   Recall regulations - intermediate airport authorizations
PLT423   Recall regulations - knowledge and skill test checks
PLT424   Recall regulations - limits on autopilot usage
PLT425   Recall regulations - maintenance reports / records / entries
PLT426   Recall regulations - maintenance requirements
PLT427   Recall regulations - medical certificate requirements / validity
PLT428   Recall regulations - minimum equipment list
PLT429   Recall regulations - minimum flight / navigation instruments
PLT430   Recall regulations - minimum safe / flight altitude
PLT431   Recall regulations - operating near other aircraft
PLT432   Recall regulations - operational control functions
PLT433   Recall regulations - operational flight plan requirements
PLT434   Recall regulations - operational procedures for a controlled airport
PLT435   Recall regulations - operational procedures for an uncontrolled airport
PLT436   Recall regulations - operations manual
PLT437   Recall regulations - overwater operations
PLT438   Recall regulations - oxygen requirements
PLT439   Recall regulations - persons authorized to perform maintenance
PLT440   Recall regulations - Pilot / Crew duties and responsibilities
PLT441   Recall regulations - pilot briefing
PLT442   Recall regulations - pilot currency requirements
PLT443   Recall regulations - pilot qualifications / privileges / responsibilities / crew complement
PLT444   Recall regulations - pilot-in-command authority / responsibility
PLT445   Recall regulations - preflight requirements
PLT446   Recall regulations - preventative maintenance

PLT447	Recall regulations - privileges / limitations of medical certificates
PLT448	Recall regulations - privileges / limitations of pilot certificates
PLT449	Recall regulations - proficiency check requirements
PLT450	Recall regulations - qualifications / duty time
PLT451	Recall regulations - ratings issued / experience requirements / limitations
PLT452	Recall regulations - re-dispatch
PLT453	Recall regulations - records retention for domestic / flag air carriers
PLT454	Recall regulations - required aircraft / equipment inspections
PLT455	Recall regulations - requirements of a flight plan release
PLT456	Recall regulations - runway requirements
PLT457	Recall regulations - student pilot endorsements / other endorsements
PLT458	Recall regulations - submission / revision of Policy and Procedure Manuals
PLT459	Recall regulations - takeoff procedures / minimums
PLT460	Recall regulations - training programs
PLT461	Recall regulations - use of aircraft lights
PLT462	Recall regulations - use of microphone / megaphone / interphone / public address system
PLT463	Recall regulations alcohol or drugs
PLT464	Recall regulations - use of safety belts / harnesses (crew member)
PLT465	Recall regulations - use of seats / safety belts / harnesses (passenger)
PLT466	Recall regulations - V speeds
PLT467	Recall regulations - visual flight rules and limitations
PLT468	Recall regulations - Visual Meteorological Conditions (VMC)
PLT469	Recall regulations - weather radar
PLT470	Recall rotor system - types / components / operating principles / characteristics
PLT471	Recall rotorcraft transmission - components / operating principles / characteristics
PLT472	Recall rotorcraft vibration - characteristics / sources
PLT473	Recall secondary flight controls - types / purpose / functionality
PLT474	Recall soaring - normal procedures
PLT475	Recall squall lines - formation / characteristics / resulting weather
PLT476	Recall stabilizer - purpose / operation
PLT477	Recall stalls - characteristics / factors / recovery / precautions
PLT478	Recall starter / ignition system - types / components / operating principles / characteristics
PLT479	Recall starter system - starting procedures
PLT480	Recall static/dynamic stability/instability - characteristics
PLT481	Recall student evaluation - learning process
PLT482	Recall student evaluation - written tests / oral quiz / critiques
PLT483	Recall supercharger - characteristics / operation
PLT484	Recall symbols - chart / navigation
PLT485	Recall taxiing / crosswind / techniques
PLT486	Recall taxiing / takeoff - techniques / procedures
PLT487	Recall teaching methods - demonstration / performance
PLT488	Recall teaching methods - group / guided discussion / lecture
PLT489	Recall teaching methods - known to unknown
PLT490	Recall teaching methods - motivation / student feelings of insecurity
PLT491	Recall teaching methods - organizing material / course of training
PLT492	Recall temperature - effects on weather formations

PLT493   Recall the dynamics of frost / ice / snow formation on an aircraft
PLT494   Recall thermals - types, characteristics, formation, locating, maneuvering, corrective actions
PLT495   Recall thunderstorms - types / characteristics / formation / hazards / precipitation static
PLT496   Recall towrope - strength / safety links / positioning
PLT497   Recall transponder - codes / operations / usage
PLT498   Recall Transportation Security Regulations
PLT499   Recall turbine engines - components / operational characteristics / associated instruments
PLT500   Recall turboprop engines - components / operational characteristics
PLT501   Recall turbulence - types / characteristics / reporting / corrective actions
PLT502   Recall universal signals - hand / light / visual
PLT503   Recall use of narcotics / drugs / intoxicating liquor
PLT504   Recall use of training aids - types / function / purpose
PLT505   Recall use of training aids - usefulness / simplicity / compatibility
PLT506   Recall V speeds - maneuvering, flaps/gear extended, V_1, V_2, r, ne, mo, mc, mg, etc.
PLT507   Recall VOR - indications / VOR / VOT / CDI
PLT508   Recall VOR/altimeter/transponder checks - identification / tuning / identifying / logging
PLT509   Recall wake turbulence - characteristics / avoidance techniques
PLT510   Recall weather - causes / formation
PLT511   Recall weather associated with frontal activity / air masses
PLT512   Recall weather conditions - temperature / moisture / dewpoint
PLT513   Recall weather information - FAA Avcams
PLT514   Recall weather reporting systems - briefings / forecasts / reports / AWOS / ASOS
PLT515   Recall weather services - TIBS / TPC / WFO / HIWAS
PLT516   Recall winds - types / characteristics
PLT517   Recall winds associated with high / low-pressure systems
PLT518   Recall windshear - characteristics / hazards / power management
PLT519   Recall wing spoilers - purpose / operation
PLT520   Calculate density altitude
PLT521   Recall helicopter takeoff / landing – slope operations
PLT522   Recall helicopter – Pinnacle / Ridgeline operations
PLT523   Recall vortex generators – purpose / effects / aerodynamics
PLT524   Interpret / Program information on an avionics display
PLT525   Interpret table – oxygen / fuel / oil / accumulator / fire extinguisher
PLT526   Recall near midair collision report
PLT527   Recall BASIC VFR – weather minimums
PLT528   Recall regulations – small UAS operations / weight limitations
PLT529   Recall physiological factors – prescription and over-the-counter drugs
PLT530   Recall regulations – small UAS aircraft registration / display of registration
PLT531   Recall regulations – operation of multiple sUAs
PLT532   Recall operating limitations – small UAS aircraft visibility / distance from clouds
PLT533   Recall regulations – small UAS operation over humans
PLT534   Recall regulations – small UAS operational control / condition for safe operation / VLOS / frequency interference
PLT535   Recall regulations – hazardous operations
PLT536   Recall physiological factors – dehydration / heat stroke
PLT537   Recall regulations – sUAS waivers